Philosophy and African Development

# Philosophy and African Development
Theory and Practice

*Edited by*
Lansana Keita

Council for the Development of Social Science Research in Africa
DAKAR

© CODESRIA 2011
Council for the Development of Social Science Research in Africa,
Avenue Cheikh Anta Diop, Angle Canal IV, BP 3304 Dakar, 18524, Senegal
Website: www.codesria.org

All rights reserved. No part of this publication may be reproduced or transmitted in any form or by any means, electronic or mechanical, including photocopy, recording or any information storage or retrieval system without prior permission from CODESRIA.

ISBN: 978-2-86978-326-3

Layout: Hadijatou Sy
Cover Design: Ibrahima Fofana
Printed by: Imprimerie Graphi plus, Dakar, Senegal
Distributed in Africa by CODESRIA
Distributed elsewhere by the African Books Collective, Oxford, UK.
Website: www.africanbookscollective.com

The Council for the Development of Social Science Research in Africa (CODESRIA) is an independent organisation whose principal objectives are to facilitate research, promote research-based publishing and create multiple forums geared towards the exchange of views and information among African researchers. All these are aimed at reducing the fragmentation of research in the continent through the creation of thematic research networks that cut across linguistic and regional boundaries.

CODESRIA publishes a quarterly journal, *Africa Development*, the longest standing Africa-based social science journal; *Afrika Zamani*, a journal of history; the *African Sociological Review*; the *African Journal of International Affairs*; *Africa Review of Books* and the *Journal of Higher Education in Africa*. The Council also co-publishes the *Africa Media Review*; *Identity, Culture and Politics: An Afro-Asian Dialogue*; *The African Anthropologist* and the *Afro-Arab Selections for Social Sciences*. The results of its research and other activities are also disseminated through its Working Paper Series, Green Book Series, Monograph Series, Book Series, Policy Briefs and the *CODESRIA Bulletin*. Select CODESRIA publications are also accessible online at www.codesria.org.

CODESRIA would like to express its gratitude to the Swedish International Development Cooperation Agency (SIDA/SAREC), the International Development Research Centre (IDRC), the Ford Foundation, the MacArthur Foundation, the Carnegie Corporation, the Norwegian Agency for Development Cooperation (NORAD), the Danish Agency for International Development (DANIDA), the French Ministry of Cooperation, the United Nations Development Programme (UNDP), the Netherlands Ministry of Foreign Affairs, the Rockefeller Foundation, FINIDA, the Canadian International Development Agency (CIDA), the Open Society Initiative for West Africa (OSIWA), TrustAfrica, UN/UNICEF, the African Capacity Building Foundation (ACBF) and the Government of Senegal for supporting its research, training and publication programmes.

# Contents

*Contributors* .................................................................................................. v
*Preface* ......................................................................................................... vii
*Introduction* ................................................................................................ ix

**Chapter 1**
Modernity and Religious Interpretations
*Samir Amin* ............................................................................................. 1

**Chapter 2**
The Human Right to Development
*Wilfred L. David* ................................................................................... 37

**Chapter 3**
On Prospective: Development and a Political Culture of Time
*Souleymane Bachir Diagne* .................................................................. 57

**Chapter 4**
Fanon and Development: A Philosophical Look
*Lewis R. Gordon* ................................................................................... 69

**Chapter 5**
Dialogue with Lansana Keita: Reflections on African Development
*Paulin Hountondji* ............................................................................... 87

**Chapter 6**
African Development and the Primacy of Mental Decolonisation
*Messay Kebede* ..................................................................................... 97

**Chapter 7**
Philosophy and Development: On the Problematic African Development
— A Diachronic Analysis
*Lansana Keita* ..................................................................................... 115

**Chapter 8**
A Relevant Education for African Development:
Some Epistemological Considerations
*Francis B. Nyamnjoh* .......................................................................... 139

**Chapter 9**

Culture: The Missing Link in Development Planning in Africa
*Kwesi Kwaa Prah* .................................................................................. 155

**Chapter 10**

Appraising Africa: Modernity, Decolonisation and Globalisation
*Sanya Osha* ........................................................................................... 169

**Chapter 11**

Philosophy, Democracy and Development: History and the Case of Cameroon
*Godfrey B. Tangwa* ............................................................................... 177

**Chapter 12**

Science, Technology and Development: Stakes of Globalisation
*Jean-Pierre Ymele* ................................................................................. 197

**Chapter 13**

Postcoloniality and Development: Development as a Colonial Discourse
*Eiman Osman Zein-Elabdin* ................................................................. 215

*Bibliography* ........................................................................................ 231

# Contributors

**Samir Amin** is Director of Third World Forum, Senegal. His most recent publications include *Eurocentrism* (1989 and 2010), *Capitalism in the Age of Globalization* (1997), and *Aid to Africa: Redeemer or Coloniser* (2009).

**Wilfred L. David** is Professor of African Studies, Howard University, USA. Among his publications are *The Conversation of Economic Development* (1997) and *The Humanitarian Development Paradigm: Search for Global Justice* (2004).

**Souleymane Bachir Diagne** is Professor of Philosophy, Columbia University, USA. His recent publications include (co-editor) *The Meanings of Timbuktu* (2008) and *Comment philosopher en Islam* (2010).

**Lewis R. Gordon** is Professor of Philosophy, Temple University, USA. Among his publications are *Fanon and the Crisis of European Man* (1995) and *Divine Warning: Reading Disaster in the Modern Age* (2009).

**Paulin Hountondji** is Professor of Philosophy, Universite' de Cotonou, Republique du Benin. He is author of *African Philosophy: Myth and Reality* (1983) and *La rationalite', une ou plurielle?* (2007).

**Messay Kebede** is Professor of Philosophy, University of Dayton, USA. He is the author of *Meaning and Development* (1994) and most recently *Education, Politics and Social Change in Ethiopia* (2010).

**Lansana Keita** is Associate Professor of Economics and Philosophy, University of The Gambia. His publications include *Science, Rationality, and Neoclassical Economics* (1992) and *Africa Development*, XXXIV, 1, 2004: Special Issue on Philosophy and Development (Guest Editor).

**Francis B. Nyamnjoh** is Professor of Social Anthropology, University of Cape Town, South Africa. Among his publications are *Insiders and Outsiders: Citizenship and Xenophobia in Contemporary Southern Africa* (2006) and *Intimate Strangers* (2010).

**Sanya Osha** is Research Fellow at the Institute of Economic Research on Innovation, Tshwane University of Technology, Pretoria, South Africa. He is the author of *Kwasi Wiredu and Beyond: The Text, Writing and Thought in Africa* and *Ken Saro-Wiwa's Shadow* (2007).

**Kwesi Kwaa Prah** is Director of the Centre for Advanced Studies of African Society (CASAS), Cape Town, South Africa. He is co-author of *Africa in Transformation: Political and Economic Transformation and Socio-Political Responses in Africa* (2000). He is also a co-author of *African Perspectives on China in Africa* (2007).

**Godfrey B. Tangwa** is Professor of Philosophy, University of Yaounde I, Cameroon. He is the author of *Road Companion to Democracy and Meritocracy* (1998) and *The Traditional African Perception of a Person: Some Implications for Bioethics* (2000).

**Jean-Pierre Ymele** is Lecturer, Department of Philosophy, University of Yaounde I, Cameroon. He is the author of 'De Descartes a Newton: la querrelle des "qualites occultes" et l'ouverture de la rationalite', *Terroirs,* April, 2007, and 'Le vanhivaux : regard sociologique', *Share. Revue de communication scientifique* , Vol. 1, No. 1, 2009.

**Eiman Osman Zein-Elabdin** is Professor, Department of Economics, Franklin and Marshall College, USA. She is co-editor of *Postcolonialism Meets Economics* (2004) and author of *Economics, Culture and Development* (2010).

# Preface

Many of the chapters of this book first appeared as journal articles in a special edition of *Africa Development* (Vol. 29, No. 1, 2004). The new additions are original chapters except for those written by Wilfred David and Kwesi Prah which have also been slightly modified to fit the present format. Research on development in general has focused mainly on issues of economics, but this collection attempts something different by looking at the topic from a phylosophical angle.

I wish to acknowledge the encouragement of former Executive Secretary of CODESRIA, Professor Adebayo Olukoshi, who first requested that the topic of development be researched from a more theoretically comprehensive position, and all my colleagues who have contributed to the volume, for this new dimension of looking at the development impasse in Africa.

**Lansana Keita**

# Introduction

## Lansana Keita

One of the noted facts about contemporary social science research on Africa is that its societies are invariably analysed as being underdeveloped or, more euphemistically, as 'developing'. These studies complete their observations with prescriptions as to what policies should be implemented so that African societies evolve from states of underdevelopment to states of development. In general, the usual method of determining levels of underdevelopment is by appeal to particular indices that measure sociological quanta such as per capita income, life expectancy, infant mortality, literacy, and so on. According to this kind of template, Africa's status as being underdeveloped is thereby seen to be justified.

In terms of the explanation of the perceived underdevelopment of Africa, a study of recent history offers some insights into the way Africa was seen as underdeveloped, and the solutions offered. In the recent past, the political dynamic of the world was seen as being driven along by a titanic struggle between the capitalist West and the Communist world. According to the argument put forward by the theoreticians of the Communist world, the Western world was historically slated to be surpassed, then replaced first by socialism, then by communism. The basis for this political diagnosis derived from the Marxian stage theory of human history. According to Marx, feudalism was a social order with a particular historical role to play according to his materialist conception of history. This social order was predicated on a particular set of productive and technological forces.

Feudalism met its sociological demise when a fortuitous conjuncture of historical forces that developed first in maritime Western Europe led to the germination and rapid growth of the economic system known as capitalism. But the development of capitalism, justified by Adam Smith as 'private vices, public benefits' while leading to great wealth for some led also to exploitation and misery for the labour inputs into the capitalist equation of land, labour and capital. This critique of capitalism was fiercely pursued by the likes of Karl Marx and his epigones. Marx argued that as capitalism developed, the workers would eventually recognize the nature of their exploitation and would then seek to replace it with a system more amenable to their interests.

The idea that economies develop was certainly engendered by the very nature of capitalism, whose *raison d'etre* was the reward of growth for capital investment. That very idea was evident in the Adam Smith's treatise *The Wealth of Nations*. In this text, Smith sought to explain the dynamics of the economic growth that led to the wealth of nations. The same idea of the accumulation of wealth and the growth of economies was also central to the subsequent shapers of theoretical political economy: Ricardo, Malthus, Say, and others. By the time Marx came along to engage in his comprehensive critique of capitalism, the idea that the essence of economics was growth was firmly entrenched. What was novel with Marx was that under the influence of the age of Darwin, he interpreted capitalism not only as a system of growth but also one of evolution. According to Marx, capitalism would eventually be forced to evolve into a new system that would develop out of capitalism. But the new system of capitalism was not only accompanied by the sociological transformation of society, but also by very important technological developments. The ultimate discovery of the steam engine together with the usage of gunpowder for warfare constitute perhaps the most important technological developments of the new age. These technological changes gradually led to a diminution of the reliance on human labour as the major factor of production. Capital now dominated the production functions of the new capitalist order with its double guise of finance capital and physical capital in the form of productive machinery. As suggested above, the major characteristics of the new capitalism were economic growth in the form of the accumulation of capital and the qualitative transformation of existing technology. In this regard, it would be instructive to refer to this new era with regard to the new capitalism as one development even though that term was not in vogue at that time.

The new capitalist system seemed to be dominated by three main characteristics: the need to exploit labour so that gains be maximised and costs reduced, the need to constantly increase capital holdings, and the need to seek out new sources of raw material and labour inputs. This was the essential basis for European colonialism and world economic globalisation according to which two elements were at work: Western Europe and North America experienced economic growth with the accumulation of capital and the raw material for such were obtained from the colonies. It was this dynamic that led Lenin and Mao to adapt Marx's critique of capital to the social conditions of Russia and China respectively to stave off the threat of becoming colonies of the economically dominant Western nations. The communist revolutions of Russia and China were founded on the principles of Marx's critique of capitalism as an exploitative economic system and the need to have a strong state to resist such.

For Lenin, the expansion of capital into all parts of the globe was an intrinsic part of the Western imperialist project. Lenin's text *Imperialism – The Highest Stage of Capitalism* bears this thesis out. The decolonisation process in Africa and other parts of the non-European world was seen by many of the anti-colonial leaders, not as a struggle against colonialism but also as a struggle against capitalism in the form of imperialism. The result was that the rise of the Soviet Union as a political and technological power was seen to represent the correct model to overcome colonialism and to rapidly develop both economically and technologically. Africa became then a contested territory for the colonising West and the Communist bloc led by the Soviet Union. The Soviet model of socialism and state power was seen as the solution to the question of transition to development as a post-colonial nation. And what was supposed to be transformed was not only existent economic systems, but also existent technologies and cultures. Marx's evolutionary stages of human sociological development was seen as the optimal path in the wake of decolonisation.

In the case of Africa, the socialist model with its statist trappings was adopted, not only by political leaders such as Nkrumah of Ghana, but also by Ben Bella of Algeria and Nyrere of Tanzania. The East-West conflict in the form of the Cold War was a fiercely contested one which ended with the West emerging triumphant at the dismantling of the Soviet experiment. Development in all its dimensions was henceforth being confidently promoted by the West as entailing a necessary adherence to the neo-liberal economic model in the context of what the West promulgated as 'free markets and democracy'. But this seemed to be mere theory, given that what actually transpired was a reformulation of the world according to the traditional division of labour. The West has accorded to itself the role of provider of high technology goods and services. Japan, Korea and Taiwan were brought into the fold as answers to the communist threat in East Asia. Other countries have been designated the role as producer of cheap low and high technology goods. Consider China and Korea in this regard. And Africa has been designated the task as supplier of raw materials only. The whole structure is kept in place by the monitoring activities of the West's global finance institutions: the WTO, the World Bank and the IMF.

Thus, what we have now, following the era of the Cold War, is a return to the global economic arrangements that held sway before the rise of the Soviet Union and the Communist bloc of nations. It is for this reason that the issue of development for those areas of the world deemed 'developing' has fallen under the almost complete purview of Western theoreticians. The obvious empirical proof of this claim is that the vast majority of books and journal articles on the development are produced in the West and acted on by Western agencies. In this regard, the African subaltern has little voice. The slogan now is 'sustainable development' ministered at the micro level by Western NGOs and at the macro level by the officials of the West's financial and credit institutions. The situation is not much different from the one that obtained during the colonial era.

## Development as Economic Development

The idea of economic development has been broadly understood as the implementation of economic ideas and policies that led to increased private and public wealth and the introduction of novel forms of technology and sociologies. Thus, the ideas about economic decision making that heralded in and directed the modern era of increased economic growth, more varied and complex divisions of labour, and most importantly novel and more efficient technologies could properly be described as ideas of economic development. In this regard, the works of European theorists such as Smith, Say, Hume, and Ricardo could be described as works in economic development. After all, there was a qualitative change in the European social order in all dimensions after the demise of feudalism.

But the term 'economic development' itself was not used in specific terms until after the second World War to refer to policies adopted by post war theorists to boost the economies of those parts of the world that were technologically less developed than those of Western Europe and North America. It should also be noted that the urgency to find solutions to the question of how to effect development was prompted especially by the economic and political model of development promised by the Communist world of the Soviet Union and China. In this highly competitive struggle, the main theorists of economics in this regard were Keynes and Marx. Those who supported the Keynesian model indirectly endorsed the free market theories of Smith and Ricardo and assumed that free trade and markets were the essentials for economic transformations in areas deemed underdeveloped. The classical model of Smith and Ricardo was revived as the neo-classical model that served as the template for subsequent works such as *The Stages of Economic Growth* authored by W.W. Rostow (1960) and *The Theory of Economic Growth* by W.A. Lewis (1955). The theories of growth that were developed out of these seminal works were myriad. But students of neoclassical economic development have been schooled on models such as the Harrod-Domar model and the Solow growth model. However, despite the plethora of research literature on the topic of economic development for the last fifty years, the results of their implementation have not been encouraging.

Those who adopted Marx's approach argued that genuine development would result only from breaking post-colonial links with the capitalist world in order to establish genuine socialist nations. In the case of Africa, only Kwame Nkrumah's Ghana chose that path. There was a negative reaction from the West which led ultimately to the erasure of the only socialist experiment in that continent. The theoretical basis for the socialist alternative was developed initially by critics of the neo-liberal international order such as Paul Baran (*The Political Economy of Growth*, 1957), Andre Gunder Frank (*Dependent Accumulation and Underdevelopment*, 1978); and of the African post-colonial order by theorists such as Frantz Fanon (*The Wretched of the Earth*, 1963).

And perhaps the most persistent African critique of the post-colonial order has come from Samir Amin who has argued that the continuing economic dependence of the post-colonial African state on Western capitalism has been the major impediment for African economic development. One might consider in this regards some of his works, such as *Accumulation on a World Scale: A Critique of the Theory of Underdevelopment*, 1974; and *Unequal Development*, 1976. One might consider too the non-radical critiques of theorists such as Stiglitz, Sen and De Soto to recognise that the topic of economic development is not wanting for committed analysts.

## Development Studies

Yet not much is changing in terms of the recommendations of those theorists who make recommendations to the World bank or IMF. It is on account of the failures of economic development theory with its tepid prescriptions for 'sustainable development' and 'poverty reduction' that theories of development have now been expanded from mere economic analysis to include considerations of history, sociology, political economy and anthropology. It is on this basis that the relatively new research area of Development Studies has been founded. In this regard, one might note the works of theorists such as Jan Pierterse (*Development Theory*, 2001) and Wilfred David (*The Humanitarian Development Paradigm*, 2004). It is on this basis that the collection of essays that constitute this anthology has been assembled. The goal here is to appraise the issue of development holistically, not only in terms of economics, but also in terms of the history of ideas, political theory, sociology, social and political philosophy, and political economy.

Introduction

Most of the chapters in this volume were prepared by philosophers who implicitly practise their discipline as one whose most effective modern function would be to appraise the human experience in all its dimensions from the standpoints of the modern social and natural sciences, all disciplinary offspring of philosophy itself. It is for this reason that the tenor of the included contributions is not only propositional but also engaged in the meta-analysis of the theories on which the concept of development is founded and practised.

The following brief statements on the text's contents support this claim. Thus, in alphabetical order, we note that Samir Amin's chapter 'Modernity and Religious Interpretations' argues that development of the Islamic world – shared by much of Africa – has been restrained by old traditions which have not been effectively challenged intellectually to yield eventually some kind of secular enlightenment that clear the path for the intellectual and technological transformations needed for development. Amin's sociology of ideas offers us insights into the relative limitations of the Nahda renaissance in Islam, as compared to what occurred in the Christian world of Western Europe.

David offers illuminating insights into the idea that economics is not just about the maximisation of expected utility according to the theorists of neo-classical economics but about the ultimate goal of human welfare. This would not be achieved by assuming that humans are mere maximising agents but anchoring the discussion of development on a paradigm founded on egalitarian human rights. His chapter 'The Human Right to Development' informs us that the world has reached the stage where such rights, though already enacted by international organisations, have been fully put into practice. David's contribution is an excellent reference text for those who would wish to compare the huge gap between the comprehensive rights due to individuals in theory and what actually occurs in practice.

The chapter by Diagne is the development explored within the context of time as 'prospective'. He examines and finds problematic the theories of 'African time' as formulated by theorists such as John Mbiti and Lucien Levy-Bruhl. Daigne makes a case for time as a dynamic 'prospective' an important ingredient for models of Africa development in the context both of a political projection for the youth and that of ongoing economic blueprints for African development in all its dimensions.

Gordon's approach to the issue of development is to examine the concept essentially from the seminal ideas of Frantz Fanon whose works focused on the idea of development as being embodied in the beings of people as problems. Fanon's solution to the problem of development was an actional one that would seek to break through the intellectual and psychological limitations imposed on the objects of underdevelopment. Gordon appeals to the ideas of Winter, Gendzier and Sen to unpack his approach to the problem of development via Fanon's critical viewing of the concept itself. In the course of the discussion, Gordon engages Wynter's interesting notion that development theory itself is more a reflection of Western narcissism than anything else. We are also led to his solution to the problem as requiring an existential and actional stance, in support of Gendzier but in critique of Sen.

Hountondji's contribution entails a lively discussion of the role that philosophy might play in the development dynamic. He adopts a historical stance as he views the present as the temporary end result of the past. In this context, we hear some incisive views on the roles that Fanon and Nkrumah have played in the ongoing dynamic of philosophy applied to politics, culture and economics.

Kebede's approach to the theme of development is to examine Africa's post-colonial comportment in the area of its psychological self conception. This leads him to offer critiques of what he regards as the three main schools of thought concerning African philosophy: ethnophilosophy, and African particularism. Regarding ethnophilosophy, Kebede engages in a critical analysis of the intellectual movement known as negritude as expounded by Senghor and Cesaire. He also engages prominent thinkers like Hountondji and Mudimbe. His solution is that Africa must seek an independent evolutionary path because development could not take place without the 'decolonisation' of the African mind.

The problem of development is often approached in static terms without regard to dynamic or historical analysis. Keita's approach is historical in that he views the particularities of African development in terms of its long archaeological and historical past. He positions his thesis in the context of a telos in which there is speculation in terms of an imagined structure of a developed Africa. He also points out the limitations of viewing development purely in terms of poverty reduction or 'sustainable development'. Keita also seeks to endorse Amartya Sen's thesis expounded in *Development as Freedom* that development comes, not only with an economic dimension, but also with the crucial one of human capabilities instantiated as substantive freedoms.

Nyamnjoh's contribution makes the point that a major impediment to development in Africa stems from the alienating effects of the colonial education to which Africans were subjected over many decades. For him, the paradigm of colonial education was one that was strictly empiricist and materialist in content, being modelled on modern science. He argues that this approach is too epistemologically restricting, given its preoccupation with answering 'what' questions instead of 'why' questions. Nyamnjoh embarks on a set of critiques of the systems of Eurocentric education that still dot the African continent. His prescription is that genuine development would necessarily require serious paradigm changes in Africa's educational structures.

Contemporary Africa is confronted with what Osha defines as three large problems: decolonisation, modernisation and globalisation. According to him, development leads in the direction of modernisation, but in the drive to attain such, Africa has to run the gauntlet of the universalising principle of Western origin which would seek to subordinate to its expression of the various particularities of Africa itself. The implicit question here is: does modernisation mean assimilating Westernisation as the form of the universal?

Kwesi Prah's chapter argues that viable solutions to the issue of African development requires a much more holistic approach than the more conventional one anchored mainly on economics. Prah argues that genuine development springs necessarily from an indigenous base. In this regard, the conversation of development must take place in a context where the maximal regard must be held for Africa's indigenous languages through which Africa's peoples view and interpret the world. Prah does not discount the assimilation of novel ideas but that they should be selectively chosen and absorbed according to local modalities.

Tangwa tackles the problematic of development with its attendant sociological, political and economic ills through a historical study of Cameroon. He discusses the triple colonial background of the Cameroon and contrasts pre-colonial sociological and political structures with those that were introduced during the colonial era. His thesis is that one of the reasons for the present politico-economic imbroglio is the evident disjunction between the social psychology of the behavioural dynamics of the leaders of the pre-colonial past and those of the contemporary era. Tangwa's key points are that democracy is a necessary condition for development and that the post-colonial era has been marked by palpable abuses of democracy, thereby establishing a cause-and-effect relationship between underdevelopment and the lack of democracy in post-independence Africa.

Jean-Pierre Ymele's contribution examines the important question of the relationship between science and technology, and its promise as the catalyst for development in an era of globalisation. He examines the crucial role that scientific and technological knowledge has played in development for the West in the past and its expansion by way of the world-wide exportation of capital under the rubric of globalisation. But there is a problem with the idea that such could be repeated in the developing world, given the constraints posed by levels of technology and variations in culture. In fact, globalisation comes with the risk of producing further occidental exploitation of attempts to assimilate modern forms of science and technology where the socio-economic and industrial conditions are not appropriate for such.

Zein-Elabdin's chapter tackles the question of development from the standpoint of postcolonial theory. For her, the question of development is a metaphysical question involving the ongoing phenomenological relationship between Western theorising about the post-colonial subaltern. In this regard, post-colonial theory seeks to interpret the discourse of 'development' not as an objective scientific analysis but as a hegemonic value-laden discourse of a post-colonial subaltern. According to Zein-Elabdin, to understand the rationale of the seemingly interminable discourse on development, it would be necessary first to recognise the post-colonial relationships between hegemon and subaltern, as the former seeks to maintain control through the power of language while the latter seeks adaptive autonomy through forms of an interactive hybridity. Zein-Elabdin's solution is one which would seek not to repeat the accumulation model of the West – given its tragic modalities in history – but to forge a new model based on human ethics.

What is evident from the above set of contributions is that the problem of development is not a purely economic one, but one which is multidimensional; hence the added insights offered by the analytical and holistic approach of theorists who approach the world epistemologically. At the core of the present African stasis is the perennial intellectual tension between claims to knowledge and their modalities of proof. Those who inquire into the issue of African development and have access to the instruments that seek solutions tend to do so from within the context of variants of neo-classical economics. The assumption is that the framework of neo-classical economics is one that is avowedly scientific and therefore appraises the social world of economics objectively. But cognitive analysis informs us that neo-classical economics, despite its objectivist pretensions, is in reality not much more than an ideological projection of a Western phenomenological interpretation onto the non-Western world, in this case Africa.

In this connection, the symbolic articulations that grace neo-classical economics and its application as economic development theory is to be properly understood as subjective and self-interested interpretations of the world of economics with its institutions and individual decision making. But the problem is that those of the non-Western world who participate in the game of development may not be aware that they are mistaking ideology for scientific analysis. This could be the main reason why development theory, despite the huge amounts of research output, achieves so little. Thus, neo-classical development theory should be recognised principally as an instance of the cultural anthropology of the West, formulated to serve its own interests in a world characterised by its own culturally particular view of the world. This view of the world is founded on the assumption that humans are naturally disposed to conflict as they seek access to the world's resources for purposes of survival. In this particular *enjeu* guile, cunning, prevarication and Machiavellian problem solving are the tools of the game. The virtue of the chapters of this volume is that such a sociobiological view of the human condition is mere ideology masquerading as objectivity. Theorists of African development would do well to acknowledge this fact.

# 1
## Modernity and Religious Interpretations

### Samir Amin

## Introduction

In the contemporary world, modernity is instinctively associated with the West; and when discussing the issue of development of the so-called underdeveloped countries, the following question is inevitably posed: Does development necessarily mean Westernisation or only modernisation? Present-day Africa is a continent where the Muslim religion has been well established since the nineteenth Century and thus, the issues of modernity and development are unavoidably linked to the Islamic culture. In this chapter, my purpose is to make a comparative analysis between religion and secularism in Europe, which ultimately leads to modernity and the parallel situation with Islam in Africa and the Middle-East. My purpose is to demonstrate that political Islam is not yet suited for making the intellectual changes necessary to accept modernity. But development in Africa and the Middle-East is not possible without modernity which, when all is said and done, is based on democracy and the freedom to alter or change traditions.

## Modernity

### *Reason and Emancipation*

There are two moments in history that were decisive for the formation of the modern world.

The first of these moments refers to the birth of modernity. It is the time of the Enlightenment (the European seventeenth and eighteenth centuries), which is also, and not coincidentally, that of the birth of capitalism. I will summarise its significance in the two following propositions.

The first of these propositions is related to the definition of modernity, which is, to my mind, the affirmation that the human being must and can individually or collectively create his own history. An affirmation that marks a rupture with the dominant thinking in all previous societies – in Europe and elsewhere – which were founded on the principle that God, having created the universe and the human being, is the ultimate 'legislator'. The ethical principles which this divine legislation erects are, of course, formulated through the historical religions or transcendental philosophers, hence opening the door to diverse interpretations through which the social realities under permanent transformation have been expressed. Reason is in that case frequently – but not always – invoked in order to serve those interpretations. But in this case, it is subjected to the duty of 'conciliating faith and reason'. The new affirmation that defines modernity frees itself from this duty, without necessarily ignoring issues of faith. The new affirmation closes a chapter, but opens another with its own problems: the freedom that human beings give themselves must be defined in turn. History, when it no longer operates as a force outside mankind, must be explained by other 'laws' whose discovery is the object of a new set of sciences, the constitution of which becomes simultaneously possible and necessary: those of man and society. Reason is mobilised anew in search of these objective determinations of the movement of societies. The new freedom that modern mankind confers on itself therefore remains subjected to the limitations of what we believe constitutes the logic of social reproduction and the dynamics of the transformation of societies.

The second refers to the bourgeois character of modernity, as expressed by the thinking of the Enlightenment. The emergence of capitalism and the emergence of modernity constitute the two facets of one and the same reality.

The thinking of the Enlightenment, therefore, offers us a concept of reason, inseparably associated with that of emancipation, without which the phrase 'the human being creates his own history' would lack meaning. It turns out that the emancipation in question is defined and limited by what is demanded and allowed by capitalism. The discourse of the Enlightenment, however, proposes a concept of emancipative Reason that claims to be transhistorical, while the examination of what it actually is will show that it is terribly historical in nature.

The most systematic fundamental expression of this discourse is the one that has been formulated by Adam Smith, unfortunately calling it 'utilitarianism', an ambiguous but spontaneous word in the tradition of English empiricism. In this view of the human world, society is conceived as an assembly of individuals, and here we have a view that breaks with the tradition of the Ancien Régime. It is therefore an unarguably emancipative ideology for the individual, once again one of the dimensions of modernity. This individual is, meanwhile, of course endowed with reason. The social order that must ensure the victory of this emancipative Reason – and therefore the happiness of human beings – is imagined as a system of 'good institutions', to employ the phrase still used today in social thinking in America. This system is in turn based on the separation, in social life, of the arena of politics and that of the economy. The 'good institutions' that must ensure the management of political life by reason are those institutions of democracy that guarantee the liberty and equality of individuals. In the management of economic life, reason imposes choosing contractual freedom (expressed in another way, 'the market') as the foundation of relations of exchange and of the organisation of the division of labour among the 'individuals' which society is composed of. The healthy operation of the economy in turn demands the protection of property, considered as of that time as a sacrosanct value in the 'good society'.

Emancipative Reason is, therefore, expressed in a classical triptych: liberty, equality, property. The formula of the successive precocious revolutions of the United Provinces and of the English 'Glorious Revolution' of 1688, before being more systematically taken up again by the United States Revolution and later by the French Revolution in its first period.

The constitutive elements of the triptych are regarded as 'naturally' and harmoniously complementary with one another. Hitherto, the statement according to which there is an equal sign between 'market' and 'democracy' has continued to be the cornerstone of bourgeois ideology. The conflict that in actual fact has, on the contrary, incessantly pitted the extension of democratic rights to all citizens, men and women, bourgeois and proletarian, whether property owners or not, against the unconditional defenders of 'the market' is removed from the debate right from the outset.

Adam Smith and the thinking of the Enlightenment certainly contain the intuition that the system of the 'good society' that they propose – rational and emancipative for all the eternity – faces some difficulties. But these, they ignore. The 'invisible hand' that guarantees the triumph of Reason in the management of economic life very often appears as an 'unpredictable' hand, for that very reason again putting into question human beings' capacity to really create their own history as modernity envisions. And the guaranteeing of freedom, of equality, of the security of property implies that the 'visible fist' of the state must complete the work of the invisible hand of the market.

The emancipative Reason of the Enlightenment does not exclude, but rather implies, the importance that is attached to an ethical principle. Reason here is not instrumental but rather inseparable from the emancipative goals and means whose triptych summarises the fundamental ethical elements.

The ethical aspect associated with the thinking of the Enlightenment may or may not be of religious inspiration. God is present for those who attribute to him the quality of being at the origin of the need for emancipation to which all human beings aspire. He disappears when this aspiration is only verified as 'natural'. The difference is minimal.

The contemporary version of bourgeois emancipative Reason, made fashionable with all the insistence that is allowed by vulgarisation through the mass media – that of the egalitarian liberalism of John Rawls – does not contribute anything new, having remained a prisoner of the liberty-equality-property triptych. Challenged by the liberty/equality conflict that is necessarily implied by the unequal distribution of property, the liberalism that is termed egalitarian is only very moderately so. The inequality is accepted and legitimised by a scarcely 'reasonable' acrobatics, which takes from vulgarised economy its pseudo-concept of 'allocations'. It is a very simple-minded analysis: the 'individuals' (society being the sum of these latter) who participate in the 'market' are endowed with differing fortunes (some are – by chance? – the heads of powerful corporations, others have nothing). These unequal 'allocations' nevertheless continue to be legitimate since they are the product (evidently an inherited one) of work done and of savings made (by their ancestors). We are therefore invited to turn backwards the chain of history until the – mythical – day when the original social contract was signed among equals. Yet, later, these formerly equal fellows became unequal because supposedly they wanted to, by virtue of the inequality of the sacrifices they consented to make. I believe that this form of facing the issues related to the specificity of capitalism does not even deserve to be considered as elegant.

But if the falsely egalitarian liberalism is stubbornly proposed as an ideological alternative in face of the bewilderment of the society of our period, it is because the front stage is no longer occupied by utilitarianism (which the so-called egalitarian liberalism barely distinguishes itself from) but by the driftage represented by the right-wing (actually an extreme right) libertarian ideology. This ideology substitutes the 'liberty-property' diptych for the Enlightenment's triptych, decisively refusing to give equality the status of a fundamental value. The Von Hayek version of this new extreme right-wing ideological formula re-establishes that of its inventors, the 'liberals' of the nineteenth century (Bastiat and company) who were at the origin of the driftage, coming as they did from a declared aversion towards the Enlightenment, responsible for the French Revolution. But the diptych in question has for a long time now constituted the kernel of the 'US ideology', establishing a contrast with European ideologies that still remain partly faithful to the Enlightenment.

In the right-wing libertarian version, ethics disappears because human beings, if they create their own history properly, are authorised to create it by behaving as if they were in the jungle: they are not responsible for the consequences of their actions, in particular for the inequalities which they may deepen, and which are even welcome. Therefore, without responsibility there is no ethics. Little, therefore, matters that some – in fact many – of these right-wing libertarians proclaim themselves to be 'believers' – in this case Christians. Their religion is in fact amoral, tending for that very reason to be transformed into simple social convenience, an expression of 'communitarian' singularity and nothing else. This is perhaps one possible interpretation of religion; the least we can say is that it continues to be arguable.

The second decisive moment is launched by the criticism that Marx directs at the bourgeois emancipative Reason of the Enlightenment. This criticism opens up a new chapter in modernity, which I call modernity critical of modernity.

Emancipative Reason cannot ignore this second moment of its deployment – more precisely, of the beginning of its redeployment. After Marx, social thinking can no longer be what it had been before him. What I wrote earlier referring to the criticism of the emancipative Reason of the Enlightenment – my second observation – certainly could not have been so without Marx. Marx is inevitable.

Emancipative Reason can no longer inscribe its analyses and its propositions under the 'liberty-equality-property' triptych. Having grasped the magnitude of the unsolvable conflict that pits the conservation of capitalist ownership against the deployment of equality among human beings, emancipative Reason cannot but suppress the third term of the triptych. And must substitute it by that of fraternity, stronger than that of 'solidarity', proposed here and there today by one and the other. 'Fraternity' thus meaning, evidently, the abolition of a capitalist ownership which necessarily pertains to some – a minority, the true dominant and exploiting bourgeois class – while depriving the others (the majority) of access to the conditions for an equality worthy of that name. 'Fraternity' thus meaning substitution of this exclusive and exclusionary form of ownership by a new form: that of social ownership, exercised by and for the benefit of the social body as a whole. Social integration would then operate by democracy, an inevitable requisite not only for the sound management of political life in the strictest sense of the term, but for social ownership as well. Integration through democracy would replace the partial and unequal integration via nature operated within the limits of respect for capitalist ownership, that is to say, for the exclusive 'market', to employ the language of the dominant vulgate.

'Liberty, equality, fraternity' – the motto was not invented by Marx, as every Tom, Dick and Harry knows. The French Revolution, like all the great revolutions, was ahead of its time and is projected far beyond its demands. For that reason, it both is a bourgeois revolution (and will tardily become stabilised on that basis) and, being projected forward, is experienced as a popular revolution and can be read today as initiating the socialist criticism of the bourgeois system; exactly in the same way that the two other great revolutions of modern times – the Russian and the Chinese – are projected in an attempt at a communist society far beyond the immediate demands and possibilities of their societies.

The 'popular ownership' that the French Revolution believes it can and therefore must guarantee is that of millions of peasants and artisans; and the 'market' that it protects, it is declared, must be authentically open and competitive, shutting out monopolies and the profits they produce. But this popular ownership is already, in that period, threatened both on the right and on the left. On the right, by the bourgeoisie of the large businessmen and capitalists who will crystallise in the symbol represented by those famous 'two hundred families' that own the Bank of France. On the left, by all those excluded in the city (proletarians and the hardscrabble poor) and in the countryside (poor and landless peasants). The jolts of the French Revolution will take up the entire nineteenth century through to its end, as of when the 'Republic' becomes stabilised, adopting the motto of the Revolution, but after having quashed the Commune and emptied the term 'fraternity' of its original content, to eventually substitute it by that which can be expressed in, and by, being a part of the 'national' community and in universalist humanism.

All the ambiguities, contradictions and diverging interpretations of 'French ideology' constitute the essence of this story, up to our time. And it is these ambiguities that we today seek to rid ourselves of by means of a brutal return to the formula that guarantees the supremacy of the security of bourgeois property.

Bourgeois Reason, placed on its feet again, is no longer and can no longer be emancipative. At the same time, it stands only on its two feet: liberty and property. From this point onwards, Bastiat and Von Hayek, who proclaim their open hostility against any fancy for attaching any importance to equality, are the true representatives of a degenerate reason, which isn't even that which the Enlightenment had conceived. And this is why the bourgeois Reason reduced to liberty and to ownership is the Reason of the 'US ideology'; this retreat – the abolition in thinking of the French Revolution and naturally of the Russian and French ones – is nothing but the expression of the essence of what we may understand by 'Americanisation of the world'.

This bourgeois Reason, deprived from that point on of every emancipative ambition, thus becomes by the force of facts an instrumental reason, summary, hollow, irresponsible (and therefore lacking in an ethical foundation).

The consummate expression of this non-emancipative Reason is displayed in the field of 'what pertains to economics', which, by the way, is defined by its inventors and defenders as 'a pure science' ('pure economics'). I shall recall here very briefly the criticism I directed on another occasion at this truncated rationality. In the first place, the fact that it never reaches the point of establishing, with consistent logical arguments (in the simplest sense of the term 'logical'), the veracity of its fundamental proposition: that market freedom produces an 'optimum general equilibrium'. Next, that it obstinately refuses to reflect on the reasons for its failure, reasons which are the result of its unreal conception of society, reduced to the sum of the individuals that compose it. On the contrary, it attempts to emerge from the confusion in which it has installed itself by reinforcing its initial axiom (the individual constitutes the exclusive cell of which society is constituted) with the invention of those famous 'anticipations'. But the integration of the latter into 'economic reasoning' worsens the chaos and leads to a sole possible conclusion: that the market shifts from imbalance to imbalance without ever tending towards equilibrium (a conclusion to which Marx and even Keynes had arrived a long time before). The cherry on the cake that the term 'social optimum' had wanted to be also has to disappear. It should not remain at that pure economics that gives up this ambition, without which, however, the emancipation of the human being – the happiness of the Enlightenment and of Adam Smith – looses sense. The human being is declared as irresponsible as the market through which he expresses himself. The cynics of pure economics will dare think and say it, and it is necessary to thank them for this courage. The market can produce three billion 'useless' human beings, a rising proportion of 'poor' in the wealthiest countries – it matters little. It seems to be 'rational'. Reason, converted into a destroyer of the alienated and/or excluded human being, of nature (something which the economic calculation that is called rational, always a short-term one, implies) and of entire societies (and therefore of human cultures), not only gives up on being emancipative, but also accepts to perform the role of a demolition company against humanity.

Other advocates of bourgeois Reason are hesitating to join the camp of cynicism and/or of Americanisation in which the system of the real world is engaged. The so-called egalitarian liberalism which I referred to above therefore tries to save the day. This trend of modern bourgeois thinking, embodied by Rawls and which some people even think may be termed 'leftist'! ignores Marx, precedes him. It experiences bitter failure, as testified by its seclusion into the chaos of the theory of inequality of the 'allocations' (to individuals) that compels one to go back up to the mythical day zero of the initial social contract.

I don't know if the 'culturalist' adversaries of the real world and of the trends in its evolution – understood as 'Americanisation' by some, 'Westernisation' (in general) by others – can be termed 'rational'. Confronting the threats of 'Americanisation', some, therefore, solely defend the 'cultural values' without questioning the general trends in the system, as if reality could be cut into slices, like salami, for the purpose of saving 'a piece for tomorrow'. Others, having previously confused capitalism with 'the West', forgetting the determining reality of the latter for the sake of a gratuitous and false affirmation of a supposedly eternal 'West', believe they can transfer the locus of the confrontation from the terrain of a social reality in permanent movement to the heaven of a trans-historical cultural imaginary for everyone.

The heteroclitical contents of these attics – the pure economics of imaginary markets, plus the falsely egalitarian liberalism, plus the trans-historical culturalist lucubrations – are pompously set up as a 'new' thinking, the so-called 'post-modernism'. Having erased the criticism of bourgeois modernism and the reason having given up of its emancipative vocation, hasn't contemporary bourgeois thought become anything other than the thinking of a system well advanced in the stage of senility?

A dangerous senility, and a danger reinforced by adherence to the principle of irresponsibility. A dangerous senility because the system has reached a degree characterised by the monstrous power of its destructive capabilities. Destruction, as I stated earlier, of the human being, of nature, of entire societies. Emancipative Reason must respond to this challenge.

### *Reason is Emancipative, or It is Not Reason?*

The concept of Reason, therefore, implies more than the creation of a set of mental procedures that allow the progress of intelligence on the relations among objects and all sort of phenomena. This intelligence on relations is also about the extent of their degree of necessity, which is absolute – or virtually so – only in situations of extreme banality of no interest. The deployment of science – knowing more but also, and above all, knowing the limits of knowledge – therefore allows the localisation of the degree of freedom with which human actions can be endowed, the definition of the possible and efficient options. But also the recognition that there is uncertainty (few absolute certainties) and the appreciation, as much as possible, of its margins.

This set of procedures does not in itself constitute Reason, even if numerous researchers in the sciences termed as sciences of nature or sciences of man can, in a first approximation, not only adhere to this (it is necessary to do so) but also be satisfied, be content with it. All live beings – and above all the higher species – put into practice, over the course of their lives, methods of action and choices that testify to a certain degree of this type of intelligence, at least in its first step, intelligence about relations.

Reason demands more. Because emancipation presupposes responsibility, without which the options among different possibilities have neither scope nor meaning. He who says responsibility says ethics, the principles of which cannot be eliminated from a reflection that aspires to be scientific.

The principles of the ethics in question can be those that non-deistic (and *a fortiori* non-religious) universalist humanism inspires since the Enlightenment (and even previously), in Marxism and in our own times. But they can also be those of a deistic Universalist humanism – even a religious one in the sense that is inscribed in a given religious tradition, Christian or other. Strong probabilities exist that these tributaries would flow into the same great river. The example that comes immediately to mind is that of the theologians of liberation whom I read as believers for whom being a Christian isn't to stop at Christ but to start out from him. There could be other religious interpretations (Islamic, Buddhist and other), or non-western philosophical ones (in the sense that their ancestry isn't the 'Hellenism' common to the peoples of the Christian and Muslim worlds), that will appear in this future to be built, common to all humanity. It is in this sense and only in this sense that one must, with regard to the diversity named as cultural (for want of a better description), more than 'respect' it ('tolerate' it is a pejorative term, you 'tolerate' what you don't like), wish to see it deployed in all its potential richness. I distinguish this diversity – oriented, in the tradition of emancipative Reason, toward the construction of the future – from the false diversity of the specificities inherited from the past, which the culturalists turn into trans-historical invariants (which they are not) in order to cling neurotically to them.

To return to the challenge which emancipative reason faces today is to invent the efficient means that may allow progress toward well-defined goals, progress in the direction of emancipation from mercantile alienation, a distancing from the practices that destroy the potential of nature and of life, a convergence toward the abolition of the gigantic disparities of the so-called (material) 'development' that the polarising expansion of world capitalism necessarily produces.

Marxism is, to my mind, the efficient instrument that makes it possible both to analyse the challenges and to define strategies capable of changing the world in the directions specified here, as long as we also consider that Marx only launched the reflection and actions in this regard. Stated differently: what we will define as arising from Marx and not ending with him.

The issues to be solved, in theory and in practice, are complex, and in their entangled condition they do not allow any one-sided solution, since the latter would ignore the conflicts arising among the different elements of the challenge. I shall select just one example, because it entails, to my mind, the greatest magnitude of the challenge on a global scale. The huge centres/peripheries contrast which capitalism has constructed must be destroyed. This will, without any doubt, demand a certain development of productive forces on the peripheries of the system – and we must admit that by doing so we run the risk of relegating the other dimensions of emancipation to the background. The contradiction resides in reality itself. Some think it can be overcome by eliminating one of its terms. They persist in ignoring 80 per cent of humanity, being content to declare that it must first 'pass through the capitalist stage' without taking into account that the polarisation that is immanent in this system will never allow them to 'catch up' with the others. They ignore the dimensions of emancipation as a whole, to the exclusive benefit of the prior development of productive forces. Emancipating Reason, must, in its living Marxist formulation, be able to combine the two contradictory terms of the challenge.

## Modernity and Interpretations of Religions

### The Flexibility of Religious Interpretations

> Modernity is based on the claim for the emancipation of human beings starting from their liberation from the bonds of social determination in its previous traditional forms. This liberation called to relinquish the prevailing forms of power legitimisation – in the family, the communities within which are organised the ways of life and production modes, in the State – so far based on metaphysics, generally of religious expression. It implies, therefore, a separation between state and religion, radical secularisation, a condition for the deployment of the modern forms of politics.

Will secularisation abolish religious belief? Some philosophers of the Enlightenment so thought and wished, who ranked religion among the absurd superstitions. This perception of religion has found an enabling ground for expansion in the nineteenth and twentieth centuries in the popular classes attaining political consciousness. If only because the working-class lefts (and the organic intellectuals who expressed their ideologies) were coming up, in practice against the conservative options of all organised Christian, Catholic, Protestant or Orthodox religious hierarchies. Anticlericalism became downright synonymous with anti-religious and, thereby, has gained ground nearly everywhere in Europe, although in various degrees of course, depending on the circumstances of the evolution of the ideological, political and social struggles. The French society, in particular, has counted among the most sensitive to the new anticlericalism – atheism, for reasons pertaining to the legacy of the radical nature of its Revolution. The Soviet ideology has resumed this fundamental atheism which it incorporated into its concept of dialectic materialism.

However, it is possible to have another reading of Marx. The often cited phrase ('religion is the opium of the people') is truncated, with what follows suggesting that the human being needs opium, because the human being is a metaphysical animal who cannot avoid posing questions concerning the meaning of life. He gives them the answers he can give, by either taking up those offered by religion, or inventing his owns, or still, avoiding to worry about them.

In any case, religions are there, are part of the picture of reality, even a significant dimension of this. It is therefore important to analyse their social functioning, i.e. in our modern world, their articulation to what constitutes the modernity in place – capitalism, democracy and secularism. I will try to do it in what follows, for the three so-called Religions of the Book. We will see then that the religions in question have been the subject of successive interpretations which enabled them to survive, to adapt to and accompany huge social transformations.

In this regard, the success of Christianity that has accompanied modernity, which was constituted in Europe (should it be reminded?) has given rise to a flowering of 'theories' that do not convince me. The commonest – which has become some sort of generally admitted platitude without it raising the slightest critical questioning – is that Christianity bore in it this exceptional evolution. The 'genius of Christianity' is thus reconstructed as one of the myths – among others (the Greek ancestor among others, 'Indo-European racism', etc.) – from which the 'European miracle' (the fact that modernity was invented there and not elsewhere) is explained. The most extremist of the ideologies of this Eurocentrism adopt an idealist theory of history according to which capitalism is supposedly the product of this evolution of religious interpretation. I propose a systematic critique of this in *Eurocentrism* (published in this book).

And the most extremist of the extremists reserve this creative genius of capitalist modernity to the Protestant Reform. One can recognise here the famous thesis of Max Weber, even less convincing in my opinion than what I called the 'Christianophily' of Eurocentrism.

The arguments developed by Weber in this regard are confused despite their apparent accuracy. Furthermore, they can be perfectly reversed; similar to those that were put forward yesterday to explain the backwardness of China because of Confucianism, then fifty years later to explain the take-off of this country, thanks to the same Confucianism! Superficial historians had explained the success of the Middle Ages Arab civilisation by Islam, whereas contemporary journalists, even more superficial, explain the stagnation of the Arab world by the same Islam. Culturalism has no possible unequivocal response to any of the major challenges of history; it has too many responses because it can prove any formulation as well as its contrary.

As counterpoint to these *idées-force* (key ideas), false, but feeding the ideology of the dominant world, I propose the following theses:

(i) Modernisation, secularism and democracy are not the outcomes of an evolution (or a revolution) of religious interpretations, but conversely, the latter have adjusted, with more or less good fortune, to their requirements. This adjustment was not the privilege of Protestantism. While it operated in the Catholic world differently, it was no less efficient. In any case, it created a new religious spirit, freed from the dogmas.

(ii) In this sense, the Reform was not the 'condition' for the blooming of capitalism, even if this thesis (by Weber) is largely admitted in the societies it flatters (Protestant Europe). The Reform was not even the most radical form of the ideological break with the European past and its 'feudal' ideologies – among others its previous reading of Christianity. It was, on the contrary, its primitive and confused form.

(iii) There has been a 'reform of the dominant classes' which led to the creation of national Churches (Anglican, Lutheran) controlled by these classes and implementing the compromise between the emergent bourgeoisie, the monarchy and the big rural property, warding off the threat of popular classes and the peasantry that is systematically regulated. This reactionary compromise – expressed by Luther and analysed by Marx and Engels as such – has enabled the bourgeoisies in the countries in question to avoid what happened in France: a radical revolution. Thus, the secularism produced in this model has remained shy to date. The regression of the Catholic idea of universality which is shown by the institution of national Churches has fulfilled only one function: establish its role of arbitrator between the forces of the Ancien Régime and those represented by the rising bourgeoisie, strengthen their nationalism and delay the progression of new forms of universalism that the socialist internationalism would propose later.

(iv) But there were also reforming movements that took hold of the popular strata victims of the social transformations produced by the emergence of capitalism. Those movements which reproduced ancient forms of struggle – those of the millenarianisms of the Middle Ages – were not ahead of their time, but behind relatively to its requirements. Therefore, we had to wait for the French Revolution – with its secular and radical democratic popular mobilisations – then socialism for the dominated classes to learn to express themselves efficiently in the new conditions. The Protestant sects in question fed on illusions of fundamentalist type. They created an enabling ground for the endless reproduction of 'sects' with an apocalyptic vision, as we can see them flourishing in the United States.

(v) There were not only 'positive' adjustments, the renovated religious interpretation offering open perspectives to social transformations. There were also involutions, with religious interpretation becoming, in turn, an obstacle to social progress. I will give the example of certain forms of the North-American Protestantism.

(vi) Christianity has no monopoly of adjustments, be they positive or negative. Islam has experienced positive adjustments in the past and is presently experiencing involution in many aspects similar to those of the American protestant sects in question. Judaism too. And I will add (what the reader will find explained in *Eurocentrism*) that this concerns both the great ideologies and religions of Asia.

(vii) That these adjustments may be positive or negative speaks in favour of an interpretation of historical materialism based on 'under-determination.' What I mean here is that each of the authorities (economic, political, ideological) has its own internal logic and that, thereby, complementarity in their evolution, necessary to ensure the global consistency of a system, does not define beforehand a given direction of a guaranteed evolution.

The three religions declare themselves 'monotheist' and take pride in this. They even pretend that they are the sole to be so, each in the 'fairest' manner of course, and, thereby, show contempt that borders on arrogance towards other religious beliefs which, having failed to conceive the God that is unique, abstract, the same for all human beings – whether they recognise him or not – would be thereby 'primitive' and 'inferior'.

Moreover, the three religions declare themselves 'revealed' (by this God that is unique) and deny others this quality. These would be thus 'invented' (therefore false) religions. Of course, the supporters of other religions believe as much in revelation. Revelation is synonymous with sacred. The distinction between the Religions of the Book and the others is ideological arrogance.

The relationship between the three so-called Religions of the Book is an obvious historical fact. They have in common a sacred book, the Bible of the Jews (the Old Testament for the Christians), even if this Bible is presented in very different variants among Jews and Muslims, each pretending of course that his version is the 'good' one, the one that was truly 'revealed'. Catholics and Protestants, on the contrary, accept the Jewish versions of the Bible, the former the corpus of Jews in the Diaspora, the latter that of Jews in Jerusalem. This relationship could be explained in a very basic manner by the geographical place of birth of the three religions. Christ lived in Palestine, besides the Jewish communities of the country, and perhaps within these communities. Islam is born in a nearby country, impregnated by the beliefs of Jews and Christians, challenged by these, in particular the Christianity of the civilised societies virtually surrounding it from Byzance to Ethiopia.

By itself, the relationship neither excludes, nor involves *a priori* the fundamental uniqueness of the metaphysics of the three religions. To answer this question, it will be necessary to measure the fundamental, minor or significant importance of the common origin they share. How did the latter mark the metaphysical options and the social experiences of the groups of people that are divided among the three religions?

All the peoples of the world have a mythology that gives an account of the Creation and their place within it. All, initially, give themselves in this universe the place of the 'chosen people', the one whose mythology is the real story of the Creation. Their gods are too, therefore, the 'real' ones; all other peoples made mistakes, or were deceived. Initially, the gods are thus conceived of as particular and different from one people to another. However, there have always been enough clear-sighted minds, even very early in history, to put in perspective the significance of mythological stories and the particularity of gods. A first salutary reaction has been to accept the plurality of the truths revealed to any of them ('every people has its truth'; it is the same, expressed in different languages) and therefore, in a way, the equivalence of the gods of each one. This reaction encourages syncretism which is found for instance in the Roman empire which associates diverse peoples, like elsewhere, up to contemporary Africa. Furthermore, the mutual borrowings between the mythologies are better known. The advances of archaeology, history and the exegesis have made it possible to discover 'ancestor mythologies' like those recounting the issue of the Deluge in the Middle-East, the myth of Gilgamesh, etc.

The Jews are, therefore, not the only people to proclaim itself 'chosen'. They all did the same. Do the Jews continue to think it seriously? I doubt it. In present-day social reality, most of the Jews, even those among them who are convinced believers, like among other peoples, probably know that they are only ordinary human beings. The nuance that can be brought in this regard is perhaps that, because of the Diaspora, the Jews were led, in order to survive as such, to stress their 'specificity' (therefore, their religious attachment). But they are not absolutely the only ones in this case.

Our modern society has made some progress all the same, for two thousands years or more (even if the concept of 'progress' should be thrown into the dustbin, as they say!). Many human beings in our modern world, even among those who remain strongly attached to their own beliefs, have somewhat put into perspective their religious references. They are perhaps more easily 'tolerant' not only in their daily external behaviours but also – and this is more important – in the intimate respect for other people's beliefs.

Owing to this progress, the mythologies of the Creation have been undermined in their turn. They are no longer construed as they were initially: to the letter. Many of our contemporaries – once again including among believers – accept that these mythologies are only mythologies, i.e., have the status of educational tales even – and precisely if – they are supposed to be inspired by the divinity. The Bible of the three religions of the Book, the mythology of the Bororo or the Dogons have the same status: that of being the original sacred text of the beliefs of one or several peoples.

The monotheist affirmation in itself is a strictly theological concept. When you say that there is only one god, you don't say much. This is neither evidence nor counter-evidence. Furthermore, monotheism is probably more widespread than the partisans of the formal distinction between monotheist/so-called polytheist religions. Many of those who are accused of polytheism hierarchically rank their divinities and often reduce them to various expressions of one and the same supernatural force. Looking at it more closely, it was realised that those who were called the 'idolaters' where in reality 'animists' and that this term improved their status because, beside the plurality of its expressions, the supernatural force was one.

For all that, are the monotheists as strongly monotheist as they declare? All religions, including Judaism, Christianity and Islam, affirm the existence of supernatural beings other than God – angels, demons, jinns, etc. In the same way as they affirm that, among human beings, some are 'inspired' by the divinity: Saints or prophets, they have conveyed God's word. The three religions of the Book know Satan as well as God, even if they organise the powers of these two beings along hierarchical lines for the benefit of the second. Before and after the religions of the Book, the same dualist conception of the supernatural has existed, with the Zoroastre, the Manicheans and others. And in Christianity, the unique God embodied in three persons (Father, Son and Holy Spirit), a mystery that is the subject of theological debates that animated the discussion between monophysit and other Christians – qualifies the concept of monotheism. How then can we really distinguish the word of God from the one that he inspires through his Prophets or his Son? From the point of view of the analysis of the metaphysical text, this is the same.

No doubt, the three religions of the Book have been more than others affirmative of this monotheist character, as they have introduced some form of rationality in other aspects of their ethical and organisational constitutive elements. One is therefore tempted to establish a correspondence between this religious evolution and that of the former Middle-East societies, with the surpassing of the lineage organisation by the building of the state. But if this mutual adjustment of the social basis of the religious instance is plausible, it does not constitute the sole historical form possible. Other no less developed societies, in India and in China for instance, have responded to these requirements by other means: in China by adopting a non religious metaphysics (Confucianism), in India by the freedom of religious invention (Hinduism).

At the risk of seeing some people protest violently, I will add that the three religions in question, like the others, have crystallised in moments where the temptations for syncretism were very powerful. Scientists were able to reveal 'borrowings', for instance of Christianity to the religion of ancient Egypt, of Judaism to the religions of ancient Orient (Baal and others), of Islam to the beliefs of the Arabic Peninsula, etc. If we come down a bit lower to rites, dietary restrictions and other things of the same type, the borrowings are even more visible. No believers will feel uncomfortable with this reconnaissance: it will only prove for them that God has inspired the human beings all along their history, even before the religion associated with him was revealed.

Among the three religions of the Book, proximity is greater between Judaism and Islam. Religions have put forward – not without argument – that Islam is largely an Arabisation of Judaism. Not only because its precepts, legislation and rites and those of the Jews are largely common but also – and more fundamental – because Islam shares with Judaism the same conception of the relationship between Religion and Society. The Arabisation of Judaism, besides, precedes the message of the Prophet of Islam. History and the Koran recognise the existence of the Hanifs who identify with the God of their ancestor, Abraham, without proclaiming themselves Jews for all that. In this spirit, Islam affirmed to be the religion revealed by God to mankind from the very beginning, having been revealed to Adam himself. Islam is supposed to have always existed, even before God spoke through his Prophet Mahomet. But is was supposedly forgotten or misunderstood by some (polytheists), and only partly understood by others (Jews and Christians).

So, we seize the importance that Muslims – or some of them – give to a curious debate. There is actually an abundant literature that is not considered as heretic by the authorities who proclaim themselves to be 'the' bearers of Islam, and that seeks to 'prove' that Abraham was not a Jew, but an Arab, etc. This demonstration appears like scientificity: there is reference here to the excavations in Mesopotamia, linguistics, the etymology of nouns, etc. For he who reads the Bible as a mythology among others, the question is meaningless. You don't 'correct' a mythology, or try to find out who was the real person behind the mythological figure.

One, therefore, understands – in the perspective of the thesis of Arabisation of Judaism (or Islamisation of Judaism) – that Islam does not resume the Bible of the Jews just as it is. It is reviewed and corrected.

The concomitance between the advent of Islam and the political unification of the Peninsula is so obvious that it led many Arab historians to saying that monotheism – substituting for the plurality of tribal divinities – had been the vehicle of the Arab national formation, because obeying the same God became synonymous with obeying the same political power. By then, the Arabs were well familiar with the Christian and Judaic monotheism. But if they had opted for Christianity, they would have run the risk to be dependant on Byzance which dominated the region, something they feared above all. On the contrary, by taking over in their own name a form of Judaism, they ran no risk, since the Jewish religion was not associated with a state system in place. There was, therefore, great temptation to make their singular reading of Judaism and to own it by refusing to see it as the proper religion of a particular Semitic people, the Hebrews, but proclaiming it as a religion revealed to their own ancestors, also Semitic, but Arab.

On the other hand, the features of the environments in which Islam and Christianity were formed are very different. Islam was formed with all its dogmas in a small homogenous environment, that of the Arab tribes of Mecca and Medina. So it was bound to bear the marks of this origin to such a point that the universal vocation of this religion was not established at first. In the first time of the Arab conquest beyond the peninsula, the dominant trend among the Arab was to reserve Islam for themselves and leave to the peoples conquered their religions. If that was the way things were, Islam would have remained a strictly Arab religion. But a double movement has opened Islam to its universal vocation: the spontaneous conversion of important segments of the populations conquered and the finally favourable reception of these conversions by the Arabs themselves. Christianity, on the contrary, was formed in the cosmopolite environment of the Hellenist culture of the Roman Empire. In addition, its formation has been slow. It was therefore marked from the very start by this multiethnic and multicultural environment which encouraged its vocation for universalism.

A final remark: is monotheism really a tremendous progress of thinking, a qualitative 'progress'? There are evil spirits (but who says evil says ill-intentioned, inspired by the Evil One, the Devil) who draw a parallel between this unique God (in popular imagery – if not in the purified vision of doctors – an old man with a white beard, symbol of wisdom and authority) and the patriarch of the patriarchy, the autocrat of power systems. In this imagery which translates well real-life experience, it is obvious that the wise old man is nearer to God than a woman or a youth. A projection in Heaven that legitimates the patriarchy and autocracy that reign here below. Among others, the elimination of female deities, always important in non-monotheist religions, could but accentuate patriarchal domination. The evil spirits will say that this almighty unique God deprives them, poor wretches, of any power because, with numerous gods that are competing and in conflict, you can call to your rescue the one that is better positioned to render service and – in the Greek style – thumb your nose at the one annoying you! Is it by chance if the Greek democracy is polytheist? Is it by chance if in the areas that will be dominated by the great religions – here Christianity and Islam – this democracy disappears? But we will make you observe that the power that adopts a non-religious metaphysics in China and Hinduist religious pluralism in India also was autocratic and nothing else.

### *Religion and Society: The Risk of Theocracy*

Religions are not merely metaphysical systems. They are expressions of major social realities. Metaphysics and social function mutually determine each other in an historical dialectic. It is thus difficult to disentangle metaphysical claims from the social systems from which they emerge and on which they operate.

A useful starting point to answer the question posed above – are the three religions of the Book mainly one or several? – consists in the vision of historical time which they propose.

Judaism believes in an end of time. This hour will sound with the advent of the Messiah who will organise his kingdom here on earth, that is to say a society which is just and happy and which will endure forever. The convinced believer does not believe that this reign of justice can be conquered by human action before the end of time. That is the reason why some Jews reject the State of Israel. Nevertheless, the Messiah has not yet arrived. The end of time is still ahead of us.

Islam has adopted a different position on this important question. The Prophet in his lifetime had already organised, at Medina, a just society. In this sense, even though he is regarded as a prophet, the last of the prophets, this Prophet can be considered as the one the Jews call the Messiah: the organiser of the Kingdom of God on earth. I know fully well that this interpretation of Islam and of the time of the Prophet is not the only one even among Muslims. Many would say – and not necessarily only a minority who claim to be enlightened – that it is not necessary to re-establish the social system which existed in Medina in the time of the Prophet, that from that epoch, one can at best derive certain general principles, and nothing more, principles which must be adapted to the changing reality of the times. If only because the Prophet is no longer there to lead society and no one could replace him.

The issue then is to adapt these principles to the changing realities of time. Hence, a large margin paves the way for discussion and diverse opinions. However, this relativistic concept has actually dominated the real history of Islam. But it is only a concept and can be rejected. We can substitute for it the idea that social organisation in the time of the Prophet is well and truly the final model of history, the one we must turn to, which should be reproduced or to which we should return if we moved away from it. An interpretation that can be termed fundamentalist if you want, since it calls for a return to the 'sources', the fundamentals. It exists and has always existed. It catches the full wind in its sails today. But it comes back in the foreground, imposes itself or seems to do so only in particular circumstances, the reasons for which would need to be analysed. Therefore, what matters here is to know that this concept places the future in the past. The end of times started fifteen centuries ago, history has stopped it for the main. What may have come since in real history hardly matters, since that history provides no lesson worthy of being retained by those among the Muslims who adhere to this interpretation of Islam.

Christianity has adopted a third position on the question of the end of time, a point of view which separates it from Judaism and Islam, and which gives it a specificity both as a metaphysics and as a force which participates in shaping social reality. But in order to see this difference, it will be necessary to come directly to the analysis of the social reality in question.

- Judaism is not merely an abstract monotheism; it is also the organiser of an historical society, that of the Jews in Palestine and later and partly, that of the Jewish communities in the Diaspora.

The real history of the Jews in ancient Palestine is not well known. Infinitely less well than that of other peoples in the region, perhaps because the latter, more powerful and more developed, have left more written and other traces. But what is certain is that Judaism produced precise and extremely detailed laws which included not only the great moral principles enshrined in the Ten Commandments – which, moreover, seem to have been inspired by others – but much more: an ensemble of rules which governed the individual, family and social life of the Jews. These laws regulated everything in the fields of personal laws, marriage, divorce, filiation, inheritance, etc. All these laws are religious and sacred, and thus difficult (if not quite impossible) to modify. These laws and regulations are accompanied by criminal laws that are no less precise and besides, very hard, even savage to contemporary eyes (lapidation of adulterous women ...), which are themselves integral part of the sacred. Lastly, they operate within a highly ritualised framework: from circumcision through absolute prohibition of all activity on the Sabbath to dietary restrictions, the list is long.

It is probably the precise formalism of all these laws, rules and rituals that permitted the Jews of the Diaspora to preserve themselves from unavoidable contagion, assimilation and conversion. It is also perhaps one of the motives for the hostility against them (a motive is not an excuse!).

What appears certain is that such a social conception of religion leaves no real place to the concept of lay society. It can only produce a theocratic concept of power, which has been preserved by the Jews of the Diaspora. Since power cannot invent laws, it is there to apply those which God has established once and for all. There is a tendency today to call theocratic only those forms of power which operate through a religious caste which lays claim to a monopoly because it alone knows the laws which it is necessary to apply, whether this caste calls itself a synod, a Church, or something else, or even, has no name. This is unfortunate. Theocracy means the power of God and in practice that of those who speak in his name. Theocracy is opposed to modernity if by modernity we mean the fundamental concept of modern democracy: that human beings freely establish their own laws and because of this are responsible for their own history.

Jewish law has relatively few provisions regarding the organisation of power, public law, to speak modern language. By comparison with other developed states in the region, Pharaoh's Egypt, Acheminid then Sassinide Iran, countries in Mesopotamia, Greece and Rome – which have produced detailed models of administrative and political organisation (little matters that these models were not democratic), the Jews have remained confined in more unpolished political forms in which the powers of the judges and the kings were ill-defined. But this weakness is only an additional argument in favour of theocracy. The power of God cannot be weighed down by precise formalisms.

Long forgotten among the Jews of the Diaspora, this natural propensity for theocracy emerged again in the Jewish State – contemporary Israel. Only those who resist understanding Judaism as a form of social organisation will be surprised.

- Islam offers, on all planes, a rigorous parallel with Judaism.

Islam regulates, in the same manner, in detail and on the basis of its sacred text, all aspects of personal law. It has a similar penal law as strict and formal as that of the Jews (again, even in the details, there is perfect analogy: lapidation of adulterous women …) and practices similar rituals, from circumcision through dietary restrictions to fixed hours of prayer (not at any moment) and in a unique repetitive formula (with no personalisation possible). It is an ensemble of rules and practices which organises society in a way which leaves little room for innovation or imagination.

It matters little here that all this may have seemed or may still seem insufficient for more demanding believers. In historical Islam, Sufism opens its doors to them and allows the blooming of non ritualised mystics.

However, Jews and Muslims – like everybody – are practical people. They need commercial law to supplement personal laws. They borrow it, therefore, to the surrounding environment adapted to the requirements of the time. Muslims 'Islamise' the practices and laws that they discover in the civilised area they conquer. In this regard, Muslim law translates sometimes literally the Byzantine law. This operation is presented as Islamic, sacred, but this is only dressing.

The Muslims, like the Jews, have little in the way of an elaborate public law. As in the case of the Jews, this presents no problem. The lack was made up with the invention of the Caliphate (that preceded the Prophet's Islam) and by adapting Byzantine and Sassinid administrative institutions. The absence of precision concerning the supreme power, which one cannot define when it comes under divine jurisdiction, meant that it was impossible to transcend autocracy, pure and simple.

Autocracy and theocracy go together, for who will speak in the name of God, if not to legislate (no human has the right), then at least to apply the law? The Caliph – or his substitute the Sultan – will do it without hesitation. And the people will see him as 'the shadow of God on earth,' even when the doctors of the law hesitate to say so.

In this sense, power in Islamic countries has always been theocratic, even if the theocracy in question is not exercised by a caste of religious specialists. Islamic states cannot conceive of themselves otherwise, at least in so far as they are Islamic states. To do so has required, in the two Islamic regions to laicise radically (Turkey and the former Soviet Republics of Central Asia), a loud and official rupture with Islam. And these countries may well be returning to the Islamic norm. But that is another story.

In this sense, contemporary political Islam is nothing new. It simply goes further, and wants to transform the 'soft' theocracies of the Islamic world, contaminated by the surrounding modernity, into theocratic states in the strong sense of the word, that is to say to give whole and absolute power to a religious caste, a quasi-Church in Iran; the Azhar in Egypt – which has a monopoly on the right to speak in the name of 'the' religion, 'the law (of God), purge social practice of anything which, in its eyes, is not genuinely Islamic in the law and rites. Otherwise, if this caste cannot succeed in imposing itself as the exclusive holder of the Islamic legitimacy, then 'anybody', especially the chief of clans or of any group of people will. The result is permanent civil war, as in Afghanistan.

I had already written this text when I read the critique of the Jewish religion by Israël Shahak. Reading this book will convince the reader of the extraordinary similarity between Judaism and Islam which share a common conception of theocracy as sole legitimate form of political power. The reasons by which Shahak thus explains the renaissance of Jewish fundamentalism in Israel can be transposed word-for-word to Islamic fundamentalism. But of course both religions, Jewish and Muslim, may also – if one so wishes – be read differently, but not without difficulty.

- Christianity deviated from the theocratic road, then returned to it, before the Christian peoples departed from it once again.

At the moment of its constitution, Christianity did not appear to break with the Jewish heritage regarding the end of time. The announcement of the final judgement and the second coming of the Messiah certainly has eschatological dimensions, which are strongly accentuated in the text of the Apocalypse. This is why there have been, throughout the history of Christianity, messianic and millenarian movements.

Nevertheless, by the very nature of its message, Christianity broke radically with Judaism. This rupture is fundamental because the message which is expressed in the dramatic story of Christ is clear: the Kingdom of God is not, and never will be, of this world. If the Son of God himself has been vanquished on Earth, crucified, it is obvious that it was not God's (The Father) intention to establish his kingdom of justice and happiness here below. But if God refuses to substitute himself for human beings and to solve their problems, then it belongs to humans themselves to take responsibility and to do so. There is no longer the end of time, and Christ does not proclaim it being here or coming. In this regard, Christ is not the expected Messiah of Judaism, and the Jews were not in error when they refused to recognise him as such. The message of Christ can then be interpreted simply as an invitation to human beings to make their own history and, if they do it well (that is inspired by the values of which the Messiah gave an example by his life and death), then they bring themselves closer to the God in whose image they have been created. It is this interpretation which imposed itself in the end, and which gives to modern Christianity its particular style founded on a reading of the Gospels which makes it possible to imagine the future as an encounter between history made by human beings themselves and divine intervention. The end of time, imagined as the product of a divine intervention from outside of history, has disappeared.

This rupture then extended itself to the whole field which up to then had been regulated by sacred law. While Christ made it quite clear that he did not come to abrogate the law (of the Jews), he did make it subject to human judgement, something which inevitably meant that it would be called into question. Christ himself will exemplify this by challenging one of the most formal and hard among these criminal laws (precisely the lapidation of adulterous women). By saying 'Let he who never sinned throw the first stone', he opens the doors of debate: what if this law was not just? What if it only hid the hypocrisy of the real sinners? The Christians will then abandon in fact the Jewish law and rituals: circumcision disappears, the rules of personal law diversify, especially as the expansion of Christianity beyond the Jewish environment adapts to different laws and statutes, for which it does not substitute a Christian law that does not exist, dietary restrictions lose strength, etc.

The same was true with respect to dogma. While not breaking openly with Judaism, and in fact admitting its sacred text (the Bible), it did so 'without discussion', neither submitting it to re-reading or to review, in a way which effectively annulled their meaning. It juxtaposes it to other sacred texts, those it produced, the Gospels. The morality proposed in its own sacred texts (love for the neighbour, pity, forgiveness, justice …) is somewhat different from the one inspired by the Old Testament. What is more, the Gospels did not propose anything sufficiently precise to inspire any positive legislation regarding the personal or criminal law status. From this point of view, the texts are neatly different from those of the Torah and the Koran.

There is no longer any possible confusion between legitimate power and God ('Give unto Caesar what is Caesar's'). This is an untenable precept in the sense that the Empire, after having combated Christianity for three centuries, suddenly embraced it and became Christian. Even before, in the clandestineness of the churches around which the Christians are organised, even more after the Emperor became the armed protector of Christianity, a new law developed, which called itself 'Christian.' First, in the field of personal law. What is a Christian family? This should be clearly outlined, legislated. The process will be long, fluctuating, and no agreement will ever be reached because previous laws and customs, different here and there, are accepted... However, gradually, these laws will take on the prestige of the sacred: the Catholics cannon laws (there is one for Oriental churches and another for Occidental churches), as the legal forms of the different orthodox and protestant churches are the outcome of this slow evolution.

Concerning the organisation of power, the relation of the political and the religious, we find the same fluctuations and the same evolution towards sacralisation. The churches, which had been constituted as clandestine parties, to use the language of our epoch, remained so after the 'seizure of power.' It was by necessity that they remained democratic by being close to the people. Now they lost this character, bringing themselves closer to power and distancing themselves from the faithful who they henceforth 'organised' on behalf of the rulers. The rulers, for their part, did not allow themselves to be domesticated by the Churches. They had their own rules of dynastic devolution; they institutionalise the requirement of the new system – feudal in the Romano-Barbarian West, imperial in Byzantine East – and subject the churches as much as possible to their own logic. The fusion progressed nevertheless, and like the Caliph, the Lord and the King became more or less sacred personages.

Christianity thus developed towards a 'soft theocratic model' managed jointly by clergy and by lay rulers who did not hesitate to proclaim themselves just as much Christians as the clergy. The result looked much like Islam. When, in the Christian world, the bourgeois revolution called into question the eternity of the social order which claimed to rest on immutable (or allegedly so) Christian principles, when this revolution opened the doors of modernity, invented the new democracy (however limited its implementation was), when the Enlightenment declared that Men (though not yet Women!) make their own history and must choose (and unmake) their own laws, the defenders of the old order denounced, in the name of Christianity, this inordinate ambition for human emancipation. Thus, Joseph de Maistre, in the France of the Restoration period, could proclaim democracy to be an absurdity, a dangerous and criminal dream, because God is the only legislator, that God alone makes laws which we only apply, without exercising his imagination for inventing better laws – A text which Ayatollah Khomeini or Sheik El Azhar could have written word for word!

It matters little that by the time Joseph de Maistre wrote, at the beginning of the nineteenth century, it was no longer possible to say just precisely what these Christian laws consisted in: the Ten Commandments? Or all the Roman, Germanic, and Slavic traditions which made up the fabric of the European societies which called themselves Christian?

By the time de Maistre wrote, it was too late. European society had developed a taste for making its own laws, without the obligation to refer to Christian principles, which continued to be invoked now and then, but without rigidity or great conviction. These societies confronted new imperatives – an established objective need to act that way. The risk of theocracy was definitively passed.

From the Old Debate – Reconciling Faith and Reason – to the New Debate – Laicising Social Power

- Proclaiming God the sole legislator is fine in theory, but hardly practical. Muslims and Christians alike will experience it in their respective areas.

Highly civilised, the societies of the Muslim and European Middle Ages faced a problem: how to reconcile Faith – or more precisely the religion which is the foundation of legitimate power – and Reason, which one needs every day not only to solve ordinary problems, but also to inspire laws and regulations in response to fundamentally new situations.

Muslims, Christians, and Jews in the Diaspora solved this problem in the same way and by the same method – Aristotelian Scholasticism – which is neither Jewish nor Christian, nor Islamic, but rather Greek! – and with the same brilliant results. The avant-garde, Ibn Rusd among the Muslims, Thomas Aquinas among the Christians, and Maimonides among the Jews went quite far. They relativised dogmas, interpreted sacred texts as much as necessary, made up for their deficiencies, and substituted for the literal reading of the text images which met their educative requirements. The most audacious were often condemned as heretics (this was the case with Ibn Rusd) by conservative interpreters in service to the powers that be. But little matters: a European society already in motion lived according to the precepts which these radicals recommended. The Muslim world on the other hand refused to and entered into a decline from which it never exited. Al-Ghazali, the spokesman of Islamic reaction, the enemy of Ibn Rusd, has remained, up to this day, among the 'revolutionary' Ayatollahs of Iran, at the El Azhar, and in Saudi Arabia, the definitive point of 'reference' in all matters.

- Beginning with the Renaissance and above all during the Enlightenment, Christian Europe abandoned this old debate for a new one.

It was no longer a matter of reconciling Faith and Reason, but rather Reason and Emancipation. Reason, having declared its independence, did not deny that there might be an appropriate field where faith might be deployed, but if there was, it was no longer interested in it. It was, henceforth, a matter of legitimating new needs: the liberty of the individual, the emancipation of a society which took the risk of inventing its own laws and of fashioning its own future. Modernity consists precisely in this qualitative rupture with the past.

This new vision implied laicism, that is to say the abandonment of all reference to religion or to any other meta-social force in the debate around laws. To be sure, the different bourgeois societies went more or less far in this regard. The more radical the bourgeois revolution, the more radical the affirmation of laicism. The more the bourgeoisie compromised with the old order, the more limited the scope of laicisation.

Modern Christianity adapted to this profound social transformation. It has had to reinterpret itself from top to bottom, renouncing the ambition to govern and settling for an effort to inspire believers while compromising with adversaries. A beneficial exercise for, in so doing, modern Christians discovered how thin the laws attributed by God to their ancestors were.

Christianity has become a religion without dogmas.

However advanced the results produced by the effort to reconcile Faith and Reason, we must recognise their limits. In effect, these advances were blocked among the Muslims and Jews, and were finally defeated in favour of a return to ancient orthodoxies. By contrast, in the Christian world these advances prepared – without having necessarily conceived it – the way for their own elimination.

How can one try to explain this failure of some and the success of others, who will become the inventors of modernity? The materialist tradition in history gives priority to social development and supposes that religions, as part of the ideological instance, will ultimately be reinterpreted in a way which satisfies the exigencies of the real movement of history. This hypothesis is certainly more fertile than its opposite, which treats religions as dogmatic ensembles which are given once and for all; transhistorical invariants. This second hypothesis – that nowadays catches the full wind in its sails – precludes all reflection on the general movement of the history of humanity as a whole and rules out any real historical explanation in favour of recourse to 'irreducible cultural differences.'

But the materialist hypothesis does not exclude reflection on the reasons why certain pathways in the evolution of religious thought seem to have had the way paved for them, and others not. For the religious instance – like all of the constitutive instances of social life (economics, politics, ideology) – moves according to its own proper logic. The logic of each of these instances can, therefore, facilitate and accelerate social evolution or block it. In this case which trend will carry the day? It is impossible to say. It is in this under-determination that lies the freedom of societies of which the choices (to submit this particular instance to the logic imposed by the evolution of another) fashions the real history.

This hypothesis of under-determination permits us perhaps to forward a response to the question posed above.

Judaism and Islam were constituted historically by the affirmation that God is the only true King of society (the Jewish or Muslim society). The principle of the 'hakimiya' reintroduced by the Islamic fundamentalists of our epoch only reaffirms this principle with greater force and draws out all of its possible conclusions. What's more, Judaism and Islam give their sacred texts (the Torah and the Koran) the strongest possible interpretation. No word is superfluous. Indeed, these traditions have historically expressed severe reservations about the translation of the sacred text. Both Jews and Muslims are peoples of exegesis. The Talmud and the Fiqh have no equivalent in the reading of the Gospels.

This double principle explains many of the visible features of the two societies. The sacred texts of both can be read as compilations of laws and even as Constitutions (Saudi Arabia proclaims the Koran the Political Constitution of the State) which regulate the details of daily life (personal law, criminal law, civil law, the liturgies), invite the believer to 'renounce his will and submit integrally to that of God' as has been written many times, imagine this life as having to be regulated in all its details in a convent.

The reconciliation of Faith and Reason was carried out within the limits imposed by this double principle, as much with Muslim Ibn Rusd as with his Jewish contemporary Maimonides. And in both cases the traditionalist reaction carried the day, with the return to the Kalam by Ashari and Ghazali, and to Talmudic exegesis with Judah Halevy. Both proclaimed that certainty lay not with Reason but with Revelation. The page of philosophy was turned for the Muslims and the Jews. Accompanying the stagnation, then the decline of the Muslim societies, this abortion of the religious reform was to lead, by force of circumstances and in both cases, to an increase in the formalist, legalist and ritualistic nature of the interpretation of religion. This form of impoverishment found compensation in both cases in the development of mythical sects: Muslim Sufis and Jewish Cabbalists who, besides, have largely borrowed their methods to traditions from India.

If Christianity proved itself more flexible and if, because of this, it eventually broke through the bounds of the debate around the relationship between Faith and Reason, this is at least in part because Christianity never proposed to establish the Kingdom of God on Earth and the Gospels never erected a system of positive laws. One can understand, then, the following paradox: although the Catholic Church is strongly organised and there is an official authority that can impose its interpretation of religion, it did not resist the assaults of the new problematic that separates Reason from Faith, and it is Christianity that has had to adapt to the new emancipative conception of reason, while the lack of such authority in Islam after the Prophet and in Judaism since the destruction of the Temple and the dispersal of the Sanhedrin did not hamper the maintenance of the orthodoxy of the origins.

- The Jews of the Diaspora in Europe could not help but be affected by the radical transformation of the society in which they were living and of conceptions regarding the relationship of this society to religion.

Moses Mendelsohn thus tried in the eighteenth century to carry out a revolution in Judaism comparable to that in which Christian society was already engaged. In interpreting the Torah not as a body of obligatory legislation, but rather as a source of inspiration which each can interpret at his pleasure, Mendelsohn set forth on the road towards laicisation. The evolution of European society contributed to this process of assimilation of the Jews, whose 'nation' was declared defunct by the French Revolution, which knew only citizens possibly of Jewish faith. Consequently, there was great risk for Judaism to disappear gradually in the indifference shared by Western Europe's Jewish bourgeoisie and all its class, including in its Christian believers' fractions.

Persistent anti-Semitism – for all sorts of religious or simply economic and political reasons – above all in Eastern Europe, did not permit this Reform to triumph in Judaism as among the Christian population. A Counter – Reformation emerged in the ghettos, in the form of Hasidism, which allowed the Jews to find compensation for their inferior status by taking up their humiliation for the love of God.

- Modern culture is neither 'Christian' nor 'Judeo-Christian', as is written now in the media. This last expression, besides, has strictly no meaning. How can we then explain its widespread use? Very simply in my opinion: Christian Europe had been very anti-Jewish (the term anti-Semite was used when the reference to the pseudo 'race' substituted for religion, in the nineteenth century (for reasons whose discussion would go beyond the scope of these reflections). Tardily, after anti-Semitism had led to the horrors of Nazism, Europe, seising then the dimension of its crime, adopted this Judeo-Christian expression in a sympathetic and commendable intent to root out its anti-Semitism. It would have been much more convincing to recognise directly the decisive contributions of so many 'Jewish' thinkers to the progress of Europe. Inverted commas are used here simply because modern culture is neither Christian nor Judeo-Christian: it is a bourgeois culture.

The point of reference has been displaced from the old field of the debate (reconcile Faith – a religion – and Reason) to a new terrain which ignores religion. Modern thinkers are fundamentally neither Christian nor Jewish. Bourgeois civilisation is neither the creation of Christianity nor of Judeo-Christianity. On the contrary, Christianity and the Judaism of Western Europe have been forced to adapt to bourgeois civilisation. One waits for Islam to do the same. It is the condition for the participation of the Islamic peoples in the fashioning of a future from which they are excluded only by themselves.

## The Reform, an Ambiguous Expression of Adaptation of Christianity to Modernity

- The Reform is an extremely complex movement in its religious doctrinal dimensions as well as in the scope of the social transformations it came with. Besides, it deploys itself in very different European fields, in some of the most advanced cores in the invention of capitalism (The United Provinces, England) and in backward regions (Germany, Scandinavia). In these conditions, it is dangerous to speak of 'Protestantism' in singular form.

On the dogmatic plane, all the great reformers have called to a 'return to fundamentals' and, in this spirit have, among others, reestablished the Old Testament which Catholicism and Orthodoxy had marginalised. I have developed above the idea that Christianity was in fact constituted not as a continuation of Judaism but as a break with it. The use, which has become frequent, of the appellation 'Judeo-Christian', popularised by the expansion of the US-Protestant discourse, testifies to this shift in the vision of the relations among these two monotheistic religions, with which the Catholics (but still not the Orthodox) have aligned themselves tardily without much conviction, but rather because of political opportunism.

The call to a 'return to fundamentals' is a method that is nearly always found in the movements that identify themselves with religion. But it means quite nothing in itself, the interpretation of the fundamentals in question being always determinant. In the Reform, the fragments of ideologies and the value systems that are expressed in this religious terrain retain all the traces of primitive forms of reaction to the capitalist challenge. The Renaissance had been further ahead in some of these aspects (Machiavelli is one of the most eloquent witnesses to this). Now, then, the Renaissance is deployed in a Catholic terrain (Italy). And the management of some Italian cities as true commercial societies led by the syndicate of the wealthiest shareholders (Venice being the prototype) establishes an even more frank relation with the first forms of capitalism than the relation that will exist between Protestantism and capitalism. Later, the Enlightenment that spreads both in Catholic countries (France) and in Protestant ones (Britain, Low Countries and Germany) is situated more closely in the secular tradition of the Renaissance than in that of religious reform. Lastly, the French Revolution, because of its radical nature, gives secularism its full bloom, deliberately abandoning the terrain of religious re-interpretations in order to situate itself in that of modern politics, which is to a large extent the product of its invention.

One understands, therefore, that according to the circumstances, the Reform may have led to either the institution of national churches at the service of the compromise between the Monarchy, the Ancien Régime and the emerging grande bourgeoisie (upper classes), or the withdrawal of dominated classes in sects that develop apocalyptic visions.

Catholicism, which by its structure is organised along hierarchical lines, has been rigid for a long time. However, the challenges of modern time have forced it to eventually open up to the reinterpretation of dogmas, with outcomes that are no less remarkable. I am not surprised, under these conditions, that the new progress in religious interpretation – I mean those represented today by the theology of liberation – found a fertile reflection ground among the Catholics rather than the Protestants. Clearly, the thesis of Weber is not up to much!

- There was also a good example of involution in the religious interpretation associated with the Reform.

The Protestant sects that found themselves compelled to emigrate from seventeenth-century England had developed a very particular interpretation of Christianity which is not shared by either Catholics or the Orthodox, or even – at least not with the same degree of extremism – by the majority of European Protestants, including of course Anglicans, predominant among the leading classes in Britain.

This particular form of Protestantism implanted in New England was destined to leave a profound mark in the American ideology with a strong imprint, up to our days, since it will be the means by which the new society will set off the conquest of the continent, legitimising it with terms drawn from the Bible (the violent conquest by Israel of the promised land, an example repeated to exhaustion in the dominant US discourse). Later, the United States would extend to the entire planet the project of carrying out the work that 'God' had reserved for them to accomplish, since the Americans perceive themselves as the 'chosen people' – a synonym for the Nazi's Herrenvolk, to take that parallel once again. This is where we are today. And this is why American imperialism (not 'empire') is going to be even more savage than were its predecessors (which did not declare that they were entrusted with a divine mission).

- In any case, whether we are dealing with Catholic or Protestant societies, with one school or another, I do not give religious interpretation a decisively independent role in the organisation and operation of the dominant real power.

The past does not become by force of circumstances an 'atavistic transmission'. History changes peoples and religious interpretations, even when they persist in apparently 'ancient' and fixed forms, and are themselves subject to the review of their articulation to other dimensions of social reality.

It is because the subsequent historic trajectories of Europe on the one hand, and the United States on the other hand, were different that the European societies and the US society, be they Catholic or Protestant, have today diverging political cultures.

Political culture is the product of history regarded over the long term which, of course, is always specific to each country. That of the United States, on this level, is marked by specificities that break with those that characterised history on the European continent: the founding of New England by extremist Protestant sects, the genocide of the aboriginal populations, the Black slavery, and the displacement of the 'communitarisms' associated with the migratory waves of the nineteenth century.

The 'American revolution', much appreciated by many 1789 revolutionaries and today praised more than ever, was nothing more than a limited independence war with no social impact. In their revolt against the British monarchy, the American colonists did not want to transform their economic and social relations; they just no longer wanted to share the profits with the ruling class of the mother country. They wanted power for themselves, not in order to create a different society from the colonial regime, but to carry on in the same way, only with more determination and more profit. Their goals were first and foremost the pursuit of the westward expansion which implied, among others, the Indian genocide. The maintenance of slavery in this framework also raised no questioning. The big chiefs of the American Revolution were nearly all slave owners and their prejudices in this area were unwavering.

The successive immigrant waves have likewise played their part in the reinforcement of the US ideology. The immigrants are certainly not responsible for the squalor and oppression that stand at the origin of their departure. On the contrary, they are their victims. Nonetheless, circumstances – i.e. their emigration – lead them to renounce the collective struggle to change the conditions common to their classes or groups in their own countries, for the benefit of adherence to an ideology of individual success in the country that receives them. This adherence is stimulated by the American system, which plays its part to perfection. It hinders the acquisition of a class consciousness which, as soon as it has begun to mature, must face a new wave of immigrants that causes its political crystallisation to be aborted. But at the same time migration stimulates the 'communitarisation' of US society, since 'individual success' does not preclude a strong insertion in a community of origin (the Irish, the Italians, etc.), without which individual isolation could become unbearable. Now, here too the reinforcement of this dimension of identity – which the American system regains and praises- is carried out to the detriment of class consciousness and of the shaping of the citizen. While in Paris the people got ready to set off to 'take heaven by storm' (I refer here to the Commune of 1871), in the United States the bands constituted by the successive generations of impoverished immigrants (the Irish, Italians, etc.) slaughtered one another, manipulated with perfect cynicism by the dominant classes.

Protestant Europe – England, Germany, Low Countries, Scandinavia – shared initially some fragments of an ideology similar to that of the United States, conveyed by the 'return to the Bible', although most certainly in mitigated forms, without comparison with the extreme forms of the sects which migrated in New England. But in the countries in question, the working class has succeeded in rising to an affirmed class consciousness, sterilised by the successive immigrant waves in the United States. The emergence of workers' parties made the difference. In Europe, it imposed combinations of the liberal ideology and value systems (equality among others) which not only are unknown to it, but even conflicting. These combinations naturally have had their own history, different from a country and a moment for others. But they have maintained the autonomy of the politics in the face of dominant economics.

In the United States, there is no workers' party; there was never one. Communitarian ideologies could not substitute for the absence of a socialist ideology in the working classes. This applies even for the most radical of these, the black community, since by definition, communitarianism is inscribed within the framework of the generalised racism that it intends to fight in the latter's terrain, nothing more.

The absence of a worker's party combined with a dominant 'Biblical' religious ideology that are proper to the historical formation of the US society have finally produced the unparalleled situation of a *de facto* single party, the party of capital.

American democracy constitutes today the advanced model of what I call 'low-intensity democracy.' It is based on a total separation between the management of political life, which rests on the practice of multiparty electoral democracy, and the management of economic life, which is governed by the laws of capital accumulation. What is more, this separation is not the object of any radical questioning, but, on the contrary, is part of what is called the general consensus. This separation eliminates all the creative potential of democratic politics. It neutralises representative institutions (parliament and others), making them impotent in the face of the dictates of the 'market.'

The US state is, for this reason, at the exclusive service of the economy (that is to say of capital, whose faithful and exclusive servant it is, without having to concern itself with other social interests). It can be so because the historical formation of US society has – in the popular classes – blocked the maturing of political class consciousness, of real citizen consciousness.

In counterpoint, in Europe the state has been (and could again become) the compulsory meeting ground of the confrontation among social interests and can, as from there, favour the historical commitments that give meaning and real scope to democratic practice. If the state is not compelled to perform this role by class struggles and political struggles that preserve their autonomy in the face of the exclusive logic of the accumulation of capital, then democracy is transformed into a derisory practice, as it now is in the United States.

Like all ideologies, the US ideology is faced with the test of time in the 'quiet' periods of history – marked by good economic growth accompanied by social benefits that are deemed satisfactory – the pressure the ruling class must exert on its people weakens. From time to time then, depending on the needs of the moment, this ruling class 'boosts' the American ideology always using the same means: an enemy (always external, the American society being declared good by definition) is designated (the Evil Empire, the Evil axis) enabling the 'full mobilisation' of all the means for annihilating it – it was communism yesterday, through McCarthyism (forgotten by the 'pro-Americans') – to engage in the cold war and subordinate Europe. It is 'terrorism' today, an obvious pretext (September 11 resembles so much the Reichstag fire), that gets the real project of the ruling class through: securing military control of the planet.

But let there be no misunderstanding about that: it is not the would-be religious fundamentalist ideology that is at the controls and that would impose its logic to the real holders of power – the capital and those who serve it within the state. It is the capital that takes alone all the decisions that suit it, then mobilises the American ideology in question to put it at its service. The means used – unparalleled systematic disinformation – are then efficient, isolating the critical spirits, and submitting them to permanent and odious blackmail. The power then succeeds in manipulating easily an 'opinion' maintained in its stupidity.

## Political Islam

- Modernity is based on the principle that human beings must and can, individually and collectively, create their own history and that, to that effect, they have the right to innovate and to disregard tradition. Proclaiming this principle meant breaking with the fundamental principle that governed all the pre-modern societies, including of course that of Feudal and Christian Europe. Modernity was born with this proclamation. It had nothing to do with rebirth; it was simply a question of birth. The qualification of Renaissance that Europeans themselves gave to history in that era is therefore misleading. It is the result of an ideological construction purporting that the Greek-Roman Antiquity was acquainted with the principle of modernity, which was veiled in the 'Middle Ages' (between the old modernity and the new modernity) by religious obscurantism. It was the mythical perception of Antiquity that in turn paved the way for Eurocentrism, whereby Europe claims to go back to its past, 'to return to its sources' (hence, the Renaissance), whereas in fact, it is engineering a break with its own history.

The European Renaissance was the product of an internal social process, the solution found to contradictions peculiar to the then Europe through the invention of capitalism. On the other hand, what the Arabs by imitation referred to as their Renaissance – the Nahda of the 19th Century – was not so. It was the reaction to an external shock. The Europe that modernity had rendered powerful and triumphant had ambiguous effect on the Arab world through attraction (admiration) and repulsion (through the arrogance of its conquest). The Arab Renaissance takes its qualifying term literally. It is assumed that, if the Arabs 'returned' to their sources, as the Europeans would have done (that is what they themselves say), they would regain their greatness, even if debased for some time. The Nahda does not know the nature of the modernity that enhances Europe's power.

This is not the place to refer to different aspects and moments marking Nahda's deployment. I will just state briefly that Nahda does not forge the necessary break with tradition that defines modernity.

In constructing their 'Renaissance', the Europeans have situated their origin, be it mythological, before Christianity, in Ancient Greece. This invention will help them relativise the religious dimension of their 'specificity'. Contrarily, the Arabs in their construction by analogy will situate their origin in Islam. They need therefore to erase of their inheritance the contribution of the civilisations of Ancient Orient, called 'Jahiliya', that is, impious time.

One can thus understand why Nahda does not recognise the meaning of secularism, in other words, separation between religion and politics, the condition to ensure that politics serves as the field for free innovation, and for that matter, for democracy in the modern sense. Nahda thinks it can substitute for secularism an interpretation of religion purged of its obscurantist drifts. At any rate, to date, Arab societies are not adequately equipped to understand that secularism is not a 'specific' characteristic of the western world but rather a requirement for modernity. Nahda does not realise the meaning of democracy, which should be understood as the right to break with tradition. It therefore remains prisoner of the concepts of autocratic State; it hopes and prays for a 'just' despot (al moustabid al adel) – even if not 'enlightened' and the nuance is significant. Nahda does not understand that modernity also promotes women's aspiration to their freedom, thereby exercising their right to innovate and break with tradition. Eventually, Nahda reduces modernity to the immediate aspect of what it produces: technical progress. This voluntarily oversimplified presentation does not mean that its author is not aware of the contradictions expressed in Nahda, nor that certain avant-garde thinkers were aware of the real challenges posed by modernity, like Kassem Amin and the importance of women's emancipation, Ali Abdel Razek and secularism, and Kawakibi and the challenge posed by democracy. However, none of these breakthroughs had any effects; on the contrary, the Arab society reacted by refusing to follow the paths indicated.

Nahda is therefore not the time marking the birth of modernity in the Arab world but rather the period of its abortion.

Since the Arab States have not yet embraced modernity, whereas they bear the brunt of the daily challenge, Arabs still accept to a large extent these principles of autocratic power, which maintains its legitimacy or loses it in fields other than its non-recognition of the principle of democracy. If it is able to resist imperialist aggression – or to give that impression – if it is able to promote a visible improvement of the material living conditions of many, if not all, the autocratic power enjoys guaranteed popularity even if it now appears as an enlightened despotic power. It is also because Arab societies have not embraced modernity that the latter's brutal pompous refusal presented as the sole ideological theme placed at the centre of the Islamic project can find a favourable echo as powerful as it is known to be.

Beyond this non-modernity principle, the autocratic power therefore owes its legitimacy to tradition. In some cases, this could refer to a tradition of national and religious monarchy like that of Morocco or of a tribal monarchy in the Arabian Peninsula. But there is another form of tradition – the one inherited from the Ottoman Empire dominant in the territory between Algeria and Iraq, and therefore influencing the largest segment of the Arab world – which I describe as the tradition of 'Mameluke power'.

What is it about? It is about a complex system that associated the personalised power of warlords (relatively structured and centralised, or otherwise scattered), businessmen and men of religion. I emphasise men, since women are obviously not allowed to assume any responsibilities. The three dimensions of this organisation are not merely juxtaposed; they are actually merged into a single reality of power.

The Mamelukes are men of war who owe their legitimacy to a certain concept of Islam that places emphasis on the opposite of Dar El Islam (Muslim world – a community governed by the rules of peaceful management) / Dar El Harb (an extra-Muslim world, the place for the pursuit of Jihad, 'Holy War'). It is not by chance that this military concept of political management was fabricated by the conquering Seldjoukide Turks and the Ottomans, who called themselves 'Ghazi' – conquerors and colonisers of Byzantine Anatolia. It is not by chance that the Mamelukes' system was built from the era of Salah El Dine, liberator of the Lands occupied until then by the Crusaders. Populist powers and contemporary nationalists always mention the name of Salah El Dine with respectful admiration without ever considering or making any allusion to the ravages of the system from which it originated. At the end of the Crusades, the Arab world (which became Turkish-Arab) entered into a military feudalisation and isolation process reflecting a decline that put an end to the brilliant civilisation of the early centuries of the Caliphate while Europe was beginning to discard feudalism and preparing to embark on the invention of modernity and move on to conquer the world.

In compensation for this service as protectors of Islam, the Mamelukes gave the men of religion monopoly in the interpretation of dogmas, of justice rendered in the name of Islam and in the moral civilisation of the society. Relegated to its purely traditional social dimension – respect for rites being the sole important consideration – religion is absolutely subjugated by the autocratic power of men of war.

Economic life is then subject to the mood of the military-political authority. Whenever possible, the peasantry is directly subjected to the whims of this ruling class and private property is jeopardised (the related principle being indisputably sacralised by the fundamental texts of Islam). The proceeds of trade are no less tapped.

The Mameluke ruling class naturally aspired to the dispersion of its autocratic power. Formally responsible to the Sultan-Caliph, the Mamelukes took advantage of the long distance then separating them from the capital (Istanbul) to personally exercise full powers within the radius of the land under their control. In areas with an age-old tradition of State centralisation, such as Egypt, there have been successive attempts to discipline the whole military corps. It is not by chance that Mohamed Ali established his centralised authority by massacring the Mamelukes, but only to re-establishing a military-real estate aristocracy under his personal authority from that time onwards. The Beys of Tunis tried to do likewise on a more modest scale. The Deys of Algiers never succeeded in doing so. The Ottoman Sultanate did so in turn, thereby integrating its Turkish, Kurdish and Armenian provinces of Anatolia and its Arab provinces of historic Syria and Iraq under an authority 'modernised' that way.

Just modernisation? Or just a modernised autocracy? Enlightened despotism? Or just despotism? The fluctuations and variants are situated in this range, which does not usher in anything making it possible to go beyond.

Certainly, the typical autocratic model of Mameluke had to reckon with the numerous and diverse realities that always defined the real limits. Peasant communities that took refuge in their fortified mountains (Kabylians, Maronites, Druzeans, Alaouites, etc.), Sufi brotherhoods almost everywhere and tribes obliged the dominant authorities to reach a compromise with and tolerate the rebellious groups. The contrast in Morocco between Maghzen and Bled Siba is of a similar nature.

Have the forms in which power was exercised in the Arab world changed so much to justify the assertion that those described here belong to a distant past? The autocratic State and the related forms of political management certainly exist to date. However, they are beset with a profound crisis that has already curtailed their legitimacy, as they were increasingly incapable of meeting the challenges posed by modernity. Some of the testimonies in this regard are the emergence of political Islam, overlapping political conflicts as well as the resumption of social struggles.

- The fatal error lies in thinking that the emergence of mass political movements identified with Islam is the inevitable outcome of the rise of culturally and politically backward people who cannot understand any language other than that of their quasi-atavistic obscurantism. Discourses based on the prejudice that only the West could invent modernity, while the Muslim peoples are believed to be locked inside an immutable 'tradition' that makes them incapable of understanding the scope of the change needed.

Muslims and Islam have a history, just like those of the other regions of the world. It is a history fraught with diverse interpretations concerning linkages between reason and faith, a history of mutual transformation and adaptation of both society and its religion. However, the reality of this history is denied not only by Eurocentric discourses but also by the contemporary movements associated with Islam. In fact, the two entities have the same cultural bias whereby the 'specific' features ascribed to the different careers of their own peoples and religions are allegedly intangible, infinite and trans-historical. To the Western world's Eurocentrism, contemporary Political Islam solely opposes an inverted Eurocentrism.

The emergence of movements claiming to be Islamic is actually expressive of a violent revolt against the destructive effects of the really existent capitalism and against its attendant unaccomplished, truncated and deceptive modernity. It is an expression of an absolutely legitimate revolt against a system that has nothing to offer to the peoples concerned.

The discourse of the Islam proposed as an alternative to the capitalist modernity (to which the modern experiences of the historical socialisms are clearly assimilated), is political by nature, and by no means theological. The 'integrist' and 'fundamentalist' attributes often ascribed to Islam by no means correspond to this discourse, which, moreover, does not even allude to Islam, except in the case of certain contemporary Muslim intellectuals who are referred to in such terms in western opinion more than in theirs.

The proposed Islam is in this case the adversary of every liberation theology. Political Islam advocates submission and not emancipation. It was only Mahmoud Taha of Sudan who attempted to emphasise the element of emancipation in his interpretation of Islam. Sentenced to death and executed by the authorities of Khartoum, Taha was not acknowledged by any 'radical' or 'moderate' Islamic group, and neither was he defended by any of the intellectuals identifying themselves with 'Islamic Renaissance' or even by those who are merely willing to 'dialogue' with such movements.

The heralds of the said 'Islamic Renaissance' are not interested in theology and they never make any reference to the classical texts concerning theology. Hence, what they understand by Islam appears to be solely a conventional and social version of religion limited to the formal and integral respect for ritual practice. The Islam in question would define a 'community' to which one belongs by inheritance, like ethnicity instead of a strong and intimate personal conviction. It is solely a question of asserting a 'collective identity' and nothing more. That is the reason why the term 'Political Islam' is certainly more appropriate to qualify all these movements in the Arab countries.

Modern political Islam had been invented by the Orientalists in the service of the British authority in India before being adopted intact by Mawdudi of Pakistan. It consisted in 'proving' that Muslim believers are not allowed to live in a State that is itself not Islamic – anticipating the partition of India – because Islam would ignore the possibility of separation between State and Religion. The Orientalists in question failed to observe that the English of the thirteenth century would not have conceived of their survival either without Christianity!

Abul Ala Al Mawdudi therefore took up the theme stipulating that power comes from God alone (wilaya al faqih), thus repudiating the concept of citizens having the right to make laws, the State being solely entrusted with enforcement of the law defined once and for all (The 'Shariah'). Joseph de Maistre had already written similar things, accusing the Revolution of inventing modern democracy and individual emancipation.

Refuting the concept of emancipative modernity, Political Islam disapproves of the very principle of democracy – the right of society to build its own future through its freedom to legislate. The Shura principle is not the Islamic form of democracy, as claimed by Political Islam, for it is hampered by the ban on innovation (ibda), and accepts, if need be, only that of interpretation of the tradition (ijtihad). The Shura is only one of the multiple forms of the consultation found in all pre-modern and pre-democratic societies. Of course, interpretation has sometimes been the vehicle for real changes imposed by new demands. However, the fact remains that by virtue of its own principle – denial of the right to break with the past – interpretation leads into deadlock the modern fight for social change and democracy. The parallel claimed between the Islamic parties – radical or moderate, since all of them adhere to the same 'anti-modernist' principles in the name of the so-called specificity of Islam – and Christian-Democrat parties of modern Europe is therefore not valid, strictly speaking, even though American media and diplomatic circles continue to make allusion to the said parallel so as to legitimise their support of possibly 'Islamist' regimes. Christian-Democracy is an element of modernity of which it upholds the fundamental concept of creative democracy as the essential aspect of the concept of secularism. Political Islam refuses modernity and proclaims this fact without being able to understand its significance.

Hence, the proposed Islam does not deserve at all to be qualified as 'modern' and the supporting arguments advanced in this regard by friends of 'dialogue' are extremely platitudinous: they range from the use of cassettes by its propagandists to the observation that these agents are recruited from among the 'educated' classes – engineers for instance! Moreover, these movements' discourse solely reflects Wahabite Islam, which rejects all that the interaction between historical Islam and Greek philosophy had produced in its epoch, as it merely turned over the unimaginative writings of Ibn Taymiya, the most reactionary of the theologians of the Middle Ages. Although some of his heralds qualify this interpretation as 'a return to the sources' (or even to the Islam of the time of the Prophet), it is actually a mere reference to the notions that prevailed two hundred years ago, notions of a society whose development has been stalled for several centuries.

The contemporary Political Islam is not the outcome of a reaction to the so-called abuses of secularism, as often purported, unfortunately.

It is because no Muslim society of modern times – except in the former Soviet Union – has ever been truly secular, let alone appalled at the daring innovations of any 'atheistic' and aggressive power. The semi-modern State of Kemal's Turkey, Nasser's Egypt, Baathist Syria and Iraq merely subjugated the men of religion (as it often happened in former times) to impose on them concepts solely aimed at legitimising its political options. The beginnings of a secular idea existed only in certain critical intellectual circles. The secular idea did not have much impact on the State, which sometimes retreated in this respect when obsessed with its nationalist project, thereby causing a break with the policy adopted by the Wafd since 1919, as testified by the disturbing evolution inaugurated even at the time of Nasser. The reason for this drift is perhaps quite obvious: whereas the democracy of the said regimes was rejected, a substitute was found in the so-called 'homogeneous community', with its danger obviously extending to the declining democracy of the contemporary Western world itself.

Political Islam intends to perfect an evolution already well established in the countries concerned and aimed at restoring a plainly conservative theocratic order associated with a political power of the 'Mameluke' type. The reference to this military caste that ruled up to two centuries ago, placed itself above all laws (by pretending to know no law other than the 'Shariah'), monopolised profits from the national economy and accepted to play a subsidiary role in the capitalist globalisation of that era – for the sake of 'realism' – instantly crosses the mind of anyone who observes the declined post-nationalist regimes of the region as well as the new so-called Islamic regimes, their twin brothers.

From this fundamental point of view, there is no difference between the so-called 'radical' movements of Political Islam and those that wanted to appear 'moderate' because the aims of both entities are identical.

The case of Iran itself is not an exception to the general rule, despite the confusions that contributed to its success: the concomitance between the rapid development of the Islamist movement and the struggle waged against the Shah who was socially reactionary and politically pro-American. Firstly, the extremely eccentric behaviour of the theocratic ruling power was compensated by its anti-imperialist positions, from which it derived its legitimacy that echoed its powerful popularity beyond the borders of Iran. Gradually, however, the regime showed that it was incapable of meeting the challenge posed by an innovative socio-economic development. The dictatorship of 'turbaned' men of religion, who took over from that of the 'caps' (military and technocrats), as they are referred to in Iran, resulted in a fantastic degradation of the country's economic machinery. Iran, which boasted about 'doing the same as Korea', now ranks among the group of 'Fourth World' countries. The indifference of the ruling power's hard wing to social problems facing the country's working classes was the basic cause of its take-over by those who described themselves as 'reformers' with a project that could certainly attenuate the rigours of the theocratic dictatorship, but without renouncing, for all that, its principle enshrined in the Constitution ('wilaya al faqih'), which formed the basis of the monopoly of a power that was therefore gradually induced to give up its 'anti-imperialist' postures and integrate the commonplace compradore world of capitalism of the peripheries. The system of Political Islam in Iran has reached deadlock. The political and social struggles in which the Iranian people have now been plunged might one day lead to the rejection of the very principle of 'wilaya al faqih', which places the college of the men of religion above all institutions of the political and civil society. That is the condition for their success.

Political Islam is in fact nothing other than an adaptation to the subordinate status of the compradore capitalism. Its so-called 'moderate' form therefore probably constitutes the principal danger threatening the peoples concerned since the violence of the 'radicals' only serves to destabilise the State to allow for the installation of a new compradore power. The constant support offered by the pro-American diplomacies of the Triad countries towards finding this 'solution' to the problem is absolutely consistent with their desire to impose the globalised liberal order in the service of the dominant capital.

The two discourses of the globalised liberal capitalism and Political Islam do not conflict; they are rather complementary. The ideology of American 'communitarianisms' being popularised by current fashion overshadows the conscience and social struggles and substitutes for them, so-called collective 'identities' that ignore them. This ideology is therefore perfectly manipulated in the strategy of capital domination because it transfers the struggle from the arena of real social contradictions to the imaginary world that is said to be cultural, trans-historical and absolute, whereas Political Islam is precisely 'communitarianism'.

The diplomacies of the G7 powers, and particularly that of the United States, know what they do in choosing to support Political Islam. They have done so in Afghanistan by describing its Islamists as 'freedom fighters' (!) 'against the horrible dictatorship of communism', which was in fact a project of enlightened, modernist, national and populist despotism that had the audacity to open schools for girls. They continue to do so from Egypt to Algeria. They know that the power of Political Islam has the virtue – to them – of making the peoples concerned helpless and consequently ensuring their compradorisation without difficulty.

Given its inherent cynicism, the American Establishment knows how to take a second advantage of Political Islam. The 'drifts' of the regimes that it inspires – the Talibans for instance – who are not drifts in any way but actually come within the logic of their programmes, can be exploited whenever imperialism finds it expedient to intervene brutally, if necessary. The 'savagery' attributed to the peoples who are the first victims of Political Islam is likely to encourage 'Islamophobia' and that facilitates the acceptance of the perspective of a 'global apartheid' – the logical and necessary outcome of an ever-polarising capitalist expansion.

The sole political movements using the label of Islam, which are categorically condemned by the G7 powers, are those involved in anti-imperialist struggles – under the objective circumstances at the local level: Hezbollah in Lebanon and Hamas in Palestine. It is not a matter of chance.

# 2
## The Human Right to Development

### Wilfred L. David

> The better life, once a decent minimum has been reached, is largely a matter of people getting along with each other and not fouling their own fairly well upholstered nests.... Freedom of movement, freedom to express ideas, a feeling of security, and, in general, a reasonable bill of rights are surely involved in creating the conditions [for] the better, more satisfying, and more constructive life.
>
> Wendell Gordon (1973)

The rights-based or egalitarian perspective of morality projects a vision of the natural right of all human beings to share and participate equally in the design of Institutions based on an overlapping consensus. Correlatively, people can be said to possess a universal 'right to development' by virtue of their common status as human beings who are endowed with capabilities to make plans, enforce shared rules, and apportion justice (Dworkin 1978). The right to development is grounded in a preconception that every human being should live a free and worthy life in his or her community. This connotes a 'right to life,' or the capability to aspire to an increasingly better quality of existence. Hence, all individuals and groups should be afforded an equal opportunity to participate in, contribute to, and benefit from the fruits of material progress.[1]

The right to development is a fundamental human right that lies at the intersection of the entire gamut of economic, social, cultural, political and civil rights. It is a focal point of Articles of 1, 55, and 56 of the United Nations *Charter*, which emphasises the joint responsibility of member states to promote development, social progress, and respect for human rights. Such themes are also adumbrated in several normative resolutions adopted by the United Nations and its specialised agencies. For example, the 1986 United Nations *Declaration on the Right to Development* affirms that 'the human person is the central subject of development and should be the active participant and beneficiary of the right to development.' A recurrent theme has centred around the collective responsibility of the global community to ensure attainment of an adequate standard of living necessary for the enjoyment of equal rights and fundamental freedoms throughout the world.

Various resolutions of the Human Rights Commission also stress the duty of all member-states and the global community jointly and severally to create the conditions necessary for the realisation of the right to development. The 1993 *World Conference on Human Rights* not only reaffirmed this right, but also reiterated that 'the human person is the central subject of development.' It was also emphasised that 'while development facilitates the enjoyment of all human rights, the lack of development cannot be invoked to justify the abridgement of internationally recognised human rights.' Hence, a relatively low level of development should not be used as an excuse for denying citizens of a country their basic rights, and in particular, as a justification for political and other forms of oppression. While it is evident that poverty and social exclusion do constitute violations of human dignity, their incidence does not absolve governments from the duty of designing programmes guaranteeing human rights, while fostering effective citizen participation in decisions governing fulfillment of needs, capabilities and aspirations.

**Universals Versus Particulars**

The fundamental goals and processes of humanitarian development are inextricably intertwined with principles guaranteeing the provision of basic rights – economic, social, cultural, civic or civil and political. Over the centuries, these principles have come to reflect forms of citizenship that provide people with access to rights and powers in most established societies (Marshall 1964).[2] The economic and social categories denote the rights of all people to a certain minimum standard of living, economic welfare and social security. Cultural rights pertain to the ability of each society to design and enforce its own norms and standards about how its citizens may or may not achieve their goals. Civic or civil rights refer essentially to legal rights, while the political dimension stresses the right of every person to participate in the exercise of political power, or more directly in the practice of politics.

These broad categories of 'first generation' rights are both indivisible and interdependent. For example, enjoyment of economic, social, and cultural rights is a *sine qua non* for the enjoyment of political rights. At the same time, abridgement of civil and political rights militates against enjoyment of social, cultural, and economic rights. A distinction is also sometimes drawn between 'individual' and 'collective' rights (Macpherson 1987). The former are supposed to be enjoyed by all persons irrespective of social class, gender, ethnicity, religion, age and political affiliation. By contrast, collective rights are normally claimed by subordinated cultural minorities such as Native Americans and Aborigines in Australia. In this context, the 1993 World Conference on Human Rights focused attention not only on the plight of indivi-duals, but also on the undesirable conditions facing specific groups at risk: women and girls; national, religious, ethnic and linguistic minorities; disabled persons; children; indigenous peoples; refugees and internally displaced persons; migrants and other vulnerable groups.

The major historical and logical conflicts among the broad categories of rights can be traced to the peculiar evolution of international laws and corresponding changes in modes of interpretation. In particular, human rights law was initially developed as a part of the constitutional codes of individual nation-states. The perception was that its substance and enforcement were primarily concerned with relations among nation-states, an area historically regarded as a domestic matter. The first set of bills of fundamental rights emerged in the *French Declaration of the Rights of Man and the Citizen* in 1789, and in the declarations of the North American colonies at the time of their independence. From the very inception, however, a major bone of contention arose over the 'human' versus the 'rights' dimension of the equation. For example, the historical debate on the French Declaration has demonstrated that while it specified the actual constitution of valued rights, there was not sufficient clarity about the individuals or groups who were entitled to them (Hunt 1996).

Along similar lines, Chirot (1994) poses the question: who is considered human or subhuman? Its import lies in the historical tendency for tyrants and dictators to dehumanise entire groups of people. The process of human rights empowerment shows that large numbers of people have become collective 'non-persons' who have been treated inhumanely and deprived of their rights. The worst kinds of abuses, Chirot opines, have occurred when authoritarian regimes implicitly categorise certain groups as 'subhuman,' not so much because of what they are perceived to have done but more because of who they are[3]. The upshot of the argument is that there has been considerable divergence between the philosophical and prescriptive dimensions of human rights on the one hand, vis-à-vis the historical realities surrounding their enforcement on the other. The same is true for related notions, such as freedom (Patterson 1991).

Through the more general lens of Western thought and practice, the ideal notion of economic justice was predicated on equality in the distribution of rights. This preconception was grounded in the classical or Enlightenment view of a good society, which espoused two broad principles: equal incomes and equal rights. It was expected that the economic and political institutions of capitalism would guarantee equal incomes and privileges for all members of society. Economic justice was to be arbitrated through the rules governing the operation of free markets, while equality was to be guaranteed by the principles of democracy (Okun 1975). But, humanitarian skeptics point out that capitalism and free markets do not necessarily guarantee equality, and democracy, in the sense of absolute majority rule, is not always consistent with human rights. The record suggests that unconstrained majorities can impose inordinate burdens on minorities, for example, through the propagation of overtly racist policies, denial of legal equality to women, or suppression of opposition voices.

While issues about the 'tyranny of the majority' remain with us, the immediate concern is more with the evolution of 'universal' human rights. Their contemporary fundamentals, especially the economic and social variety, did not enter into international law until the Second World War. The resulting atrocities led to a realisation that international security, peace, and progress could only be guaranteed through universal enforcement and protection of such rights (Forsythe 1977). The United Nations emerged in this context, and pursuant to Article 66 of its Charter, a Commission on Human Rights was established in 1946 to give precision to the scope and content of human rights. It drafted a *Universal Declaration of Human Rights*, which was proclaimed by the General Assembly on December 10, 1948 as a *de facto* code of universal human rights, even though it was merely termed a 'declaration.' It consists of thirty Articles highlighting basic rights and freedoms to which people are entitled without discrimination. Several supporting covenants and conventions have subsequently defined and further codified the contexts of these rights. Table 1 lists the major human rights agreements for ease of reference.

Thus, the United Nations Charter, through the Universal Declaration to subsequent international settlements have been responsible for enunciating a set of intrinsic rights that all established societies have a moral obligation to bring about, guarantee and protect. Our common humanity and the very fact that we live in an interdependent world tend to establish the need for shared standards of human dignity and embracement of the fundamental rights of all humankind. In concert with the humanitarian development perspective, they should not be interpreted as abstract or metaphysical constructs, but rather as concrete human goals to be progressively achieved. The enforcement of some categories (positive rights) calls for positive action, while others involve refraining from certain types of action (negative rights).

**Table 1:** International Human Rights Agreements

Charter of the United Nations (1945)
United Nations Commission on Human Rights (1946)
Universal Declaration of Human Rights (1948)
Convention on the Prevention and Punishment of the Crime of Genocide (1948)
European Convention on Human Rights (1950)
Convention Relating to the Status of Refugees (1951)
Convention on the Political Rights of Women (1952)
Convention on the Status of Stateless Persons (1954)
Convention Abolishing Slavery (1956)
ILO Convention on the Abolition of Forced Labour (1957)
Convention on Consent to Marriage (1962)
Convention on the Elimination of Racial Discrimination (1965)
International Covenants on Economic, Social, and Cultural Rights/ Civil and Political Rights (1966)
Convention on the Suppression and Punishment of the Crime of Apartheid (1973)
Convention on the Elimination of all Forms of Discrimination against Women (1979)
Convention against Torture and other Cruel, Inhuman or Degrading Treatment or Punishment (1984)
Convention on the Rights of the Child (1989)
International Criminal Tribunal for Ex-Yugoslavia (1993)
International Criminal Tribunal for Rwanda (1994)

**Source:** United Nations

Whatever the actual constitution of individual categories of rights, fundamentalists argue, they should be construed as mutually reinforcing elements of a composite that is guided by universal standards guaranteeing not only political, civil and religious liberties, but also optimal human welfare through social and economic protections such as job security, access to health, education and social security. As shown, in Table 2, the comprehensive vision is mirrored in what is nowadays termed an International Bill of Rights, which encapsulates the major provisions of the Universal Declaration of Human Rights (D) and two international covenants it engendered (International Covenants on Civil and Political Rights (C) and Economic, Social and Cultural Rights (E)).

The past fifty years or more have witnessed a very intensive debate between protagonists who share a common belief about the nature of humans and society vis-à-vis others subscribing to a more relativistic mode of interpretation. The latter stress the need to recognise how the substantive concepts have emerged and changed over time. One variant of the argument is that no uniform or monolithic standards and criteria can be used to assess disparate cultural contexts – for example, global versus regional, Western versus Asian, or liberal versus socialist regimes. The strongest claim is that the very concept of universal human rights is a product of Western civilisation and individualism. Hence, any attempt to impose human rights on other societies is a form of cultural imperialism. Such arguments are being increasingly championed by Islamic fundamentalists and exponents of Asian values based on Confucianism, Hinduism, Taoism, Shintoism and the likes.

**Table 2:** International Bill of Human Rights

| Rights to: | Document/Article* |
|---|---|
| - Life | D3, C6 |
| - Liberty and security of person | D3, C9 |
| - Freedom from slavery and servitude | D4, C8 |
| - Freedom from torture or cruel, inhuman or de-grading treatment or punishment | D5, C7 |
| - Equality before the law | D6, C16 |
| - Equal protection under the law | D7, C14, C26 |
| - Freedom from arbitrary arrest and detention | D9, C9 |
| - Fair trial by an independent and impartial tribunal | D10, C14 |
| - Presumption of Innocence | D11, C15 |
| - Inviolability of home, family, and privacy | D12, C17 |
| - Freedom of movement and residence | D13, C12 |
| - Seek asylum from persecution | D14 |
| - Nationality | D15 |
| - Marry and found a family | D16, C23, E10 |
| - Own property | D17 |
| - Freedom of peaceful assembly and association | D20, C21, C22 |
| - Vote and participate in government | D21, C25 |
| - Social Security | D22, E9 |

| | |
|---|---|
| - Work, form, and join trade unions | D23, C22, E8 |
| - Rest and leisure | D24, E7 |
| - Food, clothing, and housing | D25, E11 |
| - Health care and social services | D25, E12 |
| - Special protections for children | D25, E10, C24 |
| - Education | D26, E13, E14 |
| - Participation in cultural life of the community | D27, E15 |
| - Self-determination | C1, E1 |
| - Humane treatment when detained or imprisoned | C10 |
| - Protection against arbitrary expulsion of aliens | C13 |
| - Protection against advocacy of racial or religious hatred | C20 |
| - Protection of minority culture | C27 |

**Source**: Author

For example, China subscribes to a notion of what may be termed 'particularistic' human rights, the rationale being that so-called universal human rights are not only an infringement of national sovereignty, but are really a matter of domestic rather than international concern. It may be commented that the very idea of particularistic human rights is contradictory. Human rights would not be 'human' if certain individuals or groups were denied them. This is not meant to deny that their enforcement should always be sensitive to diverse regional and cultural differences. But, the perspective of cultural relativism also draws support from noted Western political scientists such as Samuel P. Huntington (1993), who predicts that culture rather than ideology will become the most potent causal force generating conflicts, or the 'clash of civilisations.'

Huntington claims that Western ideas such as individualism, liberalism, constitutionalism, human rights, equality, liberty, the rule of law, democracy, free markets, and separation of church and state often have little resonance in Islamic, Hindu, Confucian, Buddhist, or 'orthodox' cultures. Western attempts to propagate such ideas have produced a reaction against 'human rights imperialism' and a concomitant reaffirmation of indigenous values. Huntington's prognostication is certainly correct in the sense that all societies now pay attention to cultural values and domestic appurtenances when confronting perceptibly international or 'universal' standards imposed from outside. However, the implicit assumption that prevailing cultural patterns are more or less sedimented and will inevitably be the source of conflicts is open to question. Historically, cultural differences and the rivalry emanating from their interactions have frequently brought creative changes at both national and international levels. A useful example is Japanese confrontation with Western civilisations during the mid-19th century. This allowed the country to progressively open its door to external influences, which provided an essential catalyst in its subsequent Industrialisation. Moreover, the violent clash of civilisations is more likely to result from one civilisation trying to dominate others and/or a failure to transform systems of inequality (Rubenstein and Crocker 1994).

The fact that human rights are firmly entrenched in Western civilisation is not sufficient ground to deny their universal status. It can be argued that the human rights concept is based on an 'overlapping consensus,' or values shared across cultures. These 'transcultural universals' encapsulate a respect for the sanctity of life and human dignity, a tolerance of differences among peoples, and a desire for free-dom, equality, fairness, order and stability. Across cultures, there is no uniform or monolithic set of Western, Asian or Islamic values, as the case may be. While the world is made up of varying degrees of multi-culturalism, there may be more 'unity in diversity' than meets the naked eye.[4]

There is also a lingering proclivity to compartmentalise rights, rank them in hierarchical order, and even separate them across generations. This is reflected in the debate about the relative status of so-called 'first generation' rights such as freedom and equality vis-à-vis 'second' and 'third' generation ones such as those pertaining to women, the biophysical environment, and the right to (economic) development (see Steiner and Alston 1996; Shute and Hurley 1993; and Van Ness 1999). This is exemplified by the 'full belly' or 'bread first' thesis, or the claim that promotion and enforcement of civil and political rights can be postponed until economic needs (economic and social rights) are fulfilled. One biblical variation on this theme is implicit in Moses' admonition to the Israelites that 'man doth not live by bread only.'

In modern times, on the contrary, many authoritarian regimes and 'development dictatorships' adopted a philosophy that a full belly was more valuable than political liberty, democracy and a free press. On the one hand, the record suggests that huge economic costs have to be borne by regimes that deliberately suppress civil and political rights. In general, they have failed to generate the economic rewards that were promised. On the other hand, the spectacular economic growth experienced during the 1970s and 1980s by Hong Kong, Singapore, South Korea, Taiwan, and perhaps Chile is sometimes used to support the argument that LDCs could achieve some measure of material prosperity based on a market-oriented development path propped up by authoritarian rule. The full list of provisions contained in the International Bill of Rights reflects the organic goals of human development, which is also grounded in the principle that human rights are universal, indivisible and derive their substance from the dignity of the human person. People cannot fully exercise the freedoms inherent in their civil, political and cultural rights if they are destitute, impoverished, or face other forms of economic debilitation.[5] The provision of adequate levels of food, shelter, education, medical care and other wherewithals of human well-being cannot be divorced from the imperative of establishing a decent, fair, and ultimately free society. The argument may be taken one stage further by exploring the need for fair labour standards and the protection of workers' rights.

## Workers' Rights and Labour Security

Labour market institutions play a pivotal role in employment creation, determining the structure of earnings, and therefore in achieving equitable and fair outcomes in the real world. Unlike the textbook model of factor and commodity markets, they directly affect the living standards of workers and their families because the majority of households largely depend on income from work for their well-being. When the domestic economy falters, labour must bear the brunt of the shock because, unlike capital, it is not internationally mobile and invariably stays at home. In recent times, the problem has been exacerbated by the falling demand for labour in almost all episodes of structural adjustment. No country has been able to escape the resultant employment losses and decline in real wages.

Unfortunately, the new international division of labour inherent in the globalisation of the world economy, with its highly mobile capital, almost instantaneous communication, and spirited even cut-throat competition, has put a downward pressure on workers' wages, working conditions, labour standards and the rights of workers in every part of the world. Labour laws have been thrown out of the window, unions have lost their strength, and many employers now have the right to hire and fire workers as an incentive to increase investment. There is also a growing preference for casual and temporary workers who now have to work harder and longer in order to fulfill their basic needs. On an overall basis, therefore, there has been an erosion of labour's influence despite the fact that it has to bear the brunt of adjustment costs and is still expected to play a responsible role as social partner in the development process.

The wage bargaining process has been increasingly governed by a cost-cutting assumption on the part of powerful employers and exporters. This is supported by the notion of labour market flexibility and a 'distortionist' theoretical perspective of labour relations. The latter posits that trade union activity, traditional forms of collective bargaining, government regulation of wages, and the imposition of fair labour standards represent pervasive examples of policy-induced distortions that raise labour costs, militate against flexibility and slow up the economic and trade liberalisation process. While unions are attributed with positive qualities in terms of their potential contribution to productivity and equity, more emphasis is placed on the negative effects of their monopoly power on other groups such as employers, consumers, and unorganised workers.

In contrast to the distortionist approach, the 'contextualist' perspective views the labour market as a social institution, and collective bargaining as a mechanism facilitating achievement of societal goals (Freeman 1992; Solow 1990). This is supported by the rights-based philosophy of the United Nations and its specialised agencies, espe-cially the ILO. To illustrate, the Universal Declaration of Human Rights contains a number of provisions specifically relating to workers' rights. For example, Article 20 declares: Everyone has the right to freedom of peaceful assembly and association. Article 23 contains the following provisions: (1) Everyone has the right to work, to free choice of employment, to just and favourable conditions of work, and to protection against unemployment; (2) Everyone, without discrimination, has the right to equal pay for equal work; (3) Everyone who works has the right to just and favorable remuneration ensuring for himself and his family an existence worthy of human dignity, and supplemented, if necessary, by other means of social protection; and (4) Everyone has the right to form and join trade unions for the protection of his interests. Many other Articles of the Universal Declaration are concerned with workers' rights, for example, protection of children, freedom of opinion and expression, protection against arbitrary arrest and prohibitions against torture.

These and other provisions are grounded in the preconception that labour market intervention is beneficial, and that where efficiency criteria conflict with the social protection of labour, the latter course should be chosen. This philosophy also informs the policies of the ILO – a tripartite labour-business-government agency – that promotes fair labour practices, including the protection of minors, freedom of assembly and abolition of discrimination. As the ILO declares:

> countries which are members of the ILO are presumed to accept the value judgment that free collective bargaining between employers and autonomous pluralistic trade unions is the best method of determining terms and conditions of employment. *Access to such mechanisms is regarded as a basic human right.* Therefore, governments are expected to introduce legislative provisions to encourage the development of trade unions and free collective bargaining (ILO 1990:39; emphasis added).

The ILO's 'Core' human rights conventions are summarised in Table 3 for ease of reference. These, together with its Declaration on the Fundamental Principles and Rights at Work are deemed to constitute five 'core worker rights', even if legislatures of member-countries have not ratified ILO Conventions pertaining to these rights: (i) freedom of association; (ii) effective recognition of the right to collective bargaining; (iii) elimination of all forms of forced or compulsory labour; (iv) effective abolition of child labour; and (v) elimination of discrimination in respect to employment and occupation. Organised labour is considered the principal mechanism of collective bargaining to determine wages and working conditions. But, governments have an important role to play in setting the rules defining the rights of workers, trade unions and employers; the conditions of collective bargaining; and the system for settling disputes. Governments are also expected to intervene directly in labour markets –

**Table 3:** ILO Human Rights (Core) Conventions

**No. 29 Forced Labour Convention (1930):** Requires the suppression of forced or compulsory labour in all forms. Certain exceptions are permitted, such as military service, convict labour properly supervised, emergencies such as wars, fires, earthquakes…

**No. 87 Freedom of Association and Protection of the Right to Organize Convention (1948):** establishes the right of all workers and employers to form and join organisations of their own choosing without prior authorisation, and lays down a series of guarantees for the functioning of organisations without interference by the public authorities.

**No. 98 Right to Organise and Collective Bargaining Convention (1949):** Provides for protection against anti-union discrimination, for protection of workers' and employers' organisations against acts of interference by each other, and for measures to promote collective bargaining.

**No. 100 Equal Remuneration Convention (1951):** Calls for equal pay and benefits for men and women for work of equal value.

**No. 105 Abolition of Forced Labour Convention (1957):** Prohibits the use of any form of forced or compulsory labour as a means of political coercion or education, punishment for the expression of political or ideological views, workforce mobilisation, labour discipline, punishment for participation in strikes, or discrimination.

**No. 111 Discrimination (Employment and Occupation) Convention (1958):** Calls for a national policy to eliminate discrimination in access to employment, training and working conditions, on grounds of race, colour, sex, religion, political opinion, national extraction or social origin and to promote equality of opportunity and treatment.

**No. 138 Minimum Age Convention (1973):** Aims at the abolition of child labour, stipulating that the minimum age for admission to employment shall not be less than the age of completion of compulsory schooling.

---

Source : ILO

to achieve specific socio-economic goals: for example, protection of women, children, and other minority groups; setting minimum wages; and legislation on safety and health standards in the workplace.

In some countries, the earnings of select categories of workers such as women, girls, children and migrants are so low that they typify 'exploitation wages' or 'slave labour.' This raises a question about the effects of minimum wage policies. The conventional economic wisdom is that too high a minimum wage not only prevents wages generally from being set at market-clearing levels, but also establishes a floor under the wage distribution profile. The effect, it is claimed, is to price low-skilled and younger workers out of the formal labour market. According to one study,

> inasmuch as minimum wage and other regulations discourage formal employment by increasing wage and non-wage costs, they hurt the poor who aspire to formal employment. Hence it is difficult to argue for minimum wages in low- and middle-income countries on equity grounds (World Bank 1995:75).

From a rights-based perspective, it can be countered that appropriate application of minimum wage legislation can help to raise earnings of poor and disadvantaged groups at little or no cost to employment creation. The minimum wage tends to set the floor to the wage structure below which it becomes socially unacceptable and economically unjust for labour to cooperate fully in building a viable economy and decent society. No iron-clad generalisations can be made about the positive or negative economic effects of minimum wages, since specific outcomes ultimately depend on the structural and institutional contexts of individual countries, as defined by the labour market structure, levels at which minimum wages are set, and the ability of the state to enforce them. Furthermore, legal minimum wages are so low and labour standards so weakly enforced in many poor countries that any putative distortional effects are virtually non-existent.

The increasing deregulation of the economy in Africa, Asia, Latin America and the Caribbean has led to a deterioration of wages and labour standards for the following four reasons, *inter alia*: weak trade union bargaining power; deliberate attempts to abandon minimum wage policies due to the onslaught of structural adjustment and globalisation; removal of social safety nets; and accelerated inflation. As a result, new cadres of unprotected workers – veritable 'reserve armies' or 'labour reservoirs' – have emerged in the urban informal and rural sectors. Since the environment for public policy has been transformed by exogenous forces, national governments find it increasingly difficult to cushion workers against the adverse effects of economic dislocations. Besides the disciplinary effects of world markets on public expenditures, the state's ability to raise tax revenues has been diminished, leading to a curtailment of expenditure on health, education, housing, and other social services. In many countries, such trends continue to inhibit the use of growth-oriented macroeconomic policies to improve job prospects and wages of workers.

The general problem relates to the distribution of burdens and benefits across different segments of society. While this is primarily an issue about social legitimacy and justice, it also has implications for society's capacity to generate the human resources necessary for equitable growth. The paradox is that the global forces of adjustment have apparently given rise to economic hardship, which increases deprivation and heightens inequality. The consequent human damage, in terms of people's capabilities and future life chances, is most severe for those who are least prepared to bear it. Thus, shifting the cost of economic adjustment to workers and society's most vulnerable, or those with the least resistance, flies in the face of sustainable human development and protection of basic needs.

This calls for a new rights-based development ethic in which rules governing employment and earnings reflect the principles of social legitimacy. It entails universal standards guaranteeing jobs that pay more than the minimum wage and providing necessary protection for labour. Forging a feasible social compact requires that trade unions, employers, and other participants in the labour market are transformed from being antagonistic players of a game toward becoming representative and cooperative social partners. This imperative was at the heart of the protests by labour and environmental groups at the Seattle meetings 6f the WTO in 1999. A major bone of contention was whether labour standards should be linked to WTO trade rules. It touches on some critical aspects of labour rights, their enforcement, and the responsibilities of North-South protagonists.

Northern trade unionists and politicians have long argued that trade should be used as a lever for countries to practise minimum standards of decency. But skepticism has surfaced about the real or hidden intent, that is, whether advocacy of a link between trade liberalisation and labour standards is motivated more by self-interests of the rich North rather than by altruistic or moral feelings toward the poor South. American and European trade unions contend that low wages and labour standards in the South create 'unfair' competition by luring investments away from rich to poor countries. The counter-argument is that low wages, a reflection of lower levels of development, are a primary factor in the international competitive advantage of LDCs. They also believe that the attempt to link trade and labour standards is no more than a ploy for increased protectionism by rich nations.

In the eyes of the WTO, labour standards are the domain of the ILO whose Declaration on Fundamental Principles and Rights at Work obliges its members 'to respect, to promote and realise' the seven ILO conventions defining 'core' labour standards. The ILO does not link trade and labour standards; indeed, its Declaration stresses that labour standards should not be used for protectionist purposes. The real question concerns whether or how they will be enforced. It is envisaged that public opinion will become an important mechanism in goading governments to comply with their commitments. In this regard, the International Confederation of Free Trade Unions (ICFTU) – a Brussels-based club of 206 union federations from 141 countries – hopes that, in the absence of world government, moral suasion can be used to get the world committed to labour standards. It wants to see WTO membership made conditional on the observance of core labour standards certified by the ILO.

The available evidence suggests that there is no strong link between observance of core labour standards and trade flows, so LDC exporters are unlikely to be harmed much if they adopted the ILO conventions. By the same token, it seems that workers in rich countries have little to fear from competition with the downtrodden in LDCs. While this may be reassuring, it does not necessarily mean that the use of trade measures to enforce labour standards is a good idea. As we have argued, there is nothing wrong with the intentions behind the standards. People of goodwill would agree that slavery, child labour, other forms of bonded labour, and imprisonment of trade unionists should not be sanctioned. But enforcement of standards may not always produce the desired effect. If trade unions are recognised, wages in unionised sectors might rise but employment might fall. The displaced workers might be pushed into jobs that pay less than they earned before. It should be remembered, however, that the lion's share of labour in LDCs, especially in agriculture, remains unorganised. This is not because their rights, such as collective bargaining and freedom of association, are denied but more because it best suits their ethos and condition.

## Engendering of Human Rights

It goes without saying that the adequate functioning of labour markets and other institutions requires some perception of fairness on the part of their main constituents and society as a whole. In this regard, workers' rights and the broader right to development are inextricably linked to the imperative of 'women's rights as human rights.' 'Human development, if not engendered, is endangered' (UNDP 1995:1). A recursive relationship may be posited between women's rights and authentic development. The latter will be impossible without the full emancipation of women, and vice-versa. This requires a clear commitment to universal norms and standards of gender equality. As noted earlier, one of the major purposes of the United Nations Charter was to define and protect the rights and freedoms of every human being regardless of race, sex, language or religion. The Preamble to the Charter affirms the equal rights of men and women, a faith in fundamental human rights, and the dignity and worth of the human person.

The Universal Declaration of Human Rights and supporting international conventions also affirmed that women should participate equally in economic, social, and political development, contribute equally to such development, and share equally in improved conditions of life. The 1979 Convention on the Elimination of All Forms of Discrimination Against Women covered the broad categories of indivisible rights, and in 1980 became what is viewed as the women's international human rights treaty. As mentioned earlier, the United Nations also defined development as a human rights issue in its 1986 Declaration on the Right to Development. It states that 'the right to development is an alienable human right by virtue of which every human person and all peoples are entitled to participate in, contribute to, and enjoy economic, social, cultural and political development.'

The entire issue of women's rights should be interpreted as a part of longstanding attempts to 'mainstream' gender into the development conversation, or integrate women into the development paradigm. The ensuing debate has witnessed successive shifts (paradigmatic) in the intellectual and political focus of the discourse – from early 'welfarist' ideas about women's roles as 'mothers,' through 'Women in Development' (WID), 'Women and Development' (WAD), and 'Gender and Development' (GAD) to 'Development Alternatives with Women for a New Era' (DAWN). These perspectives have been variously influenced by the rise of Western feminism and its quest for a good and just life for both women and men. Feminist schools of thought and research programmes tend to perform what may be viewed as a 'radical hermeneutics,' or progressive mode of reinterpretation, that attempts to appropriate or modify other philosophies of life as a means of coming to grips with issues arising from women's confrontation with injustices and inequality. Hence, the *interpretive turns* are grounded in alternative preconceptions about the centrality of women to human life and development, or what constitutes a just social and economic order.

Contextually, the quest for women's liberation can also be interpreted through the lens of a 'discourse ethics'. It does not project the idea of an undifferentiated humanity, but accepts feminist and related arguments that the particularity of 'concrete others' should be recognised, respected, and perhaps celebrated. The overall idea centres around eradication of unjust forms of exclusion and the promotion of freedom and equality through overlapping and intersecting *communities of dialogue* (class-based, racial, ethnic, religious, feminist, and the like). Such conversations would 'enable multiple political authorities to develop, and to endeavor to bring harmony through dialogue to the great diversity of ethical spheres which stretches from the local community to the transnational area' (Linklater 1998:45).

Prior to the emergence of WID, the orientation of development thought and policy was in terms of women as 'better mothers,' thereby reinforcing their traditional gender roles within the family. Given the reproductive focus, development projects concentrated on family planning, nutrition, literacy and related areas that promised to improve women's welfare. During the early 1970s, it was recognised that women were not merely mothers who were passively affected by development in general and family planning programmes in particular; they were also active agents of change in key aspects of production and economic development. Hence, their inimitable contributions could be enhanced by more gender-sensitive programmes and projects. This change in orientation ushered in the WID perspective, which placed more emphasis on women's productive roles.

The integration of women into the development process was legitimised in terms of their equal productivity to men. They were presented as decision-makers and active production agents rather than as mere passive or needy beneficiaries of development (Boserup 1970). While it attempted to bring women into the mainstream, WID was essentially rooted in the ruling development paradigm of the day and its philosophical preconceptions. The potential benefits of increased productivity were implicitly linked to individualism and market-based efficiency, which were central elements of the 'growth-oriented' philosophy of development. The prevailing orthodoxy or 'global consensus' was essentially driven by a gender-neutral theory of modernisation. Its basic preconception was that women would advance through a 'trickle down' process of incremental change.

The WID perspective was anchored in a very limited conception of equality or justice. Since its primary focus was on 'merit' and individual achievement (implicit in notions such as economic growth, productivity and efficiency), very little attention was paid to other 'claims' that emphasise women's intrinsic moral worth as human beings. As it turned out, the econocentric WID discourse carried tremendous rhetorical and utilitarian appeal for influential economists and development officials in the North; but women in the South were essentially cast as passive recipients and implementers of programmes and projects emanating from aid donors. Furthermore, given its homogenising tendency, WID virtually ignored differences in interests among women belonging to diverse classes, ethnic groups, cultures and societies.

The philosophical thrust of WAD was an outgrowth of several meliorist strands of the political economy of development that emerged during the mid-1970s: growth with redistribution or equity; basic needs; and poverty alleviation (David 1997). As a result, WAD overtook WID at a time when the development debate was coming to grips with failures of the 'trickle-down' approach and new people-centred perspectives were taking shape. The focus on equity (as opposed to efficiency) became most popular during the 1975-1985 period, and attempts to adopt it were catapulted by the United Nations Decade for Women. Achievement of gender equity was predicated on women receiving their fair share of the benefits of development in the form of higher incomes, greater access to resources, better education, health and similar achievements. This orientation was supported by a needs-based argument for justice. As emphasised in the previous chapter, it entails that a society cannot be just if it treats the weakest and poorest members without compassion.

The argument for equity was supported by an 'anti-poverty' approach to poor men and women. The latter made the feminist agenda less threatening to economists, male bureaucrats and implementers who were resistant to feminist incursions into the bureaucracy. In the eyes of Buvinic (1983), the anti-poverty programme was a 'toned-down' version of the equity approach. In other words, it was interpreted more as a reaction to male resistance to fundamental claims for gender equality and justice, and therefore as a strategic tactic to enhance the feminist agenda. Given this instrumental approach, the WAD perspective failed to address the multifaceted and structural factors responsible for the marginalisation of women, such as war and civil conflict, rapid urbanisation, environmental degradation, and the social relations of gender itself.

During the 1980s and 1990s, the GAD perspective emerged as a means of capturing the holistic meanings undergirding women's lives. Primary emphasis was placed on the social realities shaping views on sex, and the corresponding assignment of specific roles, responsiblities, and expectations of both men and women. This shift was interpreted through the lens of 'gender,' which connotes the socially constructed and culturally variable roles that men and women play in their daily lives (Elson 1991). Contextually, gender refers to the historically structured relation of inequality between men and women, as manifested in the domestic household unit, markets and political systems. Hence, engenderment was predicated on the imperative of fostering a 'gender-based analysis' and its integration into development thought and policy (Moser 1993).

Like WAD, the GAD perspective consists of multiple discourses about women's social praxis. One crucial element concerns the general and daily processes inherent in human reproduction, such as rearing of children, nursing the sick, and caring for other dependents and senior citizens. The argument is that any genuine interpretation of human development must necessarily be based on effective ways of fully integrating such 'domestic labour' or 'reproductive work' into the overall processes of production. This requires a transformation of historically sedimentary relations of gender inequality, and the concomitant empowerment of women. While the idea of empowerment always lurked in the minds of WID protagonists, primary emphasis was placed on *status*, as distinct from its more intrinsic and dynamic counterpart – *power*. Insofar as empowerment was accorded any significance, it was limited to women's increased access to income-earning work and related opportunities provided for them by development agencies and through greater participation in the market.

This was a far cry from an organic concept of *self-empowerment*, which denotes women's capability of gaining more autonomy and con-trol over their lives, becoming more self-reliant as active agents in their own development, exercising their choices, and setting their own agendas. The self-empowerment concept is grounded, albeit implicitly, in a philosophy of 'development as liberation' or the pursuit of effective freedom. Income-earning opportunities are important, but they are not on the same footing as the 'human agency' of women or their ability to exercise the full range of possible options through democratisation, popular participation, and enforcement of human rights. Hence, the full engenderment of human development entails that barriers to the attainment of equal rights be identified and progressively eliminated. It is not merely sufficient for such initiatives to be consistent with national laws and development priorities. They must also conform to universality recognised human rights and cosmopolitan values.

Finally, DAWN was created during the mid-1980s by a network of women from the South who wanted to distantiate themselves from what they perceived as a white, middle class, feminist paradigm originating from the North. They challenged the WID research programme on the grounds that women in the South did not necessarily want to be integrated into mainstream development models. In their eyes, such conceptual systems not only contained gender and class biases, but the capital accumulation processes underlying them were neither neutral nor benign, that is, they are inherently hierarchical and polarising (Sen and Grown 1988). They recognised that their subjugation was multidimensional – based on the cumulative interplay of sex, class, race, and their subordinate position in the global hierarchy. Hence, strategies for the full empowerment of women can only be successful through simultaneous action in all these domains. This involves an egalitarian development trajectory based on concerted resistance to hierarchies and inculcation of positive values such as cooperation, sharing, accountability and commitment to peace. These were to be operationalised through consciousness-raising at the political level and popular education in the workplace, home, and community.

## Human Rights Programming

An intractable problematique has always surrounded human rights programming. This relates to practical issues of enforcement, promotion, and protection. The glaring gap between international aspirations for the enjoyment of human rights vis-à-vis what are perceived to be widespread violations poses an ongoing challenge at both global and national levels. Closing the gap requires concerted and credible actions in several interrelated avenues: identification and elimination of the root causes of conflicts and violations, including the panoply of economic, cultural, political, and legal barriers to the full realisation of equal rights; implementation of provisions guaranteeing the right to development; fostering and ensuring a greater respect for universal human rights; and, at the most basic level, improving the daily life of the individual – worker, woman, young person, girl-child, and so on.

An endemic source of conflict stems from the fact that many powerful sectors of interest continue to approach the issue from their own narrow and iron-clad ideological perspectives about what is desirable and practically feasible. For example, some political scientists and philosophers still harbour strong misgivings about the logical defensibility of human rights. In general, hard-nosed economists, industrialists, transnational corporations and politicians tend to be skeptical because of a fear that human rights enforcement may have negative effects on national economic growth, private profitability, market efficiency, and international competitiveness, as the case may be. By contrast, most trade unions, women's groups, human rights organisations, and NGOs usually advocate vigorous enforcement of human rights principles.

Another complicating factor is that many poor countries do not boast a strong tradition of human rights enforcement, promotion, and protection. While the majority has constitutions, institutions and other instruments subscribing to the broad principles of universal human rights, they are poorly enforced and in some cases openly flouted. For example, the Convention on Elimination of All Forms of Discrimination Against Women still remains one of the most widely disregarded international treaties, with some signatories ignoring provisions that are perceived to conflict with their customary laws. A case in point was the unanimous decision by the Zimbabwe Supreme Court in 1999 to overrule or challenge every law relating women's rights in the country.

The ruling was that Vienna Magaya could not inherit her father's estate, even though Zimbabwean laws and international treaties supported her claim. The Court gave the estate to her half-brother. The decision made explicit reference to the deep-seated roots of patriarchy in Africa. The judges opined that the 'nature of African society' relegates women to a lesser status, especially in the home. In their eyes, a woman should not be considered an adult within the family, but only as a 'junior male.' One judge went so far as to say that Zimbabwe's 1982 Majority Age Act, which said that women over 18 could be treated as minors, had been interpreted 'too widely' and had accorded women 'rights they never had under customary law.' Thus, they were stripped of almost all the rights they had gained over the past two generations.

Even if it is assumed that there is a 'separation of powers' between the judicial and executive branches of government, the Zimbabwean case clearly demonstrates the influence of cultural relativism and the conflict that can arise between requirements of international human rights law and national sovereignty. The sensitive nature of human rights law is that it challenges the way in which governments exercise power and authority over their citizens. The difficulty is that nation states assiduously guard their national sovereignty, but must simultaneously submit to international scrutiny and reluctantly accept restrictions on their domestic behaviour (Manasian 1998). In many cases, international conventions and treaties are not backed up by the political will of national governments, so that they sometimes become smokescreens for the perpetuation of human rights abuses.

The reconciliation of international standards with national purposes implies establishment of coherent frameworks of principles, objectives, legislation, and procedures for monitoring and evaluation at the domestic level. This implies the design of appropriate human rights yardsticks as goals to be attained, or performance criteria against which the success of development policies, strategies and projects can be appraised. Such a guideline takes on added significance when account is taken of the widespread incongruity between human rights norms on the one hand and the goals of many development programmes and projects, on the other. Contextually, the United Nations Committee on Economic, Social and Cultural Rights drew attention to the fact that

> development cooperation activities do not automatically contribute to the promotion of [human rights]. Many activities undertaken in the name of 'development'

have subsequently been recognised as ill-conceived and even counterproductive in human rights terms (UNHCR 1990:87).

Examples of the incompatibility between human rights norms and conventional development activities are a legion. They include: (i) abridgement of the freedom of residence and cultural rights due to mass relocations stemming from large hydroelectric and irrigation projects; (ii) unemployment caused by the introduction of labour-displacing and capital-intensive technologies; (iii) employment retrenchment and wage cuts attendant upon structural adjustment programmes; (iv) limitations placed on the basic right to a minimum level of education, health care and nutrition, due to mandated cuts in social sector spending; and (v) the tendency to turn a blind eye to international labour standards pertaining to free collective bargaining, trade unions, rates of pay, child labour, health, safety and environmental laws.

In the final analysis, the most effective means for the protection and promotion of human rights require a synergistic interplay of both national commitment and international obligation. Since human rights are universal in scope and have a global connotation, the relevant standards should apply equally to all actors, including transnational corporations (TNCs), aid donors, and recipients of development finance. Among other things, this calls for a new path of accountability whereby North-South sectors of interest openly bind themselves to adhere not only to the provisions of international agreements in general, but also to specific areas such as enforcement of fair labour standards. Concrete meaning and relevance can be given to accountability through formulation and execution of additional incentives for compliance on the one hand, and disincentives for arbitrary or willful noncompliance, on the other.

A few recent developments promise to ensure a greater degree of public commitment, transparency, and accountability. First, about 36 corporations such as Chevron, General Motors, and Proctor and Gamble have agreed to abide by the so-called 'Sullivan principles' which set standards for corporate social responsibility. Second, governments of 20 OECD countries have ratified new guidelines for safeguarding labour and environmental standards by TNCs. Third, and in the wake of this development, 50 of the world's largest TNCs have signed a 'global compact' under the auspices of the United Nations, committing them to support free trade unions, abolish child labour, and protect the environment. The list includes several firms, such as Nike and Royal Dutch Shell, which were targets of protesters at Seattle.

The UN's global compact with the private sector to promote human rights and raise labour and environmental standards seems to represent a new normative framework or progressive agenda for the reform of the ground rules that inform the current global institutional architecture. The underlying premise is that the global public good should take precedence over the private interests of financial capital and profitability of free markets. The implications for human rights are based on a recognition that the present global system does not treat all participants equally and in a fair and just manner. Markets apparently operate with double standards. Powerful industrialists from rich nations are allowed the benefit of the doubt even when they stray from the straight and narrow path of market fundamentalism. Hence, a key normative goal of the reformist agenda is to mitigate the market vulnerabilities of weaker members of the system.

In a quasi-theoretical sense, the global compact is also consistent with those research programmes of the 'post-Washington consensus' that advocate globalisation of the original Keynesian vision or compact for supranational controls over global finance and markets. The evolution of Keynesianism was predicated on a bargain between market capitalism and the state that was designed to ensure the survival of open liberalism and free markets, but tempered by mechanisms that would prevent repetition of the Great Depression and provide compensatory support systems for the most dispossessed. Historically, the Keynesian compact not only reflected the extant state of economic theory but was also an exercise in normative political economy. In today's world, it reflects a necessity to return to an economic morality that transcends the naked individualism that has apparently wrought havoc on the global economic order. In other words, the revisionist ethic would allow the private sector to operate successfully and profitably while providing adequate social protection for vulnerable participants.

# 3

# On Prospective:
# Development and a Political Culture of Time

## Souleymane Bachir Diagne

> So teach us to number our days, that we may apply our hearts unto wisdom.
>
> Psalm 90:12

Developmentalism in the spirit of the sixties is said to be *passé*. In the name of developmentalism, following the formal political independences of its nations, Africa had adopted almost everywhere on the continent one party political systems assumed to be the best tool for constructing or preserving national unity and at the same time for galvanising and channelling energies towards socio-economic betterment. Developmentalism, thus understood, has died from the political and economic failure of that spirit of the sixties and early seventies. Then, while it was repeated that a different philosophy of development was needed, what took place following that failure was the dismantling of what gave meaning to the very notion of development: planning. The actions taken under the auspices of the IMF and the World Bank aimed at restoring macroeconomic balance were presented as absolutely necessary – that is urgent and inevitable. Weak African States and impoverished populations were engaged in the same struggle to make ends meet, narrowly on a daily basis. What was lost was long-term perspective, a horizon against which actions taken would make sense, in the context of an open future; also lost was meaning.[1] Behind the recent calls for an 'African Renaissance' or for NEPAD (whatever one might think of their actual content), there is the acknowledgement that the true face of the African crisis is a crisis of *meaning* and *signification* within the context of time. Contemporary Africa is aware of its still contested-for past, the colonial interlude, and the slow disjunctive time of the present, making interpretations of the future problematic. The future is problematic because there is no clear sense of an African *telos* thereby making it possible almost by default for Western generated theories of development to be foisted on Africa without much questioning. A re-introduction of the idea of development as a long-term perspective under the aeges of African agency would be one way to confront the future. In this regard the idea of African development need not be satisfied with IMF or World Bank recommendations, or the latest position papers on economic development generated thousands of miles away in Western research centres.

For many years, the African Futures project established in Abidjan has endeavoured to build and develop long-term perspective capacity in the continent. Presenting this project and at the same time the text *Afrique 2025* produced under its auspices, here is what the coordinator of African Futures, Alioune Sall, writes:

> After having been decried and relegated to the status of an antiquity along with state-planning (to which it was assimilated), long-term perspective is now re-established in development circles. As a matter of fact, 2015 is the horizon currently considered by the United Nations for the realization of the development objectives of the millennium while 2025 – that is the span of a generation. It is the horizon agreed upon in about twenty national long term perspective studies that have been undertaken in Africa with the technical support of the UNDP program known as *African futures*. Consequently, long term perspective reflection is gaining or regaining legitimacy. We must be satisfied with this new situation and rejoice over it with all those who, not so many years ago, had to spend a great amount of energy to get decision-makers to comprehend the meaning and importance of a long term perspective approach as they were submitted to the dictatorship of urgencies and, particularly in Africa, to the hardships of structural adjustment programs (Sall 2003:11).

Two important points can be made, to comment on this quotation. One about what development is not, the other about what the essential component of the notion of development is. What development is not is dealing on a daily basis with urgencies, trying to meet the demands of structural adjustment programmes. What is essential to the very notion of development is *time* understood as *duration*, the political culture of temporality.[2] It is not only that the many social, cultural and economic transformations that a society undergoes as its 'development' need time but, more importantly that, as Alioune Sall again puts it, 'the future does not come by itself but has to be met and the conditions for its hatching have to be created' (Sall 2003:11). In other words, at the core of the notion of development, is the exploration of the future, the attitude which is best expressed by the philosophical concept of 'prospective',[3] coined by the French philosopher Gaston Berger to name the science which explores the future evolution of societies in order to light up the decisions that have to be made *today*, the actions that are to be taken *today*. In other words, the prospective attitude, which is essential to development, is grounded on the notion that the meaning of the present comes from the future. The central question of development is thus that of fostering *prospective* in African societies.[4] This means posing the philosophical question of time.

To think a political culture of time is first to get rid, theoretically and practically, of what I would call the ethnological divide between cultures concerning time. Such a question is often translated into cultural terms, very hard to dislodge, such as the

'African conception of time' the stake of which is inevitably whether or not such a conception contributes to the development of a prospective attitude. In this perspective, I would like here to first discuss this 'translation' by revisiting what John Mbiti has written about this so-called 'African notion of time' in his well known work, *African Religions and Philosophy* (Mbiti 1990).[5] I will argue that those who, like Mbiti, pretend to read a distinctly African concept of time in African cultural attitudes and languages in order to contrast it with the prospective attitude demanded by development misunderstand the very essence of time and hence, of prospective. I will demonstrate that there is nothing distinct or unique about the concept of time drawn from an African culture and I will show that in any case, 'prospective' has nothing to do with a culturally defined notion of time.

## About the Ethnological Divide between Cultures in Relation to Time

It may be useful to make a detour and consider seriously John Mbiti's analysis of African concepts of time. First, for the general reason that in prospective studies the cultural parameters are crucial. Exploring the future of values and mentalities is probably more significant than the economic parameters *stricto sensu* for a prospective exercise when considering, for example, a temporal horizon such as the span of a generation.[6] Because these parameters, on the one hand, oppose the strongest forces of inertia to change but are also, on the other hand, such that when they do change, they make the biggest difference and generate the most decisive transformations in the society. This is the sense in which one may say that development is essentially a cultural question. And at the very heart of this cultural question of development, John Mbiti places the concept of time. From their conception of time, he argues, stem the attitudes, beliefs and practices that are manifested, in particular, in the people's philosophy of work. And he calls for further research to fully take into account the centrality of time-consciousness in the studies of African philosophy in general and of the cultural dimension of development in particular.[7] The following are the main affirmations made by John Mbiti as they result from his analysis of African concepts of time:

1) *Time is a composition of events.* In other words, the concept of time cannot be understood otherwise than in connection with the events that take place. And we should not even say 'take place *in* it' because this formulation would convey the notion that time could have independent being as some sort of frame which subsists when the events are mentally taken out of it, so to speak. In the same way that 'it is the content which defines space' (Mbiti 1990:26), it is the event that defines time. Time is not the *form* for the events in any Kantian sense; it is not the *order* for their succession in any Leibnizian sense: time *is* these events and *is not* outside of them.

2) *The past is the most important dimension of time.* This is an obvious consequence of the first thesis: if time is the stock of events it can almost be totally identified with the past which is but these events once they have occurred.

3) *The present is continuously in motion towards the past.* This is again obvious from a physical perspective but also has an important 'meta-physical' corollary: the dynamic of the present and indeed its meaning is oriented towards the past. The 'now' of our consciousness and actions ultimately rests on the ocean of past events receiving again and again, as drops that add nothing to it, the events we call our 'present'.

4) *There is virtually no future.* This is of course necessary because there is, by definition, a contradiction in considering a future event. As John Mbiti writes, time really 'is a two-dimensional phenomenon, with a long past, a present and virtually no future' (Mbiti 1990:16). The only aspect of the future that can be said to 'exist' is that which is constituted by what we might call *quasi events*, meaning that the present is pregnant with them, and that they can be read in it, so to say, *now*, in the same way the harvest can be read in the blossoming of the seeds. Practically, this means that one cannot consider the future beyond the close horizon of a few months, beyond tomorrow, beyond the shadow that, already, it retro-projects, *now*.

5) *The evidence to support these affirmations comes mainly from the consideration of the African languages and calendars.* The best testimonies for Africans' concepts of time are of course the way in which they reckon time in their languages and also the way in which they cast the flow of temporality into calendars. In fact, John Mbiti presents the study of the East African languages in which he has carried out his research as a 'test [of his] findings'. So examining, in particular, the verb tenses in the Kikamba and Gikuyu languages, he comes up with the 'confirmation' that 'there are no concrete words or expressions to convey the idea of a distant future' (Mbiti 1990:17) the one that lies beyond the span of a few months, two years at most. Then he goes on to give an account of African calendars that he calls '*phenomenon* calendars' in opposition to 'numerical', mathematical calendars that are not tied up with concrete phenomena taking place and constituting time. Hence, as watch time is different from the time measured by an activity, hours and months (lunar of course) are named as the time for given events such as 'milking the cattle' in the morning and the evening, or 'the sun [being hot]', from which the month corresponding to October bears its name in the language of the Latuka people.[8]

6) *Planning for a distant future is foreign to the society.* This is one of the most crucial consequences of the affirmations made by Mbiti, especially in connection with the project of developing a prospective capacity for development. In Mbiti's words: 'African peoples have no 'belief in progress', the idea that the development of human activities and achievements move from a low to a higher degree. The people neither plan for the distant future nor 'build castles in the air''. The centre of gravity for human thought and activities is the [past] period' (Mbiti 1990:23). And Mbiti puts great insistence on the point that many sayings, seemingly based on ethnological facts, concerning some distinctive African way of *wasting* time have to be understood as stemming from this meta-

physics of time; once what time means for the Africans is fully understood that way, the attitudes associated with wasting time then appear to be truly 'waiting for time or in the process of 'producing' time' (Mbiti 1990:19).

7) *The future dimension of time has been forced into African societies from outside and is still in the process of being appropriated by them.* In other words, it took a catastrophe, in the literal meaning of this word, to have African societies discover or extend the future dimension of time. This catastrophe has taken the face of 'Christian missionary teaching' or Western-type education or modern technology and has led 'to national planning for economic growth, political independence, extension of educational facilities and so on'.[9] And the fact that this is a rupture explains why this process, far from being a smooth one, is 'at the root of (…) the political instability of our nations'. So the African crisis is structural and its ultimate philosophical meaning is to translate the disruption represented by the introduction of the future dimension of time in an environment where the centre of gravity was in the memory of the past, the emphasis on tradition.

John Mbiti's chapter on 'the concept of time' ends with a challenge to scholarship on Africa which has the function of dismissing negative or critical reactions to his affirmations, mainly from those who would think these are bordering the notion of a different African mentality understood *à la* Levy-Bruhl, and would not accept the conclusion that the future dimension of time is absent from the African languages and traditional experience. The challenge is to come up with "another sustained analysis of African concepts of time' instead of just saying 'yes' or 'no' to his theory'.[10] The burden of proof lies on the contradictors who have to produce evidence of contrary theses.

## *Opposing a Political Culture of Time to a Cultural Conception of Time*

One of those who took up John Mbiti's challenge is the Ghanaian philosopher Kwame Gyekye (Gyekye 1987) who, opposed to the Kenyan's views on the subject, gave his own exploration of Akan concepts of time. The approach is thus to come up with a counterexample in order to destroy any universal character of John Mbiti's claims about an *African* notion of time. Actually, there is no need to try to come up with counterexamples presented by this or that particular African language where the future tense is seemingly fully present or with traditional calendars used in this or that African group which do not operate the way described by J. Mbiti. The challenge, as formulated would simply lead to some kind of impasse under the form of a futile opposition between philosophical examinations of different African languages and the subtleties of their verbal systems. It is the very assumption upon which the opposition is founded that needs to be questioned and eventually dismissed.

This assumption is indeed the one expressed by Lucien Lévy-Bruhl in his account of what appeared to him to be *the* (primitive, hence) African conception of time:

(...) the primitives' minds do not represent time exactly as ours do. Primitives do not see, extending indefinitely in imagination, something like a straight line, always homogenous by nature, upon which events fall into position, a line on which foresight can arrange them in a unilinear and irreversible series, and on which they must of necessity occur one after the other. To the primitive time is not, as it is to us, a kind of intellectualised intuition, an 'order of succession'.[11]

The most appropriate answer is not to defend Africans from 'primitiveness' in their representation of time but to say that it is just not true that there is such a thing as a Western notion of time against which one would actually characterise the African conception of time as 'primitive'. And to insist on this point makes far more sense towards a political culture of time than throwing back and forth examples and counterexamples to illustrate or refute the assumption made. What linear notion of time and what conception of the future is behind the French word 'avenir', for example? This word which translates 'future' literally and etymologically means 'what is to come'. Now what indicates that we have in mind, using the word *avenir* six months rather than two or a hundred years? Nothing but the context is the good answer. And what makes it a good answer is that it is the same for all human languages. For example, the word for 'future' in the Wolof language, *ëllëg*, literally means *tomorrow*. Now does one mean literally 'tomorrow' if one says that one is working *ngir ëllëgu njaboot gi* that is to say 'for her children's future?' The context clearly shows that the scope one has in mind here is the time when the children reach adulthood. And parents often project in time when they visualise and discuss the very future adulthood of their children. Also activities within the precolonial agricultural societies of Africa were focused on planting and harvesting within the context of at least one year and often many years, as when late-bearing fruit trees are planted. But back to the word 'tomorrow': of course, in English or in French for example, the word 'tomorrow' has exactly the same use.

In the same way one could raise the question of the 'representation of time' revealed by the use of a calendar where months are named after the god of war or Julius Caesar or Junius Brutus or Augustus…The answer of course is that no one has these associations in mind when using the names 'March', 'July', June or 'August'. And incidentally this Julian calendar is of African origin being invented by the ancient Egyptians. Note too that the Dogon of Mali, whose knowledge of astronomy was surprising to French anthropologist, Marcel Griaule, celebrate the star Sirius *every sixty years*. And there are other instances to note in this regard. Thus going back to the etymology of the term itself could perfectly allow us to use Mbiti's terminology and speak of a *phenomenon calendar* for the one currently used in the West as well. The conclusion to be drawn from this is that there is not a clear divide between (African) societies using phenomenon calendars and different (Western) societies using numerical calendars. Calendars in general may have *phenomenon* origins: very quickly their use is just *numerical*.

More generally, the problem with the kind of linguistic philosophy that concludes the way Mbiti does is to *overanalyze* African languages reading, as it were, too much into them as one is too busy seeking the cultural differences they are supposed to reveal between a concrete oriented African mind and an abstract Western mind. Such a preconception leads one to forget, in the process, that the same kind of *over-analysis* can be conducted for virtually any human language and would bear the same kind of conclusions. What this type of linguistic philosophy fails to take into account is that if words do have (often concrete) *origins*, they have above all *uses* which, ultimately, determine their (often abstract) meaning.[12] In so doing, one does not only come up with an 'invented' Africa to use Valentin Mudimbe's phrase but with an invented 'West' as well.

In his posthumous works, Levy Bruhl came to acknowledge this kind of objection about 'inventing' the other's mentality. But, even more important than the way he invents the 'primitives', he missed the point that the comparison made was flawed in the first place: it was not drawn between comparable terms but between *experience* of time on the one hand and *concept* of time on the other hand. The 'straight line, always homogenous by nature, upon which events fall into position', the 'line on which foresight can arrange [these events] in a unilinear and irreversible series, and on which they must of necessity occur one after the other', that line may express a *concept* or rather an image of time. It does not describe an *experience* of time, let alone an experience presented as common to the 'West'. In the 'West' as everywhere else, it is the *human* experience of time to measure a distance by what and how long it takes to 'get there', to have not an 'always homogenous' line but rather differences between the time of our impatient desire and the time of our boredom. Everywhere human beings, to use Bergson's image, experience time when they have to wait for their sugar to melt in their coffee and not when they imagine it as a 'straight, homogenous line'. Nobody's experiential time, neither 'ours' nor 'theirs', is that mathematical time, of which we always speak in spatial terms like a 'line', a 'flow', etc. because that is the language of our intelligence (which means, according to the etymology, the faculty by which we hold things together, in the same mental place, as it were) and not our experience of time as *duration*. This Bergsonian notion of time as duration is an excellent antidote to the ethnological inclination to present an African concept of time (cyclical, futureless, and God knows what) radically different from a Western (linear, mathematical, infinite) concept of time.

In sum, both Mbiti and Levy Bruhl may be criticised for the essentialising respectively of precolonial African sociology and African cognitive processes. Proof of this is that the putative 'Western notion of time' is in reality *modern* Western time. For the most part, time in Europe was impressionistic, non-linear and finite until the period of the Renaissance and the commencement of literacy, some four hundred years ago. And then, there is the question of the isomorphism of time, well-established in modern physics. If the human mind can grasp the past, it must also grasp the future; for the past of whatever duration was at one time also a future. So political culture of time is not about how time is lived but how it is *managed* and this is done through 'prospective'.

## Developing a Political Culture of Time Through Prospective

Léopold Sédar Senghor's thought and action have undergone some eclipse now as his philosophy is considered an old story of 'essentialism'. Yet, one should not ignore the importance in his thought of the necessity of self-transformation through action[13] or the centrality of prospective in his political philosophy. He thus wrote: 'When we became an independent nation I had to interrupt my literary work to solve planning problems, those faced by our young state. Now, what is planning but a prospective project? This is what leads me to keep from the Franco-Senegalese philosopher's work only what pertains to his philosophy of action: prospective'.[14] A reader of Gaston Berger, referred to in this quotation as 'the Franco-Senegalese philosopher',[15] he understood how crucial it is to ground development on the notion that our actions today draw their orientation and significance from tomorrow. That meaning, as it were, flows back to the present from the future. This is the very foundation of his insistence on prospective and planning as the substance of development. One example often given to illustrate the failure of developmentalism is to look back at Senghor's projections for the millennium and to ridicule his views about the year 2000 as the year of Senegal's economic take off. Did the projections go wrong? Of course they did, but he was right making them, that is to say, assigning the year 2000 as the horizon of meaning for all actions of development. As a philosopher, a poet and a man of action he had grasped the essence of development as prospective and of prospective as a political culture of time.

What is prospective? John Mbiti's ethnologist view considers that planning is founded on the Levy-Bruhlian notion of a time seen as 'a line on which foresight can arrange events in a unilinear and irreversible series, and on which they must of necessity occur one after the other'. And since he considers such a conception to be a characteristic of Western culture, he naturally concludes that the spirit of foresight has to break into African societies through Westernisation and Christianity. The main lesson to be learned from Gaston Berger is precisely that prospective, the true attitude of foresight has nothing to do with an image of time and the future as a 'straight homogenous line'. More precisely, such an image is the absolute contrary of what a true understanding of what the future and its exploration mean. The most famous and striking image often used by Berger to illustrate the full significance of a prospective attitude is that of a car running faster and faster on an unknown road, racing along through the night; this car needs to have powerful headlights that can reach further and further if a catastrophe is to be avoided. This image tells us something important about the nature of time, more precisely about its future dimension. We do not know what it will be like just as we do not know what the shape of the road is while it unfolds itself under the lighting of the car speeding along on it. In other words, the concept of a future lying ahead of us and not as continuous creation of our own moving present is not a 'Western' or a 'modern' notion of time. It is an absurdity. This is to say that, contrary to what Mbiti affirms, a future void of events is not the condition for prospective thinking; that would just be an effort to grasp nothingness. On the contrary, prospective is based on the freest possible imagination, but still remains an imagination of *possible scenarios*, of what has been coined in French as *'futuribles'* ('futurable' would be the corresponding neologism in English: possible states of affairs that could become real).

One thing that is also important is that this metaphor tells us about the meaning of a prospective attitude is this: one has to continuously *anticipate* what the curves of the road will be as this is the best way to be ready to adjust to what will actually present itself. This is to say that the representation of the future changes continuously and so do the decisions we make in the present in order to shape this future. In a word, the image of the homogenous line empty of the events that will occur on it is at the opposite of the true science of the future that prospective aims to be.

There is another lesson in this image of a car speeding in the night with high beams on. A prospective attitude means that we act and operate according to our anticipations and not according to the past, or to what we hold as our 'tradition'.[16] Another way to understand this lesson is to see that prospective is radically different from *extrapolation*, from simply prolonging the past into the future. In that sense, to paraphrase Gaston Berger again, development means that a society is racing towards its youth, not towards its old age. We could define it then, in Bergsonian terms, as the movement of life and spirit which is the effort to go uphill while matter and its inertia are bound to go downhill. It would be a paradox for African societies where the youth make up everywhere the great majority of the population not to be going, through prospective and developmental political culture of time, towards their adolescence but rather towards a state of senescence signifying a crisis of planning, which in turn is the expression of a crisis of becoming. Such an attitude leaves the African youth with the feeling that it is futureless and condemned to find 'tomorrow' only in emigration. It is for this reason that there is an urgent need for new or modified paradigms of development, new theories of political economy and new critiques of received doctrines. For the African philosopher, the task with regard to development lies not with the atavistic work of Mbiti but with assiduous conversation with the futurist ideas of Fanon, Nkrumah, Senghor, Diop, Hountondji, Amin and others.

In an important reflection on African initiative titled 'From the Lagos Plan of Action to the New Partnership for African Development and from the Final Act of Lagos to the Constitutive Act: Whither Africa?', Adebayo Adedeji evokes Africa's 'fundamental right and responsibility to occupy the driver's seat of the automobile of its destiny', using the same kind of metaphor Gaston Berger adopted to illustrate the meaning of prospective (Adedeji 2002:35). He rightly states in this reflection that indeed Africans had made attempts to shape their own future with a 'transformation ethics [that] rests on the firm belief that development should not be undertaken on behalf of a people [but] rather that it should be the organic outcome of a society's value system, its perceptions, its concerns and its endeavours' (Adedeji 2002:41). That is precisely one crucial dimension of prospective: the indigenous or 'organic' character of development. Today the question is whether NEPAD could provide the answer to the crisis of initiative that followed the burial of the *Lagos Plan of Action* (1980) under the structural adjustment program built on the philosophy behind the Berg Report of 1981? This question translates itself into that 'of the extent to which the initiative can serve as the foundation for a new optimism about Africa's future' (Olukoshi 2002:88). The answer depends on the true *appropriation* of agency by Africans, expressing their mastery over the very stuff societal development is made of. That 'very stuff' is time.

But how does all of this fit into the issue of development in Africa. First, there are the exceptional parameters that Africa has to work with. This continent carries that aura of timelessness with regards to human habitation, being for a very long archaelogical time the only habitable area of the globe. And even its human constructions in history seem timeless: pyramids, Zimbabwe ruins, and so on. Modern-day liberal capitalism focuses on short term profits and constant disruptive change. Could prospective time in the African context extend the amplitudes of development so that development stretches from the next instance to far off time? In this regard, growth and development would not just be short-term endeavours but also planned efforts for the long term. With a proper configuration of the idea of 'prospective' an African *telos* would begin to take shape. It is in this context that the idea of development would assume African agency to re-fashion it according to the dictates of contemporary African political economy, politics and sociology.

## Notes

1. I explore the question of the lost meaning to be restored in a work titled *Reconstruire le sens* (Diagne 2000). A question I was also very fortunate to be able to discuss with Lansana Keita, Nasrin Qader and David Schoenbrun when writing this paper.
2. The phrase 'political culture of time' which appears in the very title of this article is penned by French writer Jean Chesneaux (1998).
3. In English, 'prospective' is an adjective so the equivalent noun for the French word should be the phrase 'long term perspective' which has been used up to this point. But in order to truly capture the philosophical content of Gaston Berger's 'science of the future' the word 'prospective' will be used in the rest of this article, both as a noun and as an adjective (in the phrase 'prospective attitude', for example.)
4. Of course, the past is important and recapturing her own history was a crucial aspect of Africa's liberation. The emphasis put here on prospective as the source of meaning is also a way of seeing the past as a site for useful prospecting. To insist that the future creates the present, which is the basis of prospective attitude, is not to consider the past as divorced from the present but somehow to try to question seriously the situation on our continent where, as Lansana Keita put it in our conversation on this issue, the leaders seem frozen and catatonic in colonial time. To recast the past in its totality is, for example, Cheikh Anta Diop's project and this implied an attitude which, ultimately, is a prospective one. I agree with L. Keita that the central issue is that of a telos for the future, ridding Africa of a catatonic state where time is standing still.
5. The first edition, published in 1969 had been reprinted not less than thirteen times!

6. Gaston Berger writes: 'previsions are more likely to be accurate when they concern a long period rather than a short one'. And he adds that this is especially true for economic prevision (Berger 1958:1).

7. '...I propose to discuss the African concept of time as the key to our understanding of the basic religious and philosophical concepts. The concept of time may help to explain beliefs, attitudes, practices and general way of life of African peoples not only in the traditional set up but also in the modern situation (whether of political, economic, educational or Church life). On this subject there is, unfortunately, no literature, and this is no more than a pioneer attempt which calls for further research and discussion' (Mbiti 1990:16) This call for further research seems to have been answered a few years ago by the many contributors to a volume entitled *Time in the Black Experience*, edited by Joseph K. Adjaye (Westport,CN, Greenwood Press, 1994). More recently, H. Kimmerle and myself have published a volume on *the concept of time* in sub-Saharan Africa (Diagne and Kimmerle, 1998).

8. He gives the example of eight months bearing such 'poetic' names as 'Give your uncle water' or 'Grain in the ear' as they are so reckoned among the Latuka people; this example is presented as an 'improvement' on the one given in 1915 in J. Roscoe's study of *The Northern Bantu* people (Mbiti 1990:20, footnote 1).

9. See p. 27. What Mbiti says of Christian missionary teaching here is also valid for the Islamic opening of the religious dimension of *expectation*.

10. Mbiti 1990:28). 'Nobody else has yet produced' such an analysis, John Mbiti claims.

11. Quoted in Joseph K. Adjaye (1994:3).

12. See, for example, the excellent work of reconstructing the etymologies and distributions of Bantu cultural vocabulary done by David L. Schoenbrun. One interesting instance in particular would be his account of the root -*langa* identified to mean 'report, announce, foresee future, prophecy' and which appears in words meaning 'announce, proclaim', or 'perceive from afar' or 'be clear, illuminated, transparent' or 'hope for, wait for something with much patience and hope'... (Schoenbrun 1997:211-212). The same David Schoenbrun in his review of Adjaye's *Time in the Black experience* rightly points out that 'claiming that 'traditional' African time is somehow concrete and that capitalist European time is abstract or mechanically severed from immediate social contexts' is but 'a rhetorical trap' into which scholars like Mazrui and Mphande fall in their contributions (Schoenbrun 1996, *International Journal of African Historical Studies*, Vol. 29, No. 1, p. 172).

13. Senghor who called 'doux ethnologues' (literally 'sweet ethnologists' which is an evocation of the phrase 'doux rêveurs', sweet dreamers) those who fancied an African essence to be kept unchanged liked to think of culture, in 1950, using these words from Marxist thinker Remo Cantoni: 'A culture that does not want to change neither the world, nor man's external relations, nor his conditions of life is a museum culture which fears the fresh air of concrete action because it likes its dust and mold' (Senghor 1964:95-96).

14. This passage from Senghor's *Hommage à Gaston Berger* is quoted by Senegalese philosopher Abib Mbaye (Mbaye 1997:62-63).

15. As a matter of fact, Gaston Berger, the 'father of Prospective', was born in Saint-Louis, Senegal, on October 1st, 1896 and had a Wolof grand-mother, on his father's side, named Fatou Diagne.

16. Berger states: 'In fact, until now, it is the past that provided the answers as it was called here tradition, elsewhere habit, elsewhere common sense, sometimes laziness... Auguste Comte's famous phrase about the dead governing the living seemed to be valid everywhere' (Berger 1958:127).

# 4

# Fanon and Development: A Philosophical Look

## Lewis R. Gordon

### Fanon's Encomia

Reflecting on the contemporary social and economic condition of Africa, Olufemi Taiwo found himself drawn to the prescient analyses of Frantz Fanon a little more than four decades ago:

> *Les Damnés de la terre* was originally published in 1961, the same year that Fanon died… [That] year takes an added significance when juxtaposed with the historical importance of the preceding year, 1960, for 1960 was the year in which many erstwhile colonial countries won independence from colonial rule. This independence provided the background for Harold Macmillan's euphoric declaration that a wind of change was blowing over Africa. His statement was symptomatic of the enthusiasm and near universal optimism that marked the advent of independent states in Africa. The optimism was not without ground. Given the violence of colonialism and its direct role in retarding the growth and development of colonial territories, it was no surprise that all and sundry thought that independence would usher in a period of development in self-governing nation-states… However, unlike most of his contemporaries, especially those who had secured for themselves alien on the fruits of independence, Fanon had been a dissenting voice in the chorus of enthusiasm that greeted the advent of flag and independence (nominal independence) and was one of the earliest to posit the limits of the phenomenon. Like a seer, Fanon the dissenter had peered into the future and left us a legacy of forebodings about how precarious that future – our present – might be (Taiwo 1996:257).

Although Fanon is often held to his word of supposedly not offering 'timeless truths' (Gates 1991 and Masolo 1998), the unfolding of history and thought seems to be such that his claim is nothing short of ironic. Form need not hover over matter, as Aristotle showed so long ago, but can meet in that powerful embrace that we have all come to know as 'reality', and in so being, sober up our thoughts under its pressing weight. Fanon was much aware of this in his classic early work, *Peau noire, masques blancs*, from which his qualification was announced. In that work, he presented a complex interplay of intratextual naïveté with metatextual insight as he, as in the fashion of Dante's *Inferno*, invited the reader to follow him through each circle of a claustrophobic, hellish condition. The black is a white construction, he admits, that is a consequence of a social world that stands between phylogenetic and ontogenetic forces (Fanon 1952, 1967: Introduction). Yet, creating alternative constructions is not so easy when we take seriously the complexity of signs and symbols which constitute the language of their transmission. The colonising signs and symbols are not simply at the level of what they assert, but also at the level of *how* they assert themselves. Thus, epistemological colonisation should also be understood as lurking even at the heart of *method* (Fanon 1952, 1967: Chapter 1). A major epistemological problem is the degrading quagmire stimulated by the dialectics of recognition. There, blackness stands as imitation instead of originality or source. All imitations face the original as standard, which makes ownership of the promised national language an elusive dream. The link between language and Fanon's sociogenic observation is that language is in principle communicable, which means that it is inherently 'public', which means that it finds its foundations in the social world. Failure at the linguistic and semiotic level means there is trouble in the social world, and trouble in the social world means that, should one continue to cling to its completeness, its inherent legitimacy, that one should retreat inward, into the bosom of love, for an affirmation of one's worth, for sanctuary.[1] Yet, there too, failure awaits so long as, under the guise of love, the desired desire is to be loved not as black but through the narcissism of whiteness, through a gift of deceiving words. That words of whiteness, words of white recognition as white, within the privacy of love are insufficient resistance against the social world calls for a further retreat to the point of constitutional fantasy. He then rehearsed the retreat autobiographically through his own encounters with words of 'niggerness', to laughter, to words of science, to the rhythms of *negritude*, to tears and then wrestling with psychopathological anxieties in a world bereft of normality. Why did Fanon take such a circuitous path in that early work? Because he knew that reality is difficult to bear; it is that for which preparation is necessary. Facing such difficulties awakens a critical, interrogative consciousness – one that, in the encomium that marks the book's denouement, is appealed to in its author's flesh.

Fanon's philosophy can be summarised by a single conviction: That maturity is fundamental to the human condition, but one cannot achieve maturity without being *actional*, which, for Fanon, is tantamount to freedom. Much of his subsequent writings explore this thesis. In *Les Damnés de la terre*, this march through concentric layers of hell, echoed in the title's reference to *les damnés*, returns, but now in the context of the wider political question of a geo-constituted realm. Recall that Fanon begins with the provocative observation of decolonisation as a violent process. Many commentators overlook his critical rejections of the 'Graeco-Latin pedestal' of Western values. For if those values were instruments of colonisation, how can they legitimate themselves as anything other than its salvation? But what happens in a world of suspended values both old and new? Is it not the case that in a world without values, all is permitted? And what could be more violent than such a world, a world without limits?

I have written of that world as one in which there is no hope of everyone both eating and then having their cake (Gordon 1995: Chapter 4). When competing communities lay claims to 'right' from value systems that render those rights 'natural' and 'absolute', the stage set is no less than a tragic one. Fanon then takes us into the world faced at the moment of decolonisation. His argument, that the absence of an infrastructure both at the level of land and idea, leads to a neocolonial situation through the auspices of a Third World elite and of the need for revolutionary mobilisation that required the peasantry and the lumpen-proletariat, stimulated outcries of heretical Marxism.[2] Having built his thought on the importance of seizing one's freedom and taking responsibility for one's values, Fanon was careful to raise the question of *how* a transition can be made from neocolonialism to a genuine *post*colonialism. He returns to criticising *negritude*, for instance, on the grounds that it is more than a negative moment in a historical dialectic but also a form of reductionism akin to nationalism, racism and all self-interests-laden models of group organisations instead of those premised upon the common good. Here, Fanon is making concrete the old problem of participatory politics, where policy can be premised upon a collective of interests or the interest of the collective. As Jean-Jacques Rousseau famously formulated it in *Du Contrat social* – between the will in general and the general will. Fanon provided case studies of nationalisms collapsed into ethnic conflicts, and offered, in their stead, the option of national consciousness where the task, as he formulated it, is to build the nation. In the course of his critique of neocolonial values, Fanon advanced both a geopolitical and a class critique. The geopolitical critique challenged the necessity of the capital city as the site of political residence and the organisation of social life. The modern African city, for example, faces the reality of the complex political demands of rural Africa. The urban elite that emerges in this structure is one, he argues, that lacks material capital but relies on political capital as mediators with colonial metropolises. The result is a neglected infrastructure, mismanaged national loans and the emergence of what can be called a 'lumpen-bourgeoisie', an elite that, he concludes, serves no purpose (Fanon 1961, 1991:217, 1963:175-176).

Fanon then returns to the colonial and decolonising moments to illustrate a chilling point. The colonial condition forces the colonised, he argues, to question their humanity. This interrogation occasions alienation of the spirit in the face of loss of land and thwarted, indigenous teleological processes. The decolonisation process unleashes an array of violent forces that bring to the surface the many double standards of the colonial system and contingency in a world that once seemed to be absolute, necessary and law. At the heart of this 'hell', is the classic direction of consumed hatred. As Virgil showed Dante's protagonist's two foes, one of whom is so consumed by hatred that he gnaws on the head of his enemy while frozen from the neck down, Fanon presented the horrific implications of being consumed by hatred. The message is clear: there are some attachments, some values, that we must let go, and in so doing, we will find a way outside at which we encounter the awesome set of possibilities raised by the stars in the night sky. This is what Fanon ultimately means by '...*il faut faire peau neuve, développer une pensée neuve, tenter de mettre sur pied un homme neuf*' (Fanon 1961, 1991:376, 1963:316).³

If we return to *Peau noire, masques blancs*, a consideration should be added to this summary. The metatextual Fanon stood in a special relation to the intratextual Fanon's naive investment in the epistemic and political promises of European society. Failing to see that the social world itself was suffering from a colonising, racist malediction, the naive black subject/Fanon failed to see that it was that *system* itself that required transformation. He thus related to that system with a *theodicean* attitude. Theodicy is the theological rationalisation of God's ultimate goodness in the presence of evil, given God's omnipotence and omniscience. On one account, God's actions are all good, so evil must be a function of our limited ability to see God's relation to His actions – one of ultimate justice; hence the term theodicy (*theo* [god's] *dike* [justice]). Another account is that God's having given human beings free will means that evil and injustice in the world are functions of humanity, the source of original sin. There is, in other words, nothing wrong with God, but there is much wrong with humanity. The modern world is, however, supposedly governed by secular rationalisations. Yet, although divine terms may not be advanced in modern rationalisation processes, it is not always the case that the *grammar* or the *form* of the divine have been eliminated. Two idols that take the place of the divine are science and politics. Where science fills the gap, it functions as a form of *science-dike* a form of ultimate rationalisation of reality. To contradict scientific claims means, then, simply to be wrong and to be a form of rationality that stands outside the bounds of reason. Where politics fills the gap, the result is the claim of a complete political system. The result is the emergence of people who contradict such a system. Since the system is complete, and therefore just, such people must be incomplete and unjust. In 1903, W.E.B. Du Bois formulated the situation of such people as one of being a problem.⁴

The problem faced by problem people is how to be actional. Such people live in a world in which the assertion of their humanity is structured as a contradiction of the system. To *assert* their humanity, then, is already structurally 'violent', 'unjust', 'wrong', 'ill-deserved' and 'ill-liberal'. How, then, does one set afoot a new humanity when the status quo's notion of humanity is treated as just? Both Fanon and Du Bois saw this problem as one of double consciousness. The metatextual relation of which I have been writing is also that second sight, that place behind the veil of false consciousness. It is what people live in the face of a world that bullies them to pretend does not exist. It is the lived world of enslavement under the banner of avowed 'freedom'. It is the world of racial limits in every place that purports to be colourblind; it is knowing that the normative always benefits from claims of 'neutrality'. It is knowing that words like 'development' and 'modernisation' sound much better than their practice in parts of the world outside of North America, Europe and Australia. This insight leads to a set of reflections that can be called critiques of development reason. Although there are many, I will, in the rest of this chapter, focus on three scholars, two of whom are influenced by Fanon and one of whom continues to keep the intratextual faith: Sylvia Wynter, Irene Gendzier and Amartya Sen. Then, I will offer my own Fanonian-existential, postcolonial, alternative philosophical conception.

### 'We the Underdeveloped': Sylvia Wynter

'Development' is a relational and teleological term. To aim at development requires not yet being developed. To be developed implies achieving more than an end but an end that *ought* to be achieved. In terms of an organism, the obvious example is maturation of that organism or its achievement of its adult form. Implicit in not being developed, then, is the condition of childhood at worst and adolescence at best, but in neither instance is there the condition of full responsibility – namely, adulthood. Without responsibility, there is no agency, and without agency, the familiar patterns of dependence follow. In 'Is 'Development' a Purely Empirical Concept or also Teleological?', Sylvia Wynter takes on Fanon's demand to develop new thoughts. She argues that such a project may require the rejection of 'development' (Wynter 1996:299).

Wynter's argument is as follows. The modern world has set Western civilisation and its concomitant white normativity as the standard of development. White normativity emerged through the rise of Europe as a global force that contrasted European humanity with those that constituted its limits, its points beyond which there is, supposedly, no longer a properly human mode of being. This limit she refers to as 'liminality, or *conceptual otherness*' (305). This conceptual otherness emerged as a function of the newly-formed cultural processes that centered Judeo-Christian practices as the foundations of religious life against which secular modernity emerged. In effect, because of the absence of even a Semitic premodern legitimation practice, such populations are twice removed from modern, normative conceptions of the human as white and secular. Although she does not refer to Hegel, a version of this argument can be seen in his infamous introduction to his lectures on history, where he denied Africans of even a *religious* moment.[5] The result of this double move – of neither a modern present or a religious past – is a designation of the absence of a subjective life that can be correlated with a European subjective life, which eliminates the analogy-oriented conditions for intersubjectivity and empathy. In philosophical language, the liminal is devoid as an epistemic correlate.[6] Wynter writes:

> The paradox here is that the category of liminality, or *conceptual otherness*, functions as the second mechanism by which the West will be able, in the words of the Royal Lady, to conquer without being in the right as traditionally and therefore religiously conceived but rather in terms of a purely secular sense of right. It also functions politically in another cognizing dimension. As the Eritrean anthropologist Asmarom Legesse argues, the liminal category is the systemic category from whose perspective alone, as the perspective of those forcibly made to embody and signify lack-of-being,

whose members, in seeking to escape their condemned statuses, are able to call into question the closure instituting the order and, therefore, the necessary 'blindness' of its normative, in this case, 'developed' subjects (Wynter 1996:305).

If white normativity requires black liminality, and development is premised upon white normativity, then it, too, requires the liminal. Development, in other words, at least in its historic instantiation, constitutes liminal people. What then happens when the liminal takes on the project of development? They, too, begin to produce their own sites of liminality. Recall Fanon's point about nationalism in the neocolonial moment, where xenophobic and racist protection of limited resources lead to the failure of not building a genuine national consciousness. The argument can be extended to the violence that marks a feature of liminality that is, in my view, not quite captured by Wynter's formulation of conceptual *otherness*. In *Peau noire, masques blancs*, Fanon challenged the dialectics of recognition in racialised slavery. The racialised slave is not considered the normative self *or* other. He or she or, in many instances 'it', is considered *below* the realm of human intersubjectivity and ethical relations. In effect, as I have argued elsewhere (Gordon 1995, 1997 and 2000), the objective of the racialised slave and the black in an antiblack society is to *achieve otherness*, wherein there is a genuine intersubjective and ethical problematic. If this thesis is correct, then all is permitted on such an 'object'.[7]

Themes of damnation return:

> This new form represents metaphysical lack, that of humankind's potential subordination to the dysselected genetically defective aspects of its own human nature on the one hand; and on the other, to that of its potential material overcoming by the Ricardo-defined threat of an external natural scarcity. For in the same way as the liminal category of the *lepers*, prescribed and segregated outside the walls of the town, signified for the feudal-Christian order the *massa damnata*, condemned to their then believed to be incurable fate, so the knight's category of the we-the-underdeveloped equally functions for the now barely secularized and global form of the original Judeo-Christian 'local culture' of Western Europe. The *underdeveloped*, proscribed like the medieval lepers outside the gates of the attained, *civitas materialis* of the developed enclaves, function as the empirical proof of subordination to natural society, and therefore of the affliction of the Malthusian 'iron laws' of nature. Consequently, its 'underdeveloped' state is an indispensable function of our present behavior-orienting projection. The only 'cure' is that of the specific behavioral pathways prescribed by the represented supraordinate *telos* of development and economic growth; of therefore *material redemption* and the *civitas materialis* as the now transumed form of spiritual redemption and the *civitas dei*, as the telos that institute our contemporary global order (Wynter 1996:306–307).

The theodicean element returns, wherein the devastation of life, safety, social institutions and the environment in Africa is treated by the current global order as indication of the failings, of the inferiority of African people. The effort, however, of African and African diasporic peoples to 'fix' themselves in the material terms of Europe, North America and Australia, locks us in the processes of a redemption that is not ours and is consequently an affirmation, instead of a negation, of our damnation. Echoing Fanon, Wynter concludes: 'Hence it is proposed here that the 'strategy' that we must now elaborate is an epistemological (and therefore culture-systemic) rather than merely economic one' (Wynter 1996:309).

## Democracy and Development: Irene Gendzier

Although Sylvia Wynter qualified her conclusions by reminding us that we should work through epistemological categories and 'not merely economic' ones, her discussion so focuses on the question of conceptual conditions that it is difficult to determine how those economic considerations configure in the analysis. Irene Gendzier, author of one of the early studies of Fanon's life and thought, took on this task, in addition to elaborating its political dimensions as well, in her 1995 history of the field of development studies, *Development against Democracy: Manipulating Political Change in the Third World*. Gendzier first points out that development studies emerged in elite, First World universities as an attempt to offer their vision of modernisation over the Marxist ones of the U.S.S.R., Communist China, and Cuba. Their model was resolute: A capitalist economy and elite (oligarchical) democracy. We see here the normative telos writ large: The United States. Although Gendzier does not present this as a theodicean argument, those elements are unmistakable. The initial phase of development studies granted the United States the status of utopia, which means that both its contradictions and those that emerge from its application abroad must be functions of the limitations of the people who manifest them. In effect, Gendzier's study is an empirical validation of much of Wynter's and Fanon's arguments. The record of those development policies is universally bad, although there seems to be no example that could meet any test of falsification that would convince, say, members of the Council for Foreign Relations, many of whom are from the neoliberal and conservative wings of the North American academic elite. Gendzier uses an apt term to describe the work such policies have done: *maldevelopment*. Here is her assessment of their record:

> For many, terms like Development and Modernization have lost their meaning. They have become code words. They refer to policies pursued by governments and international agencies that enrich ruling elites and technocrats, while the masses are told to await the benefits of the 'trickle down' effect. For many, Development and Modernization are terms that refer to a politics of reform designed to preserve the status quo while promising to alter it. And for many social scientists, those who have rationalized the interests of governments committed to such policies are accomplices in deception (Gendzier 1995:2).

North American and European development studies set the foundations for U.S. policies that supported antidemocratic regimes for the sake of preserving the economic hegemony of American business elites, and the supposed dilemma emerged, in many countries under the yoke of First World developmental dictates, of whether to reduce social inequalities, which often led to economic decline on the one hand, or increase economic prosperity, which often led to social inequalities on the other. The problem, of course, is that this is a false dilemma since no nation attempts either pole in a vacuum. How other countries respond to a nation's social and economic policy will impact its outcome. It is not, in other words, as though any nation truly functions as a self-supporting island anymore. A good example is the small Caribbean island of Antigua. To 'normalise' relations with the United States, that island was forced to create immigration laws that would stimulate the formation of an underclass, which U.S. advisors claimed would create a cheap labour base to stimulate economic investment and an increase in production and prosperity. There is now such a class in Antigua, but there has, in fact, been a decline in prosperity. The reason is obvious: There was not an infrastructure of capital in *need* of such a labour force in the first place. The island of Antigua has a good education base, which makes the type of labour suitable for its economy to be one of a trained professional class linked in with the tourist economy and other high-leveled service-oriented professions such as banking and trade, all of which, save tourism, the United States does not associate within a predominantly black country. The creation of an underclass without an education or social-welfare system to provide training and economic relief, conjoined with an absence of investments from abroad, has created a politically and economically noxious situation, and the quality of life in Antigua now faces decline.[8] This story is no doubt a familiar one in nations with very modest prosperity as in Africa.

There has been a set of critical responses to development theory, the most influential of which has been those by theorists of dependency.[9] The obvious situation of epistemological dependence emerges from the United States as the standard of development, both economic and cultural. The economic consequence is a function of the international institutions that form usury relationships with countries that are structurally in a condition of serfdom, where they depend on loans that it is no longer possible to believe they can even pay back. Fanon would add, however, that we should bear in mind that in the case of many African countries who received such loans, the situation might have been different had those funds been spent on infrastructural resources instead of as a source of wealth for neocolonial elites. That European and American banks hold accounts for leaders who have, in effect, robbed their countries and have left their citizens in near perpetual debt to the World Bank reveals the gravity of Fanon's warnings of forty years past. An additional Fanonian warning has also been updated by sociologist Paget Henry, who warns us that the epistemological struggle also includes fighting 'to save the sciences from extreme commodification and instrumentalisation' (Henry 2002–2003:51).

To these criticisms, Gendzier poses the following consideration. The critics of development have pointed out what is wrong with development studies, particularly its project of modernisation, but their shortcoming is that many of them have not presented alternative conceptions of how to respond to the problems that plague most of Africa and much of the Third World. Think, for example, of Wynter's call for a new epistemic order. Calling for it is not identical with creating it. This is one of the ironic aspects of the epistemological project. Although it is a necessary reflection, it is an impractical call for a practical response.

Gendzier regards the fundamental problem of development theory as linked to its near religious investment in a union of liberal democracy and capitalism. This commitment has led, she argues, to an endless debate on the *meaning* of development:

> Given the premises that led to support for the elitist interpretation of democratic theory, the implications of supporting capitalist development as a motor force behind social and political change appeared to be paradoxical. The former emphasis on elite theory was geared toward controlling conditions that the latter systematically generated.
>
> What, then, was to be done? The confrontation with this paradox and the predicaments in Development theories that it addressed led to a nearly permanent debate on the meaning of the term. Did Political Development imply democracy, equality, and participation? Or did it refer primarily to economic change? And what were the consequences of choosing the one or the other of the two definitions? Far from reflecting a confusion over the meaning of Political Development, these debates circled around the impossible choice clearly understood by Development theorists. To define Political Development in terms of democracy and participation meant accepting the contradiction implicit in the interpretation of political change in Development theories. To reject such a definition meant severing the connection with democracy, which would render theories of Political Development nothing more than instruments for the management of political change. Unmasked, such instruments represented a form of social and political engineering that could hardly be expected to attract the kind of support implicit in the first project (Gendzier 1995:156).

I quoted Gendzier at length here because of the prescience of her observation. Is not the current U.S. foreign policy of preemption but an 'unmasked' instance of a logical consequence of such developmental formulations?

Gendzier points out that the response of development theorists to the critique of development *process* has been a focus on *actors* or agents of change in the Third World. And this response has, following the kinds of theodicean arguments mentioned earlier, taken the form of no less than the usual blame-the-victims variety. Through butchery of Max Weber's analysis of the impact of Calvinism on the development of capitalism, the conclusion unleashed against people in Africa is that they simply lack the capitalist spirit (Gendzier 1995:165; cf. Eisenstadt 1968). The connection between such an argument against Africans and the infamous 'cultures of poverty' argument against African Americans is unmistakable. What is submerged by such arguments is the role of policy in setting the conditions for the emergence and limits of the leadership in 'underdeveloped' communities and the problem of whether such leadership is even representative of the cultural realities of the communities they supposedly lead. Gendzier's historical analysis is, in the end, affirming at least Wynter's observation of development as ultimately a symptom of Western narcissism when she writes that it '…is more revealing of a particular dimension of American political thinking than it is of Third World societies in transition. From this perspective, then, those who have relied on the paradigms of Development

Studies to understand the nature of Third World societies will have learned something of their own political tradition instead' (Genzier 1995:197).

## Liberalism Strikes Back: Amartya Sen's Defense of Development 'as Freedom'

Sylvia Wynter and Irene Gendzier exemplify, respectively, what Paget Henry (2000) has described as poeticist and historicist critiques. The former deals with the semiosis of development; the latter, its historico-material limits. In both instances, the verdict is grim. Amartya Sen (1999) has, however, attempted to rescue the project of development through taking on the struggle of its definition and presenting a case for its use in the political economy of dehumanisation, which he describes as 'unfreedom'. He argues that if unfreedom is the problem, then the transition sought should have freedom as its telos. To be developed is to be free. The task, as he sees it, is to organize society in a way that maximises freedom, and since, in almost Aristotelian fashion, one cannot live freely without certain material things such as food, water and shelter, certain social guarantees such as security, education, and affirming values, the role of development theory is to present the strongest case for such goods.[10] The strongest case is not only that they are ethical or just, but that they are completely compatible with economic prosperity. This claim he substantiates by decoupling production from distribution. Consider the case of hunger. The problem is not that countries are not producing food. The problem is the set of social conditions that regulate the distribution of food. Sen also takes on Gendzier's point about actors by pointing out that freedom as a model requires not impeding the agency of people. In other words, the actors must be taken heed of, but *the* actors must include every member of the society (cf. Sen 1999:4).

An immediate problem with Sen's position, however, rests in his use of the word *freedom*. Consider the U.S. 'war on terror'. President Bush has repeatedly sold his foreign policy as a defense of freedom, which he equates with the United States. Although Sen is willing to say that the United States is not freedom or a nation of freedom, because there are many unfree people living here, he faces the problem of formulating freedom in the light of his initial premise of unfreedom. Bush could define the U.S. as freedom precisely because he approaches the U.S. in a theodicean fashion: unfreedom, for him, is *outside* the system. Key to the argument, then, is the location of unfreedom. Although Sen is willing to look at unfreedom as intrasystemic, he encounters problems in his use of the term, which is at times incoherent. Here is an example: 'Very many people across the world suffer from varieties of unfreedom. Famines continue to occur in particular regions, denying to millions the basic freedom to survive' (Sen 1999:15). How can survival be a *freedom*? Survival is a base-level condition *for* freedom, since it doesn't make sense to talk about what one 'has' when one is no longer alive. But more, how coherent is it to talk about *a* freedom?

In Sen's analysis, we come to one of the core problems of development thought, and that is its solipsistic adherence to a conception of political thinking that may be incompatible with its avowed goals. Sen is, after all, attempting to address the problem of unfreedom in the world within the philosophical language that fostered that unfreedom in the first place – namely, modern liberal political philosophy and political economy.[11] It would take too much time to elaborate the dynamics here, so I will just summarise it thus: There are alternative philosophical traditions whose focus on the question of freedom would suggest a dialectic in which the movement is from freedom to unfreedom to liberation. The reason would be because unfreedom makes sense as the curtailment of freedom to begin with (which, in this case are the agents/adults who are the subjects who must take control over their lives and society), and liberation makes sense as the overcoming of unfreedom. Why liberation versus freedom? Because a movement from freedom to unfreedom to freedom suggests the capacity to 'return' to one's prior condition. The historical reality is that one can never return but most find a way to build something positive and new on the misery that constituted the period of bondage. But more, the problem with the analysis is that it also turns the relationship between economics and discourses of freedom on its head. Economics is a discourse that centres rationality, and rationality relies on consistency and instrumental thinking. An insight from the broader tradition to which I am referring (the one, by the way, from which Fanon's thought emerged) is that freedom is a category that is broader than rationality; it is rooted in the fundamental incompleteness of the human condition. That being so, to place freedom under a formal model or system that yokes it in a way that leads to talking about *a* freedom is to domesticate or colonise it under a particular rational order. Although there could be a good case to link freedom with reason, the problem still emerges by virtue of reason being a broader category than rationality. One of the major projects of modern science, for example, has been to elevate rationality as the model of reason. The problem, however, is that consistency works well for systems not sophisticated enough to evaluate themselves. For the more complex problems of evaluation, including self-evaluation, a more radical model of reason is needed; one that *cannot* be complete.[12]

A tradition that takes on the question of freedom in ways that adhere to its fundamental incompleteness is the existential tradition, and we can find, in the existential phenomenological tradition, one that takes very seriously the social dimensions of freedom. For the remainder of this chapter, I am going to outline my Africana existential phenomenological approach, which has also become known as postcolonial phenomenology. That it is heavily based upon Fanon's thought is already known and acknowledged (see Gordon 1995, 1997, 2000, Henry 2000). In many ways, it is sympathetic to Sen's choice of focusing on freedom, but it comes from a tradition that rejects the dependency implicit in the neoliberal framework of Sen's thought.

## A Postcolonial Phenomenological Look at Freedom

In many ways, the term 'postcolonial phenomenology' is a redundant term. Phenomenology is a form of inquiry in which one suspends one's ontological commitments for the sake of investigating meaningful features of the world. In phenomenology, one takes seriously that all objects of thought are just that – which means that there are intentional features of every epistemological or knowledge endeavour. It is odd that some systems of investigation attempt to eliminate the *investigation* dimension in the search for objectivity. What phenomenologists admit is that objectivity can only be posed as a problem by a pre-given subjectivity. Similarly, subjectivity can only be posed as a problem in the light of there not being subjectivity alone. These arguments are called transcendental arguments; they deal with the conditions for the concepts under investigation. An important feature of phenomenological work is the question of grounding phenomenology. The phenomenological approach demands that such a project be as radical as possible, which means that all methods must be subject to ontological suspension (i.e., the rejection of their presumed legitimacy). This critical position must be taken against even logic itself, for if it were not done, then phenomenology would be subordinate to logic without logic having gone through a critical process of legitimation. (And yes, this critical question applies, as well, to the critical process of legitimation that one attempts.) I bring this up to point out the spirit of resistance to epistemic colonisation that marks the phenomenological way of thinking. That is why there is some redundancy: phenomenology already means a form of postcolonial thinking.

The postcolonial/phenomenological approach suggests, then, that even phenomenology's history must be engaged with the cautious eye of ontological suspension. What that means is that the history, whether in its European, Asian or Africana forms, must be seen as factual instances but not as what *legitimates* phemomenological work.[13]

The existential element comes to the fore when we think of the dual meaning of *existence*. From the Latin words *ex* and *sistere*, it means to stand out or to emerge. It is another way of saying that if one does not stand out, even to one's self, one is as though one were not there. To exist, then, is vital to every human being; it is what it means *to live*.

To stand out or to live means that one is, in a word, metastable. That means that every act of complete containment fails to present a *living* being. Because such living requires emergence, standing out, or, in more grandiose language, *transcendence*, it *is* freedom – always more, always incomplete. How, then, could such a reality be 'unfree', when it *is* freedom?

The answer rests in the social world. The social world is the realm of meaning and creativity. In purely physical terms (for the sake of argument), the material world continues to be its exact content of the relation of energy to matter. But the social world, the world of intersubjectivity, is one in which many new 'things' are created everyday. These 'things' are meaningful in those terms, and they proliferate such things as institutions and forms of life. This is what Fanon means by *sociogenesis*.

A problem emerges, however, in the relation of individual intentions to the framework of intentions that constitute the social world, or in more familiar language, individuals and structures. The former faces the latter in a peculiar relationship that we shall call *choice* to *options*. A peculiar feature of the social world is that some practices and institutions can become so calcified that they function no differently than would a brick wall. That is to say, just as one cannot go through a brick wall without force; there are social institutions that function similarly. Those are options. They are either material reality or function as material features of reality.

Human beings live in relation to options as the transcendence of options. What this means is this: There are choices that are isomorphic with options, but when options are exhausted, choices can continue on *how to relate to the exhaustion of options*. Such choices tend to be about the chooser. One can choose *how* one deals with one's limits (e.g., happily, angrily, reluctantly, stupidly). Notice the adverbial nature of these 'choices'. With enough time, one could begin to make so many inward-directed choices that the choices become entirely about the constitution of the self. I call this 'implosivity'.[14]

Implosivity is a function of oppression. Fanon's words illuminate this observation:

> Because it is a systematic negation of the other, an unreasonable decision to refuse to the other all the attributes of humanity, colonialism forces the people it dominates to ask the question constantly, 'In reality, who am I?'[15]

The 'Who am I?' to which Fanon refers is rendered perverse by the adverb *constamment* (constantly). The constant questioning of the self, of one's value, is a function of lost hope in outward-directed choices. In Fanonian language, it is the failure to become *actional*. This failure is not, as we have been seeing, accidental. If we were to set the total number of options in a society as, say, $n$, and we were to make $x$ number of members of the society have $n$, but $y$ number of members have $n$-various random numbers of options, we would find the $y$ members exhausting their outward-directed choices sooner than the $x$ members. Now suppose $n$ becomes what every member of the society is expected to exercise choices over while their $n$ is denied. The immediate result is that the $y$ members will be seen as the 'cause' of their failure to make choices isomorphic with $n$. And while they at an earlier period begin implementing the self-inquiry or self-fixing, some of the $y$ members may never face those. The African-American comedian Chris Rock put it this way: 'For whites, the sky's the limit; for blacks, the limit's the sky'. He speaks here of two perceptions of reach.

A consequence of options-disparity is the scope of power. In cases of exhausted options, the inward-directed choices are at the physical reach of the body. Because of this, people with limited options are often associated with force or violence. They cannot have an effect on the world beyond what their body can contact. That makes the field of their actions limited. People who have options are those whose choices can affect the social world. Their bodies do not need to be in the location of their effects. This ability to have an effect on the social world is power. Power is the ability to live outwardly, to make choices that would initiate a chain of effects in the social world that would constitute the set of norms and institutions that would affirm one's belonging in the world instead of stimulating a flight from it to an infinitesimal, inwardly-directed path of madness and despair.

In effect, what Sen ultimately wanted to argue is something with which Fanon, Wynter, Gendzier and I would agree: that the goal is to increase the options available for people to live well in a world in which time and space are increasingly pressurised by the social and consumption demands of each coming generation. The reality of this goal is that it is a form of globalism for which we all would have to fight since the contemporary hegemonic policies of North America, Europe, and Australia suggest an alternative model premised upon maximizing such options for fewer people, each day at the expense of all.

**Conclusion**

There is, of course, the continued, resounding question from a century ago: What is to be done?

That the context of this discussion is philosophical presents the role of the intellectual. Given the nature of the problems at hand, it would be folly to presume a single role for intellectuals to take. The Africana intellectual tradition has, for instance, been guided by a healthy tension between concerns of identity and liberation – between questions of being and becoming (cf. Gordon 2000:chapters 1–4). It is the task of some intellectuals to work out questions of being, questions of 'what' and 'how'. And then there are those who focus on 'why' and other questions of purpose. Some do both. All should consider their work, I here submit, with the following considerations in mind.

Each epoch is a living reality. This is so because they are functions of living human communities, which, too, are functions of the social world. As living realities, they come into being and will go out of being. What this means is that societies go through processes of birth and decay. An erroneous feature of most civilisations that achieve imperial status is the silly belief that such an achievement would assure their immortality. But we know that no living community lasts forever, save, perhaps, through historical memory of other communities. Decay comes. The task faced by each subordinated community, however, is how prepared it is for the moment in which conditions for its liberation are ripe. When the people are ready, the crucial question will be of how many ideas are available for the reorganisation of social life. The ideas, many of which will unfold through years of engaged political work, need not be perfect, for in the end, it will be the hard, creative work of the communities that take them on. That work is the concrete manifestation of political imagination.

Fanon described this goal as setting afoot a new humanity. He knew how terrifying such an effort is, for we do live in times where such a radical break appears as no less than the end of the world. In the meantime, the task of building infrastructures for something new must be planned, and where there is some room, attempted, as we all no doubt already know, because given the sociogenic dimension of the problem, we have no other option but to build the options on which the future of our species rest.

## Notes

1. I won't rehearse here the many criticisms of Fanon's discussion of this retreat under the taxonomy of women of color and white men, and of men of color and white women. The error of expecting symmetric treatments of these categories abound in the critical literature. For examples, see the various anthologies of these essays in Gibson 1998, Allesandrini 1999, and the critical commentary in Sharpley-Whiting 1997. I provide a detailed discussion of this argument in Gordon (Forthcoming).
2. See, especially, Jack Woddis (1972).
3. '…make a new start, develop new thoughts, and set afoot a new man'. In Dante's *Inferno* (Canto XXXIII, lines 127–139), the redemptive reflection is posed thus:

   There is a place below, the limit of
   that cave, its farthest point from Beelzebub,
   a place one cannot see: it is discovered
   By ear—there is a sounding stream that flows
   along the hollow of a rock eroded
   by winding waters, and the slope is easy.
   My guide and I came on that hidden road
   to make our way back into the bright world;
   and with no care for any rest, we climbed-
   He first, I following-until I saw,
   through a round opening, some of those things
   of beauty Heaven bears. It was from there
   That we emerged, to see—once more—the stars.

4. '…Between me and the other world there is ever an unasked question: unasked by some through feelings of delicacy; by others through the difficulty of rightly framing it. All, nevertheless, flutter round it. They approach me in a half-hesitant sort of way, eye me curiously or compassionately, and then, instead of saying directly, How does it feel to be a problem? They say, I know an excellent colored man in my town; or, I fought at Mechanicsville; or, Do not these Southern outrages make your blood boil? At these I smile, or am interested, or reduced the boiling to a simmer, as the occasion may require. To the real question, How does it feel to be a problem? I answer seldom a word' (1903,1969:43-44).

   Du Bois is being ironic here since, in effect, his entire career as a social scientist and theorist was devoted to answering this question. For discussion, see Gordon (2000:chapter 4) and Gordon (forthcoming 2004).

5. This passage on Africans from Hegel's introduction *Philosophy of History* has received much discussion, so I won't rehearse it here. See, e.g., D.A. Masolo (1994).
6. For a more developed discussion of this problem, see Wynter's 2001 essay on Fanon.
7. Although conflicts in Africa often have political and economic causes, the extent of the deaths caused by such are often unreported in the dominant media cannot be ignored. It is as if the 'enemy', invariably racialized, were not human. What is often overlooked, however, is how this view is part of a larger, global reality. An infamous example of this is the leaked December 12, 1991 memorandum of Lawrence H. Summers, then Chief Economist and Vice President of the World Bank, and now President of Harvard University:

'Dirty' Industries: Just between you and me, shouldn't the World Bank be encouraging MORE migration of the dirty industries to the LDCs [Less Developed Countries]? I can think of three reasons:

(i) The measurements of the costs of health impairing pollution depends on the foregone earnings from increased morbidity and mortality. From this point of view a given amount of health impairing pollution should be done in the country with the lowest cost, which will be the country with the lowest wages. I think the economic logic behind dumping a load of toxic waste in the lowest wage country is impeccable and we should face up to that.

(ii) The costs of pollution are likely to be non-linear as the initial increments of pollution probably have very low cost. I've always thought that under-populated countries in Africa are vastly UNDER-polluted, their air quality is probably vastly inefficiently low compared to Los Angeles or Mexico City. Only the lamentable facts that so much pollution is generated by non-tradable industries (transport, electrical generation) and that the unit transport costs of solid waste are so high, prevent world welfare enhancing trade in air pollution and waste.

(iii) The demand for a clean environment for aesthetic and health reasons is likely to have very high income elasticity. The concern over an agent that causes a one in a million change in the odds of prostate cancer is obviously going to be much higher in a country where people survive to get prostate cancer than in a country where under 5 mortality is 200 per thousand. Also, much of the concern over industrial atmospheric discharge is about visibility impairing particulates. These discharges may have very little direct health impact. Clearly trade in goods that embody aesthetic pollution concerns could be welfare enhancing. While production is mobile the consumption of pretty air is a non-tradable.

The problem with the arguments against all of these proposals for more pollution in LDCs (intrinsic rights to certain goods, moral reasons, social concerns, lack of adequate markets, etc.) could be turned around and used more or less effectively against every Bank proposal for liberalization.

8. See the Eastern Caribbean Community Documentation Center Reports by the Caribbean Development Bank in the 1990s, which are discussed in Paget Henry's paper, 'Globalization and the Deformation of the Antiguan Working Class', presented at the UWI Country Conference on Antigua, November 13–15, 2003.

9. For a recent retrospective on dependency theory, see the special symposium on development, edited by Paget Henry and José Itzigsohn in *Radical Philosophy Review*, 2002–2003, Vol. 5, Nos. 1-2 , pp. 26–95), which includes discussions by Giovanni Arrighi (75–85) and Samir Amin (86-95).

10. By Aristotelian fashion, I am referring to Aristotle's discussion of ethical life in his *Nichomachean Ethics*.

11. Because of limitations of space, I cannot elaborate the theory of disciplinary decadence that underlay my discussion here. Disciplinary decadence emerges from the ontologizing of a discipline or particular area within a discipline. Think of physicists, for instance, who criticize other areas of thought for not presenting their ideas in terms of physics, or philosophers who collapse philosophy into epistemology. It undermines the relation of thought to being. For some discussion, see Gordon 1995: chapter 5 and Gordon 2003, and Gyekye 1995: chapter 1.

12. The European version of the traditions to which I am referring find their foundations in Kant's *Critique of Pure Reason* and Hegel's *Phenomenology of Spirit*, and their critique on existentialists from Kierkegaard and Nietzsche through to Jaspers, Heidegger, Sartre and Merleau-Ponty. In the Africana tradition, these problems have been struggled with not only from the modern encounters with slavery, as we find in Cugoano, but also in Africana existential thought. For discussions, see Gordon (1997, 2000), Henry (2000), and Bogues (2003).

13. For discussion of varieties of phenomenological traditions, see Henry (2000). For explicit discussion of the limits of historicist (and naturalist) legitimation practices, see Edmund Husserl (1910–1911).
14. A more detailed version of this discussion can be found in Gordon (1995: chapter 3, 2000: chapter 4).
15. Parce qu'il est une négation systématisée de l'autre, une décision forcenée de refuser a l'autre tout attribut d'humanité, le colonialisme accule le peuple dominé a se poser constamment la question: « Qui suis-je en réalité » ? (Fanon 1961,1991: 300, 1963:250).

# 5

# Dialogue with Lansana Keita: Reflections on African Development

## Paulin Hountondji

**Ten Questions**

Lansana Keita asked me ten revealing questions about his own personal expectations and demands as a philosopher. The first one was on the responsibilities of African philosophers and other intellectuals in relation to developments in their own society. The second one was on the future of socialism as a doctrine and its relevance to Africa, considering the collapse of communism in the former Soviet Union and the economic disruptions taking place in modern China. The third question calls for a diagnosis of development obstacles in contemporary Africa and proposed solutions. The fourth question probes the relationship between science and philosophy and the possible promotion by philosophy of the development of science and technology in Africa, instead of being submitted to the development of science as is generally the case everywhere. The fifth question is a very specific one concerning Nkrumah and the mission he assigned to philosophy in the political field. Alluding to Frantz Fanon and Cheikh Anta Diop, the sixth question wondered about the relevance of their political thought in relation to the current development tasks in Africa. The seventh question acknowledges my observations on North/South disequilibrium in the area of production and scientific knowledge management and wonders about the solution. The eighth one seeks to know what type of economic, political and cultural system can make Africa regain its sovereignty and autonomous decision-making.... The ninth question ponders over the real value of NEPAD in relation to the demands of a united and sovereign Africa. The tenth and last question concerns the possible contribution of African thinkers and philosophers of the past, from ancient Egypt up till today, to thinking what Lansana Keita named development *telos*.

Needless to say that such questions can only emanate from a philosopher and a committed one who is concerned with the destiny of his own society, and particularly the immense tragedy that contemporary Africa is going through; one who believes philosophy should address these questions and contribute to providing their solution; one who also believes in the power of philosophy and its capacity to respond to the society's concerns. I can't remember which character in Malraux called out to Miguel de Unamuno in *L'espoir* in these terms: 'I do not have anything to do with your thinking if it does not concern my tragedy. Lansana Keita would have probably liked to author this retort and use it to question both himself and all African philosophers.

I must say first that this demand is a legitimate one. Africa is calling out to us and you cannot claim to be a responsible intellectual if you remain deaf to this call, to this painful scream rising from a whole continent. Something needs to be done. Let's mobilise all the available forces, including the intellectual and scientific forces, to end the tragedy. Art for art's sake is out of place in such a context. Science for science's sake, philosophy conceived and practised for the sake of it can just not be relevant, legitimate and useless, to say the least.

But the truth is that things are not so simple. I am almost tempted to repeat, word-for-word, a presentation that I had to improvise in Cotonou at the end of the 1970s and published in 1981 in *Présence africaine* under the title: 'What Can Philosophy Do?' [1] My answer must have sounded excessively negative to many of you, and subsequently disappointing, but this disappointment is a lesser evil and even a necessary stage if you don't want to delude yourself, if you don't want to expect from philosophy more than it can give and thus be in a position to better grasp its objectives: philosophy should literally be given its legitimate place.

I therefore appealed first to lucidity and my first reaction will still be the same today. Why so? First, because the philosopher, as a philosopher, is not necessarily *committed* and when he or she is, it might not necessarily be in the right direction. In fact, there are philosophers of the left and philosophers of the right, or if you choose to avoid these lateral metaphors which also have their particular history, there have always been philosophers who conform to colonial and post-colonial Africa and who are prepared to fight tooth and nail for a social and political *status quo*, and bolder philosophers and anti-conformist thinkers who can imagine the possible beyond reality because they relativise the existing power relationship, because they have assimilated the master-slave dialectics and understood that no domination, and inversely no servitude, can be eternal. And yet, no one can rigorously argue that the philosophers of the latter calibre are more philosophical than the others.

Secondly, a philosopher, the one who is *committed* and committed in the positive way does not hold a monopoly over boldness and political clear-sightedness. He/she shares those values with tens, hundreds, thousands of other intellectuals and tens of thousands of conscious citizens who do not necessarily consider themselves intellectuals and who reject humiliation and suffering. A committed philosopher has exactly the same similar demands.

This having been said, once a philosopher is recognised as a human being among other human beings, an intellectual among others and at best, an activist intellectual among other activist intellectuals, one cannot deny the role played in history by the social doctrines invented by intellectuals who also happen to be 'philosophers'. Therefore, we need to ask ourselves two questions: first on the specific terms governing the work of a philosopher and possibly his/her function as an activist intellectual and secondly, on the relationship (accidental or essential coincidence or mutual ownership) between the complementary components of a given philosophical doctrine.

I would like to respond very quickly to the ten questions asked by Lansana Keita.

## Philosophers and the City

As you would have noticed, some of the authors mentioned tried to theorise capitalism (Adam Smith, Hume, Stuart Mill), others (Saint-Simon, Proudhon, Marx) believed they had to challenge it by proposing an alternative. While both sides should be credited with showing concern for the problems of society, they did not do it the same way nor did they follow the same orientations. It is also obvious that the philosopher's interest in social concerns did not start in the 18th or 19th centuries but well beyond those periods. Plato and Aristotle demonstrated similar interest. The author of *Gorgias, Théétète, Cratyle* also wrote *La République*. The author of *Métaphysique* and *Organon* also wrote *Le politique*.

I even think the question could be put the other way round and, instead of overplaying the philosophers who explicitly invented political doctrines or built systems of society organisation, let's wonder whether, in the history of philosophy, some authors have actually remained totally unconcerned throughout their work about the problems of society. My opinion is that you wouldn't find any. Any philosophy carries directly or indirectly a society project. The whole difference lies indeed in 'directly or indirectly' that is, in the more or less explicit nature of the project. The authors cited by Lansana Keita should be credited with clarity just like their predecessors, Plato and Aristotle, whom we mentioned and many others who could have also been cited. Their social doctrine is explicit. By laying their cards on the table, they make it easier for the reader, without making too many efforts, to adhere or not to adhere, to approve or disapprove of their proposed vision.

I would like to add a detail: anyone can propose a vision, but not anyone is a philosopher. The philosopher's originality is not only to propose a vision but to also claim to have founded it, leaving the reader with the option to appreciate the robustness or inversely the weakness of such foundation.

Now, lets' turn to Africa, since Lansana Keita himself cited the Europeans philosophers just as examples. Yes of course, we had and still have in Africa some thinkers who explicitly proposed visions of society and, more precisely, alternatives to dependency and under-development. Yes, we have Nkrumah, Frantz Fanon, Cheikh Anta Diop who were precisely mentioned in the questionnaire. We have many others including Senghor whom you may or may not like but whose contribution, after all said and done, is considerable; Julius Nyerere who proposed Ujamaa and tried in vain to put it into practice in Tanzania, Césaire, the volcanic thinker from the islands who does not consider himself a philosopher but who is more and better than a philosopher. At another level, we have had Sékou Touré whose chattering on 'communaucracy' has led us nowhere both in theory and practice.

Did you say 'philosopher'? Somebody like Samir Amin does not consider himself a philosopher, though I believe he cannot be overlooked today as a critical thinker, as an open and imaginative economist for anyone who wishes to know the origin, nature and mechanisms of under-development in Africa and have an insight into the possible alternatives.

I would therefore respond to Lansana Keita and to all those who are puzzled like him that the important thing is not philosophy as such, but critical thinking. This is the type of thinking we should today develop in our universities and research centres, making us imagine the possible beyond reality and seeing to it that the commonplaces of the present do not become the measure of everything and should also be measured, relativised, put in their legitimate place, ordered and subordinated to other exigencies and tested against higher standards if we want to pull out of conformism and resignation.

### Future of Socialism

What today is the future of socialism? More precisely (and this is the second question), does socialism as a doctrine still have a future? Does it have any relevance to African problems? Does it have any credibility considering the collapse of the governments which rightly or wrongly, claim to embody it in the Soviet Union, Eastern Europe, though not openly said, in the last countries that still claim today to represent it in a more theoretical than real way (China and Cuba)?

Cautioning against the then dominant understanding of Marxism among the would-be African left wingers, I called a few years ago for a responsible reading of Marx, Lenin and all the Marxist tradition. I warned against a catechistic and dogmatic approach to Marxism, against being tempted to swallow Marxism the way you swallow a pill, so to speak. I called for a critical appropriation of this historical and political heritage. I was speaking from Benin, a country that converted to communism overnight as you convert to a religion but in which the revolutionary claptrap, inspired by the Soviet propaganda manuals, then flowing into the country, barely concealed the most despicable police dictatorship which treated democratic freedom cheaply and tended to nip in the bud any responsible initiative or thought.

I believe the intellectuals and other executives should be more ambitious for themselves and for the country. Instead of passively consuming and worse, making the masses consume the neo-Stalinist clichés for instance on the 'dialectics law' (sic) from which strangely enough the 'law on the negation of negation' cherished by Lenin had been expurgated, they should have gone back to the roots and see clearer by themselves the troubled history of the doctrine and hold free discussions at their own level, develop a plural and contradictory Marxist theoretical traditional, as any credible theoretical traditional would do.

And yet, what has happened since then? After the global collapse of communism, indeed, there was a sudden shift from purely ideological to hundred per cent economic concerns, in other words, from a Marxist-Leninist claptrap lacking collective research back-up or local theoretical tradition to the-straight-to-the-point prose of the World Bank and IMF experts, repeated in unison by our local leaders. There was a sort of overnight 'rectification without self-criticism', which Althusser deplored in the practice of the French communist party and which clearly denotes one of the worst forms of opportunism and irresponsibility.

However, the question asked is very specific: yes or no is socialism outmoded today? The first answer might be: yes, socialism is outmoded at least in two ways: first, *it is no longer fashionable* – but this is not a serious argument against socialism as a doctrine; secondly, history has indeed demonstrated the extraordinary capacity of the capitalist system to adapt, to resolve more or less its internal contradictions, to regain balance and to excel itself precisely when deemed doomed. Marx had underestimated this invention and adaptation capacity and his predictions about the self-destruction of capitalism bound to succumb to its own contradictions were contradicted by the facts, at least up to this point.

Let's put the question this way: What was the *place* of these predictions in the overall doctrine? Should they be rejected for this single reason? Should this mistake, if it is really one, be treated as a detail? Should the real analysis of capital, which provides an unprecedented insight into the way the capitalist system operates, be thrown overboard under the pretence that it would have led, from Marx's perspective, to purely fanciful predictions? Or should these predictions be put back to their place and be relativised to the analysis itself? And which other doctrine and reading method might help us today to understand 'imperialism, the superior stage of capitalism' as Lenin called it or 'neo-colonialism, the superior stage of imperialism' as Nkrumah described it, if we rejected altogether this precious heritage? How could we understand what André Gunder Franck called the 'development of underdevelopment' or Samir Amin's 'growth without development', how could we put into historical perspective our current misery and both relativise and surpass it, if we rejected altogether the precious Marxist heritage, just to be fashionable or to be in the limelight?

I want to make it very clear that socialism as a creed, socialism as a catechism, socialism as ideological purring is not only outmoded today but it has never been fertile, it was never productive then and it is not now either. The global collapse of communism opened our eyes: it revealed in broad daylight the failure of a certain use of socialism; it encourages us to show more responsibility and judgment in the way socialism, and more generally any political and social doctrine, is appropriated. But it does not discredit socialism as an analytical method, as a policy, as a societal project, as a demand for justice and equality in the management of human communities.

## Obstacles to Development

Third question: What are the main obstacles to development? Are they purely economic, political, cultural, psychological or all at the same time? *A priori*, the obstacles are of different type. But the foregoing draws our attention to one obstacle which is much too often neglected: the absence of thinking, intellectual passivity leading us to follow changing ideological modes like an opportunist. What is the solution? I have already written it somewhere: *'start thinking again'*;[2] in other words, we should reach today beyond the ready-made solutions proposed by international experts and look into the problems of society by ourselves. I insist, therefore, on the role of intellectuals and the elite or, more precisely, on their responsibility. I insist on the need for collective appropriation of existing knowledge, a high-level internal debate on social, economic and political options, and also on their pros and cons.

## Science and Philosophy: Place of Politics

Yes, you are right: philosophy should not be viewed through a too narrow prism. Reading Althusser was enlightening to me, helping put philosophy in its place and calling on it to be more humble. Philosophy indeed claimed to have founded science, prescribed in advance the terms of its validity, define *a priori* the framework in which it should be lodged and the bounds within which it should be established. Althusser warned that in fact, it is the reverse taking place: great philosophical revolutions always follow great scientific revolutions. As a result, nothing or not much is understood of Plato if you don't realise the development of Greek mathematics during his era. You don't understand at all Descartes if you do not see in his philosophy, as Judith Miller put it, a 'metaphysic of Galilean physics'. You underrate the stakes of Kantianism if you ignore Kant's admiration of Newton and the deep fascination exerted on his thinking by the new physics. You don't quite appreciate the real significance of Husserl if you do not realise the novelty of mathematical logic in relation to the traditional bounds of science.

However, science is not the only determinant of philosophical thinking. Althusser himself admitted it in his *Eléments d'autocritique* that: philosophy is not simply science theory, it is also first and foremost class struggle in theory. Even though today the concepts of class struggle should be handled more delicately, this self-criticism says it all: science theory is not all philosophy is about. Beyond these theoretical stakes, philosophy also has practical stakes. Ignoring these practical stakes is tantamount to falling into what Althusser describes as 'theorecist deviation'.

Despite this warning, I believe the initial assumption is still an enriching one in many respects. While science theory is not all what philosophy is about, it remains an essential component and in some way the hardest nucleus, the specific concern of a genuine philosophical thinking as distinguished from the other forms of discourse. For, a thread must be found to lead us through this profusion of verbal inventions today proposed in Africa and elsewhere by all kinds of system sellers who introduce themselves as philosophers and who, alas, do not always exercise the patience of the concept.

## Nkrumah, Fanon, Cheikh Anta Diop

To be honest, the main issue is that I am suspicious of philosophy or whatever appears as such. I always ask to have a closer look at it. Since you are asking me a question on Nkrumah,[3] let me say clearly that: *Consciencism*, to me, seems to be less robust, far less convincing than books like *Africa Must Unite, Neo-colonialism, The Last Stage of Imperialism*, and even *Class Struggle in Africa*, where a remarkable fine analysis is developed and applied to economy and politics. Nkrumah's greatest contribution lies in this vision of a united and sovereign Africa, as a project now more topical than ever of building the United States of Africa. *Consciencism* wanted to supersede this political unification project with another project: conscience unification. The latter project was neither necessary nor consistent.

You are asking a question about Frantz Fanon and Cheikh Anta Diop? Of course, they are also part of our common heritage and the intellectual weapons that we have and can use to think about building a new, unified, self-reliant, sovereign Africa, which can constitute an autonomous development hub in a globalisation with many voices.

Let me make this additional observation. In the case of Nkrumah or Cheikh Anta Diop, they both lived at a time when the major issue was that of sovereignty and regaining lost autonomy in relation to colonialism and neo-colonialism. The result is that they did not address the problem of human rights and democratic freedom that have since become a hot issue in the States. We also know that in the specific case of Nkrumah, the political theoretician was also once a Head of State whose dictatorial practices were denounced by several opponents. We shouldn't close our eyes: the contribution made by these authors remains considerable but are marked in the corner by some objective limit. This contribution should today be lucidly, critically and responsibly appropriated.

## Global Knowledge Build-up

I would not elaborate on the seventh question. It is an enriching one indeed in understanding Africa' technological and scientific backwardness in applying to scientific and technological activity the same reading method that has enabled neo-Marxist economists (Samir Amin, for instance) to put 'under-development' in general into historical perspective so as to better capture its origins, development and possible remedies. I therefore tried first to describe 'the colonial research pact'; this system consisted, during the colonial era, in developing in dominated territories a feverish activity of gathering information destined for processing in the Metropolitan laboratories and research centres; then continuing the system into the postcolonial period despite the remarkable progress made in some cases in specific sectors.[4] I drew attention to this 'extraversion logics' which thus governs the African researcher's activity and always puts it directly or indirectly at the service of knowledge build-up at the system centre, in Europe or USA.

You are asking me what the remedy is. In substance, the same as the one proposed for developing economies: 'disconnection'. This metaphor is, undoubtedly, very equivocal but it clearly indicates the direction in which to search. The question is only to know what this necessary reorientation, this conquest of self-reliance would mean for peripheral scientific activity, and how it can, like a general economic activity, 'pull out of the global market'.

## What is the Worth of NEPAD?

I will answer Questions 8 and 9 together: Which economic, political and cultural system can free this balkanised, indebted Africa, which has subsequently become easy prey to the institutions of developed countries such as the World Bank and the International Monetary Fund and these hordes of paternalistic NGOs streaming onto the continent. Would NEPAD, which is today much talked about, be the system sought or is it just a deception invented by developed countries in the face of the danger of what an organised Africa would represent for them? What is the real scope of NEPAD?

I am almost tempted to say: I don't know! And this has nothing to do with coquetry. I am waiting to study the issue. But as of now, I can already express one concern: that NEPAD does not experience what happened to the Lagos Plan of Action; that is, remaining a dead letter. I should also say that I don't like too much the word 'system'. The Lagos Plan of Action bore the appropriate name; it was a plan of action. Besides, I don't see a real mobilisation of the African intelligentsia and live forces behind it. Without such a mobilisation, nothing sustainable will come out of it, regardless of the intrinsic value of the proposed programme.

## Heritage Appropriation

The tenth question looks like an ordinary one and is too obvious to dwell on. Yes, indeed, we should interrogate the ancient authors on our current problems, ask them the questions worrying us today and make the best out of their contribution and teaching. However, the most interesting thing is what lies behind this question: a project on the history of African thinking. Nobody would have thought of it forty years ago. Nobody, because the then dominant concern was for identity and this has led into imagining African thinking, an essential component of this identity, as a closed system deprived of history. The big issue then for philosophers was to describe, decipher and rebuild this system. African philosophers felt compelled in this context to practise philosophy as a particular chapter of ethnology, or as it would be called today, cultural anthropology.

Things have changed a lot since then. Perhaps ethno-philosophy has been subjected to excessive criticism, but it has at least led to freeing the project on a history of African philosophy, a history of African thinking and more generally of what Abiola Irele described as an intellectual history of Africa.[5]

I will conclude on that note. We should today appropriate this rich heritage critically and responsibly. We should equally freely appropriate, with the same critical vigilance, what is produced in other parts of the world and which may serve us because if you look at it closely, you will always discover that we have contributed in our own way to these inventions. No, history has not finished yet. It is just starting or, more precisely, re-starting.

## Notes

1. Paulin J. Hountondji, «Que peut la philosophie?», *Présence africaine* (Paris), 119, 1981 : 47-71. Translated into Hungarian by Sipos Janos in *Magyar filosofiai szemle* (Hungarian Journal of Philosophy), 1981 and English under the title 'What philosophy can do' in *Quest: Philosophical Discussions* (Lusaka), I, 2: 2-28.

2. « Alors, que faire? Au-delà du repli nationaliste sur nous-mêmes, de l'inventaire laborieux et interminable de nos valeurs culturelles, du narcissisme collectif induit par la colonisation, réapprendre à penser » (P. Hountondji, *Sur la «philosophie africaine»: critique de l'ethnophilosophie*, Paris, Maspero, 1976, p. 47). Please forgive me for citing myself. I know this is contrary to established practice. I'm doing this mostly to signal once again a regrettable misunderstanding created by the excessively literal translation of this sentence: 'So what is to be done? Apart from a nationalistic withdrawal into ourselves, a painstaking, unending inventory of our cultural values, a collective narcissism induced by colonisation, *we must re-learn how to think*» (*African Philosophy Myth and Reality*, London, Hutchinson, 1983:52-53). Part of the criticism could have been avoided if the sentence were translated as: «*we must start thinking again*».

3. I'd rather write *Nkrumah* without an apostrophe as he himself used to write his name. French speakers have got into the bad habit of writing *N'krumah*.

4. In an excellent thesis on the sociology of science presented at Bielefeld, Germany, Maxime Dahoun reported on his field studies which confirmed entirely these views. Cf. Maxime Dahoun, *Le statut de la science et de la recherche au Bénin. Contribution à une sociologie de la science dans les pays en développement*, Berlin, Logos Verlag, 1998. Up to this point in time, I still don't know whether similar studies on other countries of the sub-region exist. Anyway, this is an investigation area that needs to be systematically explored.

5. Cf. F. Abiola Irele, 'Réflexions sur la negritude', Ethiopiques N° 69, 2nd semester 2002, p. 83-106.

# 6

# African Development and the Primacy of Mental Decolonisation

## Messay Kebede

### Introduction

According to the basic belief of the modernisation school, modernisation occurs when traditional values, beliefs, and ways of doing things give way to innovative views and methods. 'A society is traditional', writes Everett E. Hagen, 'if ways of behaviour in it continue with little change from generation to generation', if it 'tends to be custom-bound, hierarchical, ascriptive, and unproductive' (Hagen 1962:56). To define modernisation by the rise of innovative capacity has the interesting twist of putting the blame for Africa's failure to modernise less on the persistence of tradition than on the internalisation of the colonialist discourse, which in itself has become a new tradition imposed on older traditions. For no resurgence of innovative capacity can take place so long as internalisation of the colonialist argument paralyses the African mind. Mental decolonisation thus emerges as the top priority in Africa's development agenda. To admit the priority of mental decolonisation is to acknowledge the precedence of the subjective factor over objective conditions, and so to recognise the importance of the philosophical debates generated by the attempts of African scholars to counter Europe's colonial discourse on Africa. This chapter reviews some key moments of the debates for the purpose of showing both how African philosophical positions constitute various attempts to disentangle the African self from colonialist constructions, perceived as the major obstacle to Africa's modernisation, and how specific limitations get in the way of these attempts.

### From Traditionality to Decolonisation

Before reviewing the position of the different schools, let us pose clearly the terms of the problem. Even though the political decolonisation of Africa occurred some forty years ago, many African scholars trace the extreme difficulties of the continent in initiating a resolute process of modernisation back to the ills of the colonial legacy. What is less frequent, however, is the equation of African societies with backward cultures as the chief infirmity of the African continent. Obvious as it is, that analysis of political and economic obstacles takes precedence over the disability induced by the colonial discourse.

The eminent French anthropologist, Lucien Lévy-Bruhl, standardised the colonial discourse when he baptised rationality as a Western appanage, thereby granting what he termed 'mystic' or 'prelogical' (Lévy-Bruhl 1985: 63) thinking to non-Western peoples. The underestimation of the repercussions of the colonial discourse by African scholars is all the more surprising as the accusation of having no contribution whatsoever to civilisation singles out blackness. Who today would argue that G. W. F. Hegel's statement that of all cultures, Africa 'is no historical part of the World; it has no movement or development to exhibit' (Hegel 1956:99), no longer preserves its original upsetting impact?

Doubtless, Africans strongly reject the characterisation of their legacy as primitive. All the same, both the process of Western education and the normative equation of modernisation with Westernisation condition them to endorse the charge of backwardness. Worse still, their denial only succeeds in pushing the charge to the dark corners of the unconscious. Take the teaching of world history. Not only are all the great breakthroughs and achievements of modern history mostly assigned to European actors, but the whole historical scheme is constructed so as to exclude Africa while presenting the West as the centre and the driving force of history. The example shows that modern schooling is for Africans nothing else than the learning of self-contempt through the systematic exposure to Africa's utter insignificance. Africans cannot but internalise this view, given that their ability to echo the Western idea of Africa is how they acquire modern education.

Africans are all the more compelled to endorse the colonial discourse as the way they defend themselves hardly avoids appealing to Western concepts. Such is notably the case each time Africans use the notion of race to articulate their solidarity and common interests in opposition to the West. The West used race attributes to codify differences through the selection of criteria favoring its normativeness, the most conspicuous of which is the exclusive claim to rationality. As a result, whatever differs from the West becomes irrational and primitive. When Africans define themselves by racial attributes, they are sanctioning this Western codification, and hence their alienation from rationality. Self-assertion, thus obtained through the denial of human capability, puts Africans at odds with the basic requirement of modernity, to wit, the ability to develop science and technology.

No exceptional insight is required to understand that Africans cannot modernise if they internally acquiesce to the allegation of backwardness. Amartya Sen's idea that economic development should be posed in terms of 'human agency' rather than just economic indicators leads to the interesting approach depicting 'development as freedom' (Sen 1999:188). When human agencies are involved and given priority, development becomes an issue of human capabilities in terms of freedoms and opportunities. The focus shifts the question of development from pure development economics to issues of entitlement and empowerment. This centrality of freedom to development issues does no more than invite the proposal that what people can do and be is largely dependent on the representations that they have of themselves. If they define themselves in enhancing terms, the likelihood is that they will set themselves great goals and will believe that they have what is required to make them happen. By contrast, if they have a low opinion of themselves, they will be less ambitious and less inclined to think that they have the calibre to achieve great goals. But more yet, self-debasing representations can lead to behaviours that militate against the idea of agencies and the creating of opportunities.

African philosophical views have emerged from the clear perception of the deep damages caused by the internalisation of the colonial discourse. Convinced that no development policy will bear fruit so long as the African self is weighed down by the spectre of backwardness, African philosophers have devised theories to counter the colonialist discourse in order to achieve the decolonisation of the African mind. Consider the basic question that feeds on debates, often acrimonious, between the various African philosophical schools, namely, the issue of the existence of a precolonial African philosophy. The importance of the issue is directly linked with the colonialist discourse, since the denial of philosophy, that is, of rational thinking, is how colonialism corroborated the undeveloped nature of African modes of thought. Each school tries to tackle the issue by inserting the refutation of the colonialist allegation into a vision liable to reconcile Africans with their legacy, given that the reconciliation must be such that it takes into account African realities, especially the undeniable technological lag of Africa. This recognition of a major shortcoming complicates the task of rehabilitation: Is there a way of finding a definition of Africans that removes the charge of backwardness even as it grants the African delay in the control of nature?

The definition of African philosophy according to the need of overcoming the aftermaths of colonisation provides the means of evaluating the various intellectual paradigms from the vantage point of modernisation. The way the question of the existence and nature of a precolonial African philosophy is resolved also provides an answer to the question of the African potential for development. To the extent that development involves scientific and technological aptitudes, it is bound to be elusive without the propensity to think rationally. Similarly, the debate over the philosophical status of the precolonial past challenges the usual definition of modernisation as a process of dissolving traditionalism. Granted that modernisation implies increasing rationalisation of life, the fact remains that the entitlement of the African past to a philosophical status raises the question of knowing whether development should not be defined in terms of continuity rather than discontinuity. If the past is valid, the question of its preservation arises, not to mention the fact that Africans cannot want the repudiation of the past without endorsing the colonial discourse. Decolonisation, it follows, is unachievable if the discontinuity imposed by the colonial conquest and its disparaging discourse on Africa's historical legacy are not radically challenged.

The best way to give an account of the complexities involved in Africas's rehabilitation as a prelude to development is to review the major schools of thought on the topic of African philosophy. Three main schools can be identified: (1) Ethnophilosophers, who consider the defence of African otherness as the only non-derogatory way of justifying the technological retardation of Africa. Otherness disputes both the normativeness of the West and the Western definition of philosophical thinking. The thinkers of negritude best represent this trend through the racialisation of identities. (2) The universalists or 'professional philosophers' who reject the defence of otherness as an endorsement of the colonial denial of rationality and perceive the African retardation as nothing more than an evolutionary lag. (3) The particularists who attempt to strike the middle course by presenting more acceptable notions of African philosophy and difference. Ranging from the hermeneutical orientation to the deconstructionist school, these attempts present the common characteristics of rejecting the negritude concept of blackness, without however succumbing to the universalist stand of the professional philosophers. To take the full measure of the complexity of the effort of rehabilitation, let us begin with the most extreme and controversial of African philosophical schools, to wit, negritude.

**Otherness as the Road to Modernity**

Without doubt, the main thrust of negritude is to explain the technological lag of 'black Africa' in terms that do not negatively affect Africa's historical sense of itself and confidence in its indigenous cultures. Though the negritude thinkers take the lag as an undeniable fact, they strongly dismiss all evolutionary explanation. Since social evolution has been defined according to criteria establishing the normativeness of the West, such as science and technological advancements, it cannot avoid presenting Africans as culturally and technologically underdeveloped peoples. Imperative, therefore, is the need to go around evolutionary concepts if decolonisation is to be achieved. Hence the conviction that the defence of otherness is the only vehicle for the refutation of the colonial discourse and the rehabilitation of Africa. Universalism sets the theoretical framework for interpreting differences as advancement or retardation by assigning similar goals to all cultures. Otherness dismantles this unilinear construction of history by defying the idea of placing all the peoples and cultures of the world in the same universal and progressive path.

Consider Hegel's notion of universal history. After placing all the cultures of the world in the same unilinear time, he devises the idea of gradual progression through the selection of characteristics peculiar to European history and culture. He then easily arrives at the belief that the selected items, especially individual freedom and rational knowledge, exist in much less developed forms in non-European cultures. This selective parallel allows him to construe differences as earlier stages and to define the evolution of universal history as a process that 'assumes successive forms which it successively transcends; and by this very process of transcending its earlier stages, gains an affirmative, and, in fact, a richer and more concrete shape' (Hegel 1956:63). The succession promotes Europe to the rank of most advanced and driving force of universal history, and so classifies those cultures that exhibit the greatest disparity with Europe as most backward or primitive. On the strength of this normative role of Europe, Hegel defines Africa (excepting pharaonic Egypt) as 'the land of childhood, which lying beyond the day of self-conscious history, is enveloped in the dark mantle of Night' (Hegel 1956:91).

Faced with this formidable construction, Léopold Sédar Senghor, one of the founders of Negritude, could find no other recourse than to appeal to otherness, which he provocatively defines by the predominance of emotion over rationality. Unlike the European who uses objective intelligence to fix and analyse the object, the African 'does not keep the object at a distance, does not analyze it'; he rather 'touches it, feels it', he writes (Senghor 1995:118). His assumption is clear enough: the ascription of a different mental orientation to the black essence is alone liable to give a non-derogatory explanation of the African technological lag. Africans did not advance technologically, not because they were primitive, undeveloped, but because their distinct mental orientation gave them different pursuits and methods. On the other hand, the European predilection for technology does not denote a normative quality, but a specific turn of mind with positive and negative outcomes. Just as the African turn of mind does not encourage technology, so too the European mental direction is not propitious for penetrating the essence of reality, still less for providing an integrated vision.

For Senghor, Europe's technological advances derive from a mental orientation dominated by a conquering impulse. For the European, to know is to dismantle, decompose the object into constituent parts for the purpose of manipulation. An approach so driven by the need to subdue is perforce little in touch with the deeper reality of things. The downside of conquest is metaphysical superficiality. By contrast, the African gift of emotivity wants to sense things, to communicate with their inner essence. The basic condition for sensing things is to give up subduing them: only a sympathetic intention can have access to their intimacy. Compared to the European way of knowing things, Senghor finds that 'what emotes an African is not so much the external aspect of an object as its profound reality' (Senghor 1995:127).

Far from being an outcome of backwardness, non-technicalness is thus the expression of a different way of being in the world and of dealing with phenomena. As Jean-Paul Sartre comments, the 'proud claim of non-technicalness reverses the situation; that which might appear to be deficiency becomes a positive source of riches. A technical rapport with Nature reveals it as a quantity pure, inert, foreign; it dies' (Sartre 1963:43). The stage approach by which peoples are defined as advanced or retarded flies in the face of civilisations perceived as different in the radical sense of having dissimilar means and goals. Nothing is more arbitrary than to ignore this dissimilarity by placing divergent civilisations in the same universal and progressive time.

To the question whether there is such a thing as an African philosophy, the answer is, therefore, a definite 'yes'. What makes the answer confident is that it points to a philosophy whose originality is imparted by a unique racial gift. In place of the dismantling technique of Western episteme, the deeper penetrating insight of negritude promises a vision of the world emphasising cohesion and integration. Whereas the West perceives the world as a collection of fixed and juxtaposed objects, African emotivity sees the world as a living reality. It thinks of being as vital force and individuals as communal beings. Being neither premodern nor antirational, negritude presents the inspiration of a different epistemology as an alternative conception of things and of being in the world that pursues integration and harmony in lieu of conquest and domination.

Predictably, a strategy of decolonisation based on the assertion of a different epistemological orientation was bound to provoke a flood of hostile reactions. In particular, rationality being the major criterion that Europe used to classify peoples as advanced or backward, the renunciation of reason in favour of emotion could not but convince critics of 'the correspondence of certain aspects of Senghor's ideas of the basic African personality with Western racist theories and with the 'primitive mentality' of Lévy-Bruhl' (Irele1990:83).

What is more, the claim to non-rationality puts Africans at variance with scientific thinking, and so deprives them of the means to catch up with the West. Since without the mastery of science and technology Africans cannot get out of their marginal existence, the surrender of the rational faculty can only perpetuate their marginality. Given this crucial role of reason, Senghor's definition of the particularity of black peoples according to cognitive styles founded on emotivity amounts to accepting the reality of different and unequal aptitudes. The inevitable outcome of this inequality is 'to leave intact . . . the racial hierarchy established by the colonial ideology' (Irele1990:83). The notion of otherness does not ensure emancipation and autonomy; it simply approves the idea of Africans playing a minor role in a world shaped and dominated by Western rationality.

According to critics, the defence of a particularism drawn from the past confirms the acquiescence of the negritude movement to a subordinate position. The return to and the apology of the past can only entail the indefinite postponement of the modernisation of Africa. To quote Abiola Irele, 'we cannot meet the challenges of the scientific and industrial civilisation of today by draping ourselves with our particularisms' (Irele 1992:213). The philosophy of negritude is problematic because the cult of peculiarities does not rehabilitate Africans. On the contrary, it steers them away from the need and the means to construct those machines that the West used to marginalise Africa. Unable to rescue Africa, the appeal to the black essence by the negritude philosopher thus leads to nothing else than the acceptance of marginality.

However strong and pertinent these objections appear to be, the impression remains that they underestimate the deconstructive message of negritude. The virtue of the explanation by otherness of the negritude thinker is that it champions self-acceptance by relativising the West. When the West is dethroned from the position of archetype, the African ceases to be a failure. Relativisation dismisses hierarchical conceptions: in being different, particular, each civilisation is good for some pursuits, less so for others. No other way exists to decolonise the African mind than the relativisation of the West. The great goal of modernisation can never become real if Africans are prone to self-debasement, which ceases only when they are reconciled with their legacy.

Modernisation cannot result from the total assimilation of Africans, the condition of which is the complete extirpation of their historical past. The requirement to wipe out the past is contradictory: although it claims to reject the colonial discourse, it defines modernisation in terms of exporting Western institutions and ideas. To import everything from the West is obviously to endorse the notion of African technological and cultural backwardness. African scholars cannot portray colonialism as unjust and colonial discourse as false and demeaning if at the same time they define modernity as a full-fledged Westernisation. Moreover, what Westernisation actively advocates is the servile imitation of the West. By passively importing Western ideas and institutions, 'all that can happen is that we [Africans] become pale copies of Frenchmen, consumers not producers of culture' (Senghor 1976:490). No mistake about it: if modernity is defined by the rise of innovative spirit, the passive imitation of the West does not promote modernisation; it simply postpones it.

For Senghor, then, the reason why Africans must retain their tradition is that its revival and adaptation makes them creative and original. So understood, modernisation becomes the adaptation of a living culture to the new condition caused by the expansion and technological advances of the West. 'When we have made this analysis' Senghor writes, 'the problem is to determine the present value of the institutions and style of life born of these [African] realities and how to adapt them to the requirements of the contemporary world' (Senghor 1959:292). Instead of Westernisation or assimilation, modernisation becomes a process of synthesis in which the peculiar legacy of Africa merges with borrowings from the West. The need to adapt a traditional culture to modern conditions makes modernisation conditional on the liberation of African creativity, in line with the spirit of modernity. Taking root in Africa's legacy while reaching out to the West remains the only promising road to modernisation.

All the more reason for positing modernisation in synthetic terms is that important values of the past concur with modern life. Contrary to the colonial stigmatisation, African tradition exhibits characteristics congruent with modern life. In the words of Senghor, 'negritude, by its ontology (that is, its philosophy of being), its moral law and its aesthetic, is a response to the modern humanism that European philosophers and scientists have been preparing since the end of the nineteenth century' (Senghor 1970:184). The African ontology of vital force emphasises force and energy, and so is more in tune with the assumptions of modern science than Aristotle's static conception of being or Descartes' mechanical view of matter. As suggested by negritude, such notions as relativity, wave mechanics, electron and neutron confirm the existence of a dynamic microscopic world behind the static appearance of things.

Equally remarkable is the fact that the abstract style of the vanguard schools of contemporary Western art attests to the neo-modernity of pre-colonial African art. It is under the direct influence of African art that contemporary Western artists, giving up their conception of art as imitation of the given object, attempted to capture, behind the given material reality, of things their intrinsic form and structure. The African influence was revolutionary, since 'a world of life forces that have to be tamed is substituted for a closed world of permanent and continuous substances that have to be reproduced' (Senghor 1970:188). The substitution clears the way for a conception that connects life with deeper realities beyond the visible and the tangible.

Another, but no less important proof of the modernity of the African past is provided by the persistent aspiration to socialist ideals emanating from the womb of capitalist societies. The contradictions of capitalism, the rise of powerful socialist movements in the West, and the impact of the doctrine of Marxism are consonant with the traditional communal life of Africa as reflecting an optimal world, notwithstanding the present popularity of neoliberal capitalism. In addition to condemning the individualistic and class-divided society of the West, the socialist aspiration proposes the communal values of African tradition as a remedy for the evils of capitalism.

This position of forerunner shifts the return to the African legacy from the unearthing of outdated and useless values to a modernising venture. In particular, it rises against the depiction of modernisation in terms of modernity versus tradition. The disclosure of the modernity of African conceptions and the Western appeal to African values to get out of the crises of capitalism refute the colonial discourse. The rejection of values even as they prove to be so supportive of modernity would be inconsistent and self-damaging on the part of Africans. Some such reversal credits negritude with an original theory of African modernisation. The dichotomy between tradition and modernity is replaced by the conviction that the major impediment is the colonisation of the mind, as evinced by the propensity of African ruling elites to 'importing just as they stand the political and social institutions of Europe, and even their cultural institutions' (Senghor 1959:290)

## No Modernity without Universalism

For the opponents of negritude, however judiciously the African past is embellished, the fact remains that the theory, far from decolonising Africa, capitulates to the colonial discourse. Though otherness is called on to defend the existence of a traditional African philosophy, the price for the recognition of such a philosophy is an identity that alienates Africans from rationality and science by imposing the defence of a collective and uncritical set of beliefs. To present negritude as the philosophy of Africans is to suggest that all Africans are so prone to think alike by virtue of their collective identity that they are incapable of individual and critical thinking. The best way to avoid these detrimental outcomes is to repudiate the very notion of precolonial African philosophy.

In whichever way the notion is contrived, a collective and unconscious philosophy is a contradiction in terms. Philosophy is an individual and systematically critical reflection; as such, it runs counter to the idea of collective thinking. Conversely, religions, mythologies, and worldviews do not appeal to the critical effort of the individual. Instead, they call for the spontaneous, uncritical adherence of individuals to a common and transmitted set of beliefs. So that having none of the attributes by which a philosophical discourse is usually defined, what is identified as traditional African philosophy presents all the characters of a religious system or worldview, not of philosophy. Marcien Towa denounces the notion of 'traditional African philosophy' as a 'dilation of the concept of philosophy to such a point that this concept becomes coextensive with the concept of culture' (Towa 1991:189). Besides being based on the fraudulent identification of philosophy with culture, a philosophical system that is particular to Africa is a direct confirmation of the colonial discourse. Those who have a different nature cannot philosophise like Westerners; they need a philosophy commensurate with their otherness, that is, a collective and uncritical philosophy. Paulin Hountondji calls the acceptance of otherness "folklorism' a sort of collective exhibitionism which compels the 'Third World' intellectual to 'defend and illustrate' the peculiarities of his tradition for the benefit of a Western public' (Hountondji 1983:67).

For Hountondji, in addition to confirming the colonial discourse, the attempt to revive the past, nay, to baptise it as philosophy, betrays the reactionary stand of negritude. Though the negritude thinkers speak of reproducing a past philosophy, in reality they disguise their own individual philosophies as African. The conservative content of this deceiving identification becomes obvious as soon as we understand that:

> Behind this [implicit and collective worldview] usage . . . there is a myth at work, the myth of primitive unanimity, with its suggestion that in 'primitive' societies – that is to say, non-Western societies – everybody always agrees with everybody else. It follows that in such societies there can never be individual beliefs or philosophies but only collective systems of belief (Hountondji 1983:60).

When an individual thinking is metamorphosed into an African trait, the purpose is to obtain a collective sanction without providing rational arguments. It is to demand unanimous approval in the name of African authenticity and the authority of tradition. Furthermore, the attribution of philosophy endows an ensemble of uncritical beliefs with the value of indispensability and permanence. As purported products of rationality, such beliefs cease to be tied to outdated particular contexts and epochs. The connection between the unanimist reading of African tradition and the various totalitarian ideologies of Africa, such as African socialism, the one-party system, authenticity, president for life, etc., is not hard to establish.

Does this mean that Hountondji recommends the complete rejection of the past? No, his position is rather to submit the traditional and collective thoughts of Africans to a critical assessment before claiming them as relevant; it is to study them as a philosopher, that is, 'outside of all apologetic perspectives' (Hountondji 1995:191). In other words, Hountondji is against ethnophilosophy because it advocates the indiscriminate consecration of traditional knowledge, not because it wants to reappropriate it. Those aspects of the traditional culture that stand the test of critical examination will be retained as being useful for modernisation. The critical appraisal of the past, be it noted, will necessarily lead, unlike the unanimist reading of negritude, to a pluralist interpretation of the traditional thinking.

For Hountondji, then, the reappropriation of past knowledge is not the revival of a traditional philosophy, for African philosophy is yet to come; 'it is before us, not behind us, and must be created today by decisive action' (Hountondji 1983:53). The creation implicates the incorporation of the useful aspects of the past, which is made possible by the submission of the past to a critical assessment. To underline his divergence from the way negritude resurrects the past, Hountondji calls the critical reflections on and reconstruction of African legacy 'learned ethnophilosophy' (Hountondji 1995:173). Hountondji's enlightened, critical ethnophilosophy follows the Marxist method of deriving the thought process from the conditions of material life. It attempts to elucidate the genesis of traditional conceptions by connecting traditional African beliefs and practices with the then prevailing conditions of life. The exposure of the correspondence of the form and contents of the thinking with the conditions of life confirms the limitation of conceptions to specific times and places. Unlike the racial fixation of negritude, the method reveals the historical and transient nature of these thoughts, and hence avoids changing them into eternal African categories.

There remains the question of knowing whether Hountondji's rejection of otherness achieves the decolonisation of the African mind. In his eyes, the only pertinent challenge to the colonial discourse is the refutation of the assumption that Africans have by nature intrinsically different ways of thinking or even a different kind of mind. For one thing, the historical genesis of traditional beliefs underscores the rationality of the thought process by displaying the relevance of the thinking to the mode of life. African thoughts and beliefs are no longer the mere products of magic; they are reflections, albeit idealised, of real conditions of life. For another, the method does not petrify the African lag in the manner of negritude; by establishing a correspondence between the mode of life and the mode of thinking, it proposes the notion of delay in development.

Delay means that the disparity between the West and Africa is 'merely in the evolutionary stage attained, with regard to particular types of achievement... merely in quantity or scale' (Hountondji 1983:61). As Hountondji sees it, what is most detrimental is not the admission of Africa's technological lag, but the ascription of the lag to an epistemological difference. Unlike otherness, the stage disparity puts Africa in the same unilinear process as the West, and so attributes the lag to the conditions of life rather than to the mental unfitness of Africans. A difference in quantity promises the rapid narrowing of the gap, given that it views Western achievements as an expression of universal qualities that are shared by Africans as well.

For critics, what Hountondji adds to qualify his harsh evaluation of African tradition does not succeed in removing his uncritical attitude toward Western philosophy. Since Africans are denied philosophy in the name of Western norms, the net outcome of the denial is the consecration of the normativeness of the West. The allegiance to Western philosophy is such that the anthropological characterisation of African thinking as collective, spontaneous, and irrational is literally reproduced. The allegiance prevents Hountondji and Towa from developing the slightest doubt about the accuracy of the terms used to describe African traditional thinking. Speaking of Hountondji, one critic writes that Hountondji 'fails to do that preliminary work of questioning the Eurocentric structures as he appropriates European notions of philosophy' (Imbo 1998:87). On account of this failure to challenge Western philosophy, Africa appears to Hountondji as the land of myths and irrational beliefs.

Unless the West is relativised, no critical view emanating from the accepted normativeness of the West will ever be fair to Africans. When a norm is erected, the outcome is the denigration of all differences. This explains the paradox of Hountondji: though he makes pertinent criticisms of anthropology, which he considers as a 'pseudo science', (Hountondji 1983:61), he does not get to the point of accusing Western concepts of misrepresenting African traditions. What failed him is the use of Marxist philosophy and concepts to criticise both the West and the African past. A Marxist critique of the West does not really question Western hegemony; it only advocates assimilation to the European culture defined as the universal and most progressive culture. Since the definition reinstates the backwardness of African cultures, real and radical criticism cannot start unless Eurocentrism and its model of philosophy questioned. Only when the normativeness of the West is rejected does the affirmation of difference become legitimate.

This means that the problem is not so much the reality of the difference as the formulation of African difference in terms that are free of Eurocentric stereotypes. The need to emancipate the representations that Africans have of themselves from Eurocentric biases posits mental decolonisation as a prerequisite to development. A serious and forceful will to develop cannot arise while the internalised Eurocentric stereotypes keep telling Africans that they are not equipped for human progress. The only way to extirpate these stereotypes is the relativisation of the West, which creates and affirms the idea of difference. True, to define the difference in terms opposed to Western rationality, in the manner of negritude, is little conducive to invigorating the resolution to modernise. Is there a way of relativising the West without placing Africans in the box reserved for ' the Other'?

## Deconstruction as a Prerequisite to Development

The need to liberate African self-representations from Eurocentrism emphasises the necessity for the deconstruction of Western concepts and methods. No view of African difference and philosophy can be authentic and liberating if it remains entangled in Eurocentric distortions. The deconstructive standpoint relativises the

West, just as it unravels the hidden motives and mechanism of its thinking. It offers the best possible tools both to critically analyse the colonial discourse on Africa and to approach Africa from a new perspective.

According to V. Y. Mudimbe, the leading thinker of the African deconstructionist school, what passes for African philosophy and knowledge of Africa is essentially a product of the Western episteme. He writes:

> Modern African thought seems somehow to be basically a product of the West. What is more, since most African leaders and thinkers have received a Western education, their thought is at the crossroads of Western epistemological filiation and African ethnocentrism. Moreover, many concepts and categories underpinning their ethnocentrism are inventions of the West (Mudimbe 1988:185).

So pervasive is the dependence of African views on Western concepts that it perverts even the attempts to argue in support of African difference, as shown by the negritude movement, which fully maintains 'the binary opposition between European and African, civilised and primitive, rational and emotional, religious and idolatrous' (Diawara 1990:82). Some such opposition reflects the Western normative standpoint and reasserts the superiority of the West over Africa. What is intended to be a protest turns into an acceptance of hierarchy. No less loyal to Western prejudices are the opponents of negritude. Houtondji finds negritude unacceptable because the primacy of rationality, as established by the West, is not consistent with the products of African thought. Likewise, the idea of a traditional African philosophy is questioned because Western thought rejects the conflation of culture with philosophy.

Yet, seeing the gross misconceptions of anthropology, the suspicion should have been that the anthropological discourse is not accidental. Nor are the demeaning descriptions of Africans mere errors. As a product born of the epistemological specificity of the West, anthropology was first conceived as a reductionist enterprise at odds with a positive idea of human diversity. Its reductionism is inscribed in the very idea of positing the European as an archetype, the outcome of which is that non-Western peoples are defined as deficient variations. To say that anthropology is a product of Western rationality is to underline the goal of domination as the initial project of anthropology. According to Mudimbe, anthropologists 'speak about neither Africa nor Africans, but rather justify the process of inventing and conquering a continent and naming its 'primitiveness' or 'disorder' as well as the subsequent means of its exploitation and methods for its 'regeneration'' (Mudimbe 1988:20).

The purpose of anthropology is not so much to study other peoples as to construct their particularity in a way that sets them against the West. The opposition marginalises these peoples, and so singles them out for domination. The epistemological inspiration of this opposition is found in Western philosophy whose essence is to manufacture representations and explanations of history drawn from epistemological values centring the West. As a means of constructing and structuring the world around the centrality of the West, the Western philosophical paradigm is unfit to provide an objective study of other cultures. Objectivity is illusory if it disregards the basic principle that 'no one enjoys the privilege of being at the center while others remain peripheralised' (Masolo 1994:179). This strong denunciation of Eurocentrism suggests that Mudimbe welcomes the idea of African difference, provided that it does not reflect the anthropological opposition between the rational and the primitive. He writes:

> There are natural features, cultural characteristics, and, probably, values that contribute to the reality of Africa as a continent and its civilisations as constituting a totality different from those of, say, Asia and Europe. On the other hand, any analysis would sort out the fact that Africa (as well as Asia and Europe) is represented in Western scholarship by 'fantasies' and 'constructs' made up by scholars and writers since the Greek times (Mudimbe 1994:xv).

As to the question of the existence of a traditional African philosophy, the best answer is to say, to paraphrase a scholar, 'No! Not yet!' (Maurier 1984:25). The main problem is to find an approach free of Western premises and stereotypes before the attempt to reconnect with the past is made. The problem is less the particularity of Africans than the misconstruction of the perception of particularity by the insidious influence of Eurocentric concepts. To underestimate the impact of these Western concepts is a great mistake. Such concepts are no longer what Westerners say about Africans; they have been internalised to the point of becoming the unconscious references of Africans.

Most interesting is the correlation that Mudimbe establishes between the socio-economic reality of Africa and its mental setup. The colonial system of economic exploitation necessitates the inculcation of a subservient mentality into colonised peoples, especially into the educated elite. It presupposes a policy of domestication based on the production of intellectual representations and beliefs inducing mental dependency. The missionary's project of disseminating Christianity and civilisation was an important tool of implanting dependency. 'The outcome of these policies was the process of underdevelopment' (Mudimbe 1988:3), which is neither poverty nor backwardness, but the product of domestication. The production of a dependent mode of thinking and producing in colonies shows that what exists in Africa is no longer the traditional society, but a peripherised, marginalised society.

By showing that economic dependency is a consequence of mental dependency, Mudimbe's theory of underdevelopment improves on the position of the neo-Marxist school of dependency. In its heyday, the dependency school, as articulated, for instance, by André Gunder Frank, associated economic dependency with the tendency to rebel rather than to submit, thereby imbuing the third world with a strong tendency to confront imperialism. The tendency was believed to be so firm that the underdeveloped world was often described as the new birthplace of socialism, in contrast to the weakening of revolutionary spirit among the working class of the West as a result of the corrupting effect of imperialist expansions. To quote Frank:

> As the solutions to the problems of underdevelopment become ever more impossible within the capitalist system which creates them . . . the long exploited people themselves are being taught and prepared to lead the way out of capitalism and underdevelopment (Frank 1976:217–218).

Mistaken also was Frantz Fanon's ascription of a revolutionary potential to the dependent word. The trend to accommodate to a world dominated by the West greatly overtook Fanon's vision of a 'Third World... rising like the tide to swallow up all Europe' (Fanon 1968:106). In revealing the injection of dependency right into the self-representation of the third world, Mudimbe portrays a situation in which the alleged rebellious stand of underdeveloped peoples is erased by the acceptance of marginality.

Clearly, Mudimbe's approach places the colonisation of the African mind at the centre of Africa's problems of modernisation. If the mental is so conditioned as to promote Western dominance, even as Africans seem to contest that dominance, liberation is unthinkable without the complete emancipation from Western categories whose purpose is to marginalise other peoples through the universalisation of the West. Subjective liberation, that is, the decolonisation of the mind, is thus the forced prerequisite to Africa's modernisation. The priority of mental liberation establishes the primacy of deconstruction: when Western concepts are deconstructed, the affirmation of difference without hierarchy or opposition becomes possible. Deconstruction debunks Eurocentrism, and so inaugurates the authentic phase of pluralism by dismissing the antagonism between Europe and Africa.

One major implication of the deconstruction of Eurocentrism is the rejection of the antithesis, so dear to modernisation school, between modernity and tradition. In view of the systematic deformation of the African past by Western concepts, nothing justifies 'the static binary opposition between tradition and modernity, for tradition (traditio) means discontinuities through dynamic continuation and possible conversion of tradita (legacies)' (Mudimbe 1988:189). The very process of modernisation in Europe and elsewhere gives confirmation of the capacity of tradition to integrate discontinuities by means of a dynamic continuity. When Europeans refer to the Greek, Roman, and Christian roots of modern Western civilisation, what else do they underline but the continuity of European history through the integration of discontinuities? If integration is good for Europeans, why would it be retarding when Africans want to achieve a similar continuity by integrating their encounters of the West into their own legacy? When Africans conceive of modernisation as a synthesis of African legacy – communalism, dynamic conception of being, etc. – and Western ideas of science and technology, they are attempting to construct a dynamic continuity that centres and protects them from alienation and dependency while opening them to novel encounters and events.

Granted that the great merit of the deconstructionist school is to have understood the extent to which the internalisation of Western representations blocks the African initiative, still critics point out that the disengagement and freedom promised by deconstruction are severely curtailed by the underlying relativist philosophy.

Though Mudimbe establishes a sharp distinction between the facts of Africa and the Western representations of these facts, critics wonder whether the deconstructive equation of knowledge with construction allows the distinction between facts and representations. Mudimbe has no valid reason to believe that his own descriptions of Africa are not also inventions. Put otherwise, the availability of an alternative way to Western rationality, by which alone Mudimbe's perceptions of Africa can claim to be real and authentic, is not perceptible. As Masolo puts it, 'he fails, in The Invention of Africa and elsewhere, to show clearly how the 'usable past' should be used by 'experts' to construct an 'authentic' African episteme' (Masolo 1994:179).

Viewed from the need to decolonise the mind, the acceptance of relativism dilutes the authenticity of identification, which is then wanting in conviction and power. Without a forceful belief in the objectivity of identities, effective decolonisation cannot be achieved. The suspicion is that this receptivity to relativist philosophical premises may well be an imprint of mental colonisation, there being no doubt that the relativisation of the West to shake off Eurocentrism leads to disbelief, not to say cynicism. Moreover, deconstruction is unable to make a discourse on Africa that secures a vision superior to or better than the one suggested by negritude. In relativising the West, it assigns the best qualities (rationality, science) to the particularity of the West so that only the lower attributes of non-rationality remain for African particularity. Add that the quest for authentic particularism tends to downplay those characteristics of the West that produced the modern world. Since African authenticity passes through these characteristics being denounced as Western, the need to be different dampens the resolution to learn from the West, to understand the secret of its power. Relativism cripples the African determination to embark on a competitive course with the West.

## Development as Freedom

The apparent drawbacks of African philosophical responses to the colonial discourse draw attention to what can be termed the African dilemma. The attempt to refute the characterisation of Africans as underdeveloped by the assertion of difference ascribes a non-rational mode of thinking to the African self, and so works toward the perpetuation of its marginality. Modernising ventures, including scientific and technological realisations, are incompatible with a turn of mind alien to rationality. Those African philosophers who reject otherness do not escape the charge of endorsement of the colonial idea of Africa. Their commitment to the universality of the human mind cannot but explain the disparity between Africa and the achievements of the West by a difference in the attainment of progress. The explanation resurrects the evolutionary terms of backwardness. Though they promise that Africa will catch up with the West, the consent to the idea of backwardness paralyses the march toward progress.

The merit of the deconstructionist school is to understand the extent to which the internalisation of Western representations blocks the African initiative. Unfortunately, its philosophical premises make the disengagement of Africa dependent on the acceptance of relativism. As a result, the liberated African self lacks the sense of its own objectivity, and hence the power of conviction, without which effective decolonisation cannot be achieved. Even so, the deconstructive standpoint correctly prioritises the issue of African modernisation. So long as the African mind is bogged down by Western representations, no development policy, however thoroughly contrived and however skillfully planned, can initiate a sustained process of development.

If the weakness of the relativist strategy, whether that of otherness or particularism, is to take away rationality in addition to racialising or relativising its commitment, such drawbacks are not without remedy. Take the case of negritude. What is wrong with negritude is less the claim to difference than the conception of difference as otherness by the appeal to racial attributes. Instead of originating the difference from racial, natural characteristics, negritude should have resorted to an act of choice, the very one that led Sartre to argue that, in the case of human beings, 'existence precedes essence' (Sartre 1957:13). The precedence of freedom over physical or cultural determinations assigns differences to historicity, thereby construing human diversity as a product of subjective contingency.

The historical approach diversifies without racialising: it relates to an initial and sui generis option unraveling potentials which, though inherently universal and human, are used diversely as a result of divergent choices. The involvement of choice overcomes the debate over the reality or non-reality of the African essence as a racial entity. Choice refers to freedom, and so excludes objective determinations even as it reinstates the universality of human potentials. The recovery of universality avoids the limitative relativism of deconstruction, just as the foundational role of freedom supplies the power of conviction that deconstruction is unable to offer. The initiative of freedom being the foundational moment of self-determination, it inserts the absolute into the relative.

This agency of choice underlines the crucial role of freedom in the generation of civilisations by tracing the particularity of each civilisation back to the contingency of human choices. Since the initial value orientation of a given culture determines the use of rationality, provided that non-technicalness is ascribed to an act of choice, the opposition between Africa and the conquering ethos of Europe is, therefore, perfectly acceptable. Not only a disparity resulting from different choices does not exclude the rationality of Africans, but by removing the racial barrier it also warrants the possibility of changing lanes, of passing from one conception to another by an act of choice. Most importantly, it invalidates all evolutionary approach. If instead of backwardness, choice accounts for differences, the West is relativised as much as Africa is. Since the selection of some goals always requires the suppression or the giving up of other equally valid goals, there is no room for the ranking enthusiasm of evolutionism. This selectiveness of choice shows that the price for the option to make Westerners 'masters and owners of nature' (Descartes 1978:46) is the inhibition or loss of other ways of relating with nature. At the same time, it salvages Africa by attributing its non-technicalness more to the pursuit of a different purpose, with its positive and negative sides, than to evolutionary retardation.

Some such approach points to what must be the first task of a serious attempt to decolonise the African mind, namely, the radical transformation of what African students learn at schools and universities. The elimination of Eurocentric concepts from the curriculum and their replacement by conceptions whose basic purpose is to centre Africa takes priority over all other de-colonising measures. In particular, the Hegelian scheme of world history advancing by stages that display the progression from the most backward to the most advanced – a notion that carries the basic tenets of most Western philosophies of history, including the Marxist approach – must be cast aside. This scheme enables Hegel to write: 'the History of the World travels from East to West, for Europe is absolutely the end of History' (Hegel 1956:103). Having arbitrarily universalised European characteristics, Hegel, as we saw, has no difficulty in painting the characteristics of other cultures as backward, lagging manifestations of Europe. This theoretical construct must be dismantled in favour of a pluralistic view of history that views each culture as evolving autonomously in pursuit of particular goals stemming from an initial and founding choice. Only thus can Africans dissolve the stigma of backwardness and regain the freedom to define themselves in terms appropriate to their own historical initiatives.

To involve choice is to replace the unilinear scheme of evolutionism by the concept of divergence. Divergence refers to splits within the same unity developing in different directions; unlike the cumulative and unilinear conception of evolution, it exhibits, in the words of Henri Bergson, the process of evolution 'splaying out like a sheaf, sunders, in proportion to their simultaneous growth, terms which at first completed each other so well that they coalesced' (Bergson 1944:130). Though the directions are particular by their development, they are also complementary by their original unity. Both the particularity and the complementariness of the directions rule out the hierarchical conception of the process. The human effort should not seek the dominance of one direction – which is what Westernisation is targeting – but the harmonious development of human potentials But note that this harmonious development remains unattainable so long as the West is infatuated with material power. The one-sidedness of the Western path gives Africans no other choice than to strive to narrow the technological gap.

To sum up, the divergent conception of social evolution is the solution to the African dilemma. To the extent that it involves choice, it dismisses the colonial discourse in terms liable to stimulate the African resolution to seek parity with the West. The relativisation of the West by the disclosure of its initial choice challenges its normativeness and invites the development of Africa as a reciprocating act of choice. When the West is raised to the level of norm, Africans are reduced to the status of imitators, or to speak a more familiar language, to dependency. When the West is relativised through a divergent conception, it becomes an object of utilitarian and pragmatic inquiry. Contrary to the mere capitulation stemming from the normative approach, the relativising impact of choice puts Africans in the self-asserting situation of asking such questions as: What can we adopt and adapt from the West? What has the West adopted from Africa? What must we reject as detrimental? How can we integrate what we borrow into our own continuities? These questions are the very ones that Africans would have raised were they not colonised. Developing this type of utilitarian relation with the West is indeed dependent on the prior decolonisation of the African mind, which is neither more nor less than the recovery of freedom.

# 7

# Philosophy and Development: On the Problematic African Development – A Diachronic Analysis

## Lansana Keita

**Introduction**

The term 'development' is generally understood etymologically to mean 'expansion by a process of growth' or 'growth and differentiation of some entity along lines natural to its kind'. The processes of transformation and growth described by the term typically apply to biological processes where the stages of growth are usually described as development. But the development of the modern social sciences in Western Europe some 200 to 150 years ago and the recognition by its practitioners that societies have undergone and do undergo transformations in history established parallels between the processes of biological change and those of society. The theories of prominent European social scientists such as Comte, J.S. Mill, and Marx, with the important North African precursor Ibn Khaldun (1868) also in mind, were founded on the idea that human societies were not static but underwent periodic transformations. What is interesting too is that the progress or movement observed in social transformations were normatively viewed in moving from states of being less developed to ones of being more developed. One recalls Marx's quasi-Darwinian thesis that human history was naturally evolutionary progressing from less developed stages to those that were more developed. Thus, for Marx, a developed capitalism would eventually give way to socialism then communism, eventually reflective of a mature human society.

It is in this context that post-Enlightenment European thinkers such as Comte and Marx argued that human society progressed from stages that were less developed to stages that were more developed. Marx specifically argued that human society progressed through the stages of 'primitive' communism, slavery, feudalism, and capitalism to culminate in the future with communism, the most developed phase of human existence. Marx's deterministic theory of the dynamics of history argued that it was the historic function of capitalism to spread itself into societies that were not as developed, thereby setting the conditions for their eventual progress into socialism and communism.

It is instructive too to note that the post-Enlightenment idea of development as intrinsic to the path of human history was central to the philosophy of history formulated by the German thinker Hegel, a major influence on Marx, in the nineteenth century. For Hegel (*Philosophy of History*), the developmental path of human history was characterised by the idea of increasing self-consciousness on the part of humans. This process was facilitated by the movement of 'Spirit'(*Geist*) as it progressed from East to West. The result of this was to be discerned in the increasing amounts of freedom gained by the individual within his or her society over time. An interesting point about Hegel's 'dialectics of history' is that his philosophy of history granted no developmental path for Africa. Africa, according Hegel, had not entered into the path of human history, therefore it did not contain the necessary criteria for development. In this regard, Africa would be permanently undeveloped.

On account of technological transformations made within Western Europe dating from the sixteenth century, the idea developed among European thinkers that in comparative terms, the societies of Western Europe were more developed than those in the non-European world. European travel to other parts of the globe, aided by the use of the compass within the context of newly acquired knowledge of the world and nature in general, should be seen as the catalyst that produced the European Enlightenment with its subsequent development of the social and human sciences. Anthropology was created to study the cultures of non-European societies and it was born necessarily with a plethora of theoretical biases. One of its major premises was that the European world was civilised and developed, while many of the non-European societies were 'primitive' and undeveloped. It was assumed that undeveloped societies would increasingly become developed, the more they resembled the developed societies of Europe.

This was the context in which the contemporary concepts of 'modern'(literally meaning *à la mode*) and 'backward', 'civilised' and 'primitive', and 'developed' and 'underdeveloped' were first formulated. When reference was made, for example, to the economic systems and technologies of Africa during the era of Europe's irruption thither, the received doctrine was that Europe was 'developed' and Africa was 'underdeveloped'. But there is an evident problematic here concerning the terms 'developed' and 'underdeveloped'. 'Developed' suggests a completed or finished process, while 'underdeveloped' tends to imply stasis or lack of progress. But the technological and economic structures of European society fifty years ago have undergone palpable changes and continue to do so. Consider the fact that computers, cellular phones, solar energy, and so on were not commonplace in European society some fifty years ago. Thus, the idea that European societies are 'developed' is obviously questionable. European societies are in the process of development just as other societies deemed 'undeveloped' or 'developing'. For this reason, the automatic contrast between 'developed' and 'developing' societies should be subject to debate.

The obviously confirmable difference between contemporary developing European societies and those of Africa is that the former societies are the producers and users of more novel forms of technology than the latter. What is also evident is that social structures of the former are eventually made to conform to the novel forms of technology.

## Was Africa Ever the Source of Novel Forms of Development?

Having established that the term 'developed' should not be used with regard to societies that are perennially in the process of transformation – as all societies are, to lesser or greater degrees – a pertinent question now is whether Africa was ever the site of novel sociological transformations.

The human species differentiates itself from other species of living organisms in that it possesses the peculiar characteristic of not only adapting to its environments as other living organisms do, but of transforming its environments to suit its needs, wants, and purposes. Presumably, the specific biological structures of the fauna of the East African savanna are the result of millennia of slow evolutionary pressures, according to the principles of natural selection. This punctilious process has never been witnessed, but it is assumed that the elongated neck of the giraffe and the running capacities of the cheetah are results of this adaptive process. It is claimed too that the present biological structure of humans is also the result of adaptive pressures deriving from the environment. But humans differentiate themselves from other biological species in that they have developed a greater active capacity for adaptation to their environments by a continuing transformation and utilisation of the environment for their own purposes. This active capacity is certainly present with some nonhuman organisms, but it is humans who have developed this capacity to the fullest extent. For example, hymenopterous insects such as bees, wasps and ants, arachnids such as spiders, and mammals such as beavers do transform nature for their own purposes but their adaptive capacities seem driven more by instinct rather than otherwise in that their capacities seem restricted only to species-specific niches. The transformational capacities that humans demonstrate seem rather to be motivated by reflexive consciousness rather than by instinct. In other words, humans are endowed with the capacity to modify their operational programmes to suit the environment as they see fit. It is for this reason that the human capacity to transform or modify the natural environment to satisfy needs and wants is a constant and ongoing phenomenon. It is in this context that one may argue that the human capacity to transform nature according to more effective techniques of such over time may be seen as forms of technological development.

This human capacity in the form of technological development was first evident in what is now known as Africa as early as 2.5 million years ago (MYA) (Klein 1989:164). The archaeological evidence suggests the manufacture of stone and bone implements by proto-humans or early members of the species *homo*. According to archaeological evidence, the species *homo* attained its most evolved level some

160 thousand years ago (KYA) in what is now known as East Africa and Southern Africa. Until some 55KYA all human technological developments took place in Africa because no *homo sapiens sapiens* lived elsewhere. Some archaeologists claim that a qualitative change in human technology and sociology took place in Europe some 40-50KYA, thereby hoping to prove that a distinction must be made between 'anatomically modern humans' and 'behaviourally modern humans'. But there is the counter-claim that this 'human revolution' took place tens of thousands of years earlier in Africa (McBrearty and Brooks 2000). Reference here is to the 'African Middle Stone Age' with its specific microlithic technologies, trade, use of pigment, bone tools, and so on.

The end of the Neolithic approximately some 10KYA witnessed a qualitative change in the way humans sought to transform their environments for survival purposes. The age of agriculture is claimed to have begun in what archeologists call the Middle East, which includes Northeast Africa and West Asia. Agriculture required domestication of animals, development of tilling technologies, plant breeding and nurturing. With the discovery of the greater effectiveness of metal implements over other types (lithic and bone especially), usage of copper and bronze increased. Eventually iron became the metal of choice for much of Africa's societies. What is of importance, though, within the context of the development of technology, is that usage of any metal for whatever purposes requires furnace construction and smelting to specific temperatures. There is some controversy over whether the practices of agriculture and metal smelting were developed independently in different parts of the globe or whether they were spread through a process of diffusion. In any case, suffice it to say that there is archaeological evidence of agriculture, settled societies and metal smelting in Africa more or less simultaneously with similar evidences elsewhere especially in West Asia and its environs. The time period in question here ranges from 5,000 BCE (the Egypto-Nubian culture complex) to 900 BCE for the earliest approximate times. It is instructive to point out too that iron working in Africa has been much studied by archaeologists with the recognition that furnace construction seems to have been accompanied by local and indigenous considerations (Miller 1997).

But what provides incontrovertible evidence for parts of Africa being more developed than anywhere else on the globe from at least 4,000 BCE until 500 BCE are the technological and sociological structures of the Egypto-Nubian complex and its environs, which is now the Sudan. Writing, engineering, astronomy (which produced the first, accurate annual time measurement – the calendar), building in stone, mathematics, surgery and all the known human arts and sciences had their origin in this sociological complex (Diop 1991). The Greek and Roman civilisations, which respectively developed in what is now called South East Europe and Southern Europe, were both founded on the technology and general knowledge developed predominantly in the African locales of Egypt-Nubia and the sub-tropical West Asian society of Sumer.

Since the present era (i.e. AD), the level of development in Africa has been comparable to and even more technologically advanced than other parts of the globe. The Islamic presence in Europe may be said to be directly responsible for the transmission and diffusion of more developed forms of knowledge to Western Europe. But it was the technical knowledge of the Egypto-Nubian complex embellished by the culturally hybrid Greeks that served as the technological catalyst for the European Renaissance. By contrast, Medieval Africa north of the Equator was technologically and sociologically more developed than most of Europe until the tenth and eleventh centuries (Diop 1987). In that part of Africa there was long distance trade, manufacture and monetary transactions using gold bullion. The towns of Jenne, Timbuktu, and Mopti in the Sahel were well known locations of trade and manufacture. In general, agriculture, animal husbandry and long distance trade all with their required technology were present in Africa. Historians of Africa are well acquainted with Africa's technological specificities not only in the Egypto-Nubian complex, but also in what is now known as Zimbabwe, Ethiopia, Nigeria (for example, leather works and other items manufactured in Kano were transshipped to Europe by way of Morocco as early as the thirteenth century), the Sahelian economic and trade areas of Ghana, Mali and Songhay, and parts of Southern Africa.

There was a decisive transformation in the world's technological level of development when Western Europe began applying the technical knowledge it acquired from other areas to travel to other areas of the globe. Travels to China and the Americas by individuals such as Magellan, Da Gama and Columbus opened up new economic opportunities for Western Europeans. The compass, printing, and gunpowder (invented in China) were used to telling effect by Europe within the context of the rapidly spreading economic system later known as capitalism. The exploitation of captive labour in the Americas and the violent acquisition of lands and gold were the crucial ingredients for the increased trade and the accumulation of capital. African labour and the gold reserves of the Americas served as the catalysts for trans-continental trade, urbanisation, and qualitative transformations in technology. Economic historians write of the Industrial Revolution which produced the steam engine and other forms of mechanical energy. The technological advantages that accrued to Western Europe under the aegis of mercantilist capitalism in turn served as the basis for further technological developments in sea transport (the steamship) and weaponry (long range cannon, and the Gatlin and maxim guns). The colonisation of vast areas of the globe first effected by force of arms then using the vanquished populations as forced labour, all served as added catalysts to a burgeoning commercial and industrial capitalism. The combination of commercial and industrial capitalism coupled with rapid technological changes resulted in a world split along zero-sum game lines. The economic and technological gains of Western Europe resulted in economic and technological losses and disadvantages for the rest of the world, especially for the indigenous peoples of the Americas and Africa. The economic relations between African societies then under European sway and the relevant West European nations were in reality those of unequal exchange. Europe advanced and developed economically at the expense of its colonies in Africa, Asia and the Americas. This is the historical explanation for the sociological structures of what are now called the 'developed' nations and the 'underdeveloped' or 'developing' nations.

Given the comparative economic and technological disadvantages experienced specifically by the nations of Africa with regard to those of Europe, the desire on the part of the disadvantaged is to eradicate those disadvantages which carry real costs in strictly economic terms. But these comparative disadvantages have been so institutionalised in structures protective of economic advantages that radical solutions are needed. Myriad theories of economic and sociological theories of development have been developed over the years, but they have not borne fruit when empirically applied, and those that would seem to augur positive results are never tested in any authentic manner. The intriguing theoretical question is an instrumental one. What would Africa look like if correct theories of development were implemented?

## The Hypothetical Structures of a Developmentally Transformed Africa

If Africa were at the vanguard of economic and technological development this would manifest itself in three areas: technological, economic, and sociological. They are explored in the following:

### *The Technological*

If Africa were now at the vanguard of human development, its technological level would be qualitatively different from its present state now. Africa would be at the forefront in the production and manufacture of those items which now require the most advanced knowledge and skills in the world today. Thus, the continent would be the area where technologically advanced items such as airplanes, automobiles, ships, computers and other durable goods would be manufactured. These enterprises would also be supported by local research centres in technology and engineering which would be attached to them. These enterprises would be for the most part owned by their workers, who would have the right to the majority of the productive stock.

The same technological self-sufficiency would apply in the area communication. The kinds of advanced research in communications technology now monopolised by Scandinavia and the East Asian nations of Japan and Korea would also be found in Africa, again supported by research centres in engineering and applied natural science.

In the area of agricultural production, Africa would be home to the most efficient and environmentally rational modes of production with all technologies and needs produced on the African continent. Technologies appropriate for all types of agricultural units and enterprises would also be produced on the continent, supported by ongoing research in Africa's research centres. There would also be serious ongoing research to reclaim the deserts in Africa for agricultural purposes with the funding and implementation of such deriving from African sources. In other words, an Africa developed in technology would be practically autonomous in supplying the most advanced technologies for whatever purposes.

## *The Economic*

An Africa at the vanguard of economic growth and development would have transcended the balkanised, economically dependent status bequeathed to it from the colonial experience. An advanced Africa would be one in which the Bantustan-like mini-states that characterize the African continent would be a thing of the past. There would be intra-African trade, movement and communication in an economic landscape in which a single monetary unit would be on par with the other major currencies of the world. One of the reasons for the persistent unequal exchange between African nations and the West especially is the greatly debased nature of Africa's currencies. Ricardo's theory of comparative advantage, based on an international division of production coupled with the flexibility of currencies as a function of balance of payment outcomes, has not proven to be viable for Africa, given that Africa's currencies continue on their debased route without respite. In short, the economic matrix for an Africa experiencing mature economic growth would be one of a common market of some 850 million individuals who would be free to trade, travel and exchange without the impediments imposed during the colonial era. One of the noted historical and archaeological facts about the African continent is that there was untrammeled trade and travel for millennia until the advent of the colonialists. Given the geographical extent of the continent and its relative ecological variety, the question of massive unemployment with individuals having to migrate extra-continentally to areas of greater capital depth would become a thing of the past. Furthermore, Africa's economic system would be one in which the major goal would be the maximisation of human welfare in a sociological context which recognised that economies exist first to satisfy human needs and not primarily for the accumulation of wealth on the part of some individuals and nations. In this regard, major and prior considerations would be given to investment in human capital for all individuals so that the individual could realize his or her full potential in terms of interests and dispositions. In this regard, it would be practically impossible for individuals to be unemployed because Africa's educational systems would guarantee that every individual be trained in a variety of skills and be privileged with access to capital for purposes of business and otherwise. In contemporary Africa, the situation is the reverse. Enterprising individuals who might have some business idea in mind experience great difficulty in obtaining capital for the purpose in mind. Lending agencies, of course, always seek to reduce risk when capital funds are made available to the public, but that situation could be easily remedied by initially offering small amounts of capital for projects that carry high probabilities of success. This is where state and public capitalisation of such institutions would be of great assistance. Capitalisation costs would be held at a minimum if the capital equipment needed for the prospective enterprise were to be leased at manageable interest rates as an option.

The contemporary age we now live in is one which touts the virtue of the market and the neo-liberal economy. With the demise of the Soviet Union, ideological arguments are routinely mounted against what are perceived as the limitations of socialism. But it must be recognised that the banking system, which is at the heart of capitalism, is admittedly founded on a socialist principle. Banks operate on the socialist principle of collecting large amounts of public capital which is then loaned to individuals singly. The incentive on the part of the public to loan funds to banks is determined in part by the returns determined by the going rate of interest.

This brings up the important question of the role of government or the state in any programme for economic development. Theorists who support liberal economic theory and market economics argue that the role of the state in economic development should be reduced to a minimum. Ideologically, they are committed to privatisation of as many economic enterprises as possible and the reduction of state funding of socially beneficial programmes such as investment in human capital, health and commonly shared infrastructure such as roads, railways and the likes. Such theorists also express much opposition to subsidies directed at enterprises, the need for whose products are subject to inelastic demand in the areas of housing, basic education and welfare.

But the economic history of those nations that have successfully broken free from the constraints of underdevelopment demonstrates that the state has played an important guiding role in rational economic decision making and economic growth. Germany's economic growth and technological development in the latter part of the nineteenth century was determined to a great extent by the mercantilist practice of protecting growing enterprises from outside competition. This theory of autarky was argued for by political economists such as Frederic List. List argued for tariff protection of infant industries imposed by the state which itself should embark on a nationalist programme of economic development (List 1983; Roussakis 1968). The same may be said for Japan in the latter part of the nineteenth century and, more recently, nations like Korea and Malaysia. Economic transformations and economic growth took place in nations such as Korea because 'they showed that the role of the state need not merely be to protect certain industries or to promote exports. It can also perform functions like planning; it can own key sectors, create social infrastructure, and serve as a focus for ideologies and identities' (Biel 2000:202). Similar arguments have been made by admittedly prominent adherents of neoclassical economic theory such as Joseph Stiglitz (Hoff and Stiglitz 2001:415-425).

Thus, an Africa that is at the vanguard of development would be one in which there would be a judicial partnership between government as an institution and a sovereign, free and politically dominant public, composed of both single individuals and collectivities. At this juncture, a crucial distinction must be made, however, between two key institutions of any modern society: that between government as consisting of cadres whose function is to attend to economic needs such as education, housing, health, public safety, and so on, that are most efficiently served in communitarian fashion, and the state whose function in this instance would be essentially and mainly ceremonial. The functions of the state and government, both completely beholden to their creators, the people will be strictly delineated and maintained by constitutional statute. One might note in this regard that there is an increasing tendency in the modern nation state for the state to be dominant over government and even to absorb it. Much has been written on the role of the state in modern society with some theorists arguing that the real function of the state is to safeguard by implicit force the economic, political and cultural interests of its dominant classes. In a revised theory of the African state, its role would be reduced to something akin to the ceremonial role played by the remnants of the traditional monarchies of Europe and elsewhere. The modern state, in most instances, has been usurped by secular governments beholden to concentrated capital that protect their rule legally by self-serving statutes and physically by security apparatuses that often operate in secret and with impunity. Caricatures of this kind of governmental structure have been adopted widely in post-colonial Africa.

In an Africa that is advanced economically, the state would be allocated very limited powers with its appointees such as presidents and prime ministers serving almost ceremoniously, and fully beholden to the populace. The different ministries whose government functions are to provide for and oversee the general welfare would be fully divorced from the state. Heads of the different ministries and their appointees would be drawn purely from the government sector with its career employees. The point of this approach to government and the state in an advanced Africa would be to demonstrate that its economic structures would necessarily entail political economic issues involving the role and function of both government and the state. As suggested above, in an advanced Africa, human welfare in all its dimensions within the context of a constitutionally enforced communitarian ethos would be the primary consideration of such an economy. Human welfare in all its dimensions within an African context would involve not only economic decision making on the part of individuals, but also economic decision-making on the part of government. But in order to ensure a maximal human welfare in the form of the human capacity for self realisation, the state would have minimal powers to control free expression within the context of a rationally determined maximum negative and positive rights for all persons. The general political-economic context would be one of individual states within a larger collectivity of politically federated states with governments at the supranational level. From a standpoint of strict rationality, an advanced Africa would contain no more than four or five nation states, all members of a wider African commonwealth whose members would include the nation states of overseas Africa.

And yet contrary to popular belief, for the most part, the practised and cherished ideas of freedom have historically been an intrinsic element of African society. Who feels more free than Africa's eternal nomadic herdsman as he leads and follows his cattle on their wandering ways, paying little attention to the arbitrarily imposed boundaries of the colonialists, now slavishly followed by their appointed governments? Who feels more free than the African peasant who tills, plants and harvests as seen fit without the controls and regulations of the imposed colonial and neocolonial government?

## On Human Capital and the Division of Labour

One of the problems faced by contemporary post-colonial African economies is that of the very evident unemployment and underemployment of individuals who graduate from Africa's institutions of modern education. The kinds of education now extant in Africa's pedagogical institutions at all levels derive for the most part from the colonial systems imposed during the colonial era. Hence, we have French, British and Portugese systems of education in various parts of Africa, all reflective of mostly colonial modes of knowledge transmission. In an advanced Africa, education would be geared necessarily to future meaningful employment to such an extent that the crucial element in education and human capital investment would be that each student would have been already apprenticed to some productive enterprise before graduation. Individuals whose interests would lead them to establish individual enterprises would also be apprenticed to other individuals in similar situations while receiving the adequate financial support from cooperative banks and other credit granting agencies.

But the essential issue here would be that in an advanced Africa educational instruction would be not only theoretical and practical but also eclectic. Thus, as a ready example, all individuals would be trained in the various arts required for modern agriculture, architecture, business operations, automotive repairs and other instruction in the mechanical and scientific arts. In this regard, every individual after the necessary period of instruction would have the real option of self employment or otherwise. Thus, the division of labour in this context would not require the specialisation that is so evident in the West and elsewhere.

## Politics and the New Republic

In a developmentally advanced Africa, the question of its political landscape is of paramount importance. The political systems imposed or bequeathed to Africa by way of the colonial project have been tried and have been found wanting. The reason for this is obvious: the political structures of contemporary Europe are the local products of historical processes that have roots in the specific feudal and post-feudal structures of Europe. It is because of these different political histories that the political systems of France, Germany, Britain and Italy are easily distinguishable. Africa itself has had its variegated political structures, all relevant to essentially agrarian, commercial and nomadic societies, but contemporary African society has been radically transformed – as European and Asian societies – in recent times, mainly on account of the impositions of the colonial era.

To answer the question concerning the political life and structures of an advanced Africa, I begin by posing a thought experiment question. The question is: If one were about to be born but without knowledge as to one's prospective economic and sociological status, gender, talents, health, family, and so on, into what kind of society would one wish to arrive? The answer is that any individual would hope to enter a society in which he or she would be guaranteed economic security for survival purposes, optimal conditions for self-development and self-realisation and maximal conditions for freedom and self-expression. In other words, the individual about to enter human society would necessarily hope to enter a society that is structured in such a way that human welfare in all its dimensions would be maximised – even for potential masochists with their perverted sense of 'welfare'.

If humans lived single and solitary lives, the issue of human welfare and the appropriate social structures would be determined by the individual. Matters involving economic arrangements, the extent of one's freedoility of rights, freedoms and autonomy. But the passive, post-serf classes of Europe allowed their recently won rights and freedoms to be confiscated by the new bourgeoisie, the class that provided the capital and assets for a growing capitalism. The superficial aspects of democracy such as voting and the temporary service in government by those appointed by capital (private or state) have been touted to post-colonial African governments as necessary and sufficient criteria for democratic 'good governance'.

But economic imbalances between those who own or control capital and those who are employed by the owners of capital have led to great distortions in the process now referred to as democratic. It is instructive to point out, in this context, that when voting was first introduced in the post-feudal societies of Europe, only individuals with adequate amounts of capital and property were accorded the right to vote. The reason for this was that capital and property owners sought to establish political mechanisms whereby the new governors of bourgeois society would attend to the specific interests of the former in terms of legislation, taxes and economic privileges. The expansion of the choice-making process took place only after literacy and knowledge spread to the working classes and the increasing numbers of the new town bourgeoisie – in short, the superficial aspects of the democratic process, that is the right to vote, became more widespread and accepted in the context of rights with the growth of what is now known as civil society.

It was this kind of system that was introduced to the new nations of Africa as they became independent. But this political graft from Europe was essentially problematic. The development of the political process in Europe was determined by local processes. Urbanisation with literacy and increased numbers of workers was a crucial element in the shaping of the political landscape of Europe. In Africa, urbanisation was taking place, but at a much slower pace than in Europe. The populations of post-independence Africa were still predominantly rural and agricultural. Literacy did not grow as quickly, given that the languages of instruction were predominantly those of the European metropolis. But what was of critical importance in this situation was that emerging civil societies were bereft of any real political power, given that such societies had relatively few organs of media expression such as newspapers, magazines, radio stations, and so on. In other words, Africa was relatively bereft of industrialising, capital-rich productive elements except in South Africa where settlers from Europe found it relatively easy to obtain capital for industrial, mineral exploiting and industrial purposes. The result of these post-colonial structures was that most political and economic power accrued to the state, often beholden to the ex-metropolis according to the dictates of neocolonialism. Under these circumstances, the political process was necessarily flawed despite the touted superficial requirements of 'free and fair elections'. But as I mentioned above, even in the European societies where the modern idea of 'democratic governance' was organically developed, there are still serious distortions of the political process on account of the imbalance of wealth and the gre at influence of capital.

The collective approach advocated here, with regard to these considerations, is one based principally on the idea of economies of scale; pooled resources yield economically more efficient results than when invested from single sources. Natural resources such as minerals and the environment would be owned collectively by all citizens. In an adequately developed Africa, the goals of the political process would entail the direct involvement of citizens at all levels, especially at local levels. The function of elected officials would be that of attending to the already prescribed functions of government. The most important functions of government for which the citizens would have agreed to support fiscally by way of their own contributions would be the maintenance and improvement of infrastructure, the collective needs of education and the collective needs of health, administered by adequately trained government officials. Again, a distinction must be made between the government and the state. Government officials would require the appropriate training for their tasks, which would be established legally by way of a general constitution. State officials who are elected according to the political process would be completely beholden to those who elected them for the sole purpose of ensuring that the prescribed tasks of government officials be efficiently effected. Questions relating to budgetary expenditures would be determined only by those individuals employed by government and deemed competent to effect such. In other words, the role of the state and its officials would be primarily ceremonial. The political situation would amount to what one might refer to as direct democracy, with citizens having direct access to those whom they have elected to serve their own interests. The problem arises however when the state and government are conflated with the state appropriating for itself the economic tasks that are better handled by government. Matters are also compounded when the state, by way of its officials, imposes its will on the people and seeks to curtail their naturally ascribable political freedoms. In all this is forgotten the fact that the state is comprised of ordinary individuals who are required to dispatch their functions at the behest of the people who remunerate them as they see fit.

## A Note on Development in Europe

The history of the world could be seen as one in which humans have sought to increase their freedoms by improving their understanding and control of the forces of nature for their own ends. These attempts at understanding and control were always attempted by appeal to the dual epistemologies of metaphysics and empirical technology. And instead of being beholden to nature and its caprices, humans have constantly and persistently sought to increase their agencies, hence, their freedoms by understanding how nature actually works. This understanding of nature has always been the major task of metaphysics (the transcendental) in its various forms, and what we now call empirical science (limited to the sensory world). But humans have also sought to increase their freedoms within their social structures over time, *pari passu*, as they expressed their increasing freedoms in their explorations of nature. In the case of Europe it must be recognised that this now-influential area is essentially an arriviste technological civilisation, having attained such status long after Africa and Asia had attained such. Until Roman civilisation became dominant a mere two thousand years ago, the sociological landscape of Europe was one of roaming groups of individuals who survived principally by plunder and mayhem. The Vikings, Vandals, and Saxons have acquired a deserved reputation in this regard.

But when Rome pacified most of Europe, a long period of unfreedom set in for Europeans in the form of slavery and serfdom. And even before the Romans, Greek civilisation, from which modern Europeans drew their cultural inspirations, was characterised by its slave classes. The same may be said for Roman civilisation. As Roman civilisation drew to a close in the fifth century, its institutions of slavery and peonage were replaced by that of another kind of servitude, historically referred to as serfdom. During the long era of serfdom, the serf was tethered to the land and subjected to the will of his lord, whose class acclaimed to itself the title of landed aristocracy. European feudalism lasted more than one thousand years, and its demise marked a central and significant point of European history. The 'freeing of the serfs' in Europe, from approximately the fifteenth century onwards, marked a quantum increase in the amounts of freedom for the European. The freeing of the serf and the birth of the new class of town burghers armed with new knowledge and novel technologies were practically simultaneous events, and the justification for the new freedoms was assigned to the new philosophers of the European post-Renaissance. But Montesquieu, Hobbes, Locke, Rousseau and others all belonged to the maturing post-feudal class of the European bourgeoisie. Their critical theories and disquisitions all established the intellectual conditions for the justified demise of feudalism and the birth of the modern European state. The French Revolution was the culminating point of this process. Liberty, Fraternity and Equality meant that hereditary rule and monarchical tenure were things of the past. The people were now ideologically justified in choosing their governmental representatives through the power accruing to them under the concept of parliamentary democracy.

But freedom is elusive. The rise of the bourgeoisie in Europe was a function of the economic power that accrued to that class according to its own ideology and practice of the economic system known as capitalism. The post-serf peasant, now an urban dweller, saw his freedoms whittled away under the power of capital. The mine and factory were now the replacements for the fields of the manor. It was this new unfreedom that inspired the idea of socialism, first with individuals like St.Simon, then later with Marx. The increasing freedoms of the bourgeoisie under capitalism were gained at the expense of the lack of freedoms for others. But the freeing of the captive serf in Europe was soon after accompanied by the organised capture of free West African labour for the plantations of the Americas and parts of Africa (Cape Verde, Angola, Mozambique, South Africa, etc.). The new captive labour of Africa was wedded to capital to produce wealth and novel technologies for Europe. Africa in captivity meant the increasing freedoms for Europe for the period dating from the fifteenth to the twentieth century. The culminating point to this formal period of unfreedom was the end of the colonial era. In the case of Africa, the departing colonialists had the last word. They imposed on Africa their own self-serving versions of government and democracy.

## Contemporary African Attempts at Development

I have argued above that the major reason for the colonisation and economic exploitation of Africa was its relative technological retardation with regard to Europe. The struggle for independence was primarily a struggle against economic exploitation and political subservience. Like Japan in the mid-nineteenth century, some leaders of African independence recognised that it was imperative to reduce the technological gap between Africa and the West. After being the world's leader in technology for 155,000 years – culminating in the autonomous and seminal technological civilisation of the Egypto-Nubian complex, and the technologically innovative structures of Axum, Zimbabwe, Ife-Nok-Benin, and so on – out of the 160,000 years that *homo sapiens* has been extant, Africa found itself in the sixteenth century in technological arrears, thereby facilitating its subsequent control and exploitation by some of the nations of Western Europe.

Since the days of decolonisation, there have been three noteworthy theoretical attempts at economic development: the Lagos Plan of Action, Tanzania's Ujamma Cooperative Development Theory, Libya's Green Book Prescriptions, and Ghana's African Pan-African Socialism. Yet, the only attempt at development which bore fruit and offered promise was that of Ghana under the leadership of Kwame Nkrumah. The reason for the success of the Ghana model was that it was based on actual empirical study of the economic development of Europe, a careful study of the history of Africa (explaining why the 'Gold Coast' of European provenance and agency became Ghana – the well-known state of medieval Africa) and the recognition of the intra-continental aspects of African history. Ghana's theory of economic development was patterned after the many theoretical writings of Nkrumah expressed in such texts as *Consciencism, Africa Must Unite,* and *Neocolonialism: The Last*

*Stage of Imperialism*. It is instructive to examine some of the ideas expressed in *Neocolonialism: The Last Stage of Imperialism* because it offers insights into the recognition by Ghana that structural changes in the organisation of post-colonial Africa had to be made before meaningful development could take place. It must be pointed out first of all that most theorists of African development tend to offer prescriptions for development without raising questions about the viability of the myriad postcolonial political entities hastily constructed by the colonial powers as they yielded formal political power to their erstwhile colonies. The idea of development is usually couched in nebulous terms about market freedom, privatisation and corruption. But consider the following from Kwame Nkrumah:

> Neo-colonialism is based upon the principle of breaking up former large united colonial territories into a number of small non-viable States which are incapable of independent development and must rely on the former imperial power for defence and even internal security (Nkrumah 1965: xiii).

Consider too these prescient observations: 'Unless small states can combine they must be compelled to sell their primary products at prices dictated by the developed nations and buy their manufactured goods at the prices fixed by them' (Nkrumah 1965:xiv). Statements such as these offer examples as to why one of the key principles in Nkrumah's theory of Pan-Africanism is the idea of continental institutions.

But for Nkrumah, the issue of development was not restricted only to the political but also to the economic. He writes:

> The existence of separate monetary zones is having a harmful effect on the growth of trade in Africa. It is leading to illegal trade and revenue losses in many countries and makes an African Common Market difficult. Like the old, artificial political boundaries which are a relic of the colonial period, the various monetary zones help to emphasize differences when the independent African States should all be working for unified economic development. They perpetuate links with former colonial powers and strengthen the forces of neocolonialism (Nkrumah 1965:227).

The idea of the political and economic pooling of resources as a necessary condition for economic development was not unique to political theorists such as Nkrumah. Consider the following, written more than thirty years ago:

The only way to achieve the economic re-construction and development essential to fulfill the aspirations, needs and demands of the peoples of Africa is through a sustained shift to continental planning, so as to unite increasingly the resources, markets and capital of Africa in a single substantial economic unit (Green and Seidman 1968:22).

But Nkrumah's programme was not just only about the political and economic integration of Africa, it also involved the restructuring of Ghana's economic system along socialist lines. Nkrumah's socialist agenda was seen as highly controversial in Euro-American and African political circles in an era when there was a fierce ideological conflict between the Soviet Union and the West. The Soviet Union, founded on the principles of Communism, was seen by many in the non-European world as a promising alternative to the Western capitalism, for purposes of development. The socialist model which Nkrumah found attractive was one which empowered the state with the major tasks of development in the form of the harnessing of capital for rapid growth in the areas of technological infrastructure and universal education. The Soviet Union under the theoretical guidance of Lenin was able to accumulate enough capital in a relatively short period of time to create sectors of state-controlled heavy industries and manufacture. It was on account of this rapid technological transformation that the West saw the Soviet Union as a very serious competitor in the area of political economy. In fact, this rapid technological change was what could be viewed as the major reason why the Soviet Union was able to defend itself during World War II and to launch outward thrusts into Eastern Europe following the defeat of Germany.

The question now is, How successful was Nkrumah's programme of development? With regard to the theory of Pan-Africanism, suffice it to say that the Organisation of African Unity (OAU) a supra-national organisation based in Addis Ababa and the founding of the Economic Community of West African States, constitutes the practical results of this idea, but extra-continental forces mindful of the potential of a genuine implementation of the Pan-African ideal were less than enthusiastic about offering the needed economic support for such. In strict economic terms, Ghana embarked on state administered seven-year plans that produced some rapid growth in areas of needed infrastructure in the construction of the Tema Harbour, and the Akosombo Dam and power grid. And it should be pointed out that the capital for such indigenous projects derived from tax duties, especially in the area of cocoa. But there were externally imposed difficulties when Ghana tried to coordinate the mining and smeltering of its own extensive deposits of bauxite with Guinea to produce aluminium *in situ*. But what makes elements of Ghana's development programme useful for the future is the rapid success it experienced in investments in human capital. The effect of Ghana's educational programme is still felt in West Africa many years after the demise of its ambitious experiment under Nkrumah.

## Contemporary Theories of Development

One of the very evident paradoxes on the issue of development is that despite the vast amounts of research done on the topic, the issue itself seems impervious to solution. This research topic was first undertaken in the 1950s with the explicit goal of explaining and offering prescriptions as to the causes of wealth and technology differentials between the nations of Western Europe and North America, and most of those of Africa, Asia and Latin America. As a result of this interest, a number of research paradigms have been formulated to this end. One standard point of departure for the development models is that, in order for development to take place, there must first be economic growth. Growth is seen as a necessary quantitative accumulation of surpluses that would eventually be transmuted qualitatively into development. One basic assumption that the development theorists made was that mechanisms had to be developed that maximised output in society's two major sectors: the agricultural and the industrial. It was argued that the developed world (mainly Northern hemisphere Western nations) was industrialised and demonstrated regular economic growth, while the developing world was primarily agricultural and experienced difficulties demonstrating economic growth. In this regard, development was seen predominantly as a matter of economics, thereby yielding theory construction to theorists in economics who normally analyzed the problematic of development from within the theoretical assumptions of their own particular paradigms. Thus, theorists in development (I name just a few) viewed the problem of development from the standpoint of classical or neoclassical economics(Hirshman 1958; Lewis 1955), Marxian political economy (Baran 1957), sociological theory (Rostow 1960), dependency theory (Prebisch 1950; Frank 1967; Furtado 1963; Emmanuel 1972; Amin 1974), and more recently critical development theory (Pieterse 2001).

What is also evident from a consultation of the research efforts on matters of development is that the vast majority of the researchers are based in the research institutes of the developed world and determined by the need for 'analytical tractability' and an ignoring of the fact that 'the human economic agents who are objects of interpretation and understanding do not represent inconcrete and disconnected entities 'out there' in the sense of being isolated from their environment in space and time, or from the theoretical and empirical constructs of would-be interpreters' (David 1997:217).

In what follows, I will offer brief analyses and discussions of the main theories of development so as to demonstrate how they differ fundamentally from the theory I have sketched above. The theories in question are the neoclassical theory, dependency theory, poststructuralism, and developmentalism.

## Neoclassical Economic Theory

The literature on the economics of contemporary development theory is dominated by theorists who have been schooled in what is called neoclassical economics. With the development of the modern social sciences as separate disciplines dating from the mid-eighteenth century, the theory of economics evolved from its classical phase into neoclassical economics, founded on the idea that economic decision making should be studied as rigorously as possible with appeal to the quantitative methods of mathematics. In its present guise, the neoclassical paradigm views itself as decidedly objective and scientific, given its reliance on a set of fundamental axioms and mathematical derivations. On account of its commitment to a scientific orientation, its theorists argue that its strictly scientific side represents positive economics, while its applied or policy side should be viewed as normative or welfare economics.

In this regard, neoclassical economics may be viewed as a species of engineering with its fundamental axioms that stress consumer sovereignty, transparent markets, transitive preferences that are conformed to by the ideal construct, *homo oeconomicus* or 'economic man'. But what is remarkable about this construct, to whom all the postulates, axioms and theorems of neoclassical economics apply, is that its behaviour is motivated only to 'maximise expected utility, subject to real costs constraints' according to a prescribed postulate of rationality. His behaviour is a function only of one value judgment, that of maximisation or gain. It is according to this foundational theory that the majority of the economists at the IMF and World Bank formulate and implement policy. In this regard, economics as a science has no tolerance for considerations regarding politics, sociology or the value judgmental considerations of political economy. The stated justification for this approach is that economics is first and foremost a scientific discipline and that its primary operational goals are results based on efficiency rather than on normative considerations, such as equity.

But is neoclassical economics a science? Science, as it is defined, consists of a set of empirically testable theories whose function is to predict and explain experiential phenomena in the world. To these ends, scientific theories must rely on general laws expressible in quantitative or structurally discrete terms. Neoclassical economics offers the appearance of a science, given its explanatory models founded on mathematical propositions. But appearance is not necessarily reality. Epistemological concerns have been raised about the predictive accuracy of neoclassical theories and the fact that some theorists have argued that the realism of a theory's assumptions is not important in determining its scientific content (Friedman 1953). This would be acceptable on instrumentalist grounds if the predictions of the theory in question were actually borne out. But as mentioned above, the predictive record of neoclassical theories have not been encouraging. It seems rather that neoclassical economics as any discipline dealing theoretically with human behaviour is necessarily founded on value judgments in the service of some chosen orientation. In this connection, neoclassical economics serves as the evaluative basis for neoliberal market economics as it presents itself as being universally valid on essentially scientific grounds. But it must be recognised that the economic behaviour of humans on strictly empirical grounds reduces to aspects of sociology or anthropology reflective of the cultural values invoked by them as they barter and exchange items among themselves. For example, the culturally derived exchange habits of some society might eschew the principle of interest altogether, while the whole dynamic of neoclassical market economics is founded on the idea that 'interest' is its major catalyst. In this regard, let us view neoclassical economics not as a universal science, but rather as a research anthropological paradigm reflective of the historical cultures of the societies of Western Europe. This is an important constraint for those who would wish to employ this particular paradigm in the service of development for contemporary Africa. For example, the relatively large amounts of debt owed by the nations of Africa to the IMF and Western banks are based on the extending of credit based on initial considerations of interest. What this means, of course, is that the fundamental principle of neoclassical economics is that of self interest.

## Key Applications of Neoclassical Economic Theory

It is instructive to discuss at this point some of the key theoretical models within the context of development theory and to demonstrate their relative ineffectiveness with regard to general economic development. Following the work of J.M. Keynes, who argued that an economy can achieve equilibrium at much less than full employment of labour resources, the theoretical question became: What role should government play in stimulating economic growth so that the maximum amount of labour resources be employed? The research programme that developed around Keynes's arguments became known as Keynesian economics. Given that the perceived problem with underdeveloped economies was that of lack of adequate and sustained growth, attempts were made by Western theorists to formulate the problem and solution in theoretical terms. In this regard, two neoclassical models became popular: 1) the Harrod-Domar (H-D) Model and the Solow Growth Model; and 2) the Lewis Growth Model.

In brief, given the assumption of general production functions Y=F(Capital, Labour, Technological Knowledge…), the Harrod-Domar model (G=s/C) claimed that the growth rate was a function of the relationship between the rate of savings and the Capital-Output ratio. This model was then tuned to the important issue of the warranted (necessary rate for constant growth) rate of growth and actual rates of growth. But the observed dynamics of the neoclassical economy showed that there were serious concerns about the accuracy of Keynes's famous Savings = Investment recipe for growth. Market economies did not grow in strict linear fashion but rather along quasi-sinusoidal lines because of the fact that dynamic growth was periodically compromised by over-capacity and under-capacity of labour resources. Later modifications to this model were attempted by Robert Solow who formulated what became known as the Solow Growth Model (Solow 1970). Solow focused on the issue of technology and argued that changing technologies was a better guarantor of constant growth than was suggested by the H-D model.

The problematic with these growth models is that they were more suited to the industrialised world than those areas where there was a constant shortage of capital whose provenance was not indigenous. With regard to the developing world, the established growth models had little relevance except maybe to demonstrate that growth was maximally an affair of macroeconomic policies. Similar criticisms could be leveled against the Lewis model that argued that the best path to growth was the utilisation of surplus rural labour in the industrialising urban sectors which would in turn be the recipient of capital inputs from the industrialised world. The empirical evidence shows that this two sector growth model proved not to be viable. The reason is that the industrialised world was not prepared to help in creating competitors from areas that traditionally produced cheap agricultural goods.

## Dependency Theory

While neoclassical economic theory produced unworkable models of economic development, its intellectual nemesis, Marxism, sought to approach the problem of development from its theory of exploitation. Dependency theory, in general, explains development as being constrained by the unequal exchange relationships that exist between the nations that are developed and those that are viewed as developing. The literature on dependency theory is substantial, so it would be preferable to list just the more important figures. Prebish (1950), Baran (1957), Frank (1966), Amin (1974), et al. are some of the better known theorists. But it should be pointed out that the issue of dependency in its broadest sense of political economy and sociology was better explicated by theorists such as Nkrumah (1965) and Fanon (1968), speaking for the African continent. What is instructive about dependency theory is that it points out that development is virtually impossible, given present existing structural relations between the industrialised nations and their ex-colonies. While neoclassical theory is shorn of all historical and sociological context, dependency theory is founded on the historical and sociological dynamic that determines the existing structural relationships between the industrialised and the non-industrialised.

The general theme is that of unequal exchange with the industrialised nations deriving surpluses from their relationships with the non-industrialised. It points out the role of the IMF, World Bank, weak currencies and the political pressures employed to maintain the unequal relationships. It is in this context that political economy is a better analytical tool than neoclassical economics. Dependency theorists argue, in general, that the solution to the problem would derive from revolutionary activity with workers in the vanguard with the ultimate goal being some version of socialism. Yet, this has not yet been tried in the vast areas of economic underdevelopment. The only possible exceptions are China and Vietnam. Cuba has made some progress, but its political situation is problematic. Furthermore, it has been unable to move from a predominantly agricultural society to one of some industrial and technological development. Yet, it must be noted that its research and production in pharmaceuticals have been impressive. The neoclassical market theorists point, on the other hand, to the East Asian nations of Taiwan, South Korea, Singapore and Malaysia as nations that have demonstrated movement towards industrialisation. But this development took place only because of great amounts of capital from the United States coordinating with investments in human capital. But these large inputs of capital were injected by the West for purely political reasons in its conflict with the communist nations, especially the Soviet Union and China. The problem of development is not a difficult problem to explain. The question is, From where would the instruments to transform the existing situation come? In the final analysis, things reduce to a question of ethics: Would capital be forthcoming on grounds of a 'win-win' situation for all, or would it be forthcoming only in terms of self-interest for those who provide it? If history should serve as precedent, then Africa is obliged to provide its own capital in whatever creative ways it can.

In response to this approach based on hard realism, one may point to the touted successes of the microfinancing of small enterprises by the Grameen bank of Bangladesh as a potential escape from the impasses of development theory in practice. But the results here are too negligible, even though useful. Such efforts do not really deal with key structural problems such as unequal exchange and the actual political economy of underdevelopment. The World Bank can easily finance with positive and genuine monitoring, hundreds of projects requiring minimal amounts of capital. But it does not do so because the providers of international capital make economic decisions purely according to principles of political *realpolitik* and zero-sum game considerations. That is why development in the case of Africa must ultimately be based on the indigenous formulation and analysis of bold and innovative paradigms.

## Post-Structuralism and Developmentalism

While dependency theory is essentially the theoretical enterprise of political economists of the non-industrialised world, the development issue in the West itself has developed a kind of trendy aura. Development has now been transformed into 'sustainable growth and development' and the need to 'reduce poverty' in the so-called 'Third World' nations. Post-structuralism is the most convenient label for this approach to development, given that it is based on fluid and inchoate structural analysis. In this regard, there is room not only for large projects but for mini-projects administered by the proliferation of what are called NGOs. But in general, this approach is reformist. It does not seek radical transformations in the relationship between the industrialised world and the non-industrialised world. Poststructuralism may be seen as just variations on the Peace Corps theme: small scale volunteer work for those who seek the 'exotic' while they prepare for something else to do when they return to their respective metropolises. In sum, this modernist version of development transports the latest fads from the industrialised world to the developing world, hence, its tendency to focus on issues piece-meal such as gender rights, environmental and ecological concerns, food security and the ever increasingly popular 'sustainable development' (Pieterse 2001). This is not to deny the importance of such issues, but implicit in these new approaches is the idea that genuine development that would lead to an Africa on par technologically with the West is not something they consider seriously.

Developmentalism is merely the name used by those who accept poststructuralist discourse and seek to counter the traditional view of development as leading to 'progress' and 'modernism'. In this regard, developmentalism is seen as embodying a 'hegemonic discourse' that would include all strands in the critique of the idea of development itself. But some authors argue that there is a progressive side to developmentalism that includes theories that argue for 'different trajectories of development of dependent societies(as with dependency theory) and advocate different logics of development for different societies(as with democratic Marxism)' with the purported goal of empowering the poor(Peet 1999:155). Thus, for Peet, it would be problematic to lump this approach with 'neoclassical economics, modernisation theory, and World Bank policies'(Peet 1999:155). In this regard, individuals who are engaged in radical practice are much more important than 'poststructural philosophers who meet in the salons of Paris...' (Peet 1999:155). It is in this context that one must understand the post-developmentalist theories that deal with 'gender and development', 'critical modernism', 'radical democracy', and 'alternative development'. Admittedly the ideas expressed in these theories may be useful, but there is an evident problematic. None of these theories emanate from the areas where development is needed most. Thus, the idea of hegemonic discourse remains. For genuine development to take place, the presumed subaltern must have the principal voice.

## Development and Real Constraints

Despite the plethora of theories and disquisitions on the question of development in Africa, there are real constraints that militate against easy solutions. The post-colonial legacy of Africa is one in which the continent is truncated into a large number of relatively small states which do not have effective agency to operate politically or economically in the world. The Washington Consensus is naturally at loggerheads with the theoretical telos of the African Union in the image of Kwame Nkrumah. The real implementation of a Pan-African telos is thwarted first of all by mentalities frozen in colonial time as the continued existence of 'francophonie' and 'Commonwealth' suggest. But there is an ongoing dynamic in which minds and resources are struggled over and competed for. Frantz Fanon explicated the African colonial and post-colonial ethos and dynamic, Cheikh Anta Diop re-established the African past according to its own internal logic while Kwame Nkrumah formulated the general outline for Africa's historical telos. Thus, an adequate theory of African development exists, but constraints against implementation are maintained both internally and externally. The draconian dictates from the West's economic taskmasters in the form of the IMF and World Bank constitute the external constraints. The internal constraints are maintained by Africa's intellectually catatonic and psychologically ahistorical neocolonial classes, creatures all of metropolitan post-colonial culture.

It is the mental structures created in post-colonial time that prevent Africa's neocolonial classes from recognising, for example, that the principles of economic transactions that govern international economics are merely normative rules reflective of Western culture. Critical analysis would make it evident that Western bank credit is created out of thin air and that the so-called 'hard currencies' of the West are made of the same paper that African currencies are made of. There seems to be a reluctance to believe that an intra-African currency could be created in exactly the same way that the European Union created the euro. In their intellectually catatonic state, Africa's neocolonial classes merely sit back and await the next bit of 'advice' from the West which they then hasten to implement in uncritical fashion.

## Conclusion

The history of the world could be seen as one in which humans *by their very nature* have sought to increase their freedoms by improving on their understanding and control of the forces of nature for their own ends. These attempts at understanding and control were always effected by appeal to the dual epistemologies of metaphysics and empirical technology. And instead of being beholden to nature and its caprices, humans have constantly and persistently sought to increase their agencies, hence, their freedoms by understanding how nature actually works. This understanding of nature has always been the major task of metaphysics (the transcendental) in its various forms and what we now call empirical science (limited to the sensory world). But humans have also sought to increase their freedoms within their social structures over time, *pari passu*, as they expressed their increasing freedoms in their explorations of nature. This could be what is meant by 'development'. In this regard, Africa has been at the forefront of this human journey for most of human history. Only in the last 2,000 years or so out of a history of at least 150,000 years have individuals who migrated to other parts of the globe been able to claim knowledge and technological ascendance over the African continent. But even so, the foundations of such knowledge derive ultimately from Africa.

In this paper, the issue of development was approached from a somewhat different position. The normal position is that not only is Africa perpetually 'developing', but also that it was never developed and that the best advice could come only from the theoreticians of those societies deemed as 'developed'. It was shown, however, that historically, Africa was for a long period of time the most developed area of the globe and that the arguments of underdevelopment apply to a relatively recent period. It was also pointed out that an Africa at the vanguard of development would not resemble the technologically advanced nations of the West in terms of civil society, government and state structure. The reason is that the political histories of Africa's societies are different from those of Europe. But in addition to the main positions taken in this essay, an Africa in the vanguard of development would be one structured along Pan-African lines with federal states linked together with free and untrammeled trade and travel. The general point is that development in Africa would entail maximal amounts of African agency on parity with other continental groupings. Thus, Africa's languages, currencies, and status in international organisations would be on par with those of the other continents and areas. This specific configuration of Africa is usually overlooked by most theorists. For such theorists, the future of Africa is to be determined by the shallow ministrations of 'experts' and NGO cohorts of Western origin. It is evident therefore that the issue of development for Africa should be primarily the responsibility of Africa's theoreticians. It is incumbent on them that they be constantly aware of Africa's technological, sociological and economic history. They should also be vigilant epistemologists in their appraisals of the myriad theories of development that emanate continuously from the think tanks of the West.

# 8

# Relevant Education for African Development: Some Epistemological Considerations

## Francis B. Nyamnjoh

### Introduction

Development for Africa is a theme fraught with a multiplicity of Western-generated ideas, models and research paradigms, all with the purported goal of 'alleviating poverty'. This discourse is carried on mainly by economists and other social scientists who limit the question of development to the problematic of achieving economic growth within the context of neo-liberal economic principles. Notwithstanding the fact that there are now novel paradigms of development that search for solutions under the theoretical rubric of 'alternative development', the problem is rarely studied in a holistic manner.

One of the important aspects of economic growth and development is investment in human capital, or more simply put, investment in education. But education is not just the inculcation of facts as knowledge, but a set of values that in turn appraise the knowledge being acquired. When the values are not appropriate for progress, the knowledge acquired is rendered irrelevant and becomes merely cosmetic. In this chapter, I propose to show how the values acquired during the colonial era that teach the superiority of the West have set the tone for the imbibing of knowledge. The obvious result is that the knowledge, needed for African development is rendered irrelevant by a dysfunctional set of values. In this regard, development in Africa is greatly hindered and retarded. Hence, the need for Africa to revisit the dominant epistemological underpinnings of Western education, that are not always sensitive to the predicaments and expectations of ordinary Africans.

### Dominant and Dormant Epistemologies in Africa

In a recent publication, I raised the issue of the problematic nature of the dominant Western epistemological export to Africa in connection with witchcraft and the occult (cf. Nyamnjoh 2001). The export reduces science to the nineteenth and twentieth centuries' preoccupation with theories of *what* the universe is, much to the detriment of theories of *why* the universe is. By rendering science 'too technical and mathematical', this epistemology has made it difficult for those interested in questions of *why* to keep pace with developments in scientific theories (cf. Hawking 1990:171–175), and increased the risk of branding as 'intellectual imposture' the appropriation of scientific concepts by philosophers and other 'non-scientists' (cf. Sokal and Bricmont 1998). Such a narrow view of science has tended to separate the universe into the physical and the metaphysical or the religious, and to ignore the fact that people are ordinarily 'not content to see events as unconnected and inexplicable'. In other words, this epistemology has little room for popular cravings to understand 'the underlying order in the world' (cf. Hawking 1990:1–13). Although science has since moved beyond this limited version to contemplate 'the big bang and black holes', and 'a quantum theory of gravity' (cf. Hawking 1990), its narrow and hegemonic 'certainties' of the nineteenth and twentieth centuries continue to make waves and to inform the social sciences, attitudes, policies and relations in general, especially between the West and the rest.

I have argued that this Western epistemological export has serious weaknesses, especially when compared with the popular and more traditional epistemologies of the African continent. It tends to limit reality to appearances, which it then seeks to justify (without explaining) with meta-narratives claiming objectivity and a more epistemologically secure truth status. Under this kind of epistemology, reality is presented as anything whose existence has, or can be, established in a rational, objective manner, with universal laws operating only in perceived space and time. In the social sciences, such a perspective has resulted in an insensitive pursuit of a *physique sociale*, informed almost exclusively by what the mind (Reason) and/or the hierarchy of senses (sight, taste, touch, sound, smell) tell us about society and social relationships. The science inspired by such an epistemology has tended to celebrate dichotomies, dualisms, teleologies and analogies, dismissing anything that does not make sense in Cartesian or behaviourist terms, confining to religion and metaphysics what it cannot explain and disqualifying as non-scientific more inclusive epistemologies. The world is perceived and presented as dichotomous: there is the real and the unreal. The real is the rational, the natural, the physical and the scientific; the unreal is the irrational, the supernatural, the religious, the metaphysical and the subjective. This epistemology's logic is simple: if truth is one and universal, then there should be a one best way of attaining it; and those who have been there before are the best guides of the rest still in search of truth. This evokes the image of a Jacob's ladder to Heaven, where those highest up the rungs are best placed to tell everyone else what paradise is or could be. We may all be blind and animated by partial theories – like 'the six blind men and the elephant', but some are more likely to claim authority and to silence others about the nature of the universe and the underlying order of things, thanks to the hierarchy of blindness made explicit in this epistemology.

This dominant epistemology has engendered theories and practices of social engineering capable of justifying without explanation almost everything, from colonialism to neoliberalism, through racism and imperialism. Whole societies, countries and regions have been categorised, depending on how these 'others' were perceived in relation to Western Cartesian rationalism and empiricism. The epistemology has resulted in disciplines and fields of studies that have sacrificed morality, humanity and the social on the altar of a false objectivity. In other words, it has allowed the insensitivities of power and comfort to assume the moral high ground, dictating to the marginalised and the disabled, and preaching salvation for individuals and groups who repent from 'retrogressive' attitudes, cultures and practices. As an epistemology that claims the status of a solution, there is little room for introspection or self-scrutiny, since countervailing forces are invariably to blame for failure. The assumption is made here that such messianic qualities have imbued disciples of this epistemology with an attitude of arrogance, superiority and intolerance towards *creative* difference and appropriation. The zeal in them to convert creative difference has not excluded violence as an option, for the epistemology from which they draw knows neither compromise nor negotiation, nor conviviality. To paraphrase Okot p'Bitek, the ways of your ancestors may be good and solid with roots that reach deep into the soil, their customs neither hollow, nor thin, nor easily breakable or blown away by the winds; but this does not deter the epistemology and its disciples from inviting you to despise these ancestral customs and world view, in favour of foreign customs you may not even understand or admire (p'Bitek 1989:19). Because this epistemology is closely entangled with ideology and hegemony, it leaves little room for critical thinking, even as it celebrates Cartesian rationalism. The result, quite paradoxically, is an emphasis on doing rather than thinking, and all attempts at serious questioning are rationalised away. This is well captured by Okot p'Bitek in the following excerpt from his *Song of Lawino*:

My Husband

Has read at Makerere University.

He has read deeply and widely,

But if you ask him a question

He says

You are insulting him;

He opens up with a quarrel

He begins to look down upon you

Saying

You ask questions

That are a waste of time!

He says

My questions are silly questions,
Typical questions from village girls.
Questions of uneducated people,
Useless questions from untutored minds.
My husband says
I have a tiny little brain
And it is not trained,
I cannot see things intelligently,
I cannot see things sharply.

He says
Even if he tried
To answer my questions
I would not understand
What he was saying
Because the language he speaks
Is different from mine
So that even if he
Spoke to me in Acoli
I would still need an interpreter.

My husband says
Some of the answers
Cannot be given in Acoli
Which is a primitive language
And is not rich enough
To express his deep wisdom.
He says the Acoli language
Has very few words
It is not like the white man's language
Which is rich and very beautiful
A Language fitted for discussing deep thoughts.

Ocol says
He has no time to waste
Discussing things with a thing like me
Who has not been to school.

> He says
> A university man
> Can only have useful talk
> With another university man or woman.
> And that it is funny,
> That he should stoop so low
> Even to listen
> To my questions (p'Bitek 1989:65-66).

Popular epistemologies in Africa are different. They create room for *why* questions, and for 'magical interpretations' where there are no obvious explanations to 'material realities' (cf. Moore and Sanders 2001). To them, reality is more than meets the eye; it is larger than logic. Far from subscribing to the rigid dichotomies of the dominant epistemological import from the West, the popular epistemologies of Africa build bridges between the so-called natural and supernatural, physical and metaphysical, rational and irrational, objective and subjective, scientific and superstitious, visible and invisible, real and unreal, explainable and inexplicable; making it impossible for anything to be one without also being the other. They constitute an epistemological order where the sense of *sight* and *physical evidence* has not assumed the same centrality, dominance or dictatorship evident in the Western export's 'hierarchies of perceptual faculties' (van Dijk and Pels 1996: 248-251). It has equal space for all the senses, just as it does for the visible and the invisible, the physical and metaphysical. The real is not only what is observable or what makes cognitive sense; it is also the invisible, the emotional, the sentimental or the inexplicable (Okri 1991). In this epistemological order, emphasis is on the whole, and truth is negotiated, something consensual, not the result of artificial disqualification, dismemberment, atomisation or mutilation by a science of exclusion.

In this popular system of knowledge, the opposite or complement of presence is not necessarily absence, but invisibility. Thus, as Mbembe (1997) argues, understanding the visible is hardly complete without investigating the invisible. We misunderstand the world if we 'consider the obverse and the reverse of the world as two opposite sides, with the former partaking of a 'being there' (*real presence*) and the latter as 'being elsewhere' or a 'non-being' (*irremediable absence*) or, worse, of the order of unreality' (Mbembe 1997:152). The obverse and its reverse are also linked by similarities which do not make them mere copies of each other, but which unite and at the same time distinguish themselves according to the African 'principle of *simultaneous multiplicities*' (Mbembe 1997:152). In others words, far from merely being the other side, the mask or substitute, of the visible, the invisible is in the visible, and vice versa, 'not as a matter of artifice, but as *one and the same* and as external reality simultaneously—or as the image of the thing and the imagined thing at the same time' (Mbembe 1997:152). The questions here, of course, are, What role could Africa's less restrictive epistemologies play in the issue of development, and

Has not the wholesale import of the modern West's epistemology so ensnared the dominant class elements of African society that they treat it as if it were some kind of invincible magic? Nowhere is this more evident than in the African attitudes to the educational systems and values of the West that exist in the European world and are transplanted directly onto African soil.

## Education as Cultural Violence in Africa

The Western epistemological export, translated into educational systems and curricula, takes the form of science as ideology and hegemony. Under it, education in Africa and/or for Africans is like a pilgrimage to the Kilimanjaro of Western intellectual ideals, but also the tortuous route to Calvary for alternative ways of life (cf. p'Bitek 1989; Ngugi wa Thiong'o 1986; Mazrui 1986, 2001; Mamdani 1990, 1993; Copans 1990; Rwomire 1992; van Rinsum 2001). The value of education in Africa is best understood in comparison with the soft currencies of the continent. Just as even the most stable of these currencies are pecked and used to taking nosedives in relation to the hard currencies of the West over the years, so has the value of education on the continent. And just as African presidents prefer to beg and bank in foreign currencies – ignoring even banknotes that bear their own faces and stamp of omnipotence, so is their preference for the Western intellectual and expert over locally produced expertise. Sometimes with justifying rhetoric on the need to be competitive internationally, the practice since independence has been to model education in Africa after educational institutions in the West, with each country drawing from the institutions of the immediate past coloniser, and/or from the USA (Crossman and Devisch 1999:20–23; Mazrui 2001:39–45). The elite have, 'often in unabashed imitativeness' and with little attempt at domestication, sought to reproduce, even without the finances to sustain, the Oxfords, Cambridges, Harvards, Stanfords and Sorbonnes of England, the USA and France (cf. Mazrui 2001:39–8). Some, like the late Presidents Banda of Malawi, and Houphouet-Boigny of Côte d'Ivoire, have sometimes carried this craving to ridiculous proportions, seeking to be identified exclusively by europhilia in education and consumption. Education in Africa has been, and mostly remains, a journey fuelled by an exogenously induced and internalised sense of inadequacy in Africans, and endowed with the mission of devaluation or annihilation of African creativity, agency and value systems. Such 'cultural estrangement' has served to reinforce in the Africans self-devaluation and self-hatred and a profound sense of inferiority that in turn compels them to 'lighten their darkness' both physically and metaphysically for Western gratification (Fanon 1967:169). Nyang has captured this predicament as 'a pathological case of xenophilia', whereby Africans are brought to value things western 'not for their efficacy but simply because of their foreignness' (Nyang 1994:434), and persuaded to consume to death their creativity and dignity, their very own humanity (cf. Soyinka 1994).

This process of culturally uprooting Africans, has been achieved often through literally uprooting children of the well-off from their communities and nurturing them in boarding schools, 'almost like potted plants in green houses' (Mamdani 1990:3). '*The European Other* haunts the *African Self* from a young age in a post-colonial school' (Mazrui 2001:41). Okot p'Bitek captures this reality eloquently through Lawino, protagonist in his *Song of Lawino*, who laments the fate of young men who have lost their manhood in classrooms where 'their testicles were smashed with large books!' Even her husband, rendered blind by the libraries of white men, has lost his dignity and authority by behaving 'like a dog of the white man', lying by the door to 'keep guard while waiting for left-overs' from the master's table. Her husband has lost his 'fire' and bull-like prowess, and has succumbed to living on borrowed food, wearing borrowed clothes, and using his ideas, actions and behaviour 'to please somebody else'. He may have read extensively and deeply and can challenge the white men in his knowledge of their books and their ancestors of the intellect, but to Lawino, this has come at a great price: '…the reading has killed my man, in the ways of his people. He has become a stump. He abuses all things Acoli, he says the ways of black people are black' (p'Bitek 1989:91-96).

Examples abound of African countries where a foreign visitor in the heart of the 'African jungle' suddenly finds him/herself surrounded by a group of Latin speaking lads and lasses, who are ready to challenge his/her 'Westernness' with classical knowledge of Aristotle, Caesar, Plato, Shakespeare and other symbols of Western intellectual and cultural traditions. These mini-Etons (Sorbonnes, Oxfords, Cambridges, Harvards, Stanfords) in the bush are set up by europhiles eager to stay competitive internationally or simply to demonstrate excellence in the knowledge systems of the West, by measuring up. They spend a sizable portion of the enfeebled national budgets on tutors imported from the West and paid European rates, to instruct the children of the well-off on how to excel in what is often irrelevant locally. In the long run, neither the children of the lowly and poor, who in effect cannot afford the same chance to excel in this type of xenophilia, nor the children of the well-off schooled in such appetites, are in a position to contribute towards solving Africa's pressing problems in a way meaningful to the bulk of the population. The latter, having spent all their time learning to do what they do not need, and the former, having been relegated to pose as custodians of dying traditions which the elite shun, and which at best, are thought of only as a means of 'base' entertainment by the urban-centred elite and their foreign guests and tourists. If and when there is any attempt at domestication, this is hardly pushed beyond the point where students are force-fed by state-appointed pro-establishment professors and administrators-doctored versions of culture and history celebrating the heroic feats of so-called *founding fathers* and/or the dominant groupings of their 'nation-states'.

From independence to date, 'African universities have been successful in Africanising their personnel but not their curricula or pedagogical structures to any real extent' (Crossman and Devisch 1999:11). The assumption has been that because one *is* or *appears* African, one is necessarily going to be critical of Western intellectual traditions and rituals in one's teaching and research, and would offer a menu more sensitive to local realities than what is served in Western academic institutions. But this is far from being the case, as even the hundreds of universities created after independence have stayed 'triumphantly universalistic and uncompromisingly foreign' to local cultures, populations and predicaments (cf. Mamdani 1993:11–15). There has been little effort at domestication or 'an epistemological shift' informed by the 'awareness that the site – or community-specific knowledges tie in with the grammatical and lexical structures of a given language, local cosmologies and worldviews' that 'must be allowed to enter into a meaningful dialogue with the universalistic stance and some of the essentialist fixities of modern science' (Devisch 2002:7). The reality is a double alienation, first by ill-adapted academic traditions internalised through an education of extraversion, and second by repressive state structures.

A good case in point of excellence at irrelevance in education is provided by the late Kamuzu Banda's Malawi. In a BBC television documentary broadcast at 9.30 pm, Tuesday, September 8, 1987, Malawi was singled out as an example of a country which had established a school that resembled Eton of England. The school, named Kamuzu Academy, was situated in the Kasungu District in the Central Region of Malawi, President Banda's home area. This school, nicknamed by some critics 'Eton of the Bush', was built in 1981, and imported all its education equipment from the UK and South Africa. When the school was short of chemicals or other equipment, those concerned had to drive for at least five hundred miles to acquire new ones. The school had cost no less than 15 million British pounds to build, and needed not less than 1 million pounds a year to run. The students, whose table manners would put many a working class Briton to shame, were made to believe that no one is truly educated unless s/he knows something about the ancient world, which should not be mistaken to mean the ancestral world of the African (pregnant with primitive savagery and to be treated with disdain), but the world of Julius Caesar, Aristotle, Plato, Socrates and other founding fathers of Western intellectual traditions.

If ancestors are supposed to lay the path for posterity, inviting Africans to forget their ancestors was an invitation for them to be born again and socialised afresh, in the image of the West, using Western-type academic institutions and rituals of ancestral worship. This renewal, in tune with Western values and institutions is achieved, by the West

> *promoting* beliefs and values congenial to [its dominance]; *naturalizing* and *universalizing* such beliefs so as to render them self-evident and apparently inevitable; *denigrating* ideas which might challenge it; *excluding* rival forms of thought, perhaps by some unspoken but systematic logic; and *obscuring* social reality in ways convenient to itself (Eagleton 1991:5-6, original emphasis).

Only through such strategies of legitimating could the West 'wipe the blackboard clean' by turning its African students into slaves of Western definitions (cf. van Rinsum 2001). As Eagleton argues, since nobody is ever '*wholly* mystified' or 'a complete dupe', an ideology can only succeed if those it characterises as inferior actually learn to be inferior. 'It is not enough for a woman or colonial subject to be defined as a lower form of life. They must be actively *taught* this definition, and some of them prove to be brilliant graduates in this process' (Eagleton 1991:xv, original emphasis).

All teachers in Kamuzu Academy were white, recruited directly from Britain, and, of course, paid British rates at a time when few local teachers could make ends meet with their own salaries in soft local currencies. As Mazrui noted of the entire continent a year before the BBC documentary was broadcast, commitment and the sense of vocation were dwindling among teachers in Africa, who were 'often underpaid and in some countries they were not paid at all for months on end', and who were sometimes forced 'to look for moonlighting opportunities to give them an additional livelihood' (Mazrui 1986:204). Meanwhile, in Malawi, imported teachers on three-year contracts lived in European-style bungalows with salaries in hard currencies. Little has changed for good, much for worse. Almost everywhere, the consultancy syndrome has triumphed over traditional academic values such as excellence in teaching, research and publication. University professors who have failed to migrate, are forced to postpone academic excellence to a later date. 'They would rather not be wasting their time publishing and perishing', and even the most inspiring of them 'are working under conditions that stymie their creativity and fail to challenge their students' (Onyejekwe 1993:3).

English was and still is the main language of instruction at the Kamuzu Academy. Not only was Chichewa, the national language, not taught, students were forbidden to speak it in the Academy. Writing about Kenya, Ngugi wa Thiong'o shows just how widespread this practice was. The postcolonial instructors who inherited condescending English attitudes to local languages, continued 'to ban African languages in schools and to elevate English as the medium of instruction from primary to secondary stages', and did not hesitate to mete out corporal punishment to and extort fines from students 'caught speaking their mother tongues' (Ngugi wa Thiong'o 1997:620). Invited to address the OAU at Addis Ababa, Ali Mazrui insisted on doing so in Kishwahili, but there was neither translator nor switch button envisaged for one of Africa's most widely spoken languages. 'You needed to see how the Heads of States were bewildered, but I had passed my message across' (Mazrui 1986 BBC *The Africans* series). This practice gave English and other Western languages status by associating them with civilisation and enlightenment, and made African languages inferior in the eyes of the African students born into these languages. Unlike Somalia, Ethiopia, Tanzania, Kenya and Botswana, many an African country has yet to demonstrate in principle and practice that literacy, even at primary school level, does not necessarily mean knowing how to read and write a Western language. Only a few African countries have bothered to adopt policies that encourage education in African languages, and even this limited number have tended to confine the importance of local languages to primary and secondary school education, thereby accentuating the remoteness and irrelevance of universities to the bulk of the population. With perhaps the exception of Tanzania, there is hardly a single sub-Saharan African university that 'offers a full diploma programme with an African language as principal medium of instruction' (cf. Crossman and Devisch 1999:7).

At Kamuzu Academy, where the neo-Etonians were trained to recite Shakespeare and glorify the classic philosophers of the West, the library that housed the classics was deliberately designed in the image of the Library of Congress in the USA. There was Western influence everywhere; an influence so successful that in a debate about whether or not Western influence corrupts, sixty-seven students 'felt' that it did not, while only fifty-five students 'felt' it did. Perhaps by the time they had imbibed an awful lot of Latin, Classical Music, Western History, Literature and Etiquette, and consumed enough McDonaldised entertainment television, not as many as one of them would 'feel' any longer that Western influence corrupts. As the presenter of the BBC documentary observed, the students knew more about Europe than they did of Malawi, so much so that once in a while, the teachers had to carry out field trips with the students 'partly to bring their own country home to them'. Parents, he went on, sacrificed too much for their children to acquire values and an education, which were alien to their cultures of origin. This, of course, is hardly news to other Africans who have drunk from the well of 'Modern Education' in similarly Western-styled institutions modelled on the colonial educational system with 'its heavy literary and non-technical emphasis' (cf. Mazrui 1986:233).

There are basically two ways of journeying to the West. One can undertake the journey physically or one can do so psychologically with facilitation from education and the media. Either way, one still succeeds in imbibing Western influences. Western-style training at Kamuzu Academy-type institutions is not just to compensate for the real West where these students have not been yet. It is seen as preparing them for Europe and North America, where they ultimately have or yearn to go to make use of the skills they have acquired. Thus, if at the Kamuzu Academy they were being taught all about Sunday barbecues, swimming pools, table etiquette, the classics, suits, ties, horse riding and straw hats (or how to be the complete gentleman or lady *à l'anglaise*), this was to purge them of that presumed backwardness that has qualified Africa to be termed 'the Dark Continent' par excellence, and Africans as people desperately in need of salvation from a *mission civilisatrice* (cf. Magubane 2004; Schipper 1990a&b). It is hard to imagine African students who have gone through all these stages of Westernisation, returning home to bear the misery and poverty of un- or under-employment with a stiff upper lip. Brain drain has been an inevitable consequence. As Mamdani observes, in its craving for centres of learning and research of international standing, Africa has produced researchers and educators with 'little capacity to work in surrounding communities but who could move to any institution in any industrialised country, and serve any privileged community around the globe with comparative ease'. The failure by the educational system in Africa to contextualise standards and excellence to the needs and conditions of Africans has resulted in an intelligentsia with little stamina for the very process of development whose vanguard they claim to be (Mamdani 1993:15). A McDonaldised educational system is too standardised, uniformised and detached to be in tune with the predicaments of ordinary and marginal Africans thirsty and hungry for recognition, representation and upliftment.

The quest for Western academic symbols of credentialism – sometimes termed *diplomania* (cf. Robinson 1981:176–192) – and respect for qualifications obtained abroad have characterised postcolonial Africa. Africans are still very much dependent on ill-adapted curricula, sources and types of knowledge that alienate and enslave, all in the name of modernity. Sometimes it does not matter whether or not school libraries are empty, since a full library may well be of little real relevance to the pressing problems and specificities of the continent, in terms of perspectives and contents. Education for Africans has, in the main, tended to be an exercise in self-evacuation and the devaluation of all that took pre-colonial generations, wisdom, cultural creativity and sweat to edify. The fact that Africans have placed and continue to place a very high premium on getting educated in the West has only compounded the problem.

In South Africa for example, despite numerous local universities and a relatively long history of university education, a doctorate from Britain is still valued higher than anything obtained locally. Like other Africans, South Africans instinctively ask one another or others: 'Where did you do your degree?', and depending on the university you name, you could be treated as a superior, an equal or an inferior by a fellow academic. If the doctorate holder is credited with the capacity to devalue those without PhDs ('Pull him Down' syndrome), PhD holders who graduate from Western universities are considered to be less 'Phenomenally Dumb' than those from local universities whose ignorance, purportedly, 'Piles higher and Deeper'. These amusing but telling puns tell the story. Some Africans would rather graduate from Oxford, Harvard or Sorbonne for example, even if this means changing their specialisations to accommodate the limited academic menu offered in these heavyweight Western universities. Africans continue to flood Europe and North America to research aspects of their own countries which normally are best studied back home in Africa, mostly for the prestige and status that studying abroad brings. Parents continue to send their children to the West for education, with the conviction that a degree even from a commercialised and second-rate Western university is worth a lot more opportunities than one from a purportedly top university in Africa.

## Epistemological Consequences of Irrelevant Education

The extraverted nature of African education in general has favoured the Western knowledge industry tremendously. It has allowed Western intellectual traditions and practitioners to write themselves into the past, present and future of Africa as civilisers, saviours, initiators, mentors, arbiters (Fonlon 1967; Chinweizu 1987; Mudimbe 1988; Schipper 1990a & b; Ngugi wa Thiong'o 1977; J. and J. Comaroff 1997a; Crossman and Devisch 1999; Mbembe 2000a:7–40; 2001:1–23; Magubane 2004). Europe and North America have for decades dominated the rest of the world with its academic products. Focusing on the social sciences, Frederick Gareau, an American sociologist of knowledge, has noted that the West has been consistently more advanced and expansionist than the underdeveloped and dependent regions of the world. In the late 1980s, he remarked that American social science, in its 'unrelenting one-way traffic', was able to penetrate countries with cultures as different from its own as those of France, Canada, India, Japan and the Republic of Korea (Gareau 1987: 599). The African continent should be included in his list. This penetration has given American social science a 'privileged position' with 'a very favourable export balance of communications' or 'talking without listening'. Not only is there little importation, American social scientists ensure that 'incoming messages are in accord with American socio-cultural norms'. This, Gareau observed, 'betrays an ethnocentric, inward-looking fixation', with little preference for anything foreign: 'if foreign, a preference for the Anglo-Saxon world; little concern for Continental Europe, and indifference or hostility towards the Second and the Third Worlds' (Gareau 1987:598–9).

Focusing on the discipline of International Relations, and writing ten years later, Kim Richard Nossal makes exactly the same observations. Nossal notes that text books in this area 'portray the world to their readers from a uniquely *American* point of view: they are reviewed by Americans; the sources they cite are American; the examples are American; the theory is American; the experience is American; the focus is American; and in ... [some cases], the voice is also explicitly American' (Nossal 1998:12). This makes it extremely difficult for thinking critical of American assumptions or (mis)representations of the rest of the world finding suffrage in mainstream American academic circles or in other circles for that matter, given America's impressive academic export record. In this connection, perspectives sympathetic with the predicaments of Africa have suffered a great rejection rate by university curricula, reviewers for publishers, and academic peers who stick to their conceptual and methodological spots however compelling arguments to the contrary have been.

Understood in terms of the centre-periphery perspective, the favourable 'export balance' for American social science is explained by the spread of American political, economic and cultural values after World War II. Following the war, America, as a superpower, exported its cultural values, through educational aid and the social sciences. "In this way, the US exported its social science sects abroad both by training social scientists in the homeland and by sending experts abroad. The expense incurred was often borne by the United States government or by private foundations" (Gareau 1987:602). In this way, America has been able, over the years, to use its doctrine of Free Flow of Information as a 'highly effective ideological club' to promote its political, economic and cultural values by whipping 'alternative forms of social organization' into a ridiculous defensiveness (Schiller 1977). In Africa, it has managed to dwarf the cultural legacies of former colonialists from Europe, including in higher education where American nomenclature and *manière de faire* have gained prominence (cf. Mazrui 1986:247–8). The advent of the internet and its purported equalising potential for the developing world, does not seem to be achieving much in redefining unequal flows of information and cultural products between the West (epitomised by America) and Africa, the internet's significant impact notwithstanding (cf. Nyamnjoh 1999; Olorunnisola 2000; van Binsbergen 2004).

Such dependence, in Africa, is compounded by the fact that the production of social scientific knowledge requires huge funds for university infrastructure from lecture halls to libraries, computers, laboratory equipment and research facilities, which not even the best scholars and institutions on the continent can afford easily. In terms of infrastructure and finance, well-endowed institutions like the University of Botswana and the historically white universities of South Africa are rare exceptions (cf. Zeleza and Olukoshi 2004). What this means in practice is that most of the time African scholars are forced to consume not books and research output of their own production or choice, but what their affluent and better placed counterparts in North America and Europe choose to share with them at the peripheries. Cooperation takes the form of Western universities calling the tune for the African pipers they have paid. Collaborative research has often worked in the interest of the Western partners, who, armed with assumed theoretical sophistication and economic resources, have usually reduced their African collaborators to data collectors and research assistants. And this concerns even the field of African studies, where Western Africanists appear as gatekeepers and Africans as gatecrashers (cf. Mkandawire 1997; Berger 1997; Zeleza 1997; Prah 1998). Because the leading journals and publishers are based in the West and controlled by Western academics, African debates and perspectives find it very difficult getting fair and adequate representation. When manuscripts by Africans are not simply dismissed for being 'uninformed by current debates and related literature', they may be turned down for challenging conventional wisdom and traditional assumptions about their continent (cf. Cabral et al. 1998; Mkandawire 1997). The few African academics who succeed in penetrating such gate-keeping mechanisms have often done so by making serious sacrifices in terms of the perspectives, methodologies and contextual relevance of their publications and scholarship (cf. Prah 1998:27–31). Unlike Steve Biko under Apartheid South Africa, they have had to conform rather than perish from daring to 'write what ... [they] like' (cf. Malusi and Mphumlwana 1996).

Migrating to the West often does not help, and could indeed exacerbate the problem. It has been observed that the most prominent voices in African studies today are 'diasporic intellectuals' whose 'inspiration comes perhaps more from nicely subtle readings of fashionable European theorists...than it does from...current local knowledge of the cultural politics of everyday life in the postcolonial hinterlands' (Werbner 1996:6). Little wonder that the study of Africa continues to be dominated by perspectives that privilege analogy over the historical processes that should qualify Africa as a unit of analysis in its own right (Mamdani 1996: 12-13). As has been observed, there is hardly ever a discourse on Africa for Africa's sake, and the West has often used Africa as a pretext for its own subjectivities, its self-imagination and its perversions. And no amount of new knowledge seems challenging enough to bury for good the ghost of simplistic assumptions about Africa (Mbembe

2000a:10-21, 2001:3-9; Comaroff 1997b:236-322; Schipper 1990a&b; Magubane 2004). In this sense, a Western epistemological export that marries science and ideology in subtle ways for hegemonic purposes has dominated social science in and on Africa, and coloured perceptions of Africa even by Africans. This dominant epistemological export has not always been sensitive to new perspectives that question conventional wisdom and myopic assumptions. It has stayed largely faithful to a type of social science induced and informed more by fantasies, prejudices, stereotypes, assumptions, ideologies or biases about Africa and Africans (cf. Nyamnjoh 2001). Given its remarkable ability to reproduce and market itself globally, this epistemological export has emptied academia of the power and impact of competing systems of knowledge by Africans (cf. Mudimbe 1988:x-xi). Mudimbe notes that 'Even in the most explicitly 'Afrocentric' descriptions, models of analysis explicitly or implicitly, knowingly or unknowingly, refer' to 'categories and conceptual systems which depend on a Western epistemological order', as if 'African *Weltanschauungen* and African traditional systems of thought are unthinkable and cannot be made explicit within the framework of their own rationality' or 'epistemological locus' (Mudimbe 1988:x). Although research on and in Africa has shaped the disciplines and our convictions of a supposedly universal truth (cf. Bates et al. 1993:xiii-xiv), the quest for such universality has meant the marginalisation of African alternatives. What obtains has been nothing short of an epistemological imperialism that has facilitated both a Western intellectual hegemony and the silencing of Africans even in the study of Africa (cf. Copans 1990:305-395; Zeleza 1997; Obenga 2001).

Under the dominant epistemological import from the West, most accounts of African cultures and experiences have been generated from the insensitive position of power and quest for convergence and homogeneity. Explicit or implicit in these accounts is the assumption that African societies should reproduce Western ideals and institutions regardless of feasibility or contextual differences. Few researchers of Africa, even in African universities, have questioned enough the theories, concepts and basic assumptions informed by the dominant epistemological import. The tendency has been to conform to a world conceived in the image of the West without the rest (Chinweizu 1987; Mafeje 1998:26-29). Often missing have been perspectives of the silent majorities deprived of the opportunity to tell their own stories their own ways or even to enrich defective accounts by others of their own life experiences. Correcting this entails paying more attention to the popular epistemologies from which ordinary people draw on a daily basis, and the ways they situate themselves in relationship to others within these epistemologies (cf. Nyamnjoh 2001). It also means encouraging 'a meaningful dialogue' between these epistemologies and 'modern science', both in its old and new forms (cf. Devisch 2002).

## Providing for Popular Epistemologies in the Study of Africa

The Western epistemological import has survived in the continent more because it suits the purposes of the agents of Westernisation than because of its relevance to understanding African situations. Those who run educational programmes along the

Western models they have adopted are seldom tolerant of challenge, stimulation, provocation and competing perspectives at any level. They protect their intellectual spots jealously, and are ready to deflate all 'saboteurs' and 'subversives'. They want their programmes to go on without disturbance, and would only select as lecturers or accept and sponsor only those research questions and findings that confirm their basic assumptions on scholarship and the African condition. But African universities, academics and researchers have the responsibility to challenge such unfounded assumptions based on vested interests and hidden agendas.

This is an easy task by no means, especially since scholars in Africa rely on these very agents of cultural devaluation of Africa to fund and disseminate their research. Few in positions of power and control would accept research that is critical of them, especially in a context where relations of unequal exchange with the outside world have already diminished that power and control considerably. They are more likely, therefore, to sponsor only such research that would produce results that justify their position and/or help them in their defence when challenged. To paraphrase Susan George, it matters little how many 'mistakes' mainstream researchers or theorists make or how insensitive to the predicaments of ordinary people they are, for 'protected and nurtured by those whose political objectives they support, package and condone, they have a licence to go on making them, whatever the consequences.' Through the university institutions they create and fund, the powerful are able to perpetuate their ideologies by ensuring that only people with the 'correct' ideas are recruited and/or retained to work there (George 1992:109 and 168-171). Neo-liberals and their institutions of legitimation for example, know only too well that in order to penetrate people's heads and acquire their hearts, hands and destinies, they have to make their ideas part of the daily life of people and society, by packaging, conveying and propagating these ideas through books, magazines, journals, conferences, symposia, professional associations, student organisations, university chairs, mass media and by other means (George 1997).

Yet domestication as a dialogical epistemological shift can only begin to take shape if research by Africans critical of conventional wisdom in academia is greeted with recognition rather than censorship, caricature or derision (cf. Obenga 2001:49-66). Only by creating space for African scholarship based on Africa as a unit of analysis on its own right could scholars begin to correct prevalent situations whereby much is known of what African states, societies and economies '*are not*' (thanks to dogmatic and normative assumptions of mainstream scholarship) but very little of what '*they actually are*' (Mbembe 2000a:21; 2001:9). Accepting the research agendas of African scholars may be not just 'a matter of ecumenism or goodwill', but also the beginnings of a conversation that could enrich scholarship in the West and elsewhere (cf. Appadurai 1999:235-237). Only the forging of this mutuality, partnership or interdependence would help re-energize African scholars and allow for a building of a genuinely international and democratic community of researchers. In this regard, Arjun Appadurai sees a future of profound internationalisation that invites academics across the globe to a conversation about research wherein 'the very elements of the ethic could be subjects of debate, and to which scholars from other societies and traditions of inquiry could bring their own ideas about what counts as new knowledge and about what communities of judgement and accountability they might judge to be central in the pursuit of such knowledge' (Appadurai 1999:237).

Global conversations and cooperation among universities and scholars are a good starting point in a long journey of equalisation and recognition for marginalised epistemologies and dimensions of scientific inquiry. But any global restructuring of power relations in scholarship can only begin to be meaningful to ordinary Africans through educational institutions and curricula that are in tune with their predicaments. In this connection, academics and researchers from and on Africa cannot afford to be blind to the plight of African scholarship whatever the pressures they may face, and regardless of their own levels of misery and need for sustenance. Nearly three decades ago Fonlon (1978) made a plea for the African university as a place for genuine intellectuals dedicated to the common weal. Thus, for African universities and researchers to contribute towards a genuine, multifaceted liberation of the continent and its peoples, they ought to start not by joining the bandwagon as has been their history, but with a careful rethinking of African concerns and priorities, and coming up with educational policies sympathetic to the needs of ordinary Africans (cf. Copans 1990, 1993; Zeleza and Olukoshi 2004). Mamdani (1993: 19) refers to rooting African universities in African soil, and Mafeje calls for a move away from 'received theory or contrived universalism', to an 'intimate knowledge of the dynamics of African culture[s] in a contemporary setting' (Mafeje 1988: 8). There is need for an insightful scrutiny of current curricula – their origin, form, content, assumptions and practicability; and then to decide whether to accept, reject or modify accordingly. The future of higher education in Africa can only be hopeful through a meticulous and creative process of cultural restitution and indigenisation even as African scholars continue to cooperate and converse with intellectual bedfellows in the West and elsewhere. All initiatives in this regard must be encouraged, and Peter Crossman's and René Devisch's *Endogenisation and African Universities* survey – premised on the assumption that only through greater adaptation to local and national socio-cultural contexts might African universities overcome some of the functional difficulties they currently face and make themselves more relevant to the needs of the countries and peoples they serve (Crossman and Devisch 1999) – could serve as a good starting point for those with research interest in this area. This is especially important, given that the relative advance in the indigenisation of the teaching of history and geography in Africa, is yet to inspire similar efforts towards making curricula for other social sciences more contextually relevant (cf. Crossman and Devisch 1999). If Africa is to be party in a global conversation of universities and scholars, it is only appropriate that it does so on its own terms, with the interests and concerns of ordinary Africans as guiding principle.

# 9

# Culture: The Missing Link in Development Planning in Africa

## Kwesi Kwaa Prah

### Introduction

Over the past five hundred years, no single phenomenon has impacted as definitively on the making and shaping of current realities in Africa as the experience of the African colonial encounter with the West. Today, at the beginning of the 21st century, it is often considered problematic to suggest that colonialism as a heritage has been the major impediment to Africa's attempt to move forward in social advancement and development. The argument is that it is too easy to put the blame for Africa's failure on outsiders when Africans have supposedly been in control of their own affairs since the end of the colonial era some forty years ago. Certainly, Africa should take responsibility for its own failings. Corrupt, dictatorial and undemocratic practices have been the hallmark of life in almost all of Africa's post-colonial states. But everything that is happening in Africa is not under the control of Africans. African governments do not control the prices of the commodities that are sold in global markets, nor do they have any real say in the setting of the prices at which commodities are bought from the developed world. Despite the endless propaganda trumpeted from the West about free markets, the reality for Africans is that most Western markets for the items, largely agricultural, which are produced cheaply and easily, are closed. The European Union is the supreme case in point. What we face are quotas, tariffs and cartels. For Africa, free trade remains a pie in the sky. The minerals we produce in abundance are controlled by Western capital from the source of production of the raw materials, their sale, and destination of sale, with no value added at source. Our economies are perpetually under siege through pernicious and unequal trade practices managed by the West and the related Bretton Woods institutions. These latter institutions have become *de facto* parallel governments in many African states.[1] With stagnating, shrinking economies and diminishing resources, it is not difficult to see (without condoning this) why the elites in Africa become so prone to corruption and the looting of the state. What I am saying is that a combination of internal and external forces is responsible for the current societal malaise in Africa.

But the deep structure of our malaise is largely entangled with the general impact of the colonial experience. While the West introduced modern techniques into pre-colonial and preindustrial Africa, it also distorted the autonomous nature of the processes of Africa's development.

In the fifty years or so of post-colonialism in Africa, no single obsession has been as overriding in the preoccupations of Africa's intellectuals as the question of development. It is the single, most obsessive object of all governments and ruling elites in Africa. It is hard to find a single regime in the post-independence experience of Africa which has not set its highest sights on the development objective.

What is noticeable, after half a century of post-independence, is that it continues to be an enduring feature of the rhetoric and espoused *raison d'etre* of African regimes. There are no exceptions to this, for the language of desired development is flaunted by military regimes, one-party states, so-called no-party states and multi-party states. The tragedy of the situation however is that, despite the copious verbiage and the related ceremonial fanfare which goes with high-level state events, the sanctimonious pronouncements of state authorities about development, the frequently touted imminence of expected successful outcomes of the endeavours of these regimes, little has been achieved in the 50 years of Africa's independence which can be seriously described as developmental.

The notion of development prominently implies the improvement and uplifting of the quality of life of people, that they are able, to a large measure, to attain their potential, build and acquire self-confidence and manage to live lives of reasonable accomplishment and dignity. The related idea of sustainable development which emerged in the late 1970s and early 1980s can be understood as a process of social transformation in which the exploitation of resources, patterns and strategies of investments and capitalisation, the ethos and direction of technological advancement and attendant institutional adaptation are in relative harmony, and facilitate both current and strategic potentials to satisfy the needs and aspirations of members of the society concerned. This concept was more European than American. In our times, and increasingly so, environmental and 'green' concerns have assumed, quite rightfully, a central position in how development objectives are pursued and implemented. Development efforts which show environmental sensitivity have become the prized approaches in development thinking.

Too often, skyscrapers, beautiful residential areas, cinemas and hotels are seen by some to represent development. The availability of champagne and whisky, ham and sausages, BMW's and Mercedes-Benz automobiles are equated with development. Ironically, the champagne and caviar life style in Africa invariably coexists with sprawling *bidonvilles,* with their unhealthy open drains and sewers. Development as a sustained, socially engaged socio-structural transformation paradigm, which augments the productive capacity and economic returns of mass society, and provides scope for the socio-economic amelioration of the quality of life of mass society, has largely eluded Africa. The elites have been content to feast on the latest choice commodities of Western consumer culture, and for as long as the availability of consumer-goods are assured, the fallacious arguments of the development rhetoricians will continue.

Development in Africa must make a difference, firstly, in the lives of the masses. This difference must mean that in all areas of the social life of the masses, perceptible and incremental growth of possibilities and opportunities, in both material and non-material senses, would need to be registered. Development must optimize the capacity of mass society to intervene intelligently, creatively and knowledgeably on the environment in pursuit of its mode of livelihood. An anthropology colleague, Prof. Simon Simonse, who had spent some years in Asia, more specifically in the Indonesian archipelago, once remarked to me that the striking feature about developing Asia is that the development and transformation of Asian societies are noticeable, first and foremost, at the village level. The significance of this point is that in the transformation and modernization of agrarian society in Asia, the ultimate goal has been that social change should transform the lives of the teeming rural underclasses. The leaps forward we have seen in Asia over the past three decades demonstrate the fact that development at the level of mass society for the Third World today is at heart an agrarian question.

In Africa, the often vaunted example of successful development is Botswana. As compared to the Asian experience, what we see in Botswana is a society awash with revenue from diamonds and which has provided lavishly for the elite to live and express themselves in evident materialistic terms. Botswana is one of the major beef producers in the world and has a lucrative market in the European Union. The human-livestock ratio for cattle is also one of the highest in the world. In rural Botswana, the effects of these enormous revenues have not been felt as a structural socio-economic process that is transforming the productive capacity of people and scientifically and technologically transforming the country-side. The semi-feudal *Mafisa/*cattle-loaning system is still prevalent. Botswana has a population of about 1.25 million. With its revenues from Diamonds and cattle rearing, Botswana now has reserves totalling approximately 7 billion US dollars invested in US government bonds. Such relatively large reserves could indeed transform Botswana in a more comprehensive way. Outside Africa, Saudi Arabia provides another classic point of reference, where enormous oil revenue has not meant the scientific and technological transformation of the society, but rather has created a basis for an opulent and vulgar consumerist life-style dominated by a feudalist aristocracy, backed up by one of the most sophisticated and expensive military machines of the contemporary world. This latter is purchased at a price from the West.

## The Search for the Development Formula

It has been almost fifty years that Africa's post-colonial intellectuals have been searching for the cure to the malaise of the economic, scientific and technological deficits of the African society. During the early period of our quest for solutions to the issue of Africa's under-development, some intellectuals were much influenced by one of the dominant theories known in the West as 'modernization'. It was particularly popular with American scholars, who, with considerable ingenuity, constructed a baseline model for understanding and tackling the problem of underdevelopment. The philosophical matrix on which the theoreticians of modernization grounded their formulae was 'functionalism'. For some of them, modernization was ultimately a question of attitudinal change. The global inequities of our times were identified as springing from differences in levels of technological development and industrialization. Invariably, in the thinking of the modernization theorists, tradition and cultural constraints were the prime inhibitors to modernization. This has been called *cultural blockage*.[2] They were generally, almost totally, silent on the global structure of production, distribution, exchange and the roots of the lopsidedness and unfavourable terms of trade underdeveloped nations experienced in relation to the developed ones. These theories, which had their heyday in the late 1950s and early 1960s, were championed by well-known theorists such as W.W. Rostow, David Apter, Wilbert Moore, S. N. Eisenstadt, J.Coleman, and many other largely American academics.[3] Their ideas greatly influenced a number of African and other Third World theorists of development. It was an approach which, in those years, found much favour in American government circles. Furthermore, it was a strategy which was uncritical of the role of the West in the construction of the premise of inequality in the global affairs of contemporary states. The two contrasting poles of opinion with regard to modernization theories are exemplified by the following two opinions from Mark Weigand and Manjur Karim.[4] Weigand wrote that:

> In my own experience, sociologists I have known who worked for the government usually were involved in 'social change' projects, which usually meant 'helping' Third World countries 'modernize' and become more like the US. Nothing too sinister, just ethnocentric projects.[5]

Karim's sharp and pungent rejoinder was that:

> But weren't the modernization theory related research project integrally connected with Cold War geopolitics? Third World countries were advised to modernize themselves after the Western model. A not so subliminal subtext of the modernization theory was to present a paradigm of development that is opposed to the socialist model of development that some post-colonial countries were attracted to. Whether individual researchers were aware of this political agenda or not is not the issue here. The issue is a larger one. Anyone who reads one of these works carefully, whether it is about the lack of 'achievement need' (read profit motivation), or 'modern and universalism' as opposed to 'traditional particularism', or 'formalized and impersonal rules of governance' in the 'traditional' societies, will know that the only kind of modernization these folk were talking about is capitalist modernization. Third World countries are backward because they haven't attained the illuminated path of capitalist modernization, not because they are forcefully articulated into a subordinate position into the world capitalist economy and locked into peripheral capitalist (or semi-feudal, or semi-colonial or whatever .....).[6]

Implicit in most modernization theories of the past has been a replay of the Victorian linear Eurocentric view that all societies are evolving and developing to become Western type societies; that non-Western societies were at various levels of development or rungs below the West. As a corrective, the way Kurimoto goes round this implicit weakness is to suggest 'multi-linear modernization'. [7]

What 50 years of post-independence history teaches us however is that the much vaunted modernization theories of the 50's and 60's nowhere provided successful cases which can with any seriousness be emulated. In spite of years of the much extolled virtues of 'Structural Adjustment Policy (SAP)' of the Bretton Woods institutions, the International Monetary Fund (IMF) and the World Bank have dismally failed to produce any unimpeachable success stories in the Third World. We still have to see the first case in Africa of a country that has achieved economic and developmental success through the IMF SAP formula. Takahashi Motoki has made the observation that by the 'mid-1990s, the failure of orthodox SAPs to save Africa from rampant poverty and stagnation became unquestionable'.[8]

Visibly, some societies, particularly in Asia, (the Asian Tigers) have succeeded in considerable measure to achieve development levels that in some instances have been quite impressive. But these achievements have been made largely through the economic creativity, judicious institutional arrangements and political astuteness of the leadership of these countries, not through the medicine of the Bretton Woods institutions.

The failure of the modernization theories to produce success, during the Cold War era, cannot be criticized on the basis of better theories or ideas emanating from the East. Indeed, the alternative paradigm offered by Soviet thinkers at the time was, what came to be known as, the 'non-capitalist road to socialism'. This idea was the officially blessed paradigm suggested by Soviet social scientists, their ideologues, and their other Third World neophytes. In brief, it suggested that Third World countries could move to scientific and technological development under a Soviet-type socialist political system which would avoid capitalism and which, as it were, would take them from where they were to socialism through Soviet tutelage. In practice, these ideas led to state capitalist approaches with nationalization under large state bureaucracies.[9] This idea like the modernization theories from the West proved, through historical experience, to be of little use to the challenges of the Third World. Indeed, the whole edifice of Soviet economy and politics has collapsed around us. In my experience, in Africa, by the late 1960s and early 1970s, modernization theory was being pilloried in lecture halls, conference rooms, symposia and workshops by African academics. Historically, almost surreptitiously, economic neo-liberalism took centre-stage position in discourses on Africa's development. But various types of Marxists, who generally had challenged modernization theories, were again back in the fray, assailing neo-liberalism and its approval and blessing of IMF-World Bank solutions. As we moved close to the end of the 1980s, in African academic circles, the assault on neo-liberalism became more philosophically generalized, at the same time, many erstwhile Marxists (particularly those who had in the past been disposed to Soviet orthodoxy) were theoretically running for cover as the Soviet system collapsed.

Bates put the blame for Africa's incapacity to economically move forwards on the African state's 'anti-developmental policies and urban bias',[10] For Gunnarsson and Lundhal, the post-colonial state was 'predatory' and prone to a developmentally negative disposition.[11] A glaring weakness in the views of these observers is their relative silence on the role of international and globalizing interests in the creation of the African malaise.

In contrast to the concept of modernization which, for the reasons I have given above and others, is tainted by both theoretical inadequacies and practical failures, some observers favour the notion of the search for 'modernity'. When applied to the problems of the Third World, this notion generically alludes to the search for the same objectives and goals as the modernization theories of old, but is not bound to any particular school of thought, and is therefore open to diverse theoretical structuring. It is used to denote the mix of ideas, ideals and practice which has emerged out of Western progress since the European Enlightenment, although some scholars, variously, choose a different time span as its historical record. While some prefer to restrict it to the whole of the post-Enlightenment West, others relate it to the West since about the 1860's while some have narrowed it further down to the post-World War II era. Pos-tmodernism is defined in reaction and contradiction to this. What needs to be remembered is that the concept of modernity is also heavily loaded with Eurocentrism and cannot serve well our understandings of African realities unless its relevance for each scholar-user is clearly defined, with its relevance for Africa amply demonstrated.

The message which has over the past few decades of experience filtered through to us is that whatever developmental formula we may be disposed to, unless we build on what people have and know, not much headway will be made. Needless to say, what people have and know are constructed in their languages and cultures.

For one thing, it is important to make a point that people best develop from the foundations of their indigenous knowledge. African societies like all non-Western, non-industrialized societies of Asia and Latin-America are made up of populations which have ancient collective memories and funds of knowledge about their environments and which they utilize in the implementation of their modes of livelihood. Such knowledge has deep and penetrating roots embedded in the cultures of the people. Development, to be meaningful, needs to acknowledge this fund of indigenous knowledge and construct new knowledge on the foundations of what the people already know. That way, new knowledge is integrated into the indigenous cultures of the people. The new knowledge thus does not bypass, avoid or diminish the relevance of the old knowledge which the people already have but, acknowledging the old, the new is added on, respecting the cultural centrality of the indigenous for their confidence and ability to relate the new to the old.

In the past, a great deal of research attention was given to what was always described as *appropriate technology*. While the term has semantic propriety, in practice it has tended to be utilized to often describe inferior technology and unimaginative technological innovations which do not significantly increase the productive capacity of poor countries. This is not to say that the idea of appropriate technology is semantically inappropriate to describe what needs to be done. Obviously, technological innovations and scientific inputs into the development efforts of poor countries, like African countries, need to be environmentally friendly. Such should be within the economic grasp of the people who need such technology and scientific input, and should be understandable by the users. The goal here is that such should make a difference in their quality of life. But this must not mean inferior technology.

Culture is a large and encompassing concept. It implies the totality of products that have resulted from the creative ingenuity of humans. Some of these products are material and are therefore tangible; while others, in such areas of social life like religion, language, beliefs, customs and values, are intangible, but are often more instrumental in the guidance of behaviour than the more recognizable material products of culture. While culture is the result of human creativity, it is also the key factor which shapes the way people behave. Inasfar as it is a historical and social product often tied to geography and environment, it tends to have specificity with respect to the peoples who create particular cultures. Thus while cultures vary from one society to another, there are also features of different cultures which are common to humanity as a whole. In an increasingly globalizing world, where we are all becoming global villagers, living in proximity to everybody else, those cultural features that are shared collectively by humanity as a whole are increasing by the day. Coca-Cola has culturally globalized us in much the same way as Chinese cuisine has. But, in spite of the universal cultural features which we increasingly all share, the specifics of culture and the particularities of cultural traits, values, artefacts, science and technology remain. Some technologies are more prevalent and are created more easily in some societies than others. In South Africa, where swimming pools have a higher per capita ratio than anywhere else in the world, the country also creates the best swimming pool technology in the world. In Japan, bathroom technology is more sophisticated and adapted to Japanese cultural values and practice than anywhere else. The adaptation of science and technology to suit the cultural and institutional foundations of the social life of a given people affirms the sense of confidence and cultural well-being of the people concerned.

## The Peculiarities of Africa

In Africa, the history of the process of the production and reproduction of knowledge since the advent of colonialism is, for our purposes here, instructive. The object of education under colonialism was not as altruistic is it is often made out to be. The idea of a civilizing mission, through which Africans were Christianized and taught to read and write, was first and foremost an attempt to produce Africans who would be serviceable for the project of colonialism; Africans who will acquiesce to the strategy and tactics of the colonial project.

The language of altruism and Christian morality were one part of the mind of the colonizer. There was another area of this mind which accommodated institutionalized racism, military patrols, punitive expeditions, genocide, looting and land-grabbing. Development under colonialism was geared towards developing the sort of infrastructure which enabled the exploitative extraction of minerals and the production of colonial agricultural produce, the disengagement of the colonized from their traditional modes of livelihood through the imposition of taxes, requiring wages and the engagement of the labour of colonial subjects, their submission to the colonial consumer market, and their compliance with the laws and by-laws promulgated under colonial sponsorship and sanctioned by police and military force. Colonial railways and roads ran from mining and agricultural cash-crop production areas to the harbours.

The educational systems established under colonial tutelage in practice produced social types who were intellectually distanced from the cultures from which they sprung. The first and most important vehicle for the removal and alienation of the educated African from his or her original cultural moorings was the use of colonial languages such as English, French or Portuguese. Africans were taught to be ashamed of their own languages, and in some areas, particularly in the French and Portuguese colonial areas, the use of indigenous languages at school was punishable, sometimes by flogging. The acquisition of knowledge was therefore, right from the start, linked to the use of the colonial languages, and this lent further spurious status of truth to the idea that knowledge is available and accessible only in the colonial languages. The other side of the logic of this argument was that it was not possible to learn science and technology or acquire knowledge of any superior kind in the languages of the people. Those who worked in colonial languages and who had acquired skills in the use of these languages were the socially elevated; they represented the basis of elite formation in the colonial order.

Western languages (like all languages) were not merely vehicles of communication. They were, and continue to be, cultural packages. These are programmes through which, in addition to the acquisition of the skills of language use, one learnt to accept the values of the language bearers. The English or French languages are also registers of the histories and cultures of the people. Immersion in these languages from the position of a colonial subject was therefore, to use a Malinowskian term, an 'acculturating' process.

This pattern of education and knowledge production was inherited with only minor revisions by the post-colonial state. Indeed, in post-colonial Africa, apart from weak attempts in Tanzania and Madagascar to use African languages as languages of education at the post-primary levels, no country has made any serious attempt at developing African languages as the basis for the production and reproduction of knowledge. In the case of both Tanzania and Madagascar, after some years of half-hearted trial and error, the policy of using indigenous languages consistently in the educational system has been, in both cases, abandoned.

Language is the main pillar in any cultural system, and literacy in a given cultural system represents the most important feature in the development of a capacity for a language to work either as a repository of past knowledge or as a basis for the development and integration of new knowledge into the society or cultural system. In all societies which are able to move forward scientifically and technologically, primacy is vested in the development and use of languages indigenous to the people. This is true not only for non-Western societies like China, Japan, Thailand, Cambodia or Indonesia, but is equally true for countries in the West like Denmark, Norway, the Netherlands, France and Germany. Each case that can be referred to as an example of an advancing and developing society would be a society which works with its own language and develops its culture and knowledge on the basis of the language or languages of the masses. It needs also to be said that the transfer of knowledge from outside a given cultural system into an indigenous cultural system, to be efficacious, needs to adapt the imported knowledge into the cultural system of the people in such a way that the imports and adaptations blend into the existing culture of the people. Development cannot be achieved in circumstances where the cultures of the masses are steadily abandoned in favour of cultures which are totally foreign to the masses and which are familiar terrain for only small sections of the elite. This point needs to be emphasized because it is the absence of cultural relevance and the need for cultural adaptation of external inputs into African development planning which, in our minds, constitutes the major obstacle to success in development planning and implementation in Africa.

## Globalization, Culture and Development Planning

It is currently frequently argued that never in the history of humanity has the lot of the human community been as intertwined as is presently the case, with globalization and the forms of international integration. These days, the term 'globalization' is easily bandied around by all and sundry. It means different things to different people. Some perceive it as a process that is desirable; the inevitable and unalterable future of the world. Others regard it with various degrees of scepticism, aversion and apprehension. Such minds argue that it is, in fact, increasing global economic, political and social inequities between countries; that it undermines employment and living standards and frustrates social progress.

Globalization could, in the best of all worlds, offer capacious promises for genuine development on a world scale, but as it is currently unfolding, its progress is developmentally uneven. Some grow fat on its spoils while others maintain stunted growth patterns and face economic ruin and damnation. Some countries are becoming integrated into the global economy more quickly than others. Countries that have been able to integrate are experiencing faster growth and reduced poverty. Export-driven policies, matched with economic innovativeness, have brought remarkable prosperity to much of East Asia, transforming it from one of the poorest areas of the world into dynamic economic powers. And as living standards improve, so has the ability to embrace, more enthusiastically, democracy and pressing issues such as the environment and the conditions of labour.

In considerable contrast, since the 1970s, many countries in Latin America and Africa in particular have been pitched into the exigencies of stagnating economies, increasing poverty levels, and runaway inflation in societies increasingly overwhelmed by an enduring kleptocratic ethos. In many cases, especially in Africa, adverse external developments have made the problems worse. The crises in the emerging markets in the 1990s have made it quite evident that volatile capital movements and the risks of social, economic and environmental degradation, created by poverty, are not being helpful. In spite of the economic growth of the West in the past decade, we still live with the threat of crashes and meltdowns in the principal stock and money markets of the world.

Of all the issues attendant on globalization, the one outcome which has not received the requisite degree of attention and scrutiny is the effect of globalization on cultures of societies on the periphery of the West. Some of the developed countries of Europe, particularly France, Denmark and Italy are sensitive to the dwarfing effect of American and Anglo-Saxon culture in general on their own. France is especially concerned about this. In Africa, the steadily overwhelming and brooding presence of Western culture is singularly blighting and is fossilizing indigenous cultures. In this respect, the structural difference between France or Denmark and African countries is that in these European countries, the linguistic and cultural basis of social life of the elite and mass society are not only coterminous but also largely shared, on an everyday basis, as a common patrimony. In the African case, the elite is culturally narrowing its base and steadily alienating itself from the cultures and languages of mass society. For African elites, the extent to which European cultural features are imitated and reproduced is representative of status and social influence. They live and exist in Africa, assuming and exercising leadership, but culturally they integrate into Western culture as marginal consumers. The centre of gravity for the creation of Western culture remains in the West. In a sense, it is therefore possible to describe African elites as surrogates for Western culture in Africa. The question that follows from this reasoning is this: can an elite which is beholden to Western culture in a more or less unquestioning fashion become the architect for a culturally indigenously oriented transformation process? This curiously is a question which only the African elite can raise and answer.

In spite of the fairly homogenous and guarded interests of the African elite, they cannot be construed to be uniform in ideas, ideals and strategy. There are positions of the philosophical right and left amongst them, reformers and conservatives, 'Africanists (cultural nationalists) and non-Africanists (cultural Westerners)'. In short, what I call elites and counter-elites. The way and the pace with which Africa accepts its historical and cultural belongings in the development process will depend considerably on the contestation between the elites and counter-elites. Ultimately, it is how these contesting social elements engage the minds and actions of the grassroots that will determine the trajectory of developmental change in Africa.

## Planners and African Developmental Options

It would appear to me, clear from the above argumentation, that Africa's development, to be successful, would need to be premised on the cultural fund embedded in the social life of Africans. The key to the door of the cultural world of Africans is African languages. In the first instance, they provide the basis of social identification and, secondly, access the knowledge of the people. It is in these languages that the creative aptitude and inventive instinct of the people are articulated. It is also in these languages that any attempt to introduce ideas on a mass scale can be achieved. It is almost farcical to assume that by working in the socially very narrowly based languages of colonialism, it will be possible to effectively achieve transformation of African societies. If we want to be able to place African languages and cultures centrally in our developmental endeavours, we need to clear up the myth of their necessity to implement modern ideas. A good example of the confusion we find in thinking about African languages is provided by Dominic Milazi's observations on South Africa. He writes that:

> Language is, of course, the very medium and heart of communication, the mainstay of cultural heritage.... We can to some extent identify language as the salient feature which demonstrates the presence of ethnicity. The challenge, of course, is to find a strategic role for indigenous languages – a role in the national scheme of things. At the same time, this vexed question of the place of African languages in national development must be broached in any future move designed to deal with language policy in a comprehensive manner.... Given the fact that national languages in many African states had very little impact as far as paving the way for nation-building – decolonization, promoting self-esteem and cultural integrity – was concerned, the choice of eleven languages in South Africa as national languages was the correct one. For one thing, it gave expression to the principle of democracy and pluralism. For another, it provides for the meaningful promotion of the policy of national languages based on language rights, particularly their recognition and application. This, in itself, should foster the principle of intercultural tolerance.[12]

Milazi fails to register the fact that in almost all African states, after independence, lip-service is being paid to elevating the status of African languages. Sometimes, this is written into constitutions and at other times not. Even when this is written into the constitution, in practice, little has been done to achieve this elevation, so that in effect the pre-eminence of the colonial languages persist long after the colonialists have left. It is also important to draw attention to the fact that the so-called eleven languages of South Africa are effectively four. The two clusters, i.e. Nguni and Sotho/Tswana consist of languages which are mutually intelligible in both instances. Xhosa, Zulu, Ndebele and Swati are the same language. Indeed, there are other dialectal variants of this cluster as far north as Tanzania and includes speakers in Mozambique, Malawi, Zimbabwe and Zambia. The same can be said for the Sotho/

Tswana cluster which has speakers in South Africa, Namibia, Lesotho, Zimbabwe, Botswana, Zambia and Angola. I have elsewhere drawn attention to these issues.[13] Why the role of African languages in development must be a 'vexed question' is unfortunate because by his account 'Language is, of course, the very medium and heart of communication, the mainstay of cultural heritage'. Fortunately, there is increasingly a realization amongst some African academics and experts that the notion of a profusion of African languages is false. The argument has been very well made by Hounkpati B. Capo in his inaugural lecture at the University of Ilorin, Nigeria – 'Let us Joke Over it: Nigeria as a Tower of Babel'.[14]

## Concluding Remarks

It needs to be emphasized that all development planning and practical efforts in Africa should be undertaken with an eye on cultural relevancies in general and the language question in particular. The people who need development, such as the peoples of Africa, speak their own indigenous languages. If we need to reach them, and need them to be able to understand and create with the innovative ideas that are offered, then the language of communication and transfer would need to be their own. In those cases where a multiplicity of languages all at work at the same time could be rather impractical, perhaps Africa's linguists could create new collective languages with inputs from multiple linguistic sources. These would serve as practical *lingua francas* for Africa's populations.

Westernization as a process of adaptation of Western thought and techniques, the establishment of bureaucratic organizational principles as ordering systems for production, distribution and exchange, the institution and consolidation of democratic principles of government, the sale of law and respect for human rights, in our times, constitute basic and fundamental requirements for the march towards modernity. But such ideas in the abstract remain empty and vacuous platitudes unless they are translated into the cultural and linguistic belongings of social majorities.

No ideas however lofty, well-meaning and humanitarian can resonate with the broader classes unless these ideas find interpretable entry points into the cultural familiarities of the people. In other words, Western ideas must melt into African culture and become African cultural adaptations of Western or universal modes of thought and social practice. This requires a discriminatory and selective approach which, while eschewing the backward conventions, values and attitudes of archaic traditionalism, is unhesitant in absorbing practices and innovations which strengthen the cultural basis of what African societies already have.

Institutions that have taken thousands of years to evolve should be cast aside with great caution. It is possible and often more useful to reform such institutions than to relegate them to the dustbin of history when, in fact, their significance in the individual and collective life of societies is often much greater than meets the eye.

## Notes

1. See, Guy Arnold, 2000, 'Monitoring – The New Colonialism', in *West Africa*, November (20-26), p.2. A good example of this is provided by Abel Mwanyungwe in the *Business Day* (South Africa) of Wednesday, 23rd May 2001, p.7. 'The World Bank has asked government not to increase funding to the Foreign Affairs Ministry in the 2001-02 fiscal budget as an expenditure saving measure. In a document, titled *Malawi Budget 2001-02: Suggestions from a World Bank Study*, the bank said the squeeze on foreign affairs would necessitate adopting measures to scale back foreign representation. Malawi has 19 embassies worldwide, with an average of five Malawian employees at each station'. See also, Joe Khamisi, 'IMF Ultimatum Shock for Kenyan Officials', *Business Day/Business Report*, Johannesburg, September 12th, 1995:15.

2. I have looked at this issue in an earlier paper titled: 'The Notion of Cultural Blockage and Some Issues of Technology Adoption Concerning the African Peasantry', 1991, in Prah, K.K. (ed.), *Culture, Gender, Science and Technology in Africa*, Schriftenreihe der Deutschen Stiftung für Internationale Entwicklung (DSE), Windhoek, Harp Publications, pp. 48 - 65.

3. A good sample of such approaches is provided by the following; Marion, J., Levy, Jr., 1952, *The Structure of Society*, Princeton, Princeton University Press. Karl W., Deutsch, 1953, *Nationalism and Social Communication*, New York, M.I.T. Press. S. N. Eisenstadt, 1961, *Essays in Sociological Aspects of Political and Economic Development*, The Hague, Mouton; S. N. Eisenstadt. 'Social Changes and Modernization in African Societies South of the Sahara', *Cahier d'Etudes Africaines* ,Vol.5. No.19, 1965. Appears also in John Middleton (ed),1970, *Black Africa*, New York, Macmillan; Wilbert Moore, *Social Change*, 1963, Englewood Cliffs, N.J., Prentice Hall; Gabriel, Almond and James, S. Coleman,1960, *The Politics of Developing Areas,* J. S., Coleman, 'The Emergence of African Political Parties', in C. Grove Haines, 1955(ed.), *Africa Today*, Baltimore, Greenwood Press; David. E., Apter, 1969, *The Politics of Modernization*, pp.18-19; Edward Shils, 1962, *Political Developments in the New States*, The Hague, Mouton.

4. Http://csf.colorado.edu/mail/psn/2000/msg01185.html

5. Ibid.

6. Ibid.

7. See Kurimoto, E., 2001,'Introduction', in Kurimoto, E. (ed.), *Rewriting Africa: Towards Renaissance or Collapse,* Japan Centre for Area Studies Symposium Series, No. 14, Osaka. p.3.

8. Motoki,T., 2001, 'The Creation of Developmental States', in Kurimoto, p.60.

9. A Good Illustrative Study of the Theory of Non-capitalist Development (NCD) is provided by Esmail Hosseinzadeh, *Soviet Non-Capitalist Development: The Case of Nasser's Egypt,* Praeger Publishers, New York, 1989. Recently, Burbach and Nunez have advanced an argument which harps on the notion of non-capitalist development while meaning something different from the original Soviet usage. Burbach and Nunez argue that, in the making, within the global context is a new non-capitalist mode of production which, all things being equal, will overwhelm capitalism from below. For these authors this new mode of production, consisting of workers, peasants, petty traders, small businesses, street vendors, casual labourers who work in the twilight areas of the periphery of the globalizing economy. For them, this growing informal economy will ultimately dethrone capitalist hegemony. There is some perceptive analysis of globalization and neo-liberalism, but the way forward as viewed by the authors is marred by much wishful thinking. See, Roger Burbach, Orlando Nunez and Boris Kagarlitsky, 1997, *Globalization and its Discontents: The Rise of Postmodern Socialism,* Pluto Press. London.

10. Bates, R.H.,1981, *Markets and States in Tropical Africa: The Political Basis for Agricultural Policies,* Berkeley, University of California Press.

11. Gunnarsson, C. and Lundhal, M., 'The Good, the Bad and the Wobbly: State Forms and Third World Economic Performance', in M. Lundhal, M. and Ndulu, B.J.(eds), 1996, *New Directions in Development Economics: Growth, Environmental Concerns and Government in the 1990s*, London, Routledge, pp. 251-281.

12. See Dominic Milazi, 2000, Ethnicity and State: Revisiting the Salience of Ethnicity in South Africa', in Prah, K.K. and Ahmed A.G. (eds.), 2000, *Africa and Transformation,* Vol. 1, OSSREA, Addis Ababa, pp. 114–115.

13. Prah, K.K.(ed).,1998, 'Between Distinction and Extinction', in *The Harmonization and Standardization of African Languages,* Johannesburg, Witwatersrand University Press.

    Prah, K.K.(ed.), 1995, *African Languages for the Mass Education of Africans,* Deutsche Stiftung fur Internationale Entwicklung (DSE), Bonn, Germany. Prah,K.K.(ed.),1995, *Mother Tongue for Scientific and Technological Development in Africa,* Deutsche Stiftung fur Internationale Entwicklung (DSE), Bonn, Germany. Prah, K.K., 1998, 'In Tongues: An Edited record of the Accra Symposium on African Languages and the Challenges of African Development', in Prah, K.K. and King, Y.(eds.), Capetown, The Centre for Advanced Studies of African Society (CASAS).

14. Hounkpati, B.C., 1992, 'Let Us Joke Over It: Nigeria as a Tower of Babel', Inaugural Lecture Series (44th), Ilorin: University of Ilorin Press (Nigeria).

# 10

# Appraising Africa: Modernity, Decolonisation and Globalisation

## Sanya Osha

In addressing the nature of the current African problematic regarding development as progress towards a viable modernity, it is necessary to identify the conceptual dimensions that created the predicament in the first place. Indeed, it is necessary to define its historical origins if we are to find solutions to it. Part of the problem of not being able to locate appropriate solutions is that we do not always address the predicament in ways that are broad or comprehensive enough. At the moment, Africa's intellectuals are showing much impatience at Africa's disappointing political and economic performance, and at a deeper level, this impatience is directed at the difficulties Africa is experiencing as it seeks to come to terms with its post-colonial status, modernity and the new economic phenomenon known as globalisation. What I intend to do in this chapter is to discuss the issue of African development in the context of its ongoing experiences with modernity, decolonisation and globalisation. An obvious impatience lies too at the heart of the politics of the Western universal, in its quest to abolish once and for all, the self/other cultural dichotomy, in its drive to reverse the gains of decolonisation and finally in its aspirations to universalise all notions and projects of modernity.

This new approach as an ethos of universalism devalues the exigencies and politics of the particular. It is an orientation that has emerged partially in the aftermath of the 'September 11' event in the United States. Part of the legacy of that tragedy is the strong critique of particularist manifestations of cultural difference that present themselves as being at odds with the Western universal (Mamdani 2004). I suggest that the September 11 tragedy in the United States has provided a moral occasion to redefine the conception of the universal. I also suggest that a new ethos of the universal can easily become complicit with a certain hegemonic logic. In other words, it can lead to a new form of social Darwinism. This could mean that the integrity of African forms of territoriality will come under assault; concepts such as sovereignty, citizenship and belonging will be reformulated. However, there are concerns that they will not be redefined according to the dictates of African agency. So, if Africa misses the most liberating gains of modernity and decolonisation, then under the order of the new ethos of the universal, it may also miss a significant degree of the propellants of the contemporary dynamics of globalisation.

The three processes – modernity, decolonisation and globalisation – are like paradigms, influenced by different world views that sometimes overlap and which also at times act in contradictory ways. African responses to them must include aspects of African creativity and forms of African agency. Again, I do not intend to imply that the three processes discussed here – modernity, decolonisation and globalisation – do not at times overlap. They do in many ways but our understanding of their conceptual potentials needs to be clearer in order to appreciate the particular problems each of them presents. For instance, the current wave of globalisation presents new kinds of challenges in terms of global security which are prompting a different kind of international response to the African crisis, one which threatens to redefine the nature of sovereignty and classical national territoriality. This kind of response is coming at the moment African nations are trying to reframe the question of the classical nation-building project as part of the ongoing process of decolonisation. It is also coming at a moment of a reconfigured pre-colonial idea that is sceptical about orders of otherness that establish and defend hierarchy rather than equality.

Within the context of this disconcerting international climate, Africa's problems have become even more amplified. This new engagement with the politics of the universal, or in more contemporary terms, the politics of the global, rather than address the historical demands and specificities of Africa's problems creates its own peculiar version of a negative African exceptionalism. It also becomes a new opportunity for the promotion of an ideology of pessimism regarding the African continent. Indeed, the new challenges of global security have provided the platform for a radical reconsideration of Africa's difficulties. In my view, three conceptual categories need to be analysed in order to grapple with the current nature of the African dynamic, and these are modernity, decolonisation and globalisation. Of course, these categories are not intended to address all the dimensions of the African problematic. They are meant to provide multilayered mechanisms for problems and issues that are not always related to the three major concepts of this discussion: modernity, decolonisation and globalisation. None of these three major conceptual processes have been fully realised or implemented within Africa itself. All three of them have assumed dramatically different and often contradictory trajectories.

If our understanding of modernity derives from the European idea of the Enlightenment; if it stems from the modern reformulation of the project of democracy and faith in the promise of science and technology; if it stems from a sense of a radical discontinuity with medievalism and in a belief in the rationalities of thinkers like Kant, Hume and J. S. Mill; if finally it stems from an espousal of a politically appropriate sense of progressivism, then all these legacies and influences have had problematic diffusion into Africa. Certainly, there are powerful moments of assimilation and acceptance just as there have been equally dramatic reversals of those moments of assimilation. The point is that Africa has not yet quite decided what to do with modernity, has not discovered what version[s] of modernity best serves its interests, and has not resolved the contradictions of the continual tussle between its indigenous traditions and the wide ranging transformations proposed by the project of modernity. This is a crucial problem that faces projects geared towards the construction of African modernities. African modernities have never been the same as Euro-modernity. Modernist expressions in Africa are instead a combination of aspects of Euro-modernity, secularism, Christian cosmology, Islamic beliefs, indigenous African systems of knowledge and other syncretic cultural forms that lie outside these categories. Indeed, African modernist expressions are an invention of post-coloniality and are as such suffused with a profound hybridity (Diouf 2000).

Perhaps there is a crisis at the heart of the project of modernity. When modernity is disentangled from this unclear logic of the hegemonic, it becomes transformed into a promise of cosmopolitan inclusiveness. In other words, it loses its aura of cultural elitism and presents itself as a kind of multicultural cosmopolitanism. So, if Africa has not discovered what to do with modernity, that is, has not defined its relationship with a promoted universalist paradigm, then it would not be able to establish what belongs to the realm of the universal and what belongs to the realm of the African particular. African tensions with modernity fold into other contradictions embedded in the process and project of the modern. In more stark political terms, the colonial legacy of modernity is often played out as a struggle between ethnic and civic categories as Peter Ekeh (1975) and Mahmood Mamdani (1996, 2001) have demonstrated in several ways. The tussle between these postcolonial categories is often seen as the bane of the formation of the nation state in Africa.

Similarly, decolonisation as a project and process all over Africa has been uneven. If colonialism assumed different features, histories and outcomes, decolonisation has also been considerably diverse in the nature of its unfolding. Decolonisation has been inflected with the politics of ethnicity (Nnoli 2003; Osaghae 1994), race, territoriality, citizenship and belonging, all of which have had profound effects on the dynamics of nationhood. Indeed, every history or project of nation-building is unique and cannot be replicated. If colonialism created the first modern African nation states, decolonisation has been with varying degrees of success an attempt to consolidate the features of these artificially imposed political geographies. Consider the relative embeddedness of thoroughly artificial identity constructs such 'francophone', 'anglophone' 'sub-Saharan Africa' and the equally incongruous 'Commonwealth nation'. It is always convenient to associate decolonisation with political liberation, but reality tells us otherwise. Decolonisation is modern Africa's first self-directed attempt at nation-building. Africa clearly suffers from some exhaustion as the era of slavery and colonisation has had an obvious impact. Also, there was the error of mistaking decolonisation with political independence alone. Decolonisation clearly entailed more than political liberation; it was rather an invitation to nation-building without adequate resources in terms of personnel and institutions.

And as Africa grappled with the incomplete processes of modernity and decolonisation, a third conceptual category enters the scene: globalisation. I will not engage in a full definition of globalisation except to say that it is a project that encompasses not only economics but also the political and the cultural, but implemented under the direction of the West. It also implies in this sense a radical acceleration of the project of universal modernity – technological, political and economic – emanating from the West. Again, just as with the two other processes – modernity and decolonisation – Africa as a globalisation object and subject has not yet decided how to deal with this new world order. I have also suggested that the notions and present realities of sovereignty, territoriality, citizenship and belonging are changing under conditions of contemporary globalisation. These changes directly affect Africa yet its institutions are not flexible and responsive enough to them. This institutional vacuum is attractive to stratagems of foreign intervention. To fill this vacuum, African nations must address the dilemmas and difficulties posed by disjointed projects and processes of modernity, nation building and globalisation.

But what exactly is the face of globalisation as it descends on Africa? First, it should be read as evidence of the open and untrammelled field that the West now has at its disposal after being straitjacketed for seventy years of rivalry with the Communist bloc. Globalisation means not much more than the West's free rein to explore its advantages of unequal economic exchange within a context of IMF, World Bank and WTO *diktats,* enforced free markets that have ruined any semblance of agricultural autonomy for African farmers' strategic agricultural items such as rice, and have pushed such farmers even further to work in macro units that produce cash crops for the international market. Globalisation has also led to an accelerated rural exodus from the countryside to cities then on to urban crime, political unrest, wars fuelled by easy access to Western weaponry, or finally escape to the Western lands of hard currency and menial labour. In all of this are the constant Machiavellian ministrations from the West: democracy, rule of law and sustainable development while the neo-colonial dictators are coddled and allowed easy access to their foreign accounts bulging with the hard currencies of their paymasters.

The question then is what ought to be Africa's response to the tidal wave of globalisation now engulfing Africa? The economic power of the Western nation-state sponsors of globalisation derives from what amounts to their politically created 'hard currencies' which have been overvalued to attract cheap labour from the non-European world and to acquire products from the non-European and African world as cheaply as possible. This is the significance of the concept of 'unequal exchange'. In response, Africa can seek to create its own continental-wide hard currency which would have as its collateral Africa's abundant mineral and petroleum resources. Given that gold is no longer held as the ultimate guarantor of value, Africa need only to have an established central bank create any amount of credit necessary for trade and economic transactions. The rate of currency exchange between the Western currencies of the dollar and the euro could be established by fiat – in exactly the same way the West has established the value of its own currencies. The ultimate goal would be intra-continental trade within an African commonwealth of nations. In this context, infant technologies could be protected by a prudent application of the principle of autarky. However, the technological and cultural transformations necessary for development and modernisation would not be possible without the implanting of the modalities that make such possible: investments not only in human scientific, technological and cognitive capital, but also in the physical infrastructure to accommodate such. This would entail Africa standing the Western project of globalisation on its head and employing it as an intra-continental project whose goal would be meaningful development in all its dimensions. Africa's response to globalisation could then be primarily the globalisation of Africa in the first instance.

Colonialism created rudimentary and barely viable modern nation-states. Projects of decolonisation sought to stabilise these fragile nation-states even as they rejoiced over the euphoria of political liberation. With the crises of the nation-state in Africa under its own specific forms of post-colonial authoritarian rule on the one hand, and under homogenising tendencies of the new ethos of the global on the other, it becomes unclear as to how to create states that address the challenges of the modern nation-state; that demand the prerequisite nimbleness of the contemporary globalised state and the tensions and interactions between the artificially created African states and their historically structured counterparts of the West. These tensions may appear manageable but they implicitly promise periods of institutional dissolution, confusion, and political collapse.

There is indeed a great deal of announced impatience with Africa on the part of its intellectuals and also persistent afro-pessimistic critiques from all intellectual sectors of the West. However, there is confusion on all sides as to what decolonisation actually entailed, given that old legacies that proved to be deleterious were maintained. As mentioned earlier, decolonisation does not mean political liberation alone. It also means the construction of viable political geographies and identities. These experiments with nation-building are not quite fifty years in the making. Obviously, the velocities of the current waves of globalisation are creating many more opportunities for critique and a whittling away of the prescribed post-colonial project that promised rapid development to culminate in modernity (Mbembe 2003). If indeed aspects of Euro-modernity are being adopted in Africa, the question then would be how can such be adopted minus its parochialism? How can the tensions between the universal and the particular within the general project be addressed? How can we best deal with the critique of Africa that globalisation now seems to foster? Posing these kinds of questions restores a certain historicity and conceptual clarity to African problems. In addition, it also re-establishes the continuing dialogue between the universal and the particular in instances where the former tends to deny the presence of the politics of difference and a future of more numerous possibilities. To encourage this kind of impatience – this conceptual closure – is to deny the presence of the particular, the local and its promise of difference. In a way, it is also a denial of the imagination to create new models and modes of being.

If the African continent is to overcome its numerous present difficulties, it has to re-evaluate its relationship with the project of modernity. As it is, an acceptance of that project entails an espousal of an ethos of the universal. African nations have to resolve the tensions and contradictions of their encounters with modernity (Wiredu 1980, 1996). They have to reformulate the question: what does modernity entail? They have to resolve the problems posed by aspects of their traditions that are in conflict with modernity. Modernity does not merely involve the creation of the appropriate institutions (Comaroff and Comaroff 1991, 1997). It is also a way of life, a total engagement with the world. If it is Africa's desire to adopt this general ethos of existence, then it is necessary to restructure and debate those institutions bequeathed to it by the colonial legacy. Those institutions, we have to note, were not meant to embrace all the dimensions of modernity. They were created to be able to have marginal interactions with modernity. They were part of the apparatus of the colonial regime. Most African nations that inherited them did not upgrade them or refashion them into fully modern institutions to serve local needs. Instead, they became syncretised as the grounds on which the struggles between tradition and modernity took place. And the products that emerged from these processes of syncretisation were not always modern in orientation. In many respects, they signalled a withdrawal from the ethos of modernity, given that they were often reformulations of indigenous African cultures that were usually in conflict with modernity (Appiah 1992).

This perennial conflict with the ethos of modernity is played out in several ways – confusions between the private and public domains which often result in the privatisation of public authority and institutions, perplexities in the subject-citizen dichotomy ( Comaroff and Comaroff, 2000), the retention of the nepotistic network of the extended family for public affairs in spite of its conflict with modernity, and the political economy of the gift in traditional African cultures and its translation into the political economy of corruption within the context of modernity (Oliver de Sardan 1999). These confusions mar the drive towards development in particular, and modernity in general. In other words, African nations must transform the typologies of their colonially-inflected institutions on the one hand, and refashion the fabric of their everyday lives on the other. Indeed, there is a certain colonial logic to be read in the conception of modernity as an espousal of the politics of the universal. The problem derives from the fact that indigenous institutions have developed organically and that African societies have repeatedly demonstrated that certain traditions and orientations are vital to their continued existence (van Binsbergen 2003).

For instance, in the African conception of people-as-wealth (Simone 2004), popular mythologies of the notion of the *human* that conflict with the rationalities of modernity are specific forms of African sociology. African institutions have always made more sense to themselves than to the rest of the world since they are based on the specific socio-anthropology of their particular life-world (Gyekye 1997). A large part of the ethos of modernity disavows this tendency. African problems rise primarily out of this set of circumstances, these tensions and contradictions. Once again, Africans must decide the nature of their relationship with modernity in order to deal with the new global interdependencies (Sindjoun 2005). Deciding this question will in turn affect the nature of its projects of global interaction. The truth is that the present ideological contestation in a supposedly post-ideological milieu has become incredibly impoverished because of a certain intellectual inflexibility. The general nature of this struggle manifests itself as a somewhat sterile conflict between the universal and the particular which, within the context of current global processes, is complicit with a popular Western intellectual paradigm. In other words, the logic of this hegemonic quest is camouflaged as the politics of the universal.

I have argued that Africa's problems with decolonisation and the nation-building process, the unresolved conflict between tradition and modernity and the tensions between the particular and the universal are largely conceptual. Indeed, African problems are part of the struggles for self definition. Immediately after decolonisation was embarked on there was optimism concerning the idea of African socialism as it was supposedly in conformity with traditional African social structures. There was an ideological conflict between those who argued for a universal socialism as opposed to its local instantiations. After the dismantling of the Soviet bloc, a new Western ideology was promoted, that of economic neo-liberalism and globalisation. In a post-colonial and post-Soviet world, Africa's response was an attempt to integrate the past into the present by appeal to the two ideas of 'renaissance' – note that this concept appeals to Africa's long archaeological and historical past – and the 'union of African states' – a response to the massive Euro-American cultural, political and economic bloc and the vast integrated economic community of East Asia. This is the template on which Africa seeks to work out its problems with the ultimate aim of development as modernity.

My guess is that the appropriate kinds of institution will eventually emerge out of these struggles. As they are waged, one must also remember to point out the hegemonic propensities of the politics of the universal. Africa is now in the midst of many problems that it must resolve on its own terms by taking stock of its indigenous traditions as they conflict dynamically with the dictates of the modern (Hountondji 2002). Thus the ongoing dynamic will express itself in any number of possible ways – political, cultural, intellectual, technological and economic. This is the intellectual task that Africa must seek to accomplish before development as modernity can be realised. In practical terms, this would express itself at three levels: the domestic, the national and the Pan-African. What does the post-colonial African expect from life other than to live in an environment where his or her talents and dispositions have the chance of being fully developed so that the opportunities for rewarding work can be pursued? He or she would also hope for the best available education for his or her children in a society where an indigenously generated modern technology will have made available and the best social conditions for such goals be pursued. At the national level, the post-colonial African would hope that his or her representatives in government would have developed the commitment to ensure that promised public goods be delivered fairly in an atmosphere of maximum freedom. At the level of the Pan-African, the hope is for freedom to travel according to the dictates of commerce and trade in much the same way that pre-colonial Africa configured itself. As such the ongoing tragic, alienating and humiliating, longing for Euro-America for employment, health care, modern technology and education will have long evaporated.

For Africa's post-colonial and modernising intellectual classes, the hope is for vibrant and free civil societies, flourishing universities and academic institutions to discuss, debate and build on the prescriptive templates for progress already formulated, courtesy of the ideas on development of Nkrumah; on the nature of colonialism bearing the seeds of neo-colonialism of Fanon, and on the recounting of the African archaeological and historical past of C.A. Diop. As mentioned above, there are ideological, cultural, political and economic forces of all kinds that are constantly seeking to derail linear progress toward development as modernity in a context of post-coloniality and globalisation. Such forces have historically taken on the guise of a self-inflicted neo-colonialism on the part of Africa's tragically alienated, anti-African and historically ignorant post-colonial and Euro-dependent managerial classes. It is these intellectually and politically irresponsible bankrupt classes that serve as a major stumbling block in Africa's struggle to attain modernity.

# 11

# Philosophy, Democracy and Development: History and the Case of Cameroon

## Godfrey B. Tangwa

### Introduction

'Development' is the most important among the key terms of the above title as it is the aim that both 'Philosophy' and 'Democracy' are brought in to achieve. Talking about development, it is necessary first to consider the preconditions of development in general, irrespective of the entity whose development is in question. In general, we can consider development as purposive (teleological) growth. Mere evolution in time and space cannot properly be described as development. Left on its own, anything whatsoever will evolve in some way or other in time and space. The first precondition of development as distinguished from mere evolution is a clear and viable aim or purpose. Thus development is a *teleological* concept. As humans we optimally lead our lives according to pre-established goals and purposes; that is why the second precondition of development requires a blueprint – a well thought out series of measures and procedures – for achieving the end in question. The first generation of modern African thinkers, many of whom also happened to have been political leaders, such as Kwame Nkrumah, Julius Nyerere, Leopold Senghor, Sékou Touré, and others, seem to have made noteworthy efforts in this regard. The third precondition requires an enabling environment for achieving the aim or purpose in question, for to choose an end or aim is to choose every means necessary for the achievement of that aim. To choose an aim and to balk at the only means necessary for achieving it is either not to have chosen the end with conviction or simply to exercise bad faith.

With this in mind, the question can now be posed: What is the purpose of development in general? To suggest a general answer to a general question, I would say that development is to be understood as a set of collective and individual decisions that ultimately lead to increased human, economic, political and cultural welfare for all persons in society according to the dictates of the most advanced knowledge and technology available. In brief, let us say that the goal of development is greater human, material, technological and cultural welfare. Some countries have indeed experienced these evolutionary trends over the centuries as is the case with the world's most advanced technological nations.

It is my contention that, in the present state of human evolution, a liberal and democratic system is an important precondition for development geared towards human wellbeing. And this being the case, the main reasons for the developmental failures of African countries must be looked for in their democratic failures. Efforts at democratisation in Africa, which started in earnest in the early 1990's, following what was termed the 'wind of change blowing from Eastern Europe', where totalitarian governing structures seemed to collapse overnight, have largely failed, with only a few notable exceptions. Democratisation is, in my view, the horse, as it were, that must be placed before the cart of African development, prosperity and well being.

The evident failure of democracy in present-day Africa and the triumph of dictatorship, under various guises, in most parts of Africa, need little demonstration. With very few arguably possible exceptions, such as South Africa, Tanzania, Ghana, Kenya (?), Nigeria (?), attempts at democratisation in contemporary Africa (mostly externally instigated by key Western nations such as Britain and the United States) have not only failed but also brought some of the countries to a situation of civil war or to the brink of total disintegration and an increase in human suffering and misery, by comparison with the past. In a country like Cameroon, with which I have direct first hand familiarity, and which can be said to have had one of the best chances of effecting a peaceful postcolonial transition from dictatorship to pluralistic democracy, on account of a fairly resilient domestic economy and elements of both Anglophone liberal thinking and Francophone centralist practice, this failure has been very obvious, in spite of what superficial observation or governmental rhetoric might mislead one to believe. Cameroon has managed to avoid civil war and to stay relatively peaceful in a region characterised by strife and turbulence; it has also managed to avoid famine and the more glaring manifestations of poverty. But this situation is due more to sheer chance than to deliberate political policy or action, as my analysis below will attempt to demonstrate.

My initial hunches for explaining the failure of democratisation in Africa revolve around the following non-exhaustive factors:

- Absence of genuine democratic structures.
- Failure to modernise traditional structures, habits and patterns of thought.
- Failure to properly domesticate and indigenise borrowed structures and modes of thought.
- Absence of the genuine political will to democratise.
- Availability of an inexhaustible stock of immunising tactics and subterfuges to incumbent dictators.
- Connivance of very influential external governments, agencies and persons.

## African Systems and the Structures of Democracy

If we understand democratic structures in the modern setting as including, *inter alia*, such things as a system in which there is separation of powers between those who make laws, those who execute them, and those charged with punishing infringements of the law; as a system in which all citizens without any exception are equally subject to the same laws; as a system which guarantees freedom of thought and expression; a system where the will of the majority holds sway on contentious issues but where the rights of minorities are protected by law; a system where fundamental human rights are respected and protected; a system, most importantly, where power is subject to strict controls and regular periodic renewal or change of mandate, then it needs no arguing that most post-independence African countries have failed in practising democracy. Some of such structures existed in the precolonial traditional governing systems of Africa, in spite of the fact that most were monarchies in which change at the top could come only at the passing of the incumbent.

Most modern African governing systems would seem to have borrowed from the traditional past the principle of non-change at the helm of power without also modernising the traditional strict control of power wielded by the pre-colonial kings. For that reason, heads of African states have been mostly *de facto* monarchs wielding power without any checks and balances, power without any responsibility. If we needed to exemplify, we could consider heads of state such as Sese Seko Mobutu of Zaire, Jean-Bedel Bokasa of Central African Republic, Houphouet Boigny of Ivory Coast, Gyasimbe Eyadema of Togo, Omar Bongo of Gabon and Paul Biya of Cameroon. On the other hand, most African countries have also borrowed from the industrialised Western countries the idea of multi-parties (usually based within the Western context on different ideologies) as one of the structures of democracy, without any attempt to indigenise it in line with local conditions. The result in many cases has been the multiplication of political parties along ethnic and sectarian lines, leading to a cacophony of divisions and civil strife.

Democracy in Africa need not necessarily follow Western models or paradigms, some of whose elements are in fact only dubiously democratic. If we consider, for instance, the effects of the use of money, paid propaganda and the skilful manipulation of public opinion on 'democratic' choices, then some Western democracies are only superficially democratic. Democracy in any actual context needs to adapt itself to the culture, world-view, values, customs and practices of the society in question, as long these do not contradict the fundamentals of democracy. Democracy is also, in principle, quite possible within a non-party[1] or a one-party system.[2] It is a well-known fact that public decision-making in traditional Africa was usually effected by the method of consensus, which in no way implied unanimity or total agreement, but rather an exhaustive discussion of differences, the recognition of the irreconcilable ones, and the fashioning of a way forward which permitted the suspension of disagreements. Such a procedural method if appropriately modernised could be quite compatible with democratic values. Julius Nyerere sufficiently demonstrated this with his idea of *UJAMAA*. But democracy, anywhere at any time, must necessarily subscribe to democratic values translated into and sustained by democratic structures.

## Political and Moral Egalitarianism

Political egalitarianism is one of the enabling conditions of democracy. One of the fundamental assumptions of an egalitarian system is the moral equality of all human beings as human, without individuating differentiations; the equality of all citizens of society as citizens. All humans, *qua* human, are equal because they have a common defining characteristic – their humanity. The equality of human beings does not imply that they have the same descriptive or individuating characteristics; those are rather what distinguish one human being from another. But all humans are equal in the sense that on the basis of their humanness they are accorded the basic human rights of freedom and moral equality. We describe such equality as **moral equality** to distinguish it from other putative types of equality. It is such equality which in the political domain justifies the rule of law and the policy of 'one person one vote'. By simple extension, it is this sense of equality which imposes respect for minority groups within any community.

We may describe a meritocratic system as one in which every individual is endowed with moral equality and is freely able to be justly held responsible or compensated for personal activities regarding the wellbeing of society in general. Although some human societies can be described as 'individualistic' and others as 'communalistic', every society must to some extent or other combine communalistic and individualistic elements. Few individuals seek to survive outside a community, while any community endures only by virtue of the collective and individual efforts and contributions of its members. From this perspective, it is perfectly possible to combine the best values of a communalistic outlook with those of an individualistic orientation.

Meritocracy is one of the indispensable road companions of democracy and development. In a meritocracy, subjective data, such as birth place, ethnicity, parentage, province of origin, gender, religious, political or ideological affiliation, etc. do not count in selection and reward procedures. However, a meritocratic system can indeed accommodate social gestures that attempt at righting or minimising past wrongs and discrimination inflicted on identifiable groups, through some form or other of affirmative action. The rationale employed in this instance is certainly based on the concept of fairness.

I would therefore say that a democracy is any system underpinned by the interconnected values and ideas of liberty or freedom and equality, that permits periodic change of leadership without bloodshed or violence. The indispensable structures and indices of a liberal democratic system include: the rule of law, separation of the main types of civil powers, freedom of thought and association, freedom of expression, respect of human rights, broadly consensual rules for belonging to, living and operating within the collectivity (usually spelled out in a constitution), clear consensual rules for accessing and vacating positions of power (usually elaborated in an electoral code), and fair practices in the social, political and economic spheres.

## History, Democracy and African Dictatorships

It needs to be recognised that pure dictatorships, that is, power without any internal controls, checks and balances, were introduced in Africa by Western colonialism. Colonialism was a system based on the imposition and acceptance of superiority – that of the coloniser over the colonised. Before the colonial intervention, many African governing systems were traditional monarchies, many of which seem, by design or accident, to have struck a viable balance between autocracy and democracy, thanks to the ritualised control of power. Within such systems, extensive powers were accorded the monarch but only on trust and in reciprocity. There was strict control of power through ritual taboos, some institutions and personalities of high moral integrity, such as *kwifon, ngwerong, takumbeng nngang*, priests/priestesses, sages, medicine persons, diviners, etc., to cite examples from the traditional kingdoms of the Western grassland areas of Cameroon. In such kingdoms, ritual safeguarding and protection were ensured for the land (kingdom) as distinct from the king, for the ordinary person, the departed ancestors, and the as-yet-unborn. Such controls acted as an effective block against dictatorial or arbitrary abuse or misuse of power and authority.

Within such settings, the privileges of power and authority were counter-balanced by its heavy responsibilities, restrictions and dangers. In traditional Africa, a monarch could sometimes be subjected to a public act of atonement for a mistake, transgression or taboo wittingly or otherwise broken or violated, as was witnessed quite recently (1989) with Ngaa' Bifon III, the Fon of the Kingdom of Nso', who reigned from 1983-1993. As an institution, the African king was often symbolically considered immortal, but as a person not only mortal but fragile, wherefore, the title *kimforkir* (fragility) accorded to some of the Fons of the Nso' kingdom. In some extreme cases, when the traditional monarch's continued rule was considered particularly dangerous or ruinous for the collectivity, he could be escorted into exile (usually by the women) as happened quite recently (2004) in the Fondom (Kingdom) of Babanki-Tungo (alias Big Babanki) in the Western grasslands area of Cameroon. In extreme cases, the monarch may be punished with death, as in fact eventually happened with the Fon of Babanki-Tungo (January 2006) when he sneaked back from exile into the Fondom and was promptly beaten to death and gruesomely burned on the borders of the village.

With only a few notable exceptions, most post-independence ruling regimes in Africa are pure dictatorships, co-extensive with the colonial regimes they replaced. Furthermore, the economic and political problems encountered by many of the post-colonial nations of Africa lead many to reflect negatively on the decolonisation process. Consider, for example, the serious problems experienced in the countries now known as the Congo, Rwanda, Burundi and the Sudan.

Under Western pressures, many African dictatorships are today successfully masquerading behind democratic rhetoric, slogans and symbolism. Such phantom democracies are presently flourishing, particularly in Francophone Africa (Togo, Gabon, Burkina-Faso, Cameroon, Chad, Equatorial Guinea), for reasons that must have some connection with the administrative structure, manner and style of French colonialism and subsisting neo-colonialism. But genuine democratic systems, erected on firm democratic foundations and structures, are an indispensable pre-condition for peaceful and enduring development anywhere.

It, however, needs to be pointed out that multi-partyism and democratic elections, often brandished as proofs of democracy, by themselves, are not necessarily signs of a genuine democratic system. In Cameroon, for example, the ruling regime constantly brandishes the peaceful nature of the numerous 'democratic' elections it has conducted since the early 1990s, and the fact that there are more than two hundred registered political parties, as a sign that Cameroon's democracy is highly advanced. Elections by themselves, even when patently democratic, are not necessarily signs of democracy itself. They may only help to replace one autocratic tyrant with another, or, more usually, confirm the incumbent autocrat in his office. The problem is not just with lack of democratic elections but rather with the highly centralised and authoritarian governing systems, which give no real chance for a peaceful and genuine alternation of power. We have seen recently in Togo, where a long reigning dictator, on the approach of his natural death, arranged with the army to use every means, including ostensibly 'democratic' means to install his son as his successor. What difference could be expected in a country like Gabon, whose minister of the armed forces is the son while the minister of finance is the daughter of the incumbent 'democratically elected' president, were the latter to follow his former Togolese counterpart to the great beyond? Izu Marcel Onyeocha[3] has advanced very plausible reasons as to why he considers the structure of multi-party democracy without qualifications as fundamentally unsuitable for a country like Nigeria.

As a consequence of the lack of genuine democracy, Africa is today a crises-ridden continent, politically, economically, sociologically and culturally. And yet, it can be said that Africa abounds in natural resources of whatever dimension. With these endowments one would expect under normal circumstances that the continent would have been well on the way towards serious economic growth and general development. So, what is the genesis and what are the causes of the present problematic of Africa, and what sustainable solutions are available or may be prescribed?

## Cameroon: Africa in Miniature

For the purposes of this chapter, allow me to focus attention on three crisis areas, namely, politics, ecology and conflict, each and all of which are highly subversive of development. I will, further, use Cameroon as my focal case and paradigm, mainly because I happen to have first-hand experience of the social scientific situation in the Cameroon, and also because Cameroon is actually in many ways paradigmatic of the rest of Africa. Cameroon is, veritably, in many ways, Africa in Miniature, as some Cameroonians are wont to call it. In Cameroon, all the macroscopic problems of Africa as well as its potentialities and possibilities seem to be present. This country is the meeting, if not melting, pot of the colonial legacies of leading ex-colonial nations of the world such as Germany, Britain and France.

Lying in Equatorial Africa, between Latitudes 2° and 13° north of the Equator, Cameroon occupies a surface area of 475,000km², with an estimated population of approximately 16.5 million inhabitants. Cameroon's neighbours are many and varied. To the west is Nigeria, 'the giant' of Africa, with whom she shares the whole length of her western border; to the north, Niger and Chad, with whom, together with Nigeria, she shares the Lake Chad basin; to the east, the Central African Republic; to the south, Congo Brazzaville, Gabon and Equatorial Guinea. The south-western end of Cameroon opens out onto the Bight of Biafra in the Gulf of Guinea within the Atlantic Ocean, with a coastline of over 350km. The Cameroon Mountain (Mount Fako), on the south west extremity is the highest peak in West and Central Africa (4070 meters), an active volcano which last erupted in 2003.

Cameroon also has about 34 crater lakes, some of which like Nyos (21 August 1986) and Manoun (15 August 1984) emitted lethal gases which killed hundreds of humans and animals. Quite surprisingly, the cause of these occasional massive lethal gas releases has not been firmly and convincingly established and, even more surprisingly, the Cameroon authorities have sometimes shown only lukewarm interest in the issue, leaving ordinary citizens to engage in the wildest of speculations. Research teams from several Western countries which rushed in and collected data following the 1986 Nyos disaster met for an international conference in 1989 in Cameroon's capital city, Yaounde, but dispersed in disarray over serious disagreements. It is only quite recently (January 1996) that an American scientist came up with, at last, a plausible-sounding scientific explanation of these lake gas disasters.[4] Only since then has some system of monitoring the lakes to ensure safety been introduced.

Cameroon's geographical, biological, historical, linguistic and cultural diversity leaves out little that is of real significance elsewhere on the African continent. The major ecosystems and climatic zones, the flora and fauna of the continent are all to be found in Cameroon; so are the different Central African peoples, from the Twa of the south-east extremity of Cameroon through the coastal Bantu speaking communities, through the Sudanese of the savannah middle-belt to the Arabic speakers of the Sahel-encroaching extreme north. Cameroon's population is also composed of almost equal proportions of ethnic religions (39%), Christians (40%) and Islamic (21%). This is a near-perfect case of that triple heritage that theorists such as Nkwame Nkrumah and Ali Mazrui have written about – where African, Euro-Christian and Islamic values meet and mix.

In terms of economic resources, Cameroon is self-sufficient in domestic food production and produces for export most of what are also produced elsewhere in Africa: cocoa, coffee, tea, banana, groundnut, palm-produce, cotton, timber, rubber, petroleum, etc. With a plethora of indigenous languages and corresponding ethnic cultures, and with French and English as official national languages, Africa's rich linguistic and cultural diversity finds an obvious instantiation in Cameroon. Now, why should an African country with such a profile as Cameroon's be the failure that it has been in all domains of development except perhaps the game of football?

## Cameroon in History

Douala is Cameroon's biggest coastal city. According to historians, one of the kings of the Douala area of Cameroon (King Bell) signed a commercial treaty with the English in 1856. Subsequently, all the kings of the Douala area wrote a joint letter to Queen Victoria, inviting England to establish a 'protectorate' over their area. But as her Britanic Majesty was tardy in answering, the Douala kings, in disappointment, turned to the Germans who quickly set up a 'protectorate' in 1884. The English later arrived (a few weeks too late!) with a mandate from Queen Victoria to do what the Germans had just done but, to their disappointment, they saw the German flag already flying triumphantly in the Douala breeze.

At the 'carving up of Africa' Berlin Conference of 1884, Germany's colonial lordship over Cameroon was confirmed by the other colonial powers. The Germans set up their capital at Buea, on the slopes of Mount Cameroon (Fako), with its relatively mild climate, free from mosquitoes, and, from there, consolidated their grip over the rest of what came to be known as Kamerun. The peace-loving peoples of the coastal areas were easily bought over with exotic gifts and promises but the politically well organised kingdoms of the hinterland had to be subdued by military force. By the eve of the First World War (1914), the Germans were in total colonial control of the territory. But when the Germans were defeated in the war, they lost Cameroon along with all of their other African colonies. The League of Nations took control and placed the western part of Cameroon under British mandate and the eastern part under French mandate, an arrangement which the United Nations maintained in 1945, when Germany again lost the Second World War and the United Nations Organisation (UNO) replaced the League of Nations.

The British administered their own areas of Cameroon, which came to be known as 'British Cameroons', composed of 'Northern Cameroons' and 'Southern Cameroons', from Lagos, as a part of Nigeria, their largest African colony. 'Northern Cameroons' was administratively attached to the Northern Region and 'Southern Cameroons' to the Eastern Region of Nigeria. In the area under French mandate ('French Cameroons'), agitation for independence started in 1948 when the UPC (Union des Populations du Cameroun) was formed. The programme of the UPC was centred on the slogan 'Immediate Independence and Unification'. The French colonials were not amused. They brutally suppressed the UPC and it went underground. Some of its militants escaped to 'Southern Cameroons'. The UPC rebellion continued in 'French Cameroons' especially in the Bassa and Bamiléké regions through 'independence' which the French 'granted' on January 1st 1960. The country became known as La République du Cameroun. The rebellion was not, however, definitively crushed until around 1971.

Meanwhile, in Cameroon under British mandate, parliamentary democracy had been established and was flourishing, with several parties in lively and healthy competition. The first ever elections organised in the territory were won by the KNC (Kamerun National Convention) which formed a government under the leadership of Dr. E.M.L. Endeley. In 1959, the ruling party lost heavily in another election to the opposition party, KNDP (Kamerun National Democratic Party), and John Ngu Foncha headed a new government.

Nigeria gained her own independence on 1 October 1960 as a Federal Republic. At that point, the United Nations proposed a plebiscite in Cameroon under British mandate with two options: (a) Do you wish to achieve independence by joining the independent Federal Republic of Nigeria? or (b) Do you wish to achieve independence by joining the independent La République du Cameroun? The plebiscite took place on 11 February 1961, and 'Southern Cameroonians' voted overwhelmingly (70.49%) to achieve independence by joining La République du Cameroun while 'Northern Cameroonians' opted for remaining as a part of the Federal Republic of Nigeria.

After the plebiscite, a constitutional conference was held in the border town of Foumban between 'Southern Cameroons' and 'La République du Cameroun' during which a Federal system was agreed upon with a provision (Article 49) that any attempt to abolish the federal structure would be null and void. And so the 'Federal Republic of Cameroon' was born, composed of two federated states: West Cameroon (with its capital at Buea) and East Cameroon (with its capital at Yaoundé).

Things went on fairly smoothly in the 'Federal Republic of Cameroon', a multicultural and officially bilingual (French and English) country with three parliaments, two legal systems (Common Law and Napoleonic Law), two educational systems, two administrative systems and two peoples with different colonial experiences, orientations and outlooks, trying to understand and learn from each other in a bold experiment in modern nation building.

But in 1966, Ahmadou Ahidjo, the leader of 'East Cameroon' (former La République du Cameroun), who was now the President of the Federal Republic while John Ngu Foncha, the leader of 'West Cameroon' (former Southern Cameroons) was the Vice President, deceived the leaders of all the other political parties into sinking their differences to merge into a single party for the purported end of accelerated development and unity. The result was the CNU (Cameroon National Union). Now under a one-party state, Ahidjo moved fast and decisively to assume dictatorial powers and to set up a highly efficient network of state repression and espionage. Then in 1972, he organised what he called a 'referendum' proposing a unitary state. Not surprisingly, his proposal 'won' by 99.99 per cent of the votes supposed to have been cast, thanks to the ubiquitous 'Préfets' and their even more ubiquitous security arm, the 'gendarmes'. Then, by decree, Ahidjo changed the name of the country from 'Federal Republic of Cameroon' to 'United Republic of Cameroon'[5].

Ten years later, in 1982, Ahidjo suddenly resigned, for reasons that remain mysterious up to the present, and handed over power to one of his most loyal collaborators, Paul Biya. In 1984, Paul Biya, without any further ado, issued a decree reverting the name of the country to 'La République du Cameroun', the name of French East Cameroon before Reunification! This was variously interpreted either as an act of unilateral secession from the union by 'East Cameroon' or as an act of annexation and assimilation of 'West Cameroon' into 'East Cameroon'. The effects of these dictatorial actions have ever since been shaping politics in Cameroon.

Ahidjo had resolutely kept Cameroon out of both La Francophonie and the Commonwealth. Biya did not hesitate to take Cameroon into La Francophonie and, to mitigate the political implications and consequences of this action, has recently (November 1995) also taken Cameroon into the Commonwealth. But, since the main preoccupation of La Francophonie, as so clearly stated by the late President François Mitterand and reaffirmed by his successor, Jacques Chirac, is to fight 'Anglo-Saxon cultural imperialism', while that of the Commonwealth is, without doubt, to spread it, it is clear that Cameroon is in a rather untenable position as a member of both.

My own suggestion, relative to Cameroon's chequered history is that the country should *first* symbolically revert its name simply to KAMERUN or to some new historical name to remind us of why two territories with very different colonial histories ever thought of merging to form one country, and then second, tidy up and lay afresh the constitutional foundations of a potential nation that would be culturally, economically and politically committed to its peoples in particular and to Africa in general, without being entangled in the tiresome wooing game of the ex-colonial powers. The question is this: in what way do the divisive notions of Anglophonie or Francophonie assist in the struggle for African development?

**Crisis Profile**

In spite of its remarkable human and natural resources and potentialities, Cameroon is today one of Africa's cases of failure: economically, politically and ecologically. These failures are fundamentally founded and grounded on dictatorship and the absence of democracy. Cameroon's economy, which, in the late 1970s and early 1980s, was being rated with triple A's by international experts as one of the most promising on the entire African continent, has been ruined by shady mismanagement, large-scale executive fraud, ever falling prices of primary products in the world market, and a fall in domestic production levels. Since 1987, when the negative results started becoming rather palpable, the leadership of Paul Biya progressively increased its promises and assurances to turn around the economy in direct proportion to the progressively worsening situation, backed by annual declarations of sighting the light at the end of the economic tunnel.

Ecologically, the encroachment of the Sahara Desert on Cameroon's northernmost region has continued unabated with only occasional token attempts at fighting it. Cameroon's appreciable reserves of tropical forests have also been depleted at an alarming rate by both piecemeal local activities and large scale commercial logging. Today, while the trend in other parts of the world is to protect and preserve forests for environmental and global ecological reasons, there are about 112 government licensed logging companies in Cameroon, frantically destroying the forests with careless abandon. As recently as July 1995, the Cameroon Government, within the propagandistic context of convincing the World Bank, the IMF and Cameroonians in general that it is capable and soon about to revive the dying economy, has been boasting that wood is now Cameroon's second foreign exchange earner after petroleum and is even poised to take the lead in the near future.[6] An indirect effect of deforestation is that it is increasingly affecting overall rainfall and water for both domestic and industrial usage. Some experts are predicting that, by the year 2050, there will be no more forests left in Cameroon. But from what I have myself personally witnessed, I do not think that Cameroon's forests could survive the next two decades at the present rate of exploitation.

Cameroon also faces pollution through improper or non-disposal of urban domestic and industrial waste. Yaoundé, Cameroon's capital city, for instance, until quite recently, ranked amongst the least efficiently maintained cities in the world. Oil exploitation in Cameroon has always been shrouded in secrecy, but its effects on the ecology of the south-western areas where it is carried out can be no different from that on the Ogoni lands just across the border, to which international attention was recently drawn by the efforts of the Nigerian writer, Ken Saro-Wiwa, murdered in 1995 by the Abacha regime. On both sides, it is a clear case of foreign interests in alliance with a corrupt dictatorship trampling, with arrogance, on the rights, safety, security and survival of helpless local peoples. An oil pipe line, nearly 1000 kilometres long has now also been laid from Chad through the whole length of Cameroon to the coastal town of Kribi. The environmental concerns and consequences of this project have constantly been swept under the carpet by the Cameroon government and the American companies responsible for it.

Politically, the process of democratisation in Cameroon, which seemed to be on course from 1990, following the launching of an opposition party, the Social Democratic Front (SDF), got arrested in 1992, when the regime in power evidently lost the presidential elections but decided, with the support of the French government, which seemed afraid that its interests would not be protected under a new democratic regime led by an Anglophone, to stay put in power. At the time, the French interior Minister clearly stated that France was not ready to accept an Anglophone President in Cameroon. French policy in Africa is no secret to anybody. In stark terms, the French, by contrast with their other comrades in colonialism and empire-building, have never decolonised their own territories where the others, at least, did so by substitution with remote control mechanisms or arrangements. In all French colonies, 'independence' was simply a euphemism for a blatant political fraud. This is the causal background for French support and maintenance of dictatorships in preference to democratically elected leaders in Africa.

Since 1992, Cameroon has remained in a state of political uncertainty and uneasiness in spite of 'democratic' elections, continuing government rhetoric and periodic declarations about reviving the economy and advancing the democratic process. The dictatorship in Cameroon has been unwilling to yield to genuine democratic pressures and has successfully taken refuge behind a myriad of subterfuges dressed up in democratic rhetoric. Furthermore, Cameroon is in constant danger of internal conflict as the Anglophone minority component of the country (formerly 'Southern Cameroons'), fed up with marginalisation, exploitation, failure of the democratisation process, and continuing assimilation, is keeping the reassertion of its autonomy ever in view. A petition to this effect was taken to the United Nations by a delegation of the 'Southern Cameroons National Council (SCNC)' in March 1995 and currently there is a case pending in the international court for the rights of minorities. If a peaceful outcome is to be expected, the United Nations and the other Western powers ought to act preventively and intervene in Cameroon before things get out of hand. Cameroon also has a standing dispute, which occasionally breaks out in armed conflict, with Nigeria, over the oil-rich Bakassi Peninsular and, in spite of a 2003 ruling at the International Court of Justice affirming Cameroon's sovereignty over the disputed area as well as a United Nations arranged joint commission between the two countries for peaceful implementation of the international court ruling, Nigerian troops are still occupying the disputed area.

## Cameroon and its Disjunctions: Precolonial, Colonial and Postcolonial Structures

My general thesis is that the present plight of Africa is a direct consequence of both colonialism with its alienating transformation of the African psyche and personality and the evident failure of the post-colonial regimes of Africa to govern democratically. Africa's present predicament is largely to be blamed on the culpable and invincible limitations and irresponsibility of the leadership of the various African countries. They have not, of course, all failed to the same degree. An exception might be cited here and there, but this does not change the stark reality any more than, say, finding a few grains of rice in a bag of corn changes the fact that it is still a bag of corn. No one would deny, for instance, that Nelson Mandela's decision to serve only one term as president of post-Apartheid South Africa was an African political anomaly. In this regard, he and Julius Nyerere are two notable exceptions of African political leaders who, instead of amassing personal wealth and clinging on to power, have done just the opposite. The truth is that most of the postcolonial governments of Africa have brought their countries and people not only economic chaos and generalised misery, but the prospect or actuality of real catastrophic disintegration. And in most cases, the damage done by the corrupt dictators will only be fully realised and assessed after the dictatorships have yielded place to more democratic systems. How then does one explain the political behaviour of Mandela and Nyerere? One answer is that both men, through long study, have understood that modern government is and ought to be radically different from what was the norm in monarchical and feudal society for centuries. They also recognised that freedom from European colonial domination would be meaningless if the new post-colonial governments offered little political change in terms of democratic governance.

Colonialism and neo-colonialism should, therefore, bear their fair share of responsibility for the present state of affairs. It was the various colonial administrations which introduced the purely dictatorial systems of government, that is to say, dictatorships without any internal controls or checks and balances, into Africa, and neo-colonialism actively supports the present state of affairs. If some of the really influential Western powers had not changed – through pressure – their position about giving covert support to the apartheid regime in South Africa, Apartheid would probably still hold sway and Nelson Mandela would probably still be imprisoned. But direct settler colonialism in South Africa was defeated because the popular struggle forced the West to desist from direct political and economic support of Apartheid. Even Britain's conservative government under Thatcher had to yield at some point.

Recently, the same weak arguments were heard in relation to the Abacha dictatorship in Nigeria before it finally collapsed on its own. Had comprehensive economic sanctions, especially on oil, been imposed on the Abacha regime following the death of Ken Saro-Wiwa and the other Ogoni people,[7] as canvassed by many people the world over, the Abacha regime, I believe, would have collapsed within a fortnight, giving Nigerians another chance for a veritable democratic breakthrough. But beneficiaries of Nigerian petroleum argued that imposing an oil boycott on Nigeria would only hurt the poor masses of Nigeria. It was evidently not the interest of the Nigerian masses that was at stake here. The same is true for the other African dictatorships under which the ordinary masses are now chafing with much stoicism. The obvious solution is that the masses resume the same kind of struggles that they waged against the colonial regimes. The struggle has certainly been more complex, given the wiles of the neocolonial governments who seek to confuse the masses by duplicitous appeal to ethnic loyalties and vain economic promises.

Because of a rather widespread fallacy that the precolonial kingships of Africa were all dictatorships and the very cynical argument of some people to the effect that Europeans have no moral right to impose democracy on Africans, just as they had no moral right to impose colonialism, let me discuss this issue at some length. This argument has been expressed by some of the African dictators as well as by some people in the West who are their witting or unwitting allies.

Many of the pre-colonial kingdoms of Africa had political structures which might have seemed authoritarian from the outside but which, internally, were in fact secured by very strict controls of power through institutions and personalities of moral authority whose main preoccupation was protection and safeguarding of the kingdom from the transgressions of those in legal authority such as kings, queens and other kinds of monarchs.

To take an example, when the German colonisers first arrived in *Nso'*, in the western Grassfields of Cameroon, in 1902, they found a relatively flourishing and rapidly expanding Kingdom, composed of originally smaller kingdoms most of which had voluntarily merged (under threat from the Fulani aggression called *'bara nyam' in Lamnso', the language of the Nso*, a ripple of the expansionist religious wars of Uthman Dan Fodio), and a few that had been militarily subdued and loosely annexed. The King (*Fon*) of Nso' who, by original consensus, was always selected by a committee headed by the leader of one of the lineage strands of the Kingdom from among the male offspring of a female of another distinct strand (the *Nso'Mmntar* or commoner class) and a male of yet another strand (the *wonnto'* or royal class) had quite extensive powers which were, however, considered as held in trust and subject to several established controls.

These controls, notable among which were those exercised by the regulatory secret society, *nwerong*, and the leaders of the commoner segments of the Kingdom, (*mmntar Nso'*), were an effective safeguard against dictatorial or arbitrary abuse of power by the King who was, moreover, often reminded of his weakness as a person as opposed to his strength as the King. Whenever he is away from the palace, it is usual for visitors to salute and pay homage to the empty royal stool (*kava*) exactly as if its occupant were sitting on it. One of the favourite titles of the King (*Fon*) of Nso' is *kimforkir* (fragility). He is 'His Royal Fragility' and if he happens to die outside the palace, as happened on two occasions in the last century, both, incidentally, during the period of German colonisation, he would forever after be referred to as *kimforkir* of wherever he had died; for example, *kimforkir ke Cisong* (Sëëm 11,1880-1907), and *kimforkir_ke_Vikuutsen* (Mapiri, 1907-1910). Of course, as King, the Fon cannot die.[8] At his burial, he is seated on the royal throne (*kava*), ritually uncapped, and his personal name, which cannot be called from the moment of installation while he remains King, is called out, with the addition that that is the person who has died (*kpu*) but that the Fon has not disappeared (*lai*), that the Fon continues shining like the sun. Obviously, in this cultural instance, the kingship is permanent while the king himself is transient.

It is very significant to note that, whenever the King (*Fon*) of Nso' dies, many eligible candidates for succession flee from the Kingdom for fear of being seized and forcibly installed as King. The successor must, however, be installed the same day, since the royal stool (*kava*) is not supposed to remain for more than a single day without an occupant. And the successor is usually always forcibly seized by *ngwerong* and installed against, at least, token frantic protestations. The responsibilities and restrictions of kingship in Nso' arguably only balance its advantages and privileges.

At the arrival of the Germans in Nso' at the turn of the century, the political set-up and general situation were such as to create a certain amount of stability and self-confidence. And one of the German officers, named Zimmermann, who provided arms to Captain Pavel, did not fail to note it in writing that although the Nso' had never seen Europeans before, they were nonetheless 'confident in their bearing unlike the timid forest people'.[9] This, however, must have been considered an undesirable disposition, at least, by Lt. Houben and his group, who arrived five months after Pavel, with conscripts from other grassfield kingdoms, notably, Bali and Babungo. Failing to bully the leadership of the Nso' Kingdom into timidity and submission, Houben and his group set the palace (*Nto' Nso'*) on fire, after picking it clean of what they considered valuable, before proceeding to Banyo.

Pavel himself had explicitly stated in writing that he and his retinue had been well received in Nso' and that the *Fon* (King) had agreed he would comply with their demands punctually.[10] But, that notwithstanding, the Germans returned to Nso' in

1905 under Captain Houptmann Glauning, Commander of the so-called *Schutztruppe* in the Bamenda *Bezirk* (district) and again attempted to intimidate the Fon of Nso' into submission, by conducting a demonstration march through all the states bordering Nso' proper – a veritable *argumentum ad bacculum*. The Fon, Sëëm II, was, however, unimpressed and is reported to have even boasted that he had nothing to fear because his subjects were as numerous as finger millet.[11]

Meanwhile, the Germans discovered that the Bamum Kingdom, ancestral brothers of the Nso', had a serious grudge against the latter on account of their late King, Sangou (father of the then incumbent, Njoya), who twenty years earlier, had been killed during a battle in Nso'. His skull was still retained in Nso' and, according to traditional custom, a new King could not properly be enthroned in Bamum without it. So, Glauning went into a strong alliance with the Bamum Kingdom which saw here a golden opportunity not only to recover Sangou's skull, but also to avenge itself against the Nso'. Using two well-equipped companies, Glauning's army and its Bamum allies invaded Nso' in April 1906 from two directions. The war lasted about forty days during which the Nso', experiencing canon and machine gun fire for the first time, suffered heavy casualties and learned timidity and how not to carry a confident bearing before Europeans. On June 6 1906, Sëëm II admitted to Glauning: '*Atav ne shaa mo*' (You have really proved stronger than I), and surrendered.[12]

Writing about the expansion of the Nso' Kingdom in the 19th and early 20th centuries, Mzeka N. Paul has noted tellingly that one of the factors which encouraged this expansion in both human and territorial terms was:

> ...the tendency to use the strategy of consensus rather than coercion in administrative pursuits. Pre-German survivors in Nso' insist that coercive use of authority in certain areas of Nso' culture was imitated from the German colonial administration, which used physical force as an instrument of administration.[13]

After independence, African governments inherited the dictatorial systems and structures of colonialism and tried to justify them by appealing to the need for national unity, integration, development, well-being, peace and prosperity. These are the lofty ideals which President Alhaji Ahmadou Ahidjo used in 1966 to impose a one-party system in Cameroon and, further, in 1972, to impose a highly centralised unitary system of government. But what, in fact, happened was that colonialism transformed itself into neo-colonialism by forging alliances of partnership with unscrupulous and opportunistic individual Africans, or a handful of such individuals, so that economic exploitation could continue on a scale, in many cases, worse than under overt colonialism.

Contemporary African heads of state and their minions are mostly unscrupulous kleptocrats who have constantly emptied the public treasury of their impoverished countries to bank and invest abroad. Democracy in Africa, or anywhere else, need not follow the Western model. But I consider the main, indispensable and irreducible minimum of a democratic system, anywhere, to be the ability to remove a bad government or, in any case, one perceived as such by the governed, without any bloodshed or violence. It is on this political principle that the post-Enlightenment modern West is founded. Consider, for example, the summarising views thereon expressed by the Western political philosopher, Karl Popper.[14] It is a view that strongly recommends itself, particularly in the present context and situation of Africa.

## Explanations

The problematic of African development is an issue that has been of great interest to social scientists over the years. In strict economic developmental terms there have been those who have advocated a whole adoption of the neo-liberal economic model, according to which free markets and minimal government constitute the necessary model for economic growth and development. One recalls the economic treatises of W.W. Rostow (*The Stages of Economic Growth*, Cambridge University Press, 1960) and W.A. Lewis (*The Theory of Economic Growth*, London, Allen and Unwin, 1955) both founded on the free market economic model. But then, there were the opposing treatises developed by theorists of anti-capitalist persuasions such as Marx, Lenin, Mao, and in the African case, Nkrumah and Nyerere. I mention this conflict between the two development paradigms of capitalism and socialism because I want to explain the developmental problematic in the case of Africa as partially derived from the post World War II Cold War conflict between the West and the Communist world. African governments were afforded licence and weaponry to run authoritarian and anti-democratic states as long as they proved themselves to be firm allies of the West or the Communist bloc.

Furthermore, it is a fact that the achieving of independence by Africa's nations could be seen as a purely formal exercise given that economic ties to the erstwhile colonising powers remained intact. The argument that colonialism was followed by neo-colonialism made by political theorists such as Kwame Nkrumah and more lately Samir Amin is a valid one. The problem was compounded by the fact that neither the West nor the socialist nations provided sufficient capital to Africa's nations so that they experience meaningful economic growth leading to development. While other nations such as Korea and Taiwan were subjected to authoritarian governments but with economic growth and development, Africa experienced only neocolonial authoritarianism with minimal economic growth.

Now that the Cold War is over, the peoples of Africa are now feeling more free to express the view that they deserve the maximum political freedoms and rights. They also believe that they are naturally entitled to the fruits of their labour and the resources of their respective nations. This was the basis for the anti-colonial struggle: freedom, democracy and economic growth and development.

In this new climate, African development needs a strong and viable civil society to force governments to make the right choices with regard to education, health, general welfare, political freedoms all with the goal of development in mind. I will not seek to analyze the situation by appeal to an unfounded African essentialism as some thinkers have done.[15] Humans are merely expressions of their history and their lived sociologies. There are no human essences that explain behaviour. It is better to explain the African situation by appeal to authors such as Nkrumah and Frantz Fanon whose *Wretched of the Earth* written on the eve of decolonisation is always relevant to the contemporary situation.

## Conclusion

It is quite clear, I believe, that there can be no development in Africa, nor peace and tranquility until the present dictatorships have, at least, yielded place to more genuinely democratic and accountable systems. The linkage between Africa's present political problems and colonialism ought to make the former colonisers feel more responsible for Africa's plight than would otherwise be fairly expected from motives of pure altruism. Any policy towards Africa today, no matter its overt or covert aim, (aid, trade, humanitarian help, mutual co-operation) would do well to realise that, although democratisation has so far, with only few notable exceptions, failed, the process of democratisation itself is clearly irreversible in a world rapidly becoming a global village. Political support for Africa's peoples today against its authoritarian governments would not only be morally right, but tactically preferable from the point of view of pure self interest.

My contention and suggestion is that any genuine attempt to assist Africa out of its present plight should give priority to the political dimension of the problem, that is to say, the instauration of genuine democratic systems based on firm and solid democratic structures. And Africa's peoples have come to realise this. In many African countries today the citizens would gladly and patiently bear extreme poverty, hardship and other privations for as long as necessary if only they were sure that that was what was really necessary to bring about a truly democratic and responsible government. In 1991, Cameroonians willingly and gladly subjected themselves to many harsh privations and hardships by boycotting French goods and services and remaining indoors in an operation termed 'Villes Mortes', in the hope of convincing the French Government to allow genuine democracy to take root in Cameroon. The French did not budge and the operation only helped in further damaging the already seriously damaged economy. Even today, many are the Cameroonians who celebrate whenever they hear news such as that the IMF or World Bank is unhappy with or considering suspending or blacklisting Cameroon. The hope here is that the collapse of the so-called structural adjustment programmes would lead to the collapse of dictatorship and a chance for a genuine democratic beginning. So, how could anyone helping to bring about such popular democratic change possibly be said to be imposing democracy on Africans? Is it conceivable to be culpable for imposing, say, health on a patient? The argument that Europeans (or whoever) have no moral right to urge African governments to practise democracy is a lame argument.

With regard to conflicts in general, it is also highly recommendable for Western governments and their arms manufacturers to seriously consider ceasing the supply of arms to African regimes, dissident groups, organisations and individuals. Such arms are generally used to crush popular dissent and to maintain neocolonial relationships between oppressive governments and their patron states. An embargo on arms sales to African governments would help in no small way towards peaceful resolution of conflicts and the advancement of democracy in Africa. The reason is that it is the unrestricted flow of arms to the undemocratic regimes in Africa that provide Africa's authoritarian governments with the means and confidence to continue their undemocratic practices. The recommendations made here should be seen in the context of the democratic struggle against neocolonial oppression with the full knowledge that the postcolonial world is a world run according to the dictates of *real politik*. Africa's peoples have always been aware of this fact long before they mounted their anti-colonial struggles. There are forces that are actively militating against Africa's development. Such forces are anti-democratic. Thus, African development will occur only within the context of genuine popular democracy.

## Notes

1. See Kwasi Wiredu, 'Democracy and Consensus in African Traditional Politics: A Plea for a Non-Party Polity' in Kwasi Wiredu, *Conceptual Decolonisation in African Philosophy* (Essays Selected and Introduced by Olusegun Oladipo), Ibadan, Nigeria: Hope Publications, 1995:53-63.

2. See Julius K. Nyerere, 'Democracy and the Party System' in *Readings in African Political Thought*, edited by Gideon-Cyrus M. Mutiso & S. W. Rohio, London, Nairobi, Ibadan, Lusaka: Heinemann, 1975:478-481.

3. See his 'Nigeria and Western Democracy: The Possibility of an African Alternative', in George F. McLean et al. (eds.), *Democracy, Culture and Values*, Volume II, Washington D.C: The Council for Research in Values and Philosophy, 2004:167-194.

4. See Youxue Zhang, 'Dynamics of $CO^2$-driven lake eruptions' in *Nature: International Weekly Journal of Science*, No. 6560, 4, Vol. 379, January, 1996.

5. For a good historical snapshot of the period 1922-1972, see Anthony Ndi, *The Golden Age of Southern (West) Cameroon 1946-1972: Impact of Christianity*, Bamenda, 2005.

6. See 'Exposé Liminaire de S.E. Bava Djingoer, Ministre de L'Environnement et des Forêts à l'occasion de la Conférence de Presse du 03 juillet 1995 à Yaoundé.'

7. These other Ogoni people, judicially murdered together with Ken Saro-Wiwa on 10 November 1995, are by name: Saturday Dobee, Barinem Kiob, Paul Levura, Nordue Eawo, Felix Nuate, Daniel Gbokoo, John Kpuinen, and Baribor Bera. To this list should be added Clement Tusima, who had earlier (August 1995) died in detention.

8. See B. Chem-Langhëë, et al., 'Nto' Nso' and its Occupants: Privileged Access and Internal Organisation in the Old and New Palaces', in *PAIDEUMA* 31, 1985:175.

9. See Mzeka, N. Paul, *Four Fons of Nso': Nineteenth and Early Twentieth Century Kingship in the Western Grassfields*, Bamenda, The Spider Publishing Enterprise, 1990:77; quoting E.M. Chilver, *Nso' and the Germans* (unpublished field research notes), p.1.

10. Ibid., p. 78.

11. Ibid., p. 77. Said Sëëm 11, while releasing a fistful of finger millet through his fingers: Mfan kaay? Amo Nso' dzeen ben! (What need I fear? Nso' people are as numerous as these!).

12. Ibid., p. 79.

13. Ibid., p. 15.
14. See especially his The *Open Society and Its Enemies*, Vols. 1 and 2, London and Henley, Routledge and Kegan Paul, 1945.
15. See Achille Mbembe, *On the Postcolony*, Berkeley, the University of California Press, 2001.

# 12

# Science, Technology and Development: Stakes of Globalisation

### Jean-Pierre Ymele

**Introduction**

One of the major phenomena of modern times is undoubtedly the intensification of information flows, capital transfers, company relocations around the world which are induced by growth and the excess capital generated in industrialised countries. As a solution to the crisis-stricken economies of West Europe which, in the aftermath of World War 2, strode to develop by adopting Nation-State as a social, political and economic reference system, this intensification caused the framework to implode and forced upon the rest of the world deregulations whose impacts resulted internally in lifting some obstacles linked to the social working conditions created by State interventionism and externally in weakening the rigidity of the national framework. The international, financial and trade institutions contributed a lot to this process by accelerating the liberalisation of potential outlets and the development of new markets, particularly in developing countries through restructuring, adjustment and liberalisation policies. These countries were thus absorbed into a global dynamics where their purported role was to offer new investment spaces. Indeed, they offer every condition for making bigger profits: abundant labour and lower salaries, barely constraining social security system, availability and closeness of raw materials, lower taxes and even negotiations facilities including possibly complacency and corruption.

According to the dominant neo-liberal discourse, the development of these countries depends on their entry into the market economy: liberalisation would open markets, facilitate productive investments and subsequently help contain poverty. Liberalisation is painted as humanism. The argument for an all-out liberalisation of markets and investment conditions in developing countries was no longer the search for new outlets to prevent devaluation of the excess capital accumulated in developed economies, but rather the desire to pull these countries out of the socio-political impasse in which they find themselves. The problem in fact does not lie there. Presumably, the collapse of the nation-state economic system in developed countries could even offer some opportunities to developing countries. Don't we have on one side, new outlets-seeking excess capital and on the other a blatant need for capital! Whatever the case may be, the constraining and almost irresistible[1] force of this globalisation is a welcome idea. It is described as a 'terrible machine' (Petrella 1997:17) swaying the world and practically leaving no other alternative. The stake involved for the economies and cultures of Third World countries is being passionately debated. Some see it like a sort of development sesame and others like a serious threat to these countries which if not cautioned will disappear in the universe (Hountondji 1997:24-26).

The fact that science and technology are the key factors of this phenomenon and that the stakes for developing countries are playing out at this level very often goes unnoticed. Indeed, the future will depend on what will have been gained or lost in the areas of science and technology. It is from this perspective that we suggest analysing here the consequences of globalisation on the practice of science and technology in developing countries. What will be the impact, on scientific and technological research in developing countries, of the planetary expansion of multinationals, company relocations and intensification of the flow of scientific and technological knowledge and all their consequences at the structural level? Will all these factors contribute to greater visibility of science and technology? Will they induce a re-appropriation of scientific and technological potentials, a necessary condition for their transformation into development activities? These are some of the questions raised by the globalisation phenomenon in relation to the development of science and technology in developing countries. These questions will be analysed a special focus on the place of technoscience as a key factor of societal development and globalisation.

## Technoscience as a Key Factor of Development[2]

It was not until recently that science actually acquired its current status in the development of industrialised countries (after World War 2). Before then, conventional science operated as a marginal phenomenon. Science usually reported retrospectively on the success of a technique which progressed essentially in an empirical manner. Science did not assist the technician, the latter helped science by devising its experimentation instruments. This was a time when science was resolutely knowledge-oriented. As we all know, the industrial revolution of the 18th and 19th centuries was not exactly the consequence of essentially scientific progress. Science cannot be said to have been decisively involved in the development of agriculture, textiles and transportation, not even in that of the primary industries. For example, the steam engine which importance in the industrial progress is well recognised, the first productions of which became operational around 1710, appeared well ahead of its explanatory theory. Newcomen, Savary and the others were rather craftsmen, blacksmiths, Cartwrights, etc., working empirically to enhance the efficiency of their machines and the yields thereof. Concurrently, theoretical science continued to develop in disciplines like physics, mathematics, chemistry and biology in particular. At the end of the 19th century, indeed, it helped dissipate many mysteries and was such a capital of knowledge that people were convinced by the idea that they held the secret of the universe. This meant that historically two approaches co-existed: one scientific and the other technological. Both converged in the second half of the last century (Hall 1956).

However, a collusion was initiated at the peak of the industrial revolution between science and technology as a result, in particular, of the work of many engineers who, with a solid scientific and technological background, took advantage of scientific knowledge to expand technological progress. Technology therefore resorted increasingly to scientific knowledge and processes to improve on its own while science became simultaneously strongly dependent on technology for its verification process. Jean Ladrière pertinently observed that this converging evolution was inscribed in the 'operational' nature of science (UNESCO 1977:16). It was the need to experiment its knowledge that led science to become allied with technology. For, science combines knowledge and practice at the time of experimentation and theorisation. Thus, by relying on technology to refine and generalise the use of the instruments and tools of which it prompted the invention, science contributed at the same time to the development of those tools. Telescope, microscope, air pump, etc., which were being used in the 17th century for scientific purposes were improved, generalised and their social practice mainstreamed. This has resulted in some 'sciencisation' of technology and a 'technicisation' of science.[3] Ladrière concluded saying that 'The penetration of *social practice* in its most diverse and central forms by science is therefore not something purely accidental to be ascribed to the enlightened will of a few individuals or groups or to a fortuitous encounter between concerns and methods. It was a historically necessary fact in that it reflected the *law of essence*' (UNESCO 1969:16).

Since World War II, with the advent of 'big science'[4] and the emergence of large-scale industrial research in which science and technology are jointly used in enhancing and inventing their products, they have become altogether a 'system' in that they maintain 'a mutual double dependence relationship and are intertwined in a double feedback process' (Ladmiral 1973:IX). This is the system today referred to as technoscience, as it becomes the real development infrastructure of modern societies and all the more so because it has become inextricably linked to power. While knowing before acting was merely an ambition at the birth of modern science with Bacon, Descartes, etc., nobody would argue today that the unique goal of science is the quest for knowledge and that any pragmatic and utilitarian deviation is done to free mankind from any burden that would prevent him/her from fully dedicating himself/herself to this search for knowledge, as Poincaré (1905) did at the start of last century. The expression 'knowledge is power' by Bacon has never been so relevant. Science, as inextricably linked to technology, has thus become a real power which determines the fate of mankind and societies (Roquepo 1973:30).[5]

This further justifies the serious consideration dedicated to science by the industry, the army, politics, etc. Of course, it also raises some serious problems which are however proportionate to the deep changes it has introduced in the life of mankind.[6] People living at the turn of this century are bending beneath the weight of the artefacts of technoscience which has 'gradually acquired a decisive influence on what makes up culture in its broadest sense that is, whatever imparts its specific features to the life of a historical community' (Ladrière 1977:41).

Science is considered here from this systemic standpoint as the 'system of science and technology' (Paty 1995) in its implications for the economy and society. Science is thus understood, not only as the set of knowledge produced by the mind, but also as a decisive element in the production line which is necessarily linked to technology and entails fundamental implications for society. This is known as the science 'technology' 'industry' society Ring.

### Technoscience as a Key Factor of Globalisation

It is commonplace to argue that surplus capital from agricultural revolution was behind the industrial revolution of the 18th and 19th centuries. The capital generated by agriculture, the resulting food security (and subsequently population growth) and the freed labour force as a result of mechanisation considerably boosted the nascent industry,[7] particularly steel manufacturing and textile.

Technoscience is to globalisation what agriculture was to industrial revolution. It is the excess capital generated by the big multinationals that was behind this far-reaching phenomenon. While these multinationals have global 'control' (Clairmont 1997) and cover naturally all sectors of activities, we are more interested here in the fact that most of them make an overwhelming use of the results of scientific and technological research in pharmacy, agriculture, mechanics and electronics, communications, etc. Science and technology-oriented sectors, which are practically at the forefront of development, are behind this growth and have allowed these societies to accumulate such a huge amount of capital.

The collapse of the national framework is therefore nothing more than one of the consequences of this development. The logic of openness is natural altogether in this sense: this is the dynamics of birth giving. And political and ideological decisions on liberalisation are just instruments to facilitate such an openness. While explaining the factors of globalisation, Samir Amin (1996) wrote: 'Crisis is manifested in the fact that, in given income distribution structures, the profits yielded by production find no sufficient outlets in the profitable investments that are likely to develop production capacities. Crisis management consists then in finding 'other outlets' for this floating excess capital so as to avoid their massive and sudden devaluation as it happened in the 1930s. (...) The recipe is the same for all. (...) The liberalisation of international capital transfers, the adoption of floating exchange rates, high interest rates, the deficit in the American trade balance, Third World external indebtedness and privatisation constitute together a perfectly rational policy offering these hot monies the outlet of making headlong rush into speculative financial investments to pre-empt the same old danger: massive and sudden devaluation of excess capital'.[8]

First, the developments in science, information and communication technologies and transportation are key factors in the expansion and acceleration of this phenomenon. In fact, the planetary village concept reflects this fastness in communication and people's movements. Satellite connections, computer communication networks which have reached, thanks to the Internet, breathtaking speed are the vectors of the phenomenon. Thanks to the developments in communication, transactions which would have taken months to complete just a few decades ago are now done in real time. Victory over space and distance has never been so close. It is therefore the possibilities offered by scientific and technological progress in communication and transportation that determine the current scope of economic globalisation.

The hypostasis of the essentially economic and monetary elements has often overshadowed these genuine factors: infrastructure as such has been neglected in most cases for economic and political superstructures. The interrogation as to the structural origin of these companies' wealth is raised only occasionally. Analysts tend to gloss over economic and financial considerations. And this neglect does have an impact on the development strategies and models applied here and there in developing countries because they place key development factors in the second position and promote super-structural elements instead. An evidence of this is the place given by structural adjustment and similar programmes to education and scientific and technological research in developing countries, understood as the capacity of a people to find solutions to their problems. In these programmes, education and scientific and technological research occupy but a footnote space for social considerations. The application of such models can only lead to dead-ends.

## Effects of Globalisation: Dead-end of Science and Technology in Developing Countries

The effects of globalisation on the development of science and technology in developing countries can be tentatively analysed at three levels: first, in terms of easy access to scientific information; secondly, in terms of the consequences arising from the establishment of multinationals; and lastly, in terms of the implications of structural adjustment policies for orientations and scientific institutions. At each of these levels, science and technology seem to have come to a dead-end: by opening to 'mainstream science', they have become externalised and contribute more to the development of the societies who have the structures and resources to operationalise them. In so doing, they got cut off from local development concerns. With the establishment of multinationals and the implementation of structural adjustment policies, science and technology have become the forgotten ones in the development process, marginalised and reduced to sheer bureaucracy.

## Globalisation, Knowledge Chains and Development

Globalisation is celebrated as a panacea because it ends the isolation of developing countries by giving them more accessibility to communication media and scientific information. Because of their significantly lower cost, compared to traditional communication media, information highways constitute the main driving force. It is now possible to look for information everywhere around the world regardless of geographical distance because editing modes, catalogues and databases can now be instantly accessed, thanks to the Internet. The world Internet expansion increased from 2.4 per cent of world population to 6.7 per cent. In Africa, in particular, it went from 0.04 to 0.4 (UNDP:36).[9] It is thus an inexhaustible source of scientific data made available to the researchers of developing countries. Data that would have taken months to reach at a prohibitively expensive cost for ordinary researchers are now very cheaply accessible.

But the criteria with which to evaluate the contribution of this broader accessibility to development-related scientific information can be defined only based on the link between research and its technological, industrial, cultural and social implications. Indeed, in which direction will scientific and technological research develop? Is the social fabric prepared to take hold of them and transform them into innovations and development activities? There lies the real issue!

Here is the danger: the easier the access to scientific data, the more productive research becomes and the more it becomes marginalised and elitist in relation to the socio-economic and industrial fabric which is yet inapt to grasp the results. Then, science in developing countries will develop to contribute more to the central 'science system' with relative effects locally. As pointed out in the *2001 World Human Development Report*, 'The investments of developing countries have come to a point where they are subsidising the economies of industrialised countries. Indeed, many are the holders of prestigious degrees who emigrate despite the fact that their countries of origin devoted very considerable resources to the training of national educated labour'. (UNDP 2001:5).[10] Emigration in this case is not simply physical. Researchers who remain in their countries also experience a kind of mental emigration, judging from the focus of their research since they are not producing for their society but rather in relation to externally-defined objectives and themes.

Indeed, there is a real schism between the societies who have been able to control science and technology and who happen to be mostly countries overseas, and those who still use them marginally. The scientific and technological development map drawn by *World Human Development Report* shows gigantic disparities. 'New product concept and development which very often derive from systematic investments in development research are something occurring almost solely in the OECD countries and a handful of developing countries in Asia and Latin America' (UNDP 2001:39). In fact, representing 14 per cent of world population, the 29 countries forming OECD, with 2.4 per cent of their average GDP devoted to development research, concentrate 86 per cent of the 836,000 patent applications deposited around the world in 1998 and 437,000 of world published scientific and technical articles.

In practice, the effects of globalisation will translate into broader accessibility and increased dependency of product consumption on technoscience, as a result in part of the research conducted worldwide but which would have materialised in contexts more prepared to grasp it and transform it into innovations. This is also confirmed by the strong growth of the telecom sector (UNDP 2001:31) as it outpaces traditional sectors like electricity, potable water, land line …)

In most developing countries, science still operates marginally. But in absolute terms, the level reached might be higher than the one attained in the 19th century by developed countries. Many Third World scientists have made major contributions to cutting edge science (Paty 1992:17), though their own society could not benefit much from them. Both in terms of the themes, outcomes and validation, scientific research in developing countries is extroverted. As such, it is of a 'colonial' nature in that the recognition, validation and operationnalisation of its results depend on the Centre. Research themes are defined in relation to the practice in developed countries where people have a clearer understanding of the application potentials which are even updated every day. This choice of themes is certainly conditioned by the validation criteria and venues.

More radically, there are several levels of research validation. The first level is the choice of research themes and their institutional acceptance, to the extent where this institutional acceptance conditions funding without which there cannot be serious research. Obviously, researchers are not completely free. The work of Waast and Gaillard has clearly demonstrated that researchers from developing countries, most of whom were trained in developed countries, tend to continue work within the same bounds of research themes and training once they return to their home country. That way, they guarantee their international exposure, opening prospects for funding and getting published. The second level is 'editorial dependence' particularly having the achieved results published in the specialised journals of 'mainstream science' (Waast 1996a) and climaxes with the award of scientific prizes. However, by generalising publication of scientific results to include databases, LDCs admittedly received the smallest or no share. LDCs are practically absent from the main databases of developed countries (ISI, Francis, BiblioSHS) (Harbo 1999-2000:115-127). The third level, an operational and economic one, is the practical uses of the results, implying meeting patent requirements. No doubt, the gap broadens at this level. The stakes of development research also play out at this level since patents define the copyrights of a technological invention and its likely induced wealth. Concerning technological inventions and copyrights of such inventions, about twenty nine countries monopolise the future. Even if the research contributing to these patents is produced by the global science system as a whole, only a few countries own it, as a result of their capacities to transform research into technological innovations.

All these validation criteria are exogenous in relation to the Third World. The major specialised journals are found in developed countries, the best scientific prizes are awarded there and they offer enough operationnalisation possibilities, leading possibly to the acquisition of patents. Thus, themes can be defined only in relation to those conditions. Yet, the interweaving of scientific and technological research with socio-economic fabric and its underlying problems, needs and priorities is one clear variable. Research funding is not neutral. It is conditioned by this close relationship and by the idea that society is made by its own development. Thus, the billions of dollars spent on atomic and nuclear physics since World War 2 have a link to the Cold War and to the 'atom diplomacy' that has become international practice. More billions of dollars went into spatial research following the same logic. This is not because there were no priority research sectors whose results could be far more beneficial in terms of improving the living conditions of mankind in general. It is quite the opposite! Little research is done on scourges like malaria which are affecting Third World countries (whose population weight is well-known in relation to the whole planet) in alarming proportions. Research is therefore all the more developed in a given area if it is associated with the ideological, industrial, military and economic circuit. The orientation of scientific and technological research is inevitably political and economic.

The real problem stems from the fact that developed country needs do not necessarily correspond to the LDCs'. The situation is even more complicated because being still at the stage of agricultural revolution, LDCs must at the same time follow through their externalist education and research programmes, the most advanced science and technology. These programmes are thus carbon copies in content of developed countries' models, resulting inevitably in a disconnection between the educational system, scientific and technological research and the social fabric, yet unprepared to benefit from their result or even understand them. Scientific and technological research is marginalised in developing countries as a result of this uncomfortable situation of straddling two worlds. On one side, part of the society has attained a relatively high consumption level and on the other, the great majority is still confronted with problems of food security.

Fears are that one will increasingly witness the development of a research cut off from its deployment conditions and the results of which can only be beneficial to those countries that have adequate structures to use them. Jean-Jacques Salomon rightly remarked that the answer to the question 'What is the impact on development of a science policy essentially devoted to fundamental research' is: 'zero!' (Salomon 1196b). In fact, he added, 'fundamental research produces information available to the international scientific community. Who can benefit from this? It is those who can transform knowledge and information into an immediate technical know-how at the service of economic and industrial concerns or the health sector'. Of course, there are a few possibilities of operationalising some of the results in various scientific fields (agriculture,[11] medicine, computer science, for instance) but these are yet to create the synergy that would produce the bandwagon effect.

However, it is important to note that the reverse of the approach asking developing countries, 'instead of trying to reproduce the feats of an Einstein' to concentrate on solving the most urgent problems, especially survival, hunger, unemployment ..., is not at all viable. Gaillard asked in this connection whether 'the future of developing countries lies with new technologies in which a limited number of them like Brazil or the Republic of Korea have engaged or, on the contrary, with development research in agriculture, an activity from which over three-quarters of African and Asian populations are earning a living?' (Gaillard 1989:21). In our view, there is no better way to perpetuate dependence than to limit oneself, as Ahmad Jalali put it, to 'subsistence research' (Jalali 2000:303-306), to the research seeking to satisfy the most primitive needs and lacking the necessary leverage to boost development. To be occupied solely with immediate needs in a competitive environment certainly amounts to opting to lag behind. Japan is often cited as an example of a country which first concerned itself with solving immediate problems, oblivious of the fact that this country's success precisely stems from its ability to *'anticipate'* and to take the lead in advanced technology. Speaking of Japan, Allen further noted that: 'The officials of the ministry of international trade and industry (MITI) and their associates from major companies contended that a concentration of labour-intensive activities would doom Japan to poverty and to an everlasting economic inferiority; that it should concentrate its efforts on creating a type of industrial structure characteristic of western developed countries' (Allen 1983:104). Whereas anticipating strictly means cutting oneself off from daily routine to attend to the problems of tomorrow and finding their solutions. Inversely, if the abstract distance is completely cut off from real conditions, research will also run open.

Science is not ready-made and cannot be simply transposed; neither does it suffice to reproduce the research themes developed in developed countries or even make groundbreaking discoveries if specific conditions are not met, in particular, the existence of 'national scientific communities and well-established educational structures [...] apt to absorb the shocks of economic globalism and put international knowledge flows to their advantage' (Gaillard 1998). Otherwise, research institutions will operate, as Jean-Jacques Salomon put it, like an ultra-modern tower in the middle of a multitude of traditional villages' (Salomon 1992:388) and completely cut off from the society and the production system. In this sense, the Internet, in most of the developing countries of the South, is much more consumption than an information producing-system. Globalisation does, at that level, a sort of levelling from the top which will further widen the gap between the North and the South on one hand, and among Third World social strata on the other. While it is good for one to benefit from advanced technical communication equipments, there is also need at the same time to be involved with a global research dynamics in order to be able to exploit the massive information inflows from communication networks, to benefit from research funding and to have research validated. The need to fit into this global dynamics controlled by developed countries conditions research themes and subsequently put them on the margin of society, as a result of development gap and differences in problems and needs.

## Expansion of Multinationals and Development of an Endogenous Science System

Let's now address one of the expressions of this globalisation, that is, the expansion of multinationals worldwide and the associated relocations. From hearsay, developing countries were going to integrate the global economy by liberalising their economic system and facilitating foreign investments. With these company expansion and relocations, one would have expected revived funding for development research activities on the new sites, implying greater technological innovation capacity and enhanced education in general. But the conditions of relocations do not seem to pursue these expectations. Relocations, as they currently unfold, have essentially involved production sectors by banking on the comparative advantages of unskilled labour. In this sense, their impact on the level of education and innovation cannot be positive, even though it translates into relatively better living conditions. It is therefore being naive first to ignore that these multinationals are seeking labour-intensive countries with lower salary scales where they can make maximum profits and pay the least taxes and secondly, to believe that they could bring about any genuine development. Far from providing a breeding ground for the development of scientific research in LDCs, the installation of multinationals is more likely to become a hindrance for various reasons.

First, instead of a veritable technology transfer, these company expansion and relocations entail, in their wake, a transfer of readily consumable technological products. This creates an illusion of endogenous development. Indeed, whether these products are mounted and assembled in developing countries does not fundamentally change the situation because basic technology has not been integrated in the entire socio-economic fabric. It is therefore wrong to count the number of TV sets or computers in a country, even if assembled on the spot, as a development index if that country is reduced to a simple consumer and cannot develop research to appropriate the underlying technology.

By liberalising to facilitate access to technological import, globalisation rather contributes to a sort of innovative potentials congestion since a technological import will only show solutions. It works like a magic box without inducing re-appropriation of technology, which is a must. Globalisation is therefore trying to kind of standardise needs and solutions by simply transposing the problems and solutions of developed countries into LDCs. The latter can see their context-specific problems coexist alongside the problems created by the importation of West European culture and technology. This co-existence creates another type of LDCs-specific problems best expressed by the separation between the urban and rural areas. So, the coercive force of imported solutions develops a spirit of receptivity, finally inhibiting innovation capacities. This translates into a common belief according to which 'Whites have invented everything'.

Secondly, globalisation accentuates the 'specialisation' of economies or the international division of labour set in place since colonial times. For, multinationals are only willing to install or relocate to LDCs the mechanical or manufacturing production sectors which require intensive labour but not advanced technology. The rationale is essentially to move, based on lower salary scales and taxes, the production sectors requiring intensive but often unskilled labour. The gains from the comparative advantage offered through the cost of unskilled labour cannot guarantee genuine development without a qualitative jump forward which is necessarily expressed through technological anticipation. It is through this anticipation alone that competitiveness can be guaranteed in a world where rapid breakthroughs in production tools no longer leave room for simple production mechanics. Yet, the advanced technology, financial and service sectors (which are part of what Samir Amin named the monopolies of the West) are the ones making considerable gains. Obviously, the most decisive and sustainable element today is for growth to be based on scientific and technological innovation. The other forms of growth turned out to be short-lived.[12] Developing countries still confine themselves to the basic sectors: agriculture, raw materials, basic and mining industries, etc., which will increasingly depreciate due to the development of substitutes. Commodity and high-tech products markets do not grow at the same pace. It is quite the opposite; commodity market tends to decline or remains relatively stable due to these substitutes. Inversely, monopolised by developed countries, high-tech products market grew at a breathtaking speed and seem to offer endless prospects. This situation is nothing new. Indeed, already in 1949, the UN published a study underscoring the deterioration of commodity prices in relation to those of manufactured goods. Between 1936 and 1938, the deterioration was estimated at 40 per cent. And yet, it was admitted that because of their scarcity (a recurrent theme then) and the possible depletion of natural resources, commodity prices tended to increase. Strangely enough, no commodity has so far been dropped because of depletion but rather because of the substitutes, and more recently, because of synthetic products.

How do you pull out of a 'specialisation' cleverly upheld and maintained by several development theoreticians[13] who see in globalisation a way to perpetuate their careers? Many of them still conceive development as a straight line process. This is why they believe agriculture should be developed first so that the excess from this sector could finance industrial development as was the case in the developed countries. In a nutshell, this amounts to saying that science and technology should be put off and agriculture developed, thus going through the same stages as developed countries did. This vision overlooks a fundamental factor: Western Europe invented its own model by itself during its revolution. It was not under the pressure of a more developed system pouring in its products and results. And even though revolution did not occur in all West European countries at the same time, those that followed it like France and Germany, Sweden and even USA, and benefited from technology transfer from the revolution centre – essentially Netherlands and Italy – were advantaged by the fact that these were relatively not too advanced and more easily transferable technologies (Bairoch 1971:79). Third World countries are experiencing a different situation altogether because most of the new technologies are the result of important scientific precedences requiring longer and more complicated education which, consequently, are less easily transferable.

Furthermore, these countries are inundated with high-tech products that have been integrated in lifestyles and are now part of the daily environment; so to return at this point to the different stages of West European development – agriculture, textile, mechanical industry, modern industries making massive use of science and technology – in order to make consumption level correspond with production level is something practically impossible. This, to some extent, tends to remind us of the various bartering between USA and the European Union, USA and Japan, USA and China, etc., or even the old GATT negotiations on non-tariff barriers. These countries are aware of the devastating effects that massive importation of a foreign product would provoke on the local industry, especially if the latter is not yet competitive in the area. Most developed countries are seeking to protect or subsidise some sectors of activities so that they can face up to international competition. USA protects its agriculture, subsidises through would-be military/industry contracts many high-tech sectors, including notably aeronautics, while Japan and several other Asian countries are trying to limit access of American products to their markets. It can thus be seen that the liberalisation policy imposed on developing countries is very staunchly resisted in Western Europe, subsequently mitigating its impact. Worse still, this neo-liberal vision is mistaken since the newly industrialised countries including even Japan neither followed this path nor gave in to specialisation. Citing them as an example is wrong, because these countries have understood that they had to bet on either technological innovation or innovation through technology transfer. The South-East Asian 'dragons' often cited as successful liberalisation models followed a different policy altogether. South Korea's case is a good illustration. Instead of disengaging and opening the market, the State limited and even banned industrial imports in sectors where the local industry was striding to establish itself (Perrin 1983) at a time when the IMF imposed, as one of its conditions, that the country opens its markets to foreign products and especially allow multinationals to acquire interest in companies behind its accomplishments.

Obviously, making foreign investments solely in labour-intensive sectors cannot favour development because it does not induce appropriation of science and technology. It is the reverse. By favouring lower salaries, the investments delay skills development and innovative capacity. By employing unskilled labour alone, the companies encourage the brain drain phenomenon. Trained researchers look for a better place with the necessary environment to do their work for the benefit of these companies.

Mostly located in OECD countries, these multinationals will obviously repatriate their generated profits. In fact, these companies can be called transnationals only by their operations and production (Clairmont 1997:16).[14] But in terms of capital and development research, each multinational is associated with the name of a region or country where the major shareholders and research units are based. The study conducted by the magazine, *Wired* gives a measure of this disequilibrium. While identifying 46 technocities or science parks (innovation centre where synergies are created between technical know-how, capital and opportunities) classified on the basis of the number of seats of investment trusts, research laboratories, universities or similar institutions, the magazine identified 13 in USA, 16 in Europe, 9 in Asia, 2 in South America, 2 in Africa, 2 in Australia, 1 in Canada and 1 in Israel (UNDP 2001:38).

The profits generated therefore belong only to those countries. Even if applied research was to be developed in the units that these multinationals will base in LDCs, it will still benefit the developed countries which are in a better position to grasp their effects. There is an urgent need to develop an endogenous scientific research integrated in the socio-economic fabric. Michel Paty noted that 'Anyway you look at it, it appears that for scientific development to mature, it requires an explicit and effective national science-oriented will' (Paty 1992:11). A national science-oriented will is one way of allowing the creation in these countries of a research level and a scientific community with the capacity to accompany technology transfer and subsequently a real industrial development. Indeed, 'paradoxically, a company or a nation planning to grow mostly through technology transfer must therefore maintain active research laboratories with a view to creating the intellectual exchanges through which such transfer can be beneficial (UNESCO 1969:26).

## Liberalisation and Scientific Policy Crisis in the LDCs

Liberalisation, one of the corollaries of globalisation, reduces considerably the State's influencing power over the practical orientation of scientific or even economic policies (French 1998). Having stripped itself of all the competitive profitable sectors with the wholesale privatisations and liberalisations dictated by the international institutions, the State has much more reduced leverage over the definition of scientific policies. Remember that in most OECD countries, the private sector provides funding for 50 to 60 per cent of development research (UNDP 2001:37). By investing in development research, the companies certainly benefit from the fundamental research potential put in place by the state structures. In fact, the state is the only one to invest in fundamental research the sort of venture capital that will allow research institutions, universities and centres to provide local industries with the knowledge potential and the people needed for their development. At present, this potential is dwindling in most countries under structural adjustment, with the decay of universities and research centres. Several research centres have simply been shut down. If you add to that the inclination towards education privatisation and if you bring it to bear on the population, then you obtain the most dramatic consequence of the liberalism policy being implemented in developing countries.

The public is well familiar with the debates over the efficiency of World Bank and IMF-led policies; both institutions are known to act as the political and ideological arm of the multinationals, with the mission of perpetuating the dominant neoliberal system. Basically, the ultimate goal of these institutions is not to develop LDCs but to create the conditions for the establishment of multinationals. The ensuing form of development is relevant only because it allows markets creation. Therefore, the World Bank or the International Monetary Fund should certainly not be trusted with boosting real development of science and technology in LDCs, not even promoting the structures with the capacity to achieve such development and allowing local appropriation. What has been done so far is quite the opposite: drastic reduction or even cancellation of the education budgets of universities and research centres through the imposition of structural adjustment programmes here and there, even though their usefulness in developing countries is yet to be demonstrated in a system that has hypostasised material consumption and neglected technoscience as a veritable engine of development. Worse still, under the poverty reduction programmes implemented in Highly Indebted Poor Countries (HIPC), it appears as though scientific and technological research could be set aside for, it is being more successfully done elsewhere. Here is the logic behind such an attitude: Why should investment be made in an activity which is comparatively done better elsewhere and whose results can still be generalised through globalisation? Why continue funding research centres whose past performance was very mixed? Why not resolve the immediate problems rather than investing in activities with uncertain results?

### The Specific Case of Africa

Within the LDCs in general, African research is more marginalised and extrovert. Beyond the reasons often mentioned (brain drain, theoretical nature of research...), we believe that one single fundamental factor appears to constitute the real bottleneck: the absence of real *scientific and technological demand*. Indeed, in African countries, most of the scientific systems were developed after World War 2 or after independence. This development occurred, not in relation to local concerns, but in the spirit of the periphery providing service to the centre. It is true that the orientation of themes focusing on local concerns have been deeply changed to reflect local concerns.

The issue is neither to deny the existence of these problems, a potential research subject nor the relevance of the themes. The issue is the capacity to translate such problems into *scientific and technological demand*. The scientific demand concept presupposes a need where political, intellectual, social, industrial, economic and health concerns intersect... The need can exist or be provoked. But until it is turned into demand, the research concerned with it still remains marginal and extrovert. This is so because scientific and technological research is not simply demand for knowledge, it also demand for wealth. If science and technology cannot produce value-added, they are indeed bound to become marginalised or extrovert (since they are likely to produce it in the medium or long run for other countries).

And yet, what do we notice? When the needs are specifically African, they attract little attention from both African and international policies and are considered a marginal problem. For the past several decades, the marginal character of pharmaceutical research on malaria has been widely noticed, compared to what international pharmaceutical research is devoting to the other diseases, notably cancer.... This is indeed because malaria is considered a demand for knowledge but not a demand for wealth by global development research.

When the needs involve products and 'civilisation artefacts', technological research is all the more extrovert as common opinion has their eyes riveted on West European solutions and products. It may be argued that as a result of relocations, multinational companies recruit in host countries local researchers who contribute locally or through emigration to the development of such products, but as always, these (internal and external) migrations never appear to lead to local appropriation of development research. The production or reproduction-geared local industry sees no real interest in promoting development research, not only because of the expensive costs of such an exercise, but also because the belief is that solutions exist or can be developed elsewhere. As it appears, innovation and anticipation capacity are wrecked in the production sector. They may develop in the knowledge sectors that contribute more to enriching 'mainstream science'.

## In Conclusion: What Can We Do?

The prerequisites for the appropriation of science and technology include developing an endogenous industrial fabric with an upstream and downstream integration of scientific and technological research, generalising education, defining scientific policies which are no longer based solely on West European themes and also reflecting local problems. But none of these conditions is likely to be fulfilled at this time of globalisation despite broader access to information media and sources. Such access will no doubt contribute to raising research level and quality in developing countries. But if the appropriation conditions are not met, this intensification of research, regardless of the results, will have little consequence on development in general. Besides, such access will more likely facilitate isolated research than a real synergy-creating one, especially in the absence of veritable institutional and socio-economic dynamics which are likely to boost significant research and encourage the exploitation of its fallouts.

A concept of globalisation, different from the conventional model that preaches economy specialisation and rid off the neo-liberal imperialistic strait jacket might effectively create the conditions of this re-appropriation at the industrial and economic levels.

First, the myth of economism must disappear, particularly in African countries where development, under the pressure of the international institutions, is formulated exclusively in economic and monetary terms as though for a people lacking the invention capability to find solutions to their own problems, development could be achieved solely through economic or monetary policies.

Furthemore, instead of the manufacturing and mass labour sectors alone, multinationals should also establish themselves in sectors requiring some control of scientific and technological potential that is adapted to local needs. Their installation should be accompanied by development research units working under contract with local research centres. In recent years, African countries have been able to demand that multinationals integrate social and environmental dimensions in their projects. Now, a thought should also be given to integrating development research dimensions to be undertaken in partnership with university institutions or local research centres. Development research is today dominated by the private sector. But particularly in Africa, where the structures of public research have been completely dismantled by structural adjustment policies, political constraints must be imposed on multinational production structures by requiring them to implement a development research component which should be more important than the social one which, so far, have been leading the continent into the vicious circle of assistance.

In this sense, local research would be stimulated, as it will locally benefit from the conditions for development, validation and operationnalisation of its results. Through a retroactive effect, research training programmes will be updated to meet the local demand thus generated. This will offer a double advantage: adapting training and research contents and creating employment opportunities for those trained, and subsequently reducing extraversion and the brain drain.

The creation of transnational research teams should also be reinforced with a view to pooling them together and establishing the scientific communities who are likely to revive development. This old ambition was visibly caught in the intricate problems of state funding and bureaucracy.

The ambitions of China, as reflected in the words of Stephen S. Cohen, can illustrate this point: 'In the sectors of aerospace, fine chemistry, high-tech manufactured goods, transport equipments, pharmaceuticals, telecom, etc. it needs European, Japanese and American large multinational companies. The latter are bound to become the main aids of its trade and industrial policy by playing two key roles: technology transfer and technical know-how in exchange for access to its market...' (Cohen 1998:19). The recent discussions between China and Europe on the concept and production of Airbus 380 did confirm these terms of trade as the Chinese required Europe to base some of the development research units in China.

## Notes

1. 'There is no alternative' is one of the most recurrent expressions when it comes to discussing the relevance of neo-liberal policies. The expression is now even consecrated by the English acronym TINA.
2. For a more detailed presentation of this point, read Ymelé Jean-Pierre. 'La technoscience comme infrastructure de développement des sociétés modernes', in *Informatique Individuelle*, n° 2, March-April, 1995.
3. Read more on the subject in Jean Réné Ladmiral, prefaced by Habermas(1973). A quite explicit explanation of the role of science and technology as the 'primary productive force' is given. p. XI.

4. 'Big science' refers, as Michel Paty puts it, to the 'machinery of high-tech and industry now supportive of progress in the state-of-the-art science of the matter, life and the universe'. Read Paty (1996).

5. 'It is also in its power (or rather: in the power that it can confer because it is power by itself) that science can be practically justified; to be convinced, one simply needs to listen to the arguments put forth by the scientists themselves when they are claiming for research credits. If the situation were different, science would not have its current social importance; it would not disturb the forms of our existence; it would be an 'art' among others and would have no more resources than the 'fine arts'.

6. This issue has led to the development of a whole school of thought which sees science, in Castoriadis' words, as a 'hammer without master'. Read on the subject *Les Scientifiques parlent*, under the direction of Albert Jacquard (1987); *Le jaillissement des biotechnologies*, under the direction of P. Darbon et J. Robin (1987). However, our focus here is not to discuss the negative consequences of the domination of culture and nature by science and technology, though developing countries do face this type of problems. From another perspective, we also wish to insist on the fact that it would be dangerous in present times to make a mechanical reproduction of anti-science movements in societies where science is marginal and where primary superstitions are still deeply rooted. Focusing on this theme would certainly provoke more mistrust in science and this, we believe, would seriously jeopardise development. In developed countries, scientific and technological potential has largely reached the critical threshold enabling them to 'sustain' society and to contain anti-science movements, which is not the case in developing countries where that potential is yet to be built up.

7. For more insight into the subject, read Bairoch (1963).

8. Excerpt from a summary of the author's theses entitled 'les défis de la mondialisation', available on the Internet. A slightly different version of this excerpt is found in Amin (1995), p.11. Read also Amin (1996).

9. But this growth is still far from reaching the penetration rate of 50 per cent which is estimated to be the threshold from which computer and Internet benefits are manifested.

10. The report added that it is expected that 100,000 Indians would receive visas to emigrate to USA which would represent for India more than two billions in resource losses.

11. Agriculture and health represent indeed over 80 per cent of African scientific production in the 1980s. But in this area, paradoxically, it is estimated that the low growth of production in Africa was not the result of higher yields that is, science but rather of the expansion of cultivable surface areas while during the same period, three-quarters of the world production growth was attributed to higher yields. Read Gaillard & Waast (1988).

12. According to the reflections series devoted to the development of science, one might distinguish between four types of growth: extensive growth which is achieved by increasing the number of production units; growth through capital accumulation at constant technology, growth by improving the structure and organisation of production relations and growth resulting from technological innovation. The last mode of growth is the only one that cannot be saturated as the results of its own effects. It is therefore indefinitely extensible. Read Unesco (1969).

13. Read, for example, the comparative costs theory by David Ricardo (1817, Chapter VII) for a systematic preliminary analysis of specialisation theory. Read also Assidon (1892).

14. Eight countries possess 96.5 per cent of the first two hundred multinationals and 96 per cent of their turn-over.

# 13

# Postcoloniality and Development: Development as a Colonial Discourse

## Eiman Osman Zein-Elabdin

> Mad, Caesar?
> Why, you set the standard of sanity for the whole habitable world.
> Tiberius Claudius[1]

It seems rather foolish, or at best smacks of unrealism, to speak of postcoloniality in the current global geopolitical climate in which empire seems to take hold before our very eyes. Invoking the term postcolonial today calls back questions that critics of postcolonial theory raised many years ago.[1] Notably, Ama Ata Aidoo, the Ghanaian author, argued that 'applied to Africa, India, and some other parts of the world, 'postcolonial' is not only a fiction, but a most pernicious fiction, a cover-up of a dangerous period in our people's lives' (1991:152). For critics like Aidoo, postcolonial theory seemed to substitute a dream of a borderless, multicultural world for the reality of global disparity and persistence of oppressive structures. Aidoo admonished the term postcolonial for its implications of 'something finished' while Africa remained bogged down in debt and multinational corporate piracy.

> I would like to argue that, although I understand and appreciate the place from which Aidoo's comment is made, this comment misses the mark because it is rooted in an emphasis on postcoloniality as a purely historical marker (post-colonial), whereas postcolonial theory offers a profound critique of hegemony and domination rather than a mere depiction of the state of affairs since the formal end of the colonial era. In particular, I believe it presents a most promising philosophical entry point for grappling with the question of 'development' and with living in a contemporary world in which Africans are both discursively constructed and materially exploited in ways that secure them in a location of subalternity and loss of agency.[2] Of course, debates about the residue of European colonialism, and the extent to which it may offer an explanation of current tremors on the continent, are legion. My purpose here is not to delve into these debates but to examine how the insights of postcolonial theory might contribute to an understanding of development in relation to Africa.

Furthermore, it must be made clear that in order to extend the idea of postcoloniality from a limited historical reference to a general critique of hegemony, the term colonial must be read as a metaphor for all forms of oppression – past and present – without necessarily overlooking the historical specificities of colonialism.

I will arrive at my conclusions by first giving a brief introductory outline of postcolonial theory, focusing primarily on Homi Bhabha's (1983) theory of colonial discourse. Needless to say, this is my own reading of a highly contested and not altogether unproblematic field (see Zein-Elabdin and Charusheela 2004); others may disagree or wish to point up different themes. In the second section, I discuss the 20th century discourse of development, which continues to prevail as the line of thought organising international relations despite failures and theoretical challenges.[3] By discourse I, like many postcolonial critics, adopt the Foucauldian idea to refer to the totality of mental space, theories, texts, language, and conventions that set the parameters of what is to be thought and uttered and which do – directly and indirectly – produce whatever material reality is experienced. For the past half century, the development discourse has defined what I call a global *regime of sanity*, namely, the cognitive normative structure that governs all of its participants. As I explain in this section, postcolonial theory suggests reading development as an orientalist, colonial discourse rather than a culturally neutral, scientifically knowable path of an economy. In the final section, I elaborate on postcoloniality as a concept that I believe comes closest to capturing Africa's present realities and location, and contributes to a better understanding as well as reconstruction of a contemporary African space.[4]

## Postcolonial Theory and Colonial Discourse

Postcolonial theory evolved from readings of 19th and early 20th century European novels and other documents by some pioneering literary critics who came to the conclusion that classics such as Rudyard Kipling's *Kim*, George Eliot's *Middlemarch* (Said 1978), Charlotte Bronte's *Jane Eyre* (Spivak 1985), or Conrad's *Heart of Darkness* (Bhabha 1985) could not be fully understood and evaluated as 'pure' artifacts.[5] These texts carried far too political implications and references to Europe's imperial position and cultural encounters than the reading made possible by conventional disciplinary methods. Such texts had to be read as *colonial discourse*.

As a result of this reading, some key concepts emerged. Most crucially, *orientalism* came to be understood as more than just the academic exercise of studying the history and cultures of the 'Orient;' it was an epistemological political phenomenon, with far reaching historical consequences (Said 1978). The idea of *the postcolonial*, as a cross-cultural outcome of modern European hegemony, soon followed. At the risk of great crudity, I would schematically summarise the most defining elements of postcolonial theory in the following three propositions:

- Modern Europe had a historical ability to produce the Orient – a theoretical representation of all dominated regions – as *subaltern* through the 'knowledge'

produced by Orientalists, which set up certain derogatory representations of the Orient that in turn authorised its domination.[6]
- Cultural hegemony, in the Gramscian sense, is never complete or simple – the colonial is as much constituted by its subaltern Others as they are by its dominant position. (The import of the colonies to Europe's imagination of its own self was such that Said concluded Orientalism was less about the Orient than it was about the Occident).
- The subaltern postcolonial, the product of this historical process of domination, is a *hybrid* state of mutual constitution, irreversibly inflected by the colonial encounter.[7]

These propositions, although not exhaustive, indicate clearly that the 'postcolonial' is not 'post-colonial,' i.e. a mere historical marker, as significant as this may be. It is also a critical move, a reference to the formerly colonised as well as a critique of their domination.

At first blush, the themes of orientalism, subalternity and hybridity may appear to have little to do with development or material conditions in general. But this is precisely the appearance that gave rise to charges against postcolonial theory as misleading (Aidoo 1991) or even complicit with 'global capitalism' (Dirlik 1997). The charges, to me, reflect the common (mis)understanding of economy and economics to be an extra-cultural universally applicable rationality, a self-contained 'science.' This general failure to recognise economic theory, in all its ideological shades, as a classic instrument of cultural hegemony largely underlies the resilient power of the development discourse.[8]

For the longest time, development has been construed as a set of macroeconomic targets to be obtained with the appropriate policy mix, or at best broadened to include distributive and 'quality of life' goals, but as a whole, the perception remained of the final objectivity and universal desirability of these goals. As I have argued elsewhere (Zein-Elabdin 1998), however, development is a philosophical question; it is part of a total cosmology rooted in metaphysical assumptions that transcend the realm of the limited disciplines of social science. It is ultimately a question of social meaning – or collective understanding of purpose; therefore, making it futile to attempt a substantial challenge to it without first treading the philosophical and cultural grounds on which it firmly rests. Postcolonial theory goes a long way to unravel these grounds because, in the end, it *is* a philosophical endeavour; as Spivak (1990:204) suggested, 'a deconstructive philosophical position.'[9] So far, the philosophers of postcolonialism have not pointed up development as a prominent single theme, yet the crux of their intellectual struggles has everything to do with the development discourse once this is clearly seen as a cultural product.[10] A brief look at Bhabha's theory of colonial discourse illustrates the philosophical depth of postcolonial critique and reveals its direct relevance to the problem of development.

As I have noted, the major breakthrough of postcolonial theory has been to read European literary texts as colonial discourse – in other words, documents written in the era of colonialism and therefore imbued with imperialist conceptions of Europe's place in the world, general understandings of itself vis-à-vis other cultures, and hierarchical representations of Europeans and 'natives.' One of Bhabha's scholarly gifts to the field has been to articulate a concise theory of such discourse. In 'The Other Question' (1983), Bhabha interprets colonial discourse as an 'apparatus of power,' following Foucault's concept of *dispositiff* (apparatus): 'strategies of relations of forces supporting, and supported by, types of knowledge' (Foucault 1980: 196). In Bhabha's interpretation, colonial discourse exercises this power through an articulation of difference, racial or cultural, in order to justify subjugation. The main discursive strategy of articulating this difference is *stereotyping*, where alterity is fixed by deploying stereotypes such as the native, the savage, or the cannibal. In short, colonial discourse:

- 'turns on the recognition... of racial/cultural/historical *differences*,'
- creates 'a space for a *'subject peoples'* through the production of knowledges... of colonizer and colonised which are stereotypical,'[11]

   and

- construes 'the colonised as *a population of degenerate types* on the basis of racial origin, in order to justify conquest and to establish systems of administration and instruction' (Bhabha 1996: 70).

Despite these strong terms Bhabha reads colonialism, on the whole, as an *ambivalent* mode of power/knowledge rather than an impenetrable system of domination. This is a marked departure from Said's first account of the colonial discourse of orientalism as a 'corporate institution for dealing with the Orient – dealing with it by making statements about it, authorising views of it, describing it, teaching it, settling it, ruling over it' (Said 1978:3). Here, Europe's authority appears complete and unassailable. Bhabha, on the other hand, stresses the ambivalence of colonial discourse in which the stereotype, e.g., the oriental, is a site of conflicting emotions and imagery – desire and derision, savagery and exoticism. It is both strange and familiar, 'at once an 'other' and yet entirely knowable' (Bhabha 1996:70-1) since for the stereotype to have any credibility, it must manifest substantial 'knowledge'.

Even more crucial, from the point of view of interest in the development discourse, is the argument that the cultural authority of colonial discourse is never complete. For Bhabha, this authority was challenged in every instance where natives presented missionaries or colonial administrators with difficult questions, 'questions of authority that the authorities cannot answer' (ibid:115). By way of example, he recounts the story that, early in the 19th century, a group of Indians happened to come upon a translated copy of the Bible and to fall in love with it. But they had questions – 'How can the word of God come from the flesh-eating mouths of the English?' 'How can it be the European book, when we believe that it is God's gift to us?' (ibid:116). Not having their questions answered, the natives adopt the holy book in a manner that troubles their catechist: they refuse to take the Sacrament which in their vegetarian eyes amounted to eating flesh. Bhabha uses the term *hybridity* to indicate the natives' tendency to question and appropriate colonial discourse in ways that deflect its authority, and additionally to refer to the ensuing state of postcoloniality as a product of this cultural exchange.[12]

Hybridity has been interpreted, especially by critics of postcolonial theory, as a simple pastiche of multiculturalism that in effect mutes current polarisation and hierarchy (e.g. Dirlik 1997). No doubt there is such a conception, but this is a rather shallow meaning. In this paper, I draw on its far more radical and philosophically productive dimensions.

In the instance of *translating* Christianity in India, the cultural authority of the colonial has been hybridised, i.e. 'contaminated' with another (here, non-European) culture.

The upshot is that, even though colonialism is a dominant mode of power/ knowledge, it is riddled with ambivalence at the same time that its power is troubled and vulnerable. The significance of this insight for challenging development cannot be over-estimated as it offers grounds for subversion by empowering the subaltern's conception of its own authority relative to that of its colonisers. In other words, it opens the door for disrupting the authority of development rather than take it as given.

## Development as a Colonial Discourse

The idea of development has deep historical roots but it has become the reigning trope of our own time. It is hardly an exaggeration to say that the discourse of development has 'set the standard of sanity for the whole world.' When the majority of African 'states' broke away from European rule, the development imperative was firmly in place, with the UN officially designating 1960-70 as the 'development decade.' African leaders took this imperative as given and began the monumental task of retracing the path of industrial modernity. The sense of urgency was clear as President Nyerere stated: 'what has taken the older countries centuries should take us decades' (1968:93). Tom Mboya went even further to claim that it was 'not necessary to explain why these (African) countries must develop;' it was that axiomatic (Mboya 1970:266). To my mind, the pre-occupation with 'development' among African leaders, and at least a generation of intellectuals and students, has been an integral part of the interminable 'African crisis.'[13]

To understand the current problematic of development, one must distinguish between development as a historical process and as a discursive fetish, although, of course, the two are dialectically inseparable. Development – as the process of large-scale material accumulation that took place in the north Atlantic and later on other world regions – is a historical 'fact.'[14]

In some instances, industrialisation was set off by the 'exceptional encounter' – to use Amin's (1976:157) term – of events and processes that created extraordinary commitment to economic growth. This was true for the 'less developed' countries that have achieved the highest rises in income (e.g. Singapore, South Korea), which were helped by the exceptional encounter of the Cold War and the commitment of the north Atlantic bloc to development in this region as part of its stated strategy to contain communism. Here, I am not concerned with this process or with development in the protean sense of growth, evolution or positive change. I am interested in the 'fact' that this north Atlantic experience has been deployed into a discourse that helped to silence and subdue 'underdeveloped' regions in largely the same way that orientalism served Europe's domination of the 'Orient'. The development discourse proceeds on the premise that this experience offers the prototype for all.

To fully understand development as discourse, I return to Foucault's more encompassing concept of *dispositiff*, which he explains as a 'heterogeneous ensemble consisting of discourses, institutions, architectural forms, regulatory decisions, laws, administrative measures, scientific statements, philosophical, moral and philanthropic propositions – in short, the said as much as the unsaid' (1980:194). Thus, the discourse is part of a larger, more pervasive structure. The complexity of the apparatus explains the daunting task of forming a grip on and undoing the development discourse, and its ability to repeatedly transform itself and reappear in new guise – alternately highlighting gender (gender and development), the environment (sustainable development), or capabilities (human development).[15] In Escobar's words, development has functioned as a discursive practice that sets the rules of the game: who can speak, from what points of view, with what authority, and according to what criteria of expertise; it sets the rules that must be followed for this or that problem, theory, or object to emerge and be named, analysed, and eventually transformed into a policy or a plan (1995:41)

In other words, it set the parameters for what may be said or unsaid, and effectively produced the regime of sanity that equally governed its participants – development 'experts' as well as 'clients.'

Postcolonial theory exposes development as a direct parallel to orientalism. In Said's (1978) account, orientalism is: a distinct academic field, a 'style of thought' that perceived a deep ontological and epistemological divide between East and West, and a corporate institution of power (2-3). Any faithful application of Said reveals *developmentalism* as the name of orientalism's 20th century descendant.[16] It is an academic field of specialisation; a style of thought that divides the world into developed and underdeveloped based on perceived ontological and epistemological differences between the two; and an institution of power, a set of authorities that hold the final word on development and the financial and technological means to intervene and reconstruct the lives of the underdeveloped. The Orient is simply displaced onto the Third World. As orientalist scholars presented the Orient as exotic, mystic, and mysterious to the Western imaginary, developmentalists represent the Third World as backward, pre-modern, pre-capitalist, or deviant in one form or another.

Can development also be read as a colonial discourse in line with Bhabha's theory? As we have seen, colonial discourse requires the presence of a difference, a space for a stereotypical subject people, and degenerate types that justify their own subordination. The development discourse clearly turns on an articulation of difference, but moreover on problematising this difference, with the beginning point in any given textbook being that 'Third World nations share a common set of problems... problems that in fact define their state of underdevelopment' (Todaro 2000: 29). Bhabha's emphasis on racial and cultural distinctions is replaced by the economic dimension, and the level of income now serves as the supreme gauge of difference. Second, a 'space for subject peoples,' that is to say, people whose lifeways require development, is carved out in specialist texts where their 'problems' are discussed and dissected based on the stereotypical knowledges produced.[17]

I borrow the term 'lifeways' from Grim (1994) who uses it in the context of Native American religion and ethics.

Finally, intervention is justified on the basis of construing those subjects as 'degenerate types.' Their degeneracy is figured not in the old colonial sense of being savage, cannibalistic, or lustful, but in the new developmentalist terms of being poor, malnourished and illiterate. Development, then, may be read as a colonial discourse proper, a structured set of hierarchical representations of different cultures that justifies 'conquest.'

This orientalist colonial discourse of development is carried to extremes in Africa's case.[18] Any cursory survey of the extensive literature on the 'African crisis' uncovers the rhetoric of disaster and tragedy that aggressively solicits intervention. For instance, Easterly and Levine's frequently cited article announces that 'Africa's economic history since 1960 fits the classical definition of tragedy' (1997:1203). Howard Stein more recently confirms that 'Africa is mired in a developmental crisis, ... a crisis of a more profound and protracted nature' (2003:153). In fact, Africa 'poses the greatest challenge to world development efforts to the end of the century and beyond' (Todaro 2000:708).[19] Thus, Said's almost 30 years old conclusion that orientalism had less to do with the Orient than with Europe's imagination of its own world is borne out. Development, even more so than the Orient, has become a field of imagination and fantasy – in this case, for human challenges and possibilities – that has less to do with Africa than with a universal campaign.

To serve the purposes of this campaign, Africa remains a representation of the challenges ahead. This representational bias was revealed by Sender's (1999) critical analysis of the current economic consensus on the continent. Using the same World Bank and UN database, Sender produced a starkly different profile of trends in 'human capital,' 'quality of life,' infrastructure, and agricultural production over the past 40 years rarely presented in development texts. For instance, he found an impressive uniform decline in infant mortality even in beleaguered, war-torn countries such as Ethiopia and The Sudan.[20] The most remarkable change has been in the area of women's education where the female proportion of all secondary school students is now higher than in some rapidly growing economies such as China. In Madagascar, the country with the smallest improvement in this area, the gain from 1960 to 1991 was almost three fold (ibid:94). Yet, the point of citing Sender's findings is not to 'prove' that Africa is developing – despite wars, debt, and epidemics. The point is to highlight the orientalist bias in the development discourse, and to suggest that this discourse offers a version of 'truth' that locks Africa firmly in a subaltern location by constructing it as tragic, marginal and dependent.

Drawing on postcolonial theory tells that it is time to shift from a theoretical framework of 'dependency' to one of subalternity. The idea of subalternity has been invoked mainly in reference to marginalised classes within national borders (Guha 1982), but it may be extended to also highlight the subordination of the 'underdeveloped' within the current world hierarchy. Although space is limited, it is necessary to briefly spell out the significance of this shift. Dependency theory was revolutionary in pointing out the historical contribution of formerly colonised regions to the development of industrial capitalist economies. Unfortunately, the theory also helped generate the mistaken impression that today's 'peripheral' economies are the dependent partner in the centre-periphery relationship. But, of course, this impression can be sustained only if one accepts the present calculus of economic value, which as Amin (1976) and other unequal exchange theorists made clear long ago, merely reflects the highly skewed terms of trade between manufactured goods and raw materials. A conceptual framework of subalternity exposes the perverse logic by which those who provide the very materials that fuel industrial economies and allow such high levels of consumption are discursively produced as dependent and thereby maintained in a subaltern position. The potential results of this revision are far reaching.[21]

Understanding development as a colonial discourse opens up space for disrupting its authority. In the same way that postcolonial critics have approached European literary texts as world constructions that embody a relationship of power between Europeans and Others, by extension, development economics must be read as texts that contain dynamics of power and cultural-epistemic hegemony.[22]

Even though in his analysis Said (1978) focused primarily on literary documents, he was very much aware of the potential implication of disciplines such as economics in orientalism (p. 15). For an exposition of the role of economics in classical as well as contemporary orientalism, see Zein-Elabdin and Charusheela (2004), particularly the chapters by Robert Dimand and Jennifer Olmsted.

This reading is instrumental for breaking apart the dominant single vision of social meaning and progress.

## Postcoloniality and Africa – Hybridity and Resistance

If development is understood as a colonial discourse, what does this engender for resistance and for better understanding of contemporary Africa? I believe theorising Africa as postcolonial offers rich possibilities. This is not simply a matter of semantics – substituting postcoloniality for development – but of a substantive epistemological political transformation, because it brings to the fore the narratives of how communities live in the present and allows these narratives to hybridize the authority of the development discourse and, more importantly, to offer a different social ethics.

Postcoloniality naturally obtains on both sides of empire; but here, I am primarily concerned with its subaltern side.[23] As a subjective consciousness, postcoloniality is best captured by Spivak who suggests the postcolonial presents a doubleness of being or a conflictual existence, an 'impossible 'no' to a structure, which one critiques, yet inhabits intimately' (1990:204). This is the inevitable result of having been 'worked over by colonialism' (Prakash 1992:8). Bhabha sees postcoloniality inscribed in any situation of cultural displacement; it is a moment of in-betweenness, diaspora, refuge, and exile; being 'neither 'one' nor 'other'' (1996:127). In all the variedly stated expressions, it is clear that there is a hybridity that renders obsolete the binarisms of tradition and modernity, development and underdevelopment.

To elicit the full potential of postcoloniality, however, requires extending it more directly to the realm of political-economy. Accordingly, it may be also be taken as both an unavoidable contemporary material condition,... (and) a consciousness of resistance to the current cultural hegemony powerfully maintained in place by monopoly over economic resources as well as the discursive construction of what constitutes economy and economics (Zein-Elabdin and Charusheela 2004:6).

As such, postcoloniality may encompass not only a subjective awareness of hybridity but, in addition, an existence in and social consciousness of a global environment marked by political/cultural domination and material inequality. Resistance to this environment can draw from both an ethical commitment to a different, less oppressive time-world, and from recognition of the cultural authority of the subaltern. Therefore, far from being a condition of political aporia, 'wilderness', or limbo, postcoloniality can offer a powerful mode of resistance to despotic representations of being and becoming.

Theorising African societies as postcolonial entails understanding them as contemporary constructions, with coeval modes of being and provisioning, where social institutions and processes express a continuum of regional and worldwide encounters, mixing different technologies, lifeways and philosophies. This hybridity problematises any claims to 'authenticity' or a secure original identity, for example, in the way that Negritude perceived the African character. In the present context, authenticity can only refer to actual social patterns as they exist and perform now, not as built up in either nativist or developmentalist discourses. Most African communities today are far from the level of technological capability and material affluence found in the 'developed' world, but they are also distances away from the social formations that prevailed only a few decades ago. They have been transformed – in different ways – by immense and multiple forces of change, including colonialism, development programmes, and general contact and movement, synergistically with their own internal dynamics, whatever their sources may be. A theoretical perspective of postcoloniality allows an examination of these communities in their present fullness.

What is perhaps of more consequence is that this perspective helps free some of the social ethics that have all along been denied in the development discourse. In the following, I give a broad sense of these ethics and how they might offer a strong critique of the current conception of development, abstracting away from immediate problems and policy limitations in order to stress the importance of recovering agency. Substantivists in economic anthropology have long studied African economies as cultural creations and were, therefore, able to grasp social patterns typically dismissed in economic literature. For example, they saw the centrality of the family and kinship, reciprocity, and gift giving to economic provisioning, and the predominance of obligatory over contractual relations across a wide range of African societies.[24] More recent scholarship documents the continued presence of these patterns, which raise questions to the assumption of autonomous, self-interested choice that undergirds the current archetype of economic development.

A first narrative of postcolonial African sociality can be found in Trulsson's (1997) institutional economic study of industrial entrepreneurs in northwest Tanzania. One of the questions Trulsson set out to answer was 'why do they (African entrepreneurs) often appear irrational to a Western observer?'[25] He found that, like all firms, Tanzanian businesses relied on a set of *ad hoc* rules to respond to contingencies as they materialised. Yet, their desire for profit was subject to almost every familial priority, often against the dictates of economic efficiency. Such commitment was reflected in the 'irrationality' of importing costly labour-saving technologies while employing unnecessary numbers of relatives and friends. Trulsson found that family obligations were the leading cause behind the shortage of liquidity among his sample of entrepreneurs. Another example was earlier documented in MacGaffey's (1991) ethnography of the 'second economy' in Zaire (now Congo), defined as production for own-consumption and monetised but unrecorded or illegal activities. Her study established the role of kinship and personal obligation in both basic provisioning and business ventures, manifested in diffused reciprocity between families, clans, and trading partners. This reciprocity played an important part in the movement of food and other supplies between rural and urban areas, and helped support Zaire's economy in the midst of gross mismanagement by Mobutu's regime.

Indeed, many years ago, Hyden (1983) generalised such patterns as observed by MacGaffey and Trulsson in what he called 'the economy of affection:' 'a network of support, communications and interaction among structurally defined groups connected by blood, kin, community or other affinities' (8).[26] These networks operated in all aspects of life, including basic survival – which comprised anything from day-to-day living to disaster relief; social maintenance such as marriage and burial expenses; and 'development,' for instance, helping to pay for education or business ventures. Hyden's developmentalist Marxian premise prompted him to see this economy as an evolutionary link between a peasant and a capitalist mode of production, and therefore to argue that its persistence was an obstacle to the emergence of capitalism as a necessary historical precursor to socialism.

Accordingly, if one were to follow the colonial discourse of development, the stereotype would be the inefficient wasteful African, who must be replaced with the self-cantered sybaritic economic agent. Public policy should then seek to accelerate movement away from the 'economy of affection.' On the other hand, if one were to frame these same social patterns – regardless of the extent of their generalisability for now – in terms of postcoloniality, they can be seen as contemporary valid reality, with positive and serviceable attributes. Africans would then be in a position to participate in the construction of meaning and definitions of social being; to set not only the terms of their own sanity, but to also suggest a more socially sympathetic and generous example. Thus, Hyden must be turned on his head altogether to embrace African familial obligation and social commitment as a positive ethic rather than an obstacle to development.

But, how is this any different from the common call for cultural preservation? To show the postcolonial departure, I will give just one example. Lopes (1994) has argued that some African attitudes that have thus far been seen as an economic handicap should form the basis for an indigenous development platform. In the context of evaluating structural adjustment programmes, he identified an 'African economic behaviour' or a 'psychology,' which included a tendency toward 'wasteful' conduct, 'disdain for accumulation,' and 'need for family cohesion and security' (20). He argued that Africans' concern with preserving social relations at the expense of individual gain was a source of excessive spending and chronic indebtedness and, accordingly, he questioned the effectivity of emphasising austerity in structural adjustment directives. Instead, he asked: 'Do we have a basis for a genuine and indigenous reform process?' (21).[27] Some of this behaviour clearly converges with the social patterns discussed above, and Lopes' contribution is welcome to the extent that it takes them as equally valid modes of organisation rather than inferior aberrations.

Nonetheless, from a postcolonial standpoint, the call for an indigenous this or that is difficult to endorse because it suggests a recoverable authentically African 'tradition' that has persisted in the face of all change, something permanent and unshakable. In contrast, a postcolonial perspective demands understanding African communities in their full present depth and dynamism. Much of what is seen on the continent today are *'translations'* of European institutions introduced in the process of colonialism; an obvious example would be 'the market economy.' Surely, Trulsson's Tanzanian entrepreneurs display a profit-driven business ethic, but one that is highly incongruent with the logic of a market economy, structural adjustment, or 'development.' The developmentalist text of self-interest and efficiency, thus, has been hybridised in an African context of hospitality and connectedness. Similarly, the transactions that MacGaffey observed in Zaire (Congo) were no barter trades removed from the market economy; they existed in complex hybrid formations that amalgamate market and non-market exchange (Zein-Elabdin 2003).

I do not claim that all African communities are hybrid to the same extent, but let's also realize that nothing at hand resembles the sharp dichotomy sometimes drawn between an indigenous or traditional and a modern Africa.[28] It may be true that some know or think they know their 'roots', and I would not dismiss or trivialize this sensibility. But, even though the words and melodies of these roots echo and call deep, perhaps even ancient, associations and longings, those cannot be lived except in the present. At this point, the indigenous is a historical impossibility. The most it can do, and may be that is enough to invoke it, is to serve as a psychic anchoring mechanism in the face of change and uncertainty, to account for all the absences in a new historical context. My concern is that the appeal to the indigenous often becomes an appeal to diachronic oppressive social structures. In contrast, again, postcoloniality, as a strong critique of domination and oppression – past and present, European or African – demands redefining the terms of reference with regard to all subalterns, redrawing intra-African individual and social relations of all orders – religion, ethnicity, gender, or any others. The call for embracing certain social patterns is to be done not so much in the name of preserving a phantasmagoric indigenous culture, but from the point of view of their present vitality and service-ability, of what they might offer to help manoeuvre the way out of the present socio-ecological impasse.

The world today is faced with an acute need to re-think the received wisdom on development. It is now clear that material accumulation of the magnitudes reached in 'model' societies inheres on building immense productive capacities and engenders tremendous dislocation. It entails command over vast reserves of nature and a great deal of brutality against multitudes of human communities, with such heavy ecological and social cost that Africans should not wish to repeat. This accumulation was historically facilitated by processes of enslavement and colonialism that provided access to such reserves and allowed such brutality. The perspective I have suggested here enables Africans to possess the discursive authority to offer a different direction – in short, one might say, an ethic for a post-hegemonic world where the positive may be understood as a qualitative change in ethics more than quantitative additions to material comfort.[29] This may seem utopianist, and at the moment it remains an ideal. All I can do in this space is to extend the invitation for collective and patient reflection on the elements necessary for its realisation, but I hope that I have already pointed toward some.

### Conclusion – Philosophy and Development

As I have argued elsewhere (Zein-Elabdin 1998), development is a metaphysical question. It is ultimately about social meaning and unknowable directions. Long ago, J. B. Bury (1932) suggested there were two types of ideas: those that are within human will or knowledge and can be influenced by humans, and those beyond human will and knowledge and therefore cannot be determined or verified. They may be questions of 'fact' but a fact that we do not know. The idea of development, I think, falls under the second category. The colonial discourse of development rests on the peculiar premise that the lifeways of the overwhelming majority are ontologically inferior and it, thereby, 'sets the standard of *(in)sanity* for the whole habitable world.'

Theorising African communities as postcolonial, ontologically no higher nor lower than others, affirms what they constitute and experience today, and decentres development as an epic in which the present can only be read as an insignificant overture to the future. This need not imply isolationism, certainly not resistance to change, or denial of problems that call for attention. Instead, it restores some agency to the location from which conditions may be considered problematic and from which remedies may be proposed. I suggest, therefore, that the postcolonial, far from being a 'pernicious fiction,' is a necessary and hopeful critical outlook capable of illuminating the complexity of today's world, interrogating hegemony, and restoring agency to the subaltern.

## Notes

1. Responding to his uncle the Emperor Gaius Caligula's question: 'Do you think I'm mad?' (Robert Graves, *I, Claudius* 1934: 464).
2. By general assent, the 'beginning' point of postcolonial theory is considered the Palestinian author Edward Said's landmark book *Orientalism* (1978), which was followed by key contributions from Homi Bhabha (1983, 1985) and Gayatri Chakravorty Spivak (1985, 1988, 1990). The term 'postcolonial theory' is typically associated with these authors' approach and insights, while 'postcolonial critique' more broadly incorporates other literature that explores questions of cross-cultural interaction and the legacy of colonialism. Of course, historicising origins is not so simple; strong traces of similar themes can be found in the writings of earlier thinkers, most prominently Fanon who inspires much of Bhabha's work. For more background, see Williams and Chrisman (1994), Mongia (1996), Gandhi (1998), and Charusheela and Zein-Elabdin (2003).
3. The terms hegemony and subalternity are derived from Gramsci's analysis of the domination of the 'popular masses' by the 'intellectual strata' in Fascist Italy. Hegemony may be effected by creating the social climate that elicits the subaltern (subordinated) groups' consent to the ruling ideology. See Charusheela and Zein-Elabdin (2003). The Subaltern Studies historians adopted the term subaltern to refer to 'subordination in South Asian society whether this is expressed in terms of class, caste, age, gender and office or any other way' (Guha 1982: vii). My usage of the term is consistent with this formulation.
4. Challenges to development have arisen from diverse quarters. The most forceful have been presented by the 'post-development' literature, which sees development as a historical work of ideology. Post-development work is salutary. However, much of it contains a somewhat romantic idea of 'tradition.' See Rahnema (1997).
5. One must always struggle with the complexity and even legitimacy of 'Africa' as a category or analytical unit. Here, Africa may be taken as the quintessential representation of cultural and economic subalternity in the development discourse.
6. Examples of other colonial documents examined by postcolonial critics include Macaulay's *Minute on Education* (see Bhabha 1996, especially 'Of Mimicry and Man') and Lord Cromer's *Modern Egypt*, in particular, the passage in which he describes the difference in mental composition between Europeans and Orientals (Said 1978: 38).
7. Europe here is not confined to the geographical location but includes extensions of the same broad culture in European settlements in other regions such as north America and the south Pacific. Notice that all parts of these regions, including, for example, New Zealand, automatically acquire the emblem of development and are classified as such in the literature. I do not, of course, take Europe as a coherent, incontestable place, but I do want to single out its unifying substance vis-à-vis its Others.

8. This is, arguably, a crucial departure from anti-colonial or 'nativist' reactions to colonialism, which tended to isolate a 'native' that is ontologically different from Europeans. The classic example in the context of Africa is Negritude. As is well known, Negritude philosophy drew a razor sharp essentialist distinction between 'Europeans' and 'negroes,' with Senghor (1962) claiming that the latter's psychology was grounded in an 'emotive attitude towards the world' (p. 15). Of course, Negritude poets were themselves a hybrid product of colonialism, and concurred – perhaps in nothing more than a shrewd political move – with European characterisations of Africans. After all, it was Sartre who defined 'negrohood' as 'a certain affective attitude towards the world' (ibid.:10). For more on the relationship between postcolonialism and Negritude, see Williams and Chrisman (1994) and Mongia (1996).

9. The volume *Postcolonialism Meets Economics* (Zein-Elabdin and Charusheela 2004) highlights this cultural nature of economics. In particular, see the introduction. By culture I continue to mean an 'incomplete, unpredictable, historically specific social frame of reference that gives rise to different practices and ideas, including economy and economics' (Zein-Elabdin 2004: 28). It is not to be understood in the classical Marxian sense of a superstructure.

10. For an exploration of the philosophical character of postcolonial theory, see Gandhi (1998). Postcolonial critique has followed a particular disciplinary trajectory, beginning in literary criticism and moving on to history and other fields. Its explicit extension to the discipline of philosophy has been carried out primarily by African scholars, see Mudimbe (1988), Appiah (1992), and Eze (1997).

11. Although development does not figure as a distinct major theme, critical engagements with this discourse are scattered throughout the literature. For example, Spivak (2000) has commented on 'gender and development' and the curious notion of 'gender training'. Escobar's ethnography of development (1995) was, to my knowledge, the first move in the direction of extending postcolonial scholarship to the horizons of economics.

12. Memmi (1965) anticipated this claim although he did not develop a theory of stereotyping or even used the term. His 'mythical portrait of the colonized' sums up the composite European representation of the native that contains all *his* stereotypical traits – laziness, weakness, wickedness, greed, dishonesty, and ingratitude. He also anticipated the idea of mutual constitution in his discussion of the 'bond' between the colonizer and the colonized.

13. Hybridity has been interpreted, especially by critics of postcolonial theory, as a simple pastiche of multiculturalism that in effect mutes current polarization and hierarchy (e.g. Dirlik 1997). No doubt there is such a conception, but this is a rather shallow meaning. In this paper, I draw on its far more radical and philosophically productive dimensions.

14. Ake (1996) has argued that African leaders were never genuinely concerned with development; it was simply a matter of rhetoric for the masses. This is also implied in Ki-Zerbo (1997). This argument, I think, underestimates the power of the development discourse. In fact, as Mkandawire (2001) suggests, one might say there was all along a 'developmental state' in postcolonial Africa. I have commented elsewhere (Zein-Elabdin 1998) on the attitude of the first generation of leaders (Senghor, Nyerere, and Nkrumah) with respect to development. Their pronouncements on the subject clearly support Mkandawire's claim. Still, my concern here is with the effectivity of the discourse rather than its motivations. What matters is that the development paradigm was there to be exploited by some politicians.

15. In some instances, industrialisation was set off by the 'exceptional encounter' – to use Amin's (1976:157) term – of events and processes that created extraordinary commitment to economic growth. This was true for the 'less developed' countries that have achieved the highest rises in income (e.g. Singapore, South Korea), which were helped by the exceptional encounter of the Cold War and the commitment of the north Atlantic bloc to development in this region as part of its stated strategy to contain communism.

16. The capabilities approach, currently spearheaded by Amartya Sen and Martha Nussbaum, may be the most invasive articulation of development so far as it conceives the individual – rather than an economy or a society – as an unfinished product. Its most troubling aspect, however, is the level of universality and unilateral vision at which it is being proposed. For a critical comment on Sen's perspective on development, see the chapter by Antonio Callari in Zein-Elabdin and Charusheela (2004).

17. See Escobar (1995). Although he follows Said closely, Escobar rejects implications of clearly malicious intentions. The self-serving capitalist impulse was there, but to a credible extent there was also a strong belief in 'helping' the 'third world' break out of 'poverty.' He, therefore, describes the project of international development as a blend of philanthropy and greed.

18. I borrow the term 'lifeways' from Grim (1994) who uses it in the context of Native American religion and ethics.

19. The literature is too vast to cite but two notable examples can be found in the Symposium on Economic Growth in Africa in the *Journal of Economic Perspectives* (Summer 1999), and the special issue on African Economic Development in a Comparative Perspective in the *Cambridge Journal of Economics* (May 2001). See Zein-Elabdin (1998, 2004) for more on the construction of Africa in the development discourse. To be sure, there is plenty of developmentalist scholarship by Africans. Many work faithfully for international development agencies. I do not see this as a form of 'false consciousness' or misguidance. It simply shows that Africans may hold a diversity of convictions.

20. This statement was made in a joint report by the International Institute for Environment and Development and the World Resources Institute, *World Resources 1987*.

21. Of course, the absolute mortality rates are still higher than world average but the gains, which after all is what grounds the idea of development, are remarkable. Improvements in infrastructure are equally impressive (p. 96). Even in agriculture, the most neglected sector, average yields have improved significantly (p. 99). Sender calls this phenomenon 'development without growth.'

22. Consider, for instance, the difference between estimating Africa's contribution to the world economy in monetary terms (gross domestic product of less than 2%) and calculating it on the basis of the quantitative percentage of natural materials it provides (for example, oil and other minerals). I refrain from using the term neocolonialism to describe this exploitative relationship simply because of its historicist origins in dependency theory. See Zein-Elabdin and Charusheela (2004: 5) for a comment on this literature.

23. Even though in his analysis Said (1978) focused primarily on literary documents, he was very much aware of the potential implication of disciplines such as economics in orientalism, p. 15. For an exposition of the role of economics in classical as well as contemporary orientalism, see Zein-Elabdin and Charusheela (2004), particularly the chapters by Robert Dimand and Jennifer Olmsted.

24. Even as applied to the subaltern, postcoloniality has been a matter of furious contestation. Some have given it highly unflattering connotations. For example, Appiah (1992) suggested it is 'the condition of what we might ungenerously call a comprador intelligentsia: of a relatively small, Western-style, Western-trained, group of writers and thinkers who mediate the trade in cultural commodities of world capitalism at the periphery' (149). See Williams and Chrisman (1994) for early debates about 'the postcolonial.'

25. For instance, Bohannan and Dalton (1962). Although in this respect anthropologists transcended the theoretical error of economics, their analyses were cast in the conceptual framework of 'primitive' society, which reinforced the assumptions of the development discourse.

Contemporary anthropology (e.g. Gudeman 1986) has significantly surpassed this limitation. For more on the treatment of Africa in economic anthropology, see Zein-Elabdin (1998).

26. I have discussed these patterns in the context of the feminist critique of economics. Much of feminist economics questions neoclassical economic theory on the basis of the observation that the model of individual welfare maximisation stands at odds with behavioural norms found in the family, which require an ethic of 'altruism.' In the literature, however, this ethic has been largely theorized as 'feminine' (see Zein-Elabdin 2003). The exclusion of the family from 'History' and 'Economics' has deep roots in European philosophy and social science. Any serious attempt to reposition Africa discursively and materially will need to address this in substantial and unapologetic terms.

27. This call is inspired by the fashionable sentiment that east Asia's economic success has not been purchased at the expense of cultural integrity. Notice his remark that '(for) a long time Asian archaism was blamed on Confucius. Today Confucius is the hero that explains Asian progress' (1994: 35). Of course, the notion of an indigenous development strategy is not new, going back to post-independence 'indigenization' efforts across the continent.

28. For example by Ayittey (1998) who states 'There are two Africas that are constantly clashing. The first is traditional or indigenous Africa that historically has been castigated as backward and primitive... The second Africa is the modern one, which is lost. Most of Africa's problems emanate from its modern sector' (14). Such statements give the impression that the author is largely unaware of the overlap between these 'two Africas,' and the continuity of individual and communal lives from village to African city, to the metropoles of Europe and America, with kin and friends traversing these worlds over and over and contributing to further cultural and economic hybridity. For an analysis of such 'transnational subjects,' see Zein-Elabdin and Charusheela (2004), in particular the chapter by Colin Danby.

29. For more on postcolonial ethics, see the chapter by S. Charusheela in Zein-Elabdin and Charusheela (2004). Also see Gandhi (1998).

# Bibliography

Adams, Edwin, 1997, *A Society Fit for Human Beings*, Albany, NY: State University of New York Press.

Adams, John, 1986, 'Peasant Rationality: Individuals, Groups, Cultures', in *World Development*, vol. 14, pp. 273-82.

Adedeji, A., 2002, 'From the Lagos Plan of Action to the New Partnership for African Development and from the Final Act of Lagos to the Constitutive Act: Whither Africa?', in Anyang' Nyong'o, P., Asegedech, G. and Davinder, L. eds., *New Partnership for Africa's Development: NEPAD. A New Path?*, Nairobi: Heinrich Böll Foundation.

Adjaye, J. K. ed., 1994, *Time in the Black Experience*, Westport: CN, Greenwood Press.

Adorno, T., and M. Horkheimer, 1972, *Dialectic and the Enlightenment*, New York: Herder and Herder.

Aidoo, Ama Ata, 1991, 'That Capacious Topic: Gender Politics', in Philomena Mariani, ed., *Critical Fictions: The Politics of Imaginative Writing*, Seattle, WA: Bay Press.

Ake, Claude, 1996, *Democracy and Development in Africa*, Washington DC: The Brookings Institution.

Ake, Claude, 1996, *Democracy and Development in Africa*, Washington DC: Brookings Institution.

Almond, G. and Coleman, J.S., 1960, *The Politics of Developing Areas*, Princeton, NJ: Princeton University Press.

Amin, Samir, 1974, *Accumulation on a World Scale: A Critique of the Theory of Underdevelopment*, New York: Monthly Review Press.

Amin, Samir, 1976a, *Unequal Development: An Essay on the Social Formations of Peripheral Capitalism*, London: Monthly Review Press.

Amin Samir, 1976b, *Uneven Development*, New York: Monthly Review Press.

Amin Samir, 1990, *Maldevelopment*, London: Zed Books.

Appiah, Kwame Anthony, 1992, *In My Father's House: Africa in the Philosophy of Culture*, Oxford: Oxford University Press.

Apter, D.E., 1969, *The Politics of Modernization*, Chicago: The University of Chicago Press, pp.18-19.

Argyle, Michael, 1987, *The Psychology of Happiness*, London: Methuen.

Arnold, G., 2000, 'Monitoring – The New Colonialism', in *West Africa*, 20-26 November, p.2.

Arthur, J. and W. Shaw, 1991, *Justice and Economic Distribution*, Englewood Cliffs, NJ: Prentice Hall.

Ayittey, George B.N., 1998, *Africa in Chaos*, New York: St. Martin's Press.

Baran, P., 1957, *The Political Economy of Economic Growth*, New York: Monthly Review Press.

Bardhan, Pranab, 1988, 'Alternative Approaches to Development Economics', in H. Chenery and T.N. Srinivasan, eds., *Handbook of Development Economics*, Vol. 1, Amsterdam: North Holland, pp. 39-71.

Bardhan Pranab, 1989, *Economic Theory and Agrarian Institutions*, Oxford: Oxford University Press.

Bardhan Pranab, 2001, 'Distributive Conflicts, Collective Action, and Institutional Economics', in G. Meier and J. Stiglitz, eds., *Frontiers of Development Economics*, New York: Oxford University Press.

Barry, Brian, 1970, *Sociologists, Economists and Democracy*, London: Collier-Macmillan.

Bates, R.H., 1981, *Markets and States in Tropical Africa: The Political Basis for Agricultural Policies*, Berkeley: University of California Press.

Bates R.H. 1990, 'Capital, Kinship and Conflict: The Structuring Influence of Capital in Kinship Societies', in *Canadian Journal of African Studies*, vol. 24, pp. 151-64.

Bates, Robert, 1988, 'Contra Contractarianism: Some Reflections on the New Institutionalism', in *Politics and Society*, vol. 16, pp. 387-401.

Bauer, Peter, 1981, *Equality, the Third World and Economic Delusion*, London: Weidenfeld and Nicolson.

Becker, Gary, 1976, *The Economic Approach to Human Behavior*, Chicago: University of Chicago Press.

Beitz, Charles, 1979, 'Global Egalitarianism: Can We Make A Case?' in *Dissent*, vol. 26, pp. 59-68.

Beitz Charles, 1983, 'Cosmopolitan Ideals and National Sentiment', in *Journal of Philosophy*, vol. 80, pp. 591-600.

Ben-Porath, Y., 1990, 'The F-Connection: Families, Friends, Firms, and Organization of Exchange', in *Population and Development Review*, vol. 6, pp. 1-29.

Bentham, Jeremy, 1970 [1789], *An Introduction to the Principles of Morals and Legislation*. London: Athlone Press.

Berger, G., 1958, 'L'attitude prospective', in *Prospective*, Paris: Publication du Centre d'Etudes prospectives, no. 1, Mai.

Berger, P. and T. Luckmann, 1967, *The Social Construction of Reality*, New York: Anchor Books.

Bergson, H., 1944, *Creative Evolution*, New York: The Modern Library.

Berlin, Isaiah, 1961, 'Equality', in F. Olafson, ed., *Justice and Social Policy*, Englewood Cliffs, NJ: Prentice Hall.

Berlin Isaiah, 1969, *Four Essays on Liberty*, Oxford: Oxford University Press.

Bernstein, Richard, 1988, *Beyond Objectivism and Relativism*. Philadelphia, PA: University of Pennsylvania Press.

Bhabha, Homi K., 1983, 'The Other Question: Stereotype, Discrimination and the Discourse of Colonialism', in *Screen*, 24 (6): 18-36. (Copy cited is reprint in Homi Bhabha, *The Location of Culture*, 1996).

Bhabha, Homi K., 1985, 'Signs Taken for Wonders: Questions of Ambivalence and Authority Under a Tree Outside Delhi, May 1817', in *Critical Inquiry* 12 (1): 144-65. (Copy cited is reprint in Homi Bhabha, *The Location of Culture*, 1996).

Bhabha, Homi K., 1996, *The Location of Culture*, New York, NY: Routledge.

Bhatnagar, G. and A. Williams, 1994, *Participatory Development and the World Bank*, Washington DC: The World Bank.

Biel, R., 2000, *The New Imperialism – The Crisis and Contradictions in North/South Relations*, London: Zed Books.

Biggs, T. and P. Srivasta, 1996, 'Structural Aspects of Manufacturing in Sub-Saharan Africa', *World Bank Discussion Paper No. 346*, Washington DC: The World Bank.

Bohannan, Paul and George Dalton, eds., 1962, *Markets in Africa*, North Western University Press.

Bohman, James, 1991, *New Philosophy of Social Science*, Cambridge, MA: MIT Press.

Boserup, Ester, 1970, *Women's Role in Economic Development*, New York: St. Martin's Press.

Boulding, Kenneth, 1973a, *The Economy of Love and Fear*, Belmont, CA: Wadsworth Publishing Co.

Boulding Kenneth, 1973b, 'Equality and Conflict', in *Annals of the American Academy of Political and Social Science*, vol. 409, pp. 1-8.

Bouvier, L.H. Shyrock, and H. Henderson, 1977, *International Migration*, Washington DC: Population Reference Bureau.

Brown, D., 1991, *Human Universals*, Philadelphia, PA: Temple University Press.

Bruton, Henry, 1997, *On the Search for Well-Being*, Ann Arbor, MI: University of Michigan Press.

Bryant, Ralph, 1987, *International Financial Intermediation*, Washington DC: Brookings Institution.

Buchanan, James, 1986, *Liberty, State and Market*, New York: New York University Press.

Burbach, R., Nunez, O. and Kagarlitsky, B., 1997, *Globalization and its Discontents: The Rise of Postmodern Socialism*, London: Pluto Press.

Bury, J., 1920, *The Idea of Progress*, London: Macmillan.

Bury, J.B., 1932, *The Idea of Progress: An Inquiry Into Its Origin and Growth*, New York: Dover Publications.

Buvinic, M., 1983, 'Women's Issues in Third World Poverty: A Policy Analysis', in M. Buvinic, M. Lycette, and W. McGreevy, eds., *Women and Poverty in the Third World*, Baltimore, MD: Johns Hopkins University Press, pp. 14-31.

Buvinic M., 1986, 'Projects for Women in the Third World: Explaining their Missing Behavior', in *World Development*, vol. 14, pp. 653-64.

Caldwell, Bruce, 1991, 'Clarifying Popper', in *Journal of Economic Literature*, vol. 29, pp. 1-33.

Cantril, Hadley, 1965, *The Pattern of Human Concerns*, New Brunswick, NJ: Rutgers University Press.

Capo, H.B., 1992, *Let Us Joke Over It: Nigeria as a Tower of Babel*, Inaugural Lecture Series (44th), Ilorin, Nigeria: Unilorin Press and Benin City, Nigeria: Labo Gbe Int.

Castells, Manuel, 1993, 'The Informational Economy and the New International Division of Labor', in M. Carnoy et al., eds., *The New Global Economy in the Information Age*. University Park, PA: Pennsylvania State University Press.

Castells, Manuel, and Alejandro Portes, 1989, 'World Underneath', in A. Portes et al., eds., *The Informal Economy*, Baltimore, MD: Johns Hopkins University Press.

Chambers, Robert, 1983, *Rural Development*, London: Longmans.

Chambers, Robert, 1997, *Whose Reality Counts: Putting the Last First*, London: Intermediate Technology Publications.

Charusheela, S. and Eiman Zein-Elabdin, 2003, 'Feminism, Postcolonial Thought, and Economics', in Marianne A. Ferber and Julie A. Nelson eds., *Feminist Economics Today: Beyond Economic Man,* Chicago, IL: University of Chicago Press.

Chenery, Hollis, 1975, 'A Structural Approach to Development Policy', in *American Economic Review*, vol. 65, pp. 310-16.

Chesneaux, J., 1998, 'Pour une culture politique du temps. Quel dialogue entre passé, présent et avenir', in *Futuribles*, no. 234, September.

Cheung, Stephen, 1989, 'Economic Organization and Transaction Costs', in J. Eatwell, M. Milgate, and P. Newman, eds., *The New Palgrave: Allocation, Information, and Markets*, New York: Norton, pp. 77-82.

Chilver, E.M., *Nso' and the Germans*, (unpublished field research notes).

Chirot, D., 1994, *Modern Tyrants*, Princeton, NJ: Princeton University Press.

Codevilla, A., 1997, *The Character of Nations*, New York: Basic Books.

Cohen, A., 1985, *The Symbolic Construction of Community*, London: Tavistock Publications.

Cole, Ken, 1995, *Understanding Economics*, London: Pluto Press.

Coleman J., 1960, *The Politics of Developing Areas*, Princeton: Princeton University Press.

Coleman, J., 1989, 'Equality', in J. Eatwell, M. Milgate and P. Newman, eds., *The New Palgrave: Social Economics*, New York: Norton, 1989, pp. 49-57.

Coleman, J.S., 1955, 'The Emergence of African Political Parties' in C. Grove Haines, ed., *Africa Today*, Baltimore.

Coleman J.S., 1990, *Foundations of Social Theory*, Cambridge, MA: Harvard University Press.

Collier, P., and J. Gunning, 1999, 'Explaining African Performance', *Journal of Economic Literature*, vol. 37, pp. 64-111.

Comaroff, J.L. and J. Comaroff, 1991, *Of Revelation and Revolution, Volume 1, Christianity Colonialism and Consciousness in South Africa*, Chicago: Chicago University Press.

Comaroff, J.L. and J. Comaroff, 1997, *Of Revelation and Revolution, Volume II*, The *Dialetics of Modernity on a South Africa Frontier,* Chicago: Chicago University Press.

Comaroff, J.L. and J. Comaroff, 2000, 'Naturing the Nation: Aliens, Apocalypse, and the Postcolonial State', *HAGAR: International Social Science Review,* Vol. 1.

Cornia, G., R. Jolly and F. Stewart, 1987, *Adjustment with a Human Face*, London: Oxford University Press.

Crook, John, 1980, *The Evolution of Human Consciousness*, Oxford: Oxford University Press.

Daly, Herman and John Cobb, Jr., 1989, *For the Common Good*, Boston, MA: Beacon Press.

Dasgupta, Partha, 1993, *An Inquiry into Well-being and Destitution*. Oxford: Clarendon Press.

David, W.L., 1985, *The IMF Policy Paradigm*. New York: Praeger.

David, W.L., 1986, *Conflicting Paradigms in the Economics of Developing Nations*, New York: Praeger.

David, W.L., 1988, *Political Economy of Economic Policy*, New York: Praeger.

David, W.L., 1997a, *The Conversation of Economic Development – Historical Voices, Interpretations and Reality*, Armonk, New York: M.E. Sharpe.

David W.L., 1997b, 'The Washington Consensus and Prospects for Authentic Development in the Caribbean', in R. Palmer, ed. *Repositioning of US-Caribbean Relations in the New World Order*, Westport, CT: Praeger.

David, Wilfred, 1973, 'Development from Below: Aspects of Local Government and Finance in a Developing Economy', in W. David, ed., *Public Finance, Planning and Economic Development: Essays in Honor of Ursula Hicks*, London: Macmillan.

David, Wilfred and Peggy David, 1995, 'Resolving the African Development Cachexia: Empowerment of the People', in F. Shams, ed., *State and Society in Africa*, Lanham, MD: University Press of America.

Davidson Paul, 1980, 'Post Keynesian Economics: Solving the Crisis in Economic Theory', in *The Public Interest*, Special Edition, pp. 151-73.

Davidson, Paul, 1978, *Money and the Real World*, London: Macmillan.

De Soto, Hernando, 1989, *Another Path*, New York: Harper and Row.

De Soto Hernando, 2000, *The Mystery of Capital*, New York: Basic Books.

De Tocqueville, Alexis, 1946, *Democracy in America*, London: Oxford University Press.

De Waal, Francis, 1989, *Peacemaking Among Primates*, Cambridge, MA: Harvard University Press.

De Waal, Francis, 1996, *Good Natured: The Origins of Right and Wrong in Humans and Other Animals*, Cambridge, MA: Harvard University Press.

DeBreu, Gerard, 1959, *Theory of Value*, New Haven, CT: Yale University Press.

DeBreu Gerard, 1991, 'The Mathematization of Economic Theory', *American Economic Review*, 81, pp. 1-7.

Descartes, R., 1978, 'Discourse on the Method', in *Descartes: Philosophical Writings*, Indianapolis: Bobbs-Merrill Educational Publishing.

Deutsch, K.W., 1953, *Nationalism and Social Communication*, New York: Willey.

Dewey, John, 1929, *The Quest for Certainty*, New York; Minton, Balch and Co.

Diagne, S.B. and Kimmerle, H., 1998, *Time and Development in the Thought of Subsaharan Africa*, Amsterdam and Atlanta, GA: Rodopi.

Diagne, S. B., 2000, *Reconstruire le sens: textes et enjeux de prospectives africaines*, Dakar, CODESRIA.

Diamond, Jared, 1999, *Guns, Germ, and Steel*, New York: Norton.

Diawara, M., 1990, 'Reading Africa Through Foucault: V. Y. Mudimbe's Re-Affirmation of the Subject', in *Quest*, Vol. 4, No. 1, pp. 76-88.

Diop, C.A., 1987, *Precolonial Black Africa*, New York: Lawrence Hill Books.

Diop, C.A., 1991, *Civilization or Barbarism – An Authentic Anthropology*, New York: Lawrence Hill Books.

Diouf, Mamadou, 2000, 'The Senegalese Murid Trade Diaspora and the Making of a Vernacular Cosmopolitanism', in *Public Culture,* 12.

Dirlik, Arif, 1997, 'The Postcolonial Aura: Third World Criticism in the Age of Global Capitalism', in Anne McClintock, Aamir Mufti and Ella Shohat, eds., *Dangerous Liaisons: Gender, Nation, and Postcolonial Perspectives,* Minneapolis: University of Minnesota Press.

Domar, Evsey, 1970, 'The Causes of Slavery and Serfdom: A Hypothesis', in *Journal of Economic History,* vol. 30 (1970), pp. 18-32.

Donahue, T., 1994, 'International Labor Standards: The Perspective of Labor', in US Department of Labor,' *International Labor Standards and Global Economic Integration: Proceedings of Symposium,* Washington DC: US Department of Labor.

Downie, Robert, 1989, 'Moral Philosophy', in J. Eatwell, M. Milgate, and P. Newman, eds., *The New Palgrave: The Invisible Hand,* New York: Norton, pp. 213-22.

Dreze, Jean, and Amartya Sen, 1989, *Hunger and Public Action,* Oxford: Clarendon Press.

Dummett, Michael, 2001, *On Immigration and Refugees,* London: Routledge.

Durning, Alan, 1989, 'Action at the Grassroots', *Worldwatch Paper No. 88,* Washington DC: Worldwatch Institute.

Durning Alan, 1992, *How Much Is Enough,* London: Earthscan.

Dworkin, Ronald, 1987, *Taking Rights Seriously,* London: Gerald Duckworth.

Eagleton, T., 1991, *Ideology: An Introduction,* London: Verso Books.

Easterly, William and Ross Levine, 1997, 'Africa's Growth Tragedy: Policies and Ethnic Divisions', in *Quarterly Journal of Economics* 112 (November), pp. 1203-50.

Easterly, William, 2000, *The Middle Class Consensus and Economic Development,* Washington DC: The World Bank (processed).

Eisenstadt, S.N., 1961, *Essays on Sociological Aspects of Political and Economic Development,* The Hague: Mouton.

Eisenstadt, S.N., 1965, 'Social Change and Modernization in African Societies South of the Sahara', in *Cahier d'Etudes Africaines,* Vol.5. No.19. (Appears also in John Middleton ed., *Black Africa,* New York: The Free Press.

Ekeh, Peter, 1975, 'Colonialism and the two Publics in Africa: A Theoretical Statement', *Comparative Studies in Society and History* Vol. 17.

Elson, D., ed., 1991, *Male Bias in the Development Process,* Manchester, UK: Manchester University Press.

Elster, Jon, 1989, *The Cement of Society.* Cambridge: Cambridge University Press.

Emmanuel, A., 1972, *Unequal Exchange: A Study of the Imperialism of Trade,* New York: Monthly Review Press.

Engels, Friedrich, 1972 [1884], *The Origins of Family, Private Property and the State.* New York: International Publishers.

Escobar, Arturo, 1995, *Encountering Development: The Making and Unmaking of the Third World,* Princeton, NJ: Princeton University Press.

Esman, Milton, 1991, *Management Decisions of Development,* West Hartford, CT: Kumarian Press.

Esman, Milton and Norman Uphoff, 1984, *Local Organizations*, Ithaca, NY: Cornell University Press.

Etzione, Amitai, 1983, *The Immodest Agenda*. New York: McGraw Hill.

Etzione Amitai, 1993, *The Spirit of Community*, New York: Crown.

Evans, Peter, 1995, *Embedded Autonomy*, Princeton, NJ: Princeton University Press.

Eze, Emmanuel Chukwudi, ed., 1997, *Postcolonial African Philosophy: A Critical Reader*. Oxford: Blackwell Publishers.

Fanon, F., 1968, *The Wretched of the Earth*, New York: Grove Press, Inc.

Fieldhouse, David, 1986, *Black Africa 1945-1960*, London: Alien and Unwin,

Forsythe, David, 1977, *Humanitarian Politics*, Baltimore, MD: Johns Hopkins University Press.

Foucault, Michel, 1980, 'The Confession of the Flesh', in Colin Gordon, ed., *Power/Knowledge: Selected Interviews and Other Writings 1972-1977*, New York: Pantheon Books.

Frank, A.G., 1967, *Capitalism and Underdevelopment in Latin America*, New York: Monthly Review Press.

Frank A.G., 1981, *Crisis in the Third World*, London: Heinemann.

Freeman, A., 1973, R. Haveman and A. Kneese, *The Economics of Environmental Policy*, New York: Wiley.

Freeman, Richard, 1992, 'Labor Market Institutions and Policies: Help or Hindrance to Development?' in World Bank, *Proceedings of the World Bank Annual Conference on Development Economics*, Washington DC: The World Bank, pp. 117-44.

Friedman, M., 1953, *Essays in Positive Economics*, Chicago: University of Chicago Press.

Fukuyama, Francis, 1991, *The End of History and the Last Man*, New York: Free Press.

Fukuyama Francis, 1995, *Trust*, New York: Free Press.

Furtado, C., 1963, *The Economic Growth of Brazil*, Berkeley, CA: The University of California Press.

Furtado C., 1983, *Accumulation and Development*, Oxford: Martin Robertson.

Furtado, Celso, 1965, *Development and Underdevelopment*, Berkeley, CA: University of California Press.

Gadamer, Hans-Georg, 1979, 'The Problem of Historical Consciousness', in P. Rabinow and W. Sullivan, eds., *Interpretive Social Science: A Reader*, Berkeley, CA: University of California Press.

Galbraith, John Kenneth, 1958, *The Affluent Society*, Boston, MA: Houghton Mifflin.

Gandhi, Leela, 1998, *Postcolonial Theory: A Critical Introduction*, New York: Columbia University Press.

GATT [General Agreement on Tariffs and Trade], 1993, *Analysis of the Proposed Uruguay Round Agreement, with Particular Emphasis on Aspects of Interest to Developing Countries*, Geneva: GATT Secretariat.

Geertz, Clifford, 1962, 'The Rotating Credit Association: A 'Middle Rung' in Development', in *Economic Development and Cultural Change*, vol. 10, pp. 240-63.

Geertz Clifford, 1973, *The Interpretation of Cultures*, New York: Basic Books.

Georgescu-Roegen, Nicholas, 1971, *The Entropy Law and Economic Process*. Cambridge, MA: Harvard University Press.

Gerschenkron, Alexander, 1962, *Economic Backwardness in Historical Perspective*, Cambridge, MA: Harvard University Press.

Giddens, Anthony, 1979, *Critical Problems in Social Theory*, Berkeley, CA: University of California Press.

Giddens Anthony, 1984, *The Constitution of Society*, Cambridge: Polity Press.

Giddens Anthony, 1991, 'Structuration Theory: Past, Present and Future', in C. Bryant and D. Nary, eds., *Theory of Structuration*, London: Routledge, pp. 201-21.

Giddens Anthony, 2002, *Runaway World*, London: Profile Books.

Gilpin, Robert, 1981, *War and Change in World Politics*, Cambridge: Cambridge University Press.

Gilpin, Robert, 1987, *The Political Economy of International Relations*, Princeton, NJ: Princeton University Press.

Goldin, I., O. Knudsen and D. van der Mensbrugghe, 1993, *Trade Liberalization: Global Economic Implications*, Paris: OECD.

Goode, William, 1986, 'Individual Choice and Social Order', in J. Short, Jr., ed., *The Social Fabric*, Berkeley, CA: Sage.

Gordon, Wendell, 1973, *Economics from an Institutional Viewpoint*. Austin, TX: University of Texas Press.

Goulet, Denis, 1978, *The Cruel Choice*, New York: Atheneum.

Goulet Denis, 1979, 'Development as Liberation: Policy Lessons from Case Studies', in *World Development*, vol. 7, pp. 556-66.

Gran, Guy, 1983, *Development by People*, New York: Praeger.

Granovetter, M., 1985, 'Economic Action and Social Structure: A Theory of Embeddedness', *American Journal of Sociology*, vol. 91, pp. 481-510.

Graves, Robert, 1934, *I, Claudius, From the Autobiography of Tiberius Claudius*, New York: Harrison Smith and Robert Haas.

Gray, John, 1998, *False Dawn: The Delusion of Global Capitalism*, London: Granta Books.

Green, R. and Seidman A., 1968, *Unity or Poverty? The Economics of Pan-Africanism*, Baltimore, MD: Penguin Books.

Greif, Avner, 1992, 'Institutions and International Trade: Lessons from the Commercial Revolution', in *American Economic Review*, 82, pp. 128-33.

Grene, Marjorie, 1967, 'Martin Heidegger', in *Encyclopaedia of Philosophy*, vol. 3&4, pp. 459-65.

Griffin, J., 1986, *Well-Being*, Oxford: Clarendon Press.

Grim, John A., 1994, 'Native North American Worldviews and Ecology', in Mary Evelyn Tucker and John A. Grim, eds., *Worldviews and Ecology: Religion, Philosophy and the Environment*, Cranbury, NJ: Associated University Presses.

Grindle, Merilee, 2001, 'In Quest of the Political: The Political Economy of Development Policymaking', in G. Meier and J. Stiglitz, eds., *Frontiers of Development Economics*, New York: Oxford University Press, pp. 345-80.

Group of Green Economists, 1992, *Ecological Economics*, London: Zed Books.

GTZ [German Agency for Technical Cooperation], 1998, *Beyond the Toolkit*, Eschborn: GTZ.

Gudeman, S., 1996, 'Sketches, Qualms, and Other Thoughts on Intellectual Property Rights', in S. Brush and S. Stabinsky, eds. *Valuing Local Knowledge*, Washington, DC: Island Press, pp. 102-21.

Gudeman, Stephen, 1986, *Economics as Culture: Models and Metaphors of Livelihood*, London: Routledge and Kegan Paul.

Guha, Ranajit, ed., 1982, *Subaltern Studies I: Writings on South Asian History and Society*, Delhi: Oxford University Press.

Gunnarsson, C. and Lundhal, M., 1996, *The Good, the Bad and the Wobbly: State Forms and Third World Economic Performance* in M. Lundhal and B. J. Ndulu, eds., New Directions in Development Economics: Growth, Environmental Concerns and Government in the 1990s, London: Routledge, pp.251-281.

Gyekye, K., 1987, *An Essay on African Philosophical Thought: The Akan Conceptual Scheme*, New York: Cambridge University Press.

Gyekye, Kwame, 1997, *Tradition and Modernity: Philosophical Reflections on the African Experience*, New York and Oxford: Oxford University Press.

Habermas, Jurgen, 1973, *Knowledge and Human Interests*, Boston, MA: Beacon Press.

Habermas Jurgen, 1984, 'Reason and the Rationalization of Society', in *The Theory of Communicative Action*, Vol. 1., Boston, MA: Beacon Press.

Habermas, Jurgen, 1987, 'Lifeworld and System', in *The Theory of Communicative Action*, Vol. 2. Boston, MA: Beacon Press.

Habermas Jurgen, 1993, *Justification and Application*, Cambridge: Polity Press.

Habermas Jurgen, 1998, *The Inclusion of the Other*, Cambridge: Polity Press.

Hadenius, A., and F. Uggla, 1996, 'Making Civil Society Work, Promoting Democratic Development: What States and Donors Do?' in *World Development*, vol. 24, pp. 1621-39.

Hagen, E.E., 1962, *On the Theory of Social Change*, Homewood, Ill: The Dorsey Press.

Haines, C.G., *Africa Today*, Baltimore: Greenard Press.

Haq, Mahbubul, 1995, *Reflections on Human Development*, New York:Oxford University Press.

Hardin, Russell, 1982, *Collective Action*. Baltimore, MD: Johns Hopkins University Press.

Harsanyi, J., 1977, *Essays on Ethics, Social Behavior, and Scientific Explanation*, Dordrecht: Reidel.

Hayek, Friedrich, 1960, *The Constitution of Liberty*, London: Routledge.

Hayek Friedrich, 1976, 'The Mirage of Social Justice', in *Law, Legislation and Liberty*, Vol. 2. Chicago: University of Chicago Press.

Hayter, Teresa, 2001, *Open Borders*, London: Pluto Press.

Hazen, R. and M. Singer, 1997, *The Unanswered Questions at the Frontiers of Science*, New York: Anchor/Doubleday.

Hegel, G.W.F., 1956, *The Philosophy of History*, New York: Dover Publications.

Herrick, B., and C. Kindleberger, 1983, *Economic Development*, New York: McGraw Hill, 1983.

Hicks, John, 1969, *A Theory of Economic History*, Oxford: Clarendon Press.

Hicks, Ursula, 1961, *Development from Below*, Oxford: Oxford University Press.

Higgins, Benjamin, 1977, 'Economic Development and Cultural Change: Seamless Web or Patchwork Quilt?', in M. Nash, ed., *Essays in Economic Development and Cultural Change in Honor of Bert F. Hoselitz*, Chicago: University of Chicago Press.

Hirsch, Fred, 1976, *The Social Limits to Growth*, Cambridge, MA: Harvard University Press.

Hirschleifer, Jack, 1985, 'Expanding the Domain of Economics', in *American Economic Review*, vol. 75, pp. 53-68.

Hirshman, A., 1958, *A Strategy of Economic Development*, New Haven, CT, Yale University Press.

Hirschman, Albert, 1970, *Exit, Voice, and Loyalty*, Cambridge, MA: Harvard University Press.

Hirschman Albert, 1971, *A Bias for Hope*, New Haven, CT: Yale University Press.

Hirschman Albert, 1981, *Essays in Trespassing*, Cambridge: Cambridge University Press.

Hirschman Albert, 1984a, *Getting Along Collectively*, Oxford: Pergamon Press.

Hirschman Albert, 1984b, 'Against Parsimony: Three Easy Ways of Complicating Some Categories of Economic Discourse', *American Economic Review*, vol. 74, pp. 89-96.

Hirschman Albert, 1992, *Rival Views of Market Society*, Cambridge, MA: Harvard University Press.

Hoff, K., A. Braverman and J. Stiglitz., eds., 1993, *Economics of Rural Organizations*, New York: Oxford University Press.

Hopkins, Anthony, 1986, 'The World Bank in Africa: Historical Reflections on the African Present', in *World Development*, vol. 14, pp. 1473-87.

Horkheimer, Max, 1947, *The Eclipse of Reason*. London: Oxford University Press.

Horkheimer Max, 1974, *Critique of Instrumental Reason*, New York: Seabury Press.

Horkheimer Max, 1982, *Critical Theory: Select Essays*, New York: Herder and Herder.

Hosseinzadeh, E., 1989, *Soviet Non-Capitalist Development: The Case of Nasser's Egypt*, New York: Praeger Publishers.

Hountondji, P., 1983, *African Philosophy: Myth and Reality*, Bloomington: Indiana University Press.

Hountondji, P., 1995, 'The Particular and the Universal', in Albert G. Mosley, ed., *African Philosophy: Selected Readings*, New Jersey: Prentice-Hall, Inc., Englewood Cliffs.

Hountondji, Paulin, 2002, *The Struggle for Meaning: Reflections on Philosophy, Culture and Democracy in Africa*, Athens: Ohio University Center for International Studies.

Hunt, Lynn, 1996, *The French Revolution and Human Rights*, New York: St. Martin's Press.

Huntington, Samuel, 1968, *Political Order in Changing Societies*, New Haven, CT: Yale University Press.

Huntington Samuel, 1993, 'The Clash of Civilizations', *Foreign Affairs*, vol. 72, pp. 22-49.

Huntington, Samuel and Joan Nelson, 1986, *No Easy Choice*, Cambridge, MA: Harvard University Press.

Hyden, Goran, 1980, *Beyond Ujamaa in Tanzania*, London: Heinemann.

Hyden, Göran, 1983, *No Shortcuts to Progress: African Development Management in*

Hyden, Göran, 1986, 'African Social Structure and Economic Development', in R. Berg and J. Whitaker, eds., *Strategies for African Development*, Berkeley, CA: University of California Press, pp. 52-80.

Ibn Khaldun, 1868, *Prolegomenes Historiques*, translated Slane, 3 vols., Paris.

IFAD [International Fund for Agricultural Development], 1992, *The State of World Rural Poverty*, Rome: IFAD.

ILO [International Labor Organization], 1990, *Wages, Labor and their Impact on Adjustment, Employment and Growth*, Geneva: ILO.

ILO, 1993, *Multinationals and Employment*, Geneva: ILO.

ILO, 1997, *World Employment 1996/97*, Geneva: ILO.

ILO, 1998a, *Child Labor in Africa*, Geneva: ILO.

ILO, 1998b, *Promoting Gender Equality at Work*, Geneva: ILO.

ILO, 1999a, *World Employment Report 1998/99*, Geneva: ILO.

ILO, 1999b, *New Challenges for Employment Policy*, Geneva: ILO.

Imbo, S. O., 1998, *An Introduction to African Philosophy*, New York, Rowman & Littlefield Publishers.

Inter-American Development Bank, *Facing Up to Inequality in Latin America*. Baltimore, MD: Johns Hopkins University Press, 1998.

Irele, A., 1990, *The African Experience in Literature and Ideology*, Bloomington: Indiana University Press.

Irele, A., 1992, 'In Praise of Alienation', in V. Y. Mudimbe, ed., *The Surreptitious Speech: Présence Africaine and the Politics of Otherness*, Chicago and London: The University of Chicago Press.

Isham, I., D. Nayaran and L. Pritchett, 1995, 'Does Participation Improve Performance?: Establishing Causation with Subjective Data', in *World Bank Economic Review*, vol. 92, pp. 175-200.

James, William, 1907, *Pragmatism*, Cambridge, MA: Harvard University Press.

Kant, Immanuel, 1948 [1785], *Groundwork of the Metaphysics of Morals*, London: Hutchison.

Kant Immanuel, 1970, *Kant's Political Writings*, Cambridge: Cambridge University Press.

Kaplan, Robert, 1994, 'The Coming Anarchy', in *The Atlantic Monthly*, February 1994, pp. 44-76.

Kazmin, A., 2000, 'Gandhi and the Milk of Indian Self-Reliance', *Financial Times*, August 24, p. 8.

Keohane, Robert, 1984, *After Hegemony*, Princeton, NJ: Princeton University Press.

Keohane, Robert and Joesph Nye, Jr., 1989, *Power and Interdependence*, Boston, MA: Scott Foresman.

Keynes, John Maynard, 1936, *The General Theory of Employment, Interest and Money*, London: Macmillan.

Keynes John Maynard, 1980, 'Shaping the Post-War World: Bretton Woods and Reparations', in D. Moggridge, ed., *The Collected Writings of John Maynard Keynes*, Vol. 26. London: Macmillan.

Khamisi, J., 1995, 'IMF Ultimatum Shock for Kenyan Officials', *Business Day/Business Report,* Johannesburg, 12 September, p.15.

Kindleberger, Charles, 1988, *The International Economic Order,* Cambridge, MA: MIT Press.

Ki-Zerbo, Joseph, 1997, 'Silence! We Are Developing!' in Majid Rahnema, ed., *The Post-Development Reader,* London: Zed Books, p. 88.

Klein, R.G., 1989, *The Human Career-Human Biological and Cultural Origins,* Chicago: The University of Chicago Press.

Kornai, Janos, 1971, *Anti-Equilibrium,* Amsterdam: North Holland.

Krasner, Stephen, 1984, *International Regimes,* Ithaca, NY: Cornell University Press.

Krueger, Anne, 1990, 'Government Failure in Development', *Journal of Economic Perspectives,* vol. 4, pp. 9-23.

Kuhn, Thomas, 1970, *The Structure of Scientific Revolutions,* Chicago: University of Chicago Press.

Kuttner, Robert, 1997, *Everything for Sale,* New York: Knopf.

Kuznets, Simon, 1966, *Modern Economic Growth,* New Haven, CT: Yale University Press.

Lakatos, Imré, 1976, 'Falsification and the Methodology of Scientific Research Programmes', in I. Lakatos and A. Musgrave, eds., *Criticism and the Growth of Knowledge,* Cambridge: Cambridge University Press, pp. 91-196.

Lal, Deepak, 1983, *The Poverty of Development Economics,* London: Institute of International Affairs.

Lal, Deepak, 1999, *Unintended Consequences,* Cambridge, MA: MIT Press.

Landes, David, 1990, 'Why Are We So Rich and They So Poor?' *American Economic Review,* vol. 80, pp. 1-13.

Landes, David, 1998, *The Wealth and Poverty of Nations,* New York: Norton.

Lange, Oskar, 1965, *Wholes and Parts,* Oxford: Pergamon Press.

Lappe, F. and P. Dubois, 1995, 'From Devolved to Involved Community', in *Annual Report of the Johnson Foundation,* Minneapolis: The Johnson Foundation, pp. 7-10.

Lasch, Christopher, 1995, *The Revolt of the Elites and the Betrayal of Democracy,* New York: Norton.

Lastarria-Cornheil, S., 1997, 'The Impact of Privatization on Gender and Property Rights in Africa', *World Development,* vol. 25, pp. 1317-33.

Latsis, Spiro, 1976, *Method and Appraisal in Economics,* Cambridge: Cambridge University Press.

Levins, R., and R. Lewontin, 1985, *The Dialectical Biologist* Cambridge, MA: Harvard University Press.

Levy, M. Jr., 1952, *The Structure of Society,* NJ: Princeton University Press.

Lewis, W.A., 1995, *The Theory of Economic Growth,* London: Allen and Unwin.

Lévy-Bruhl, L., 1985, *How Natives Think,* Princeton, NJ: Princeton University Press.

Linklater, Andrew, 1998, *The Transformation of Political Community,* Cambridge: Polity Press.

Lipton, Michael, 1997, 'Editorial: Poverty - Are There Holes in the Consensus?' in *World Development,* vol. 25, pp. 1003-1007.

List, F., 1983, *The Natural System of Political Economy*, London: Frank Cass.

List, Friedrich, 1904 [1841], *The National System of Political Economy*, London: Longman, Green.

Loevinger, June, 1976, *Ego Development*, San Francisco, CA: Jossey Bass.

Lopes, Carlos, 1994, *Enough is Enough! For an Alternative Diagnosis of the African Crisis*, Uppsala: The Scandinavian Institute of African Studies.

Loury, Glen, 1977, 'A Dynamic Theory of Social Income Differences', in P. Wallace and A. Lamond, eds., *Women, Minorities and Employment Discrimination*, Lexington, MA: Lexington Books.

Loury, Glen, 1998, 'Discrimination in the Post-Civil Rights Era: Beyond Market Interactions', *Journal of Economic Perspectives*, vol. 12, pp. 117-26.

Lovelock Glen, 1988, *The Ages of Gaia*. Oxford: Oxford University Press.

Lovelock, James, 1979, *Gaia*, Oxford: Oxford University Press.

Lukes, Steven, 1978, 'Power and Authority', in T. Bottomore and R. Nisbet, eds. *A History of Sociological Analysis*. New York: Basic Books, pp. 633-76.

MacGaffey, Janet (with V. Mukohya, R. wa Nkera, B. G. Schoepf, M. ya Beda, and W. Engundu), 1991, *The Real Economy of Zaire: the Contribution of Smuggling and Other Unofficial Activities to National Wealth*, Philadelphia, PA: University of Pennsylvania Press.

MacIntyre, Alasdair, 1981, *After Virtue*, Notre Dame, IN: University of Notre Dame Press.

Macpherson, C.B., 1987, *The Rise and Fall of Economic Justice and Other Essays*, Oxford: Oxford University Press.

Macy, J., 1985, *Dharma and Development*, West Hartford, CT: Kumarian Press.

Maddison, Angus, 1995, *Monitoring the World Economy, 1820-1992*, Paris: OECD Development Center.

Mamdani, Mahmood, 2001, *When Victims become Killers: Colonialism, Nativism and the Rwandan Genocide*, Princeton: Princeton University Press.

Mamdani, Mahmood, 2004, *Good Muslim, Bad Muslim: America, the Cold War and the Roots of Global Terror*, New York: Pantheon Books.

Manasian, David, 1998, 'A Survey of Human Rights', *The Economist*, December 5, No. 62, pp. 1-16.

Marcuse, H., 1964, *One-Dimensional Man*, Boston, MA: Beacon Press.

Marcuse, H., 1968, *Negations*, Boston, MA: Beacon Press.

Markandya, A., and D. Pearce, 1991, 'Development, the Environment, and the Social Discount Rate', *The World Bank Research Observer*, vol. 6, pp. 137-52.

Marshall, T.H., 1964, *Class, Citizenship and Social Development*, New York: Doubleday.

Maruyama, M., 1972, 'Toward Human Futuristics: Trans-epistemic Process', *Dialectica*, vol. 26, pp. 156-83.

Maruyama, M., 1996, 'Logic, Cultures and Individuals', *The UNESCO Courier*, vol. 10, pp. 31-35.

Maslow Abraham, 1954, *Motivation and Personality*, New York: Harper and Row.

Maslow Abraham, 1962, *Toward a Psychology of Being*, New York: Van Nostrand.

Masolo, D.A., 1994, *African Philosophy in Search of Identity*, Bloomington, Indiana University Press.

Mason, E., and R. Asher, 1973, *The World Bank Since Bretton Woods*, Washington, DC: Brookings Institution.

Maurier, H., 1984, 'Do We Have an African Philosophy?' in Richard A. Wright, ed., *African Philosophy*, Lanham: University Press of America.

Max-Neef, Manfred, 1982, *From Outside Looking In: The Experiences in Barefoot Economics*. Uppsala: Dag Hammarskjold Foundation.

Mbaye, A., 1997, 'Léopold Sédar Senghor et Gaston Berger', in S.B. Diagne, ed., *Gaston Berger: Introduction à une philosophie de l'avenir*, Dakar: Neas.

Mbembe, Achille, 2001, *On the Postcolony*, Berkeley: The University of California Press.

Mbembe, Achille, 2003, 'Necropolitics', *Public Culture*, Vol.15, No. 1.

Mbiti, J. S., 1990, *African Religions and Philosophy* (second edition), Oxford: Heinemann.

Mboya, Tom, 1970, *The Challenge of Nationhood: A Collection of Speeches and Writings by Tom Mboya*, New York: Praeger.

McBrearty, S. and Brooks, A.S., 2000, 'The Revolution that Wasn't: A New Interpretation of the Origin of Modern Human Behaviour', in *Journal of Human Evolution*,Vol. 39, No.5, pp. 453-563.

McLean, George F. et al., (eds.), 2004, *Culture and Values*, Washington DC: The Council for Research in Values and Philosophy.

Mearsheimer, John, 2001, *The Tragedy of Great Power Politics*, New York: Norton.

Meier, G., and J. Stiglitz., eds,. *Frontiers in Development Economics*. New York: Oxford University Press, 2001.

Memmi, Albert, 1965, *The Colonizer and the Colonized*, Boston, MA: Beacon Press.

Merton, R., 1973, *The Sociology of Science*, Chicago: University of Chicago Press.

Micklethwait, J., and A. Wooldridge, 2000, *A Future Perfect*, New York: Crown.

Milanovic, Branco, 1998, *Income Inequality and Poverty during the Transition from Planned to Market Economy*, Washington DC: The World Bank.

Milazi, D., 2000, *Ethnicity and State: Revisiting the Salience of Ethnicity in South Africa* [Earlier in Moore, W., 1963, *Social Change*, Englewood Cliffs].

Miller, D., 1997, 'Ironworking Technology', in J.O. Vogel, ed., *Encyclopedia of Precolonial Africa*, London: Altamira Press.

Mkandawire, Thandika, 2001, 'Thinking about Developmental States in Africa', *Cambridge Journal of Economics*, 25: 289-313.

Mongia, Padmini (ed.), 1996, *Contemporary Postcolonial Theory: A Reader*, London: Arnold.

Moore, Barrington, 1966, *Social Origins of Dictatorship and Democracy*, Boston, MA: Beacon Press.

Moore, G.E., 1903, *Principia Ethica*, Cambridge: Cambridge University Press.

Moore, W., 1963, *Social Change*, Englewood Cliffs, NJ: Prentice Hall.

Morgenstern, Oskar, 1972, 'Thirteen Critical Points in Contemporary Economic Theory: An Interpretation', *Journal of Economic Literature*, vol. 10, pp. 1163-89.

Morishima, Michio, 1982, *Why Japan Has Succeeded?*, Cambridge: Cambridge University Press.

Mosca, G., 1939 [1896], *The Ruling Class*, New York: McGraw Hill.

Moser, Carolyn, 1993, *Gender Planning and Development Theory, Practice and Training*, London: Routledge.

Motoki, T., 2001, 'The Creation of Developmental States: Arguments and the Reality in Africa', in Kurimoto, E., ed., *Rewriting Africa: Toward Renaissance or Collapse*, pp. 59-77.

Mudimbe, V.Y., 1988, *The Invention of Africa: Gnosis, Philosophy, and the Order of Knowledge*, Bloomington: Indiana University Press.

Mudimbe, V.Y., 1994, *The Idea of Africa*, Bloomington, Indiana University Press.

Mutiso, G.M. and Rohio, S. W., 1975, *Readings in African Political Thought*, London, Nairobi, Ibadan: Heinemann.

Mwanyungwe, A., 2001, in *Business Day* (South Africa) on Wednesday 23 May, p.7.

Myrdal, Gunnar, 1968, *Asian Drama*, New York: Pantheon.

Mzeka, Paul, N., 1990, *Four Fons of Nso': Nineteenth and Early Twentieth Century Kingship in the Western Grassfeilds*, Bamenda: The Spider Publishing Enterprise.

Nair, Kusum, 1966, *Blossoms in the Dust*, New York: Praeger.

Nair Kusum, 1969, *The Lonely Farrow*, Ann Arbor, MI: University of Michigan Press.

Nair Kusum, 1979, *In Defense of the Irrational Peasant*, Chicago: University of Chicago Press.

Nardin, Terry, 1983, *Law, Morality and the Relations of States*, Princeton, NJ: Princeton University Press.

National Research Council, 1997, *The New Americans*, Washington, DC: National Academy Press.

Ndi, Anthony, 2005, *The Golden Age of Southern (West) Cameroon 1946-1972: Impact of Christianity*, Bamenda.

Neufeld, Mark, 1995, *The Restructuring of International Relations*, Cambridge: Cambridge University Press.

Nkrumah, K., 1965, *Neocolonialism: The Last Stage of Imperialism*, London, Heinemann.

Nnoli, Okwudiba, 2003, 'Globalisation and African Political Science', *Journal of Political Science*, Vol. 8, No. 2.

North, Douglass, 1981, *Structure and Change in Economic History*, New York: Norton.

North Douglass, 1990, *Institutions, Institutional Change and Economic Development*, Cambridge: Cambridge University Press.

North Douglass, 1991, 'Institutions', *Journal of Economic Perspectives*, vol. 5, pp. 97-112.

Nozick, Robert, 1974, *Anarchy, State, and Utopia*, New York: Basic Books, 1974.

Nussbaum, Martha, 1986, *Fragility of Goodness*, Cambridge: Cambridge University Press.

Nye, Joseph, 2002, *The Paradox of American Power*, New York: Oxford University Press.

Nyerere, Julius K., 1968, *Ujamaa: Essays on Socialism*, Dar es Salaam: Oxford University Press.

Odum, E., 1971, *Fundamentals of Ecology*, Philadelphia, PA: Saunders College Publishing.

OECD [Organization of Economic Cooperation and Development], 1998, *Open Markets Matter*, Paris: OECD.

Okun, Arthur, 1975, *Equality and Efficiency: The Big Trade-Off*, Washington DC: Brookings Institution.

Olivier de Sardan, Jean-Pierre, 1999, 'African Corruption in the Context of Globalisation'.

Olukoshi, A., 2002, 'Governing the African Political Space for Sustainable Development: A Reflection on NEPAD', in Anyang' Nyong'o, P., Asegedech, G., and Davinder, L. eds., *New Partnership for Africa's Development: NEPAD. A New Path?*, Nairobi, Heinrich Böll Foundation.

Osaghae, Eghosa, 1994, *Ethnicity and its Management in Africa*, Lagos: Malthouse Press.

Pagden, A., 2001, *Peoples and Empires*, New York: Modern Library.

Pareto, V., 1963, *The Mind and Society*, New York: Dover.

Passmore, John, 1970, *The Perfectibility of Man*, London: Duckworth.

Patel, S., 1966, 'Can the Intellectual Property Rights System Serve the Interests of Indigenous Knowledge?' in S. Brush and D. Stabinsky, eds. *Valuing Local Knowledge*, Washington DC: Island Press, pp. 305-22.

Patterson, Orlando, 1991, *Freedom and the Making of Western Culture*, New York: Basic Books.

Peet, R. and Hardwick, E., 1999, *Theories of Development*, New York: Guilford Press.

*Perspective*, Berkeley, CA: University of California Press.

Pieterse, J.N., 2001, *Development Theory – Deconstructions/Reconstructions*, London: Sage Publications.

Pogge, Thomas, 1989, *Realizing Rawls*. Ithaca, NY: Cornell University Press.

Polanyi, Karl, 1944, *The Great Transformation*. Boston, MA: Beacon Press.

Popkin, S., 1979, *The Rational Peasant*, Berkeley, CA: University of California Press.

Popper, Karl R., 1945, *The Open Society and Its Enemies*, London and Henley: Routledge and Kegan Paul.

Popper, Karl, 1959, *The Logic of Scientific Discovery*, New York: Harper and Row.

Popper, Karl R., 1962, *Conjectures and Refutations*. New York: Basic Books.

Popper, Karl R., 1972, *Objective Knowledge*, Oxford: Clarendon Press.

Popper, Karl R., 1982, *The Rise and Decline of Nations*, New Haven, CT: Yale University Press.

Popper, Karl R., 1989, 'Collective Action', in J. Eatwell, M. Milgate, and P. Newman, eds., *The New Palgrave; The Invisible Hand*, New York: Norton, pp. 61-69.

Popper, Mancur, 1965, *The Logic of Collective Action*, Cambridge, MA: Harvard University Press.

Porter, Michael, 1990, *The Competitive Advantage of Nations*, New York: Free Press.

Powelson, John, 2000, *The Moral Economy*, Ann Arbor, MI: University of Michigan Press.

Prah, K.K., 1991, 'The Notion of Cultural Blockage and Some Issues of Technology Adoption Concerning the African Peasantry', in *Culture, Gender, Science and Technology in Africa*, Schriftenreihe der Deutschen Stiftung für Internationale Entwicklung (DSE), Harp Publications, Windhoek, pp.48-65.

Prah, K.K., (ed.), 1991, *Culture, Gender, Science and Technology in Africa* Windhoek: Harp Publications.

Prah, K.K., (ed.), 1998, *Between Distinction and Extinction. The Harmonization and Standardization of African Languages*, Jo'burg: Witwatersrand University Press.

Prah, K.K., 1995a, *African Languages for the Mass Education of Africans*, Bonn, Germany: Deutsche Stiftung für Internationale Entwicklung (DSE).

Prah, K.K., 1995b, *Mother Tongue for Scientific and Technological Development in Africa*, Bonn, Germany: Deutsche Stiftung für Internationale Entwicklung (DSE).

Prah, K.K., 1998, *In Tongues: An Edited record of the Accra Symposium on African Languages and the Challenges of African Development*, K.K. Prah and Y. King (eds.), Cape Town: The Centre for Advanced Studies of African Society (CASAS).

Prah, K.K., and Ahmed A.G.M., 2000, (eds.), *Africa and Transformation*, Volume One, Addis Ababa: OSSREA.

Prakash, Gyan, 1992, 'Postcolonial Criticism and Indian Historiography', *Social Text*, 31/32: 8-19.

Prebisch, R., 1960, *Economic Development for Latin America and Its Principal Problems*, New York, United Nations.

Pred, Allan. 'Out of Bounds and Undisciplined: Social Inquiry and the Current Moment of Danger', *Social Research*, vol. 82 (1995) pp. 1065-91.

Putnam Robert, *Bowling Alone*. New York: Basic Books, 2000.

Putnam, Robert, *Making Democracy Work*. Princeton, NJ: Princeton University Press, 1993.

Rahnema, Majid (ed., with Victoria Bawtree) 1997 *The Post-Development Reader*, London: Zed Books.

Ranis, G., F. Stewart, and A. Ramirez. 'Economic Growth and Human Development', *World Development*, vol. 28 (2000), pp. 197-215.

Rawls John, *Justice as Fairness: A Restatement*. [Ed. E. Kelly]. Cambridge, MA: Harvard University Press, 2001.

Rawls John, *Political Liberalism*. New York: Columbia University Press, 1993

Rawls John, *The Law of Peoples*. Cambridge, MA: Harvard University Press, 1999.

Rawls, John, *A Theory of Justice*. Cambridge, MA: Harvard University Press, 1971.

Repetto, Robert, *World Enough and Time*. New Haven, CT: Yale University Press, 1986.

Repetto, Robert., ed. *The Global Possible*. New Haven, CT: Yale University Press, 1995.

Richard Fardon, et al., eds., *Modernity on a Shoestring: Dimensions of Globalisation, Consumption and Development in Africa and Beyond*, Leiden and London: EIDOS.

Rifkin, Jeremy, *The End of Work*. New York: Putnam, 1995.

Rorty, Richard, *Objectivism, Relativism and Truth*. Cambridge: Cambridge University Press, 1991.

Rose. S., *Lifelines*. London: Allen Lane, 1997.

Ross, W.D. ed., 1925, *The Works of Aristotle Translated into English*, Oxford: Oxford University Press.

Rostow, W.W., 1960, *The Stages of Economic Growth: A Non-Communist Manifesto*, Cambridge: Cambridge University Press.

Rostow, W.W., 1971, *Politics and the Stages of Growth*, Cambridge: Cambridge University Press.

Rostow W.W., 1990, *Theories of Economic Growth from David Hume to the Present*, New York: Oxford University Press.

Roussakis, E.N., 1968, *Freidrich List, The Zollverein, and the Uniting of Europe*, Bruges, Belgium: College of Europe.

Rubenstein, R., and P. Crocker, 1994, 'Challenging Huntington', *Foreign Policy*, vol. 96, pp. 113-28.

Said, Edward, 1978, *Orientalism*, New York: Pantheon Books. [Copy cited is Vintage Books edition, 1979].

Sall, A., 2003, *Afrique 2025, Quels futurs possibles pour l'Afrique au sud du Sahara?* Paris: Karthala.

Samuelson, Paul, 1983, *Foundations of Economic Analysis*. Cambridge, MA: Harvard University Press.

Sartre, J-P., 1957, *Existentialism and Human Emotions*, New York: Philosophical Library.

Sartre, J-P., 1963, *Black Orpheus*, Paris: Présence Africaine.

Sartre, Jean-Paul, 1961, 'Introduction', in Frantz Fanon, *Wretched of the Earth*, New York: Grove Weidenfeld.

Schoenbrun, D.L.,1997, *The Historical Reconstruction of Great Lakes Bantu Cultural Vocabulary: Etymologies and Distributions*, Koln, Rüdiger: Köppe Verlag.

Schultz, Theodore, 1964, *Transforming Traditional Agriculture*, New Haven, CT: Yale University Press.

Schultz Theodore, 1980, 'Nobel Lecture: The Economics of Being Poor', *Journal of Political Economy*, vol. 88, pp. 639-51.

Schutz, Alfred, 1962, *The Phenomenology of the Social World*, Evanston, Ill: Northwestern University Press.

Scitovsky, Tibor, 1976, *The Joyless Economy*, Oxford: Oxford University Press.

Scott, James, 1997, *Seeing Like a State*, New Haven, CT: Yale University Press.

Seabrook, J., 1993, *Victims of Development*, London: Verso.

Seers, Dudley, 1983, *The Political Economy of Nationalism*, Oxford University Press.

Sen, A., 1999, *Development as Freedom*, New York: Alfred A. Knopf.

Sen, Amartya, 1981a, *Poverty and Famines*, Oxford: Clarendon Press.

Sen, Amartya and Bernard Williams, eds., 1981b, 'Ethical Issues in Income Distribution: National and International', in S. Grassman and E. Lundberg, eds. *World Economic Order: Past and Present*, New York: St. Martin's Press, pp. 464-93.

Sen, Amartya, and Bernard Williams, eds., 1982, *Utilitarianism and Beyond*, Cambridge: Cambridge University Press.

Sen, Amartya and Bernard Williams, eds., 1983, 'Economics of the Family', in A. Sen. *Resources, Values and Development*, Cambridge, MA: Harvard University Press.

Sen, Amartya and Bernard Williams, eds., 1985, *Commodities and Capabilities*, Amsterdam: North Holland.

Sen, Amartya and Bernard Williams, eds., 1987, 'Gender and Cooperative Conflict', *WIDER Working Paper No. 18.* Helsinki: WIDER.

Sen, Amartya and Bernard Williams, eds., 1988, 'The Concept of Development', in H. Chenery and T.N. Srinivasan, eds., *Handbook of Development Economics,* Vol. 1. Amsterdam: North Holland, pp. 9-26.

Sen, Amartya and Bernard Williams, 1989, eds., 'Development as Capability Expansion', in *Journal of Development Planning,* vol. 19, pp. 41-48.

Sen, Amartya and Bernard Williams, eds.,1990, *On Ethics and Economics,* Oxford: Blackwell.

Sen, Amartya and Bernard Williams, eds., 1999, *Development as Freedom,* New York: Knopf.

Sen, Amartya, et al., 1988, *The Standard of Living,* [Ed. G. Hawthorn], Cambridge: Cambridge University Press.

Sen, G., and C. Grown, 1988, *Development, Crises and Alternative Visions,* London: Earthscan.

Sender, John, 1999, "Africa's Economic Performance: Limitations of the Current Consensus," *Journal of Economic Perspectives,* 13 (3): 89-114.

Senghor, L.S., 1959, 'Constructive Elements of a Civilization of African Negro Inspiration', Paris: Présence Africaine.

Senghor, L.S., 1964, 'Le problème de la culture', in *Liberté, négritude et humanisme,* Paris: Seuil.

Senghor, L.S., 1970, 'Negritude: A Humanism of the Twentieth Century', in Wilfred Cartey and Martin Kilson, eds., *The Africa Reader,* New York: Vintage Books.

Senghor, L.S., 1976, 'Prose and Poetry', in John Reed and Clive Wake, eds., London, Heinemann.

Senghor, L.S., 1995, 'On Negrohood: Psychology of the African Negro', in Albert Mosley, ed., *African Philosophy: Selected Readings,* Englewood Cliffs, N.J., Prentice-Hall.

Senghor, Léopold Sédar, 1962, 'On Negrohood: Psychology of the African Negro,' in *Diogenes,* 37 Spring: 1-15.

Serres, M., 'Espace et temps', 1981, in Philippe Choquard and Jean-Louis Ferrier eds., *Sur l'aménagement du temps. Essai de chronogénie,* Paris, Denoël/Gonthier.

Shackle, George, 1972, *Epistemics and Economics,* Cambridge: Cambridge University Press.

Shils, E., 1962, *Political Development in the New States,* The Hague: Mouton.

Shiva, Vandana, 1994, *Close to Home,* Philadelphia, PA: New Society Publishers.

Shute, S., and S. Hurley., eds., 1993, *On Human Rights: The Oxford Amnesty Lectures.* New York: Basic Books.

Sidanius, J., and F. Pratto, 1999, *Social Dominance,* Cambridge: Cambridge University Press.

Siggi, M., 1970 [1939], *Economic Society in Islam,* Lahore: Kazi Publishers.

Simon, Herbert, 1978, 'Rationality as a Process and Product of Thought', in *American Economic Review,* vol. 68, pp. 1-16.

Simone, AbdouMaliq, 2004, *For the City Yet to Come: Changing Life in Four African Cities,* Durham and London: Duke University Press.

Sindjoun, Luc, 2005, 'Ethics and Politics in Africa: Praise of Positivism to Values, Presidential address delivered at the 15th Biennial Congress of the African Association of Political Science, Cairo.

Smith Adam, 1976 [1776], *An Inquiry into the Nature and Causes of the Wealth of Nations*. Oxford: Clarendon Press.

Smith, Adam, 1974 [1759], *Theory of Moral Sentiments*, Oxford: Clarendon Press.

Solow, R.M., 1970, *Growth Theory and Exposition*, Oxford: Oxford University Press.

Solow, Robert, 1990, *The Labor Market as a Social Institution*, Oxford: Blackwell.

Soros, George, 1998, *The Crisis of Global Capitalism*, New York: Public Affairs.

Soyinka, Wole, 1999, *The Burden of Memory, The Muse of Forgiveness*, New York: Oxford University Press.

Spivak, Gayatri Chakravorty, 1985, 'Three Women's Texts and a Critique of Imperialism', in *Critical Inquiry* 12 (Autumn), pp. 243-61.

Spivak, Gayatri Chakravorty, 1990, 'Poststructuralism, Marginality, Postcoloniality and Value', in Peter Collier and Helga Geyer-Ryan, eds., *Literary Theory Today*, Ithaca, NY: Cornell University Press. [Copy cited is reprint in Padmini Mongia, ed., 1996, *Contemporary Postcolonial Theory: A Reader*, London: Arnold.]

Spivak, Gayatri Chakravorty, 2000, 'Other Things are Never Equal: A Speech', in *Rethinking Marxism*, 12 (4), pp. 37-45.

Spivak, Gayatri Chakravorty, 1988, 'Can the Subaltern Speak?', in Cary Nelson and Lawrence Grossberg, eds., *Marxism and the Interpretation of Culture*, Urbana, Ill: University of Illinois Press.

Standing Guy, 2000, *Beyond the New Paternalism*, New York: Verso.

Standing, Guy, 1997, 'Globalization, Labor Flexibility and Insecurity: The Era of Market Regulation', in *European Journal of Industrial Relations*, vol. 3, pp. 7-37.

Standing, Guy, and Viktor Tokman., eds., 1991, *Towards Social Adjustment*, Geneva: ILO.

Stein, Howard, 2003, 'Rethinking African Development', in Ha-Joon Chang, ed., *Rethinking Development Economics*, London: Anthem Press.

Steiner, H. 'Entitlements', 1989, in J. Eatwell, M. Milgate,and P. Newman, eds., *The New Palgrave: Social Economics*, New York: Norton, pp. 40-44.

Steiner, H., and P. Alston, 1996, *International Human Rights in Context*, Oxford: Clarendon Press.

Stenhouse, David, 1974, *The Evolution of Intelligence*, London: Allen and Unwin.

Stewart, Frances, 1995, *Adjustment and Poverty*, London: Routledge.

Stiefel, M., 1994, *A Voice for the Excluded*, London: Zed Books.

Stiglitz J.,, 1989, 'Markets, Market Failure, and Development', in *American Economic Review*, vol. 79, pp. 197-203.

Stiglitz J., 1986b, 'More Instruments and Broader Goals: Moving Towards the Post-Washington Consensus', in *WIDER Annual Lecture*, January 7, Helsinki: WIDER.

Stiglitz J., 1998a, 'The Private Uses of Public Interests: Incentives and Institutions', *Journal of Economic Perspectives*, vol. 12, pp. 1-22.

Stiglitz J., 2002, *Globalization and its Discontents*, New York: Norton.

Stiglitz, J., 1988, 'Economic Organization, Information, and Development', in H. Chenery and T.N. Srinivasan, eds., *Handbook of Development Economics*, Vol. 1, Amsterdam: North Holland, pp. 93-160.

Stiglitz, J.E., and Hoff, K., 2001, 'Modern Economic Theory and Development', in G.M. Meir and J.E. Stiglitz, eds., *Frontiers of Development Economics*, New York, Oxford University Press, pp. 389-459.

Streeten, Paul, 1958, 'Introduction' in Gunnar Myrdal, in *Value and Social Theory*, New York: Harper and Row.

Streeten Paul, 1988, 'International Cooperation', in H. Chenery and T.N. Srinivasan, eds. *Handbook of Development Economics*, Vol. 1, Amsterdam: North Holland.

Streeten Paul, 1995, *Thinking about Development*, Cambridge: Cambridge University Press.

Swindler, Ann, et al., 1997, *Habits of the Heart*, Berkeley, CA: University of California Press.

Taylor, Charles, 1991, 'The Dialogical Self', in D. Hiley, J. Bohman, and R. Shusterman, eds., *The Interpretive Turn*, Ithaca, NY: Cornell University Press.

Tendler, J., and S. Freedheim, 1994, 'Trusting in a Rentseeking World: Health and Environment Transformed in Northeast Brazil', in *World Development*, vol. 22, pp.1771-92.

Thomlinson, R., 1965, *Population Dynamics*, New York: Random House.

Timbergen, Jan, 1976, *RIO: Reshaping the International Order*, New York: Dutton.

Tinker, Irene, 1990, *Persistent Inequalities*, Oxford: Oxford University Press.

Todaro, Michael P., 2000, *Economic Development*, New York: Longman.

Toulmin, Stephen, 1990, *Cosmopolis*, Chicago: University of Chicago Press.

Towa, M., 1991, 'Conditions for the Affirmation of a Modern African Philosophical Thought', in Tsenay Serequeberhan, ed., *African Philosophy: The Essential Readings*, New York: Paragon House.

Toye, John, 1987, *Dilemmas of Development*, Oxford: Blackwell.

Trulsson, Per, 1997, *Strategies of Entrepreneurship: Understanding Industrial Entrepreneurship and Structural Change in Northwest Tanzania,* Linköping, Sweden: Linköping University.

Ullman-Margalit, E., 1977, *The Emergence of Norms*. Oxford: Oxford University Press.

UN [United Nations], 1992, *Agenda 21, UNCED Concluding Document,* New York: UN.

UN, 1986, General Assembly, *Declaration on the Right to Development*. New York: UN.

UN, 1979, *The International Dimensions of the Right to Development as a Human Right*, New York: UN.

UN, 1993, *The Vienna Declaration and Program of Action,* New York: UN.

UNCTAD [United Nations Conference of Trade and Development], 1994, *Structural Adjustment and Poverty Alleviation,* Document PA/7, Geneva: UNCTAD.

UNCTAD, 1997, *World Investment Report*, Geneva: UNCTAD.

UNCTAD, 1998, *World Investment Report*, Geneva: UNCTAD.

UNCTAD, 2002, *World Investment Report*, Geneva: UNCTAD.

UNDP [United Nations Development Programme], 1992, *Human Development Report 1992*. New York: Oxford University Press.

UNDP, 1993, *Human Development Report 1993*, New York: Oxford University Press.
UNDP, 1994, *Human Development Report 1994*, New York: Oxford University Press.
UNDP, 1995, *Human Development Report 1995*, New York: Oxford University Press.
UNDP, 1996, *Human Development Report 1996*, New York: Oxford University Press.
UNDP, 1997, *Human Development Report 1997*, New York: Oxford University Press.
UNDP, 1998, *Human Development Report 1998*, New York: Oxford University Press.
UNDP, 1999, *Human Development Report 1999*, New York: Oxford University Press.
UNECA [United Nations Economic Commission for Africa], 1989, *African Alternative Framework to Structural Adjustment and Economic Recovery*, Addis Ababa: UNECA.
UNESCO [United Nations Education, Scientific, and Cultural Organization], 1982, *Declaration of MONDIACULT: World Conference on Cultural Policies*, Paris: UNESCO.
UNESCO, 1994, *The Cultural Dimension of Development*, Paris: UNESCO.
UNFPA [United Nations Population Fund], 1991, *Population and Development*, New York: UNFPA.
UNFPA, 1998, *The State of the World Population 1998*. New York: UNFPA.
UNFPA, 1999, *The State of the World Population 1999*, New York: UNFPA.
UNHCR [United Nations Commission on Human Rights], 1990, *Global Consultation on the Right to Development as a Human Right*, Document E/CN.4/9/Rev., New York: UNHCR.
UNICEF [United Nations Children's Fund], 1998, *The State of the World's Children 1999*. New York: Oxford University Press.
UP Norman, 1992, *Learning from Gal Oya*, Ithaca, NY: Cornell University Press.
UP Norman, 1993, 'Grassroots Organizations and NGOs in Rural Development: Opportunities with Diminishing States and Expanding Markets', in *World Development*, vol. 21, pp. 607-22.
Uphoff, Norman, 1988, 'Assisted Self-Reliance: Working With, Rather than For, the Poor', in J. Lewis, et al., eds., *Strengthening the Poor: What Have We Learned?* New Brunswick, NJ: Transaction Books.
Valette, J., 'Larry Summer's War Against the Earth', 1992, *Counter Punch* at http://www.counterpunch.org/summers.html.
Van Arcadie, Brian, 1989, 'The Role of Institutions in Economic Development', in World Bank. *Proceedings of the World Bank Annual Conference on Development Economics 1989*. Washington, DC: The World Bank.
Van Binsbergen, Wim, 2003, *Intercultural Encounters: African and anthropological lessons towards a philosophy of interculturality*, Hamburg: LIT Verlag.
Van Ness, P., ed., 1999, *Debating Human Rights*, London: Routledge.
Veblen, Thorstein, 1965 [1899], *The Theory of the Leisure Class*, New York: Kelley.
Wachtel, Paul, 1989, *Poverty and Affluence*, Philadelphia, PA: New Society Publishers.
Waddington, C., 1977, *Tools for Thought*, London: Jonathan Cape.
Wade, Robert, 2001, 'Global Inequality', *The Economist*, April 28, pp. 72-74.
Wade, Robert, 1990, *Governing the Market*. Princeton, NJ: Princeton University Press.

Wallerstein, Immanuel, 1979, *The Capitalist World Economy*, Cambridge: Cambridge University Press.

Wallerstein, Immanuel, 2001 [1974], *The Modern World System*, New York: Academic Press, .

Walzer, Michael, 1983, *Spheres of Justice*, New York; Basic Books.

Ward, Barbara, 1962, *The Rich Nations and the Poor Nations*, New York: Norton.

Warnock, M., ed., 1962, *John Stuart Mill: Utilitarianism, On Liberty, Essay on Bentham*, Cleveland, OH: World Publishing Co.

Weber Marx, 1949, *The Methodology of the Social Sciences*, Glencoe, Il: Free Press.

Weber, Max, 1968 [1922], *Economy and Society*, New York: Bedminster Press.

Welch, C. 'Utilitarianism', 1989, in J. Eatwell, M. Milgate and P. Newman, eds., *The New Palgrave: The Invisible Hand*, New York: Norton.

Whitehead, Alfred North, 1925, *Science and the Modern World*, New York: Macmillan.

Whitehead, Alfred North, 1929, *Process and Reason*, New York: Harper.

Williams, Bernard, 1985, *Ethics and the Limits of Philosophy*, London: Fontana/Collins.

Williams, Patrick and Laura Chrisman, eds., 1994, *Colonial Discourse and Post-Colonial Theory: A Reader*, New York: Columbia University Press.

Williamson, John, 1985, *The Economic Institutions of Capitalism*, New York: Free Press.

Williamson, John, *Latin American Adjustment: How Much Has Happened?* Washington, DC: Institute for International Economics, 1990.

Williamson, Oliver, 1975, *Markets and Hierarchies*, New York: Free Press.

Wiredu, Kwasi, 1980, *Philosophy and an African Culture*, Cambridge: Cambridge University Press.

Wiredu, Kwasi, 1995, *Conceptual Decolonization in African Philosophy* (Essays Selected and Introduced by Olusegun Oladipo), Ibadan, Nigeria: Hope Publications.

Wiredu, Kwasi, 1996, *Cultural Universals and Particulars: An African Perspective*, Bloomington and Indianapolis: Indiana University Press.

World Bank, 1992a, *Third Report on Adjustment Lending*, Washington, DC: The World Bank.

World Bank, 1992b, *Poverty Reduction Handbook and Operational Directive*, Washington DC: The World Bank.

World Bank, 1995a, *World Development Report 1995: Workers in an Integrating World*, New York: Oxford University Press.

World Bank, 1995b, *Monitoring Environmental Progress*, Washington DC: The World Bank.

World Bank, 1995c, *Toward Greater Gender Equality: The Role of Public Policy*, Washington DC: The World Bank.

World Bank, 1997a, *Global Development Finance*, Washington DC: The World Bank.

World Bank, 1997b, *World Development Indicators*, Washington DC: The World Bank.

World Bank, 1998a, *Global Development Indicators*, Washington DC: The World Bank.

World Bank, 1998b, *Global Economic Prospects and the Developing Countries*, Washington DC: The World Bank.

World Bank, 1990, *World Development Report 1990: Poverty*, New York: Oxford University Press.

World Bank, 1994, *World Development Report 1994: Infrastructure*, New York: Oxford University Press.

World Bank, 1999, *World Development Report 1999: Knowledge for Development*, New York: Oxford University Press.

World Bank, 2003, *World Development Report 2003: Sustainable Development in a Dynamic World*, New York: Oxford University Press.

World Commission on Environment and Development, 1987, *The Common Future*, New York: Oxford University Press.

Worster, D., 1985, *Nature's Economy*, Cambridge: Cambridge University Press.

Zeidin, Theodore, 1997, *The Ultimate History of Humanity*, Oxford: Oxford University Press.

Zein-Elabdin, Eiman O. and S. Charusheela, eds., 2004, *Postcolonialism Meets Economics*, London: Routledge.

Zein-Elabdin, Eiman O., 1998, 'The Question of Development in Africa: A Conversation for Propitious Change', *African Philosophy*, 11 (2): 113-25.

Zein-Elabdin, Eiman O., 2003 'The Difficulty of a Feminist Economics', in Drucilla K. Barker and Edith Kuiper, eds., *Toward a Feminist Philosophy of Economics*, London: Routledge.

Zein-Elabdin, Eiman O., 2004 'Articulating the Postcolonial (with Economics in Mind)', in Eiman O. Zein-Elabdin and S. Charusheela, eds., *Postcolonialism Meets Economics*, London: Routledge.

Zinam, Oleg, 1983, 'Quality of Life, Quality of the Individual, Technology and Development', *American Journal of Economics and Sociology*, vol. 48, pp. 55-68.

www.ingramcontent.com/pod-product-compliance
Lightning Source LLC
Chambersburg PA
CBHW071348290426
44108CB00014B/1479